Learning Computer Architecture with Raspberry Pi®

Learning Computer Architecture with Raspberry Pi®

Eben Upton, Jeff Duntemann, Ralph Roberts, Tim Mamtora, and Ben Everard

WILEY

Learning Computer Architecture with Raspberry Pi®

Published by
John Wiley & Sons, Inc.
10475 Crosspoint Boulevard
Indianapolis, IN 46256
www.wiley.com

Copyright © 2016 by John Wiley & Sons, Inc., Indianapolis, Indiana

Published simultaneously in Canada

ISBN: 978-1-119-18393-8

ISBN: 978-1-119-18394-5 (ebk)

ISBN: 978-1-119-18392-1 (ebk)

Manufactured in the United States of America

For general information on our other products and services please contact our Customer Care Department within the United States at (877) 762-2974, outside the United States at (317) 572-3993 or fax (317) 572-4002.

Library of Congress Control Number: 2016945538

Publisher's Acknowledgements

VP Consumer and Technology Publishing Director:
Michelle Leet

Professional Technology & Strategy Director:
Barry Pruett

Marketing Manager:
Lorna Mein

Acquisitions Editor:
Jody Lefevere

Project Editor:
Charlotte Kughen

Copy Editor:
Grace Fairley

Technical Editor:
Omer Kilic

Editorial Manager:
Mary Beth Wakefield

Editorial Assistant:
Matthew Lowe

About the Authors

EBEN UPTON is a founder of the Raspberry Pi Foundation, serves as the CEO of Raspberry Pi (Trading) Ltd, its trading arm, and is the co-author, with Gareth Halfacree, of the *Raspberry Pi User Guide*. In an earlier life, Eben founded two successful mobile games and middleware companies (Ideaworks 3d and Podfun), held the post of Director of Studies for Computer Science at St John's College, Cambridge and wrote the *Oxford Rhyming Dictionary* with his father, Professor Clive Upton. He holds a BA in Physics and Engineering, a PhD in Computer Science, and an Executive MBA, from the University of Cambridge.

JEFF DUNTEMANN has been professionally published in both technical nonfiction and science fiction since 1974. He worked as a programmer for Xerox Corporation and as a technical editor for Ziff-Davis Publishing and Borland International. He launched and edited two print magazines for programmers and has 20 technical books to his credit, including the best-selling *Assembly Language Step By Step*. He wrote the "Structured Programming" column in *Dr. Dobb's Journal* for four years and has published dozens of technical articles in many magazines. With fellow writer Keith Weiskamp, Jeff launched The Coriolis Group in 1989, which went on to become Arizona's largest book publisher by 1998. He has a longstanding interest in "strong" artificial intelligence, and most of his fiction (including his two novels, *The Cunning Blood* and *Ten Gentle Opportunities*) explore the consequences of strong AI. His other interests include electronics and amateur radio (callsign K7JPD), telescopes and kites. Jeff lives in Phoenix, Arizona with Carol, his wife of 40 years, and four bichon frise dogs.

RALPH ROBERTS is a decorated Vietnam Veteran who worked with NASA during the Apollo moon-landing program and has been writing about computers and software continuously since his first sale to *Creative Computing* magazine in 1979. Roberts has written more than 100 books for national publishers and thousands of articles and short stories. In all, he's sold more than 20 million words professionally. His best sellers include the first U.S. book on computer viruses (which resulted in several appearances on national TV) and *Classic Cooking with Coca-Cola®*, a cookbook that has been in print for the past 21 years and has sold 500,000 copies.

TIM MAMTORA works as a master engineer in IC Design for Broadcom Limited and is currently the technical lead for the internal GPU hardware team. He has worked in mobile computer graphics for nearly seven years and previously held roles developing internal IP for analog TV and custom DSP hardware. Tim holds a Masters in Engineering from the University of Cambridge, and he spent his third year at the Massachusetts Institute of Technology, which sparked his interest in digital hardware design. He is passionate about promoting engineering and has dedicated time to supervising undergraduates at the University of Cambridge and giving talks about opportunities in engineering to his old school. Outside of work he enjoys a variety of sports, photography and seeing the world.

BEN EVERARD is a writer and podcaster who spends his days tinkering with Linux and playing with robots. This is his second book; he also wrote *Learning Python with Raspberry Pi* (Wiley, 2014). You can find him on Twitter at @ben_everard.

About the Technical Editor

OMER KILIC is an embedded systems engineer who enjoys working with small connected computers of all shapes and sizes. He works at the various intersections of hardware and software engineering practices, product development and manufacturing.

In memory of Alan Drew, without whom I would have stopped before I got started.
—Eben Upton

To the eternal memory of Steve Ostruszka 1917-1990, who gave
me his daughter's hand and honored me with his friendship.
—Jeff Duntemann

Table of Contents

Learning Computer Architecture with Raspberry Pi®

Introduction

WHEN I WAS 10 years old, one of my teachers sat me down in front of a computer at school. Now, this isn't what you think. I wasn't about to be inducted into the mysteries of computer programming, even though it was a BBC Micro (the most programmable and arguably the most architecturally sophisticated of the British 8-bit microcomputers, on which I would subsequently cut my teeth in BASIC and assembly language). Instead, I was faced with a half-hour barrage of multiple choice questions about my academic interests, hobbies and ambitions, after which the miraculous machine spat out a diagnosis of my ideal future career: microelectronic chip designer.

This was a bit of a puzzler, not least because what I really wanted to be was a computer game programmer (okay, okay, astronaut) and there was nobody in my immediate environment who had any idea what a 10-year-old should do to set him on the path to the sunlit uplands of microelectronic chip design. Over the next few years, I studied a *lot* of maths and science at school, learned to program (games) at home, first on the BBC Micro and then the Commodore Amiga, and made repeated, not particularly successful, forays into electronics. As it turned out, and more by luck than judgment, I'd happened on a plausible road to my destination, but it wasn't until I arrived at Cambridge at the age of 18 that I started to figure out where the gaps were in my understanding.

Cambridge

Cambridge occupies a special place in the history of computer science, and particularly in the history of practical or applied computing. In the late 1930s, the young Cambridge academic Alan Turing demonstrated that the halting problem (the question "Will this computer program ever terminate, or halt?") was not computable; in essence, you can't write a computer program that will analyse another arbitrary computer program and determine if it will halt. At the same time, working independently, Alonzo Church proved the same result, which now shares their names: the Church-Turing thesis. But it is telling that while Church took a purely mathematical approach to his proof, based on recursive functions, Turing's proof cast computation in terms of sequential operations performed by what we now know as *Turing machines*: simple gadgets that walk up and down an infinite tape, reading symbols, changing their internal state and direction of travel in response, and writing new symbols. While most such machines are specialised to a single purpose, Turing introduced the concept of the *universal* machine, which could be configured via commands written on the tape to emulate the action of *any* other special-purpose machine. This was the first appearance of a now commonplace idea: the general-purpose programmable computer.

After the outbreak of the Second World War, Turing would go on to play a central role in the Allied code-breaking effort at Bletchley Park, where he was involved (as a member of a team—don't believe everything you see at the movies) in the development of a number of pieces of special-purpose hardware, including the electromechanical *bombe*, which automated the process of breaking the German Enigma cipher. None of these machines used the specific "finite state automaton plus infinite tape" architecture of Turing's original thought experiment; this turned out to be better suited to mathematical analysis than to actual implementation. And not even the purely electronic Colossus—which did to the formidably sophisticated Lorentz stream cipher what the bombe had done to Enigma—crossed the line into general-purpose programmability. Nonetheless, the experience of developing large-scale electronic systems for code-breaking, radar and gunnery, and of implementing digital logic circuits using thermionic valves, would prove transformative for a generation of academic engineers as they returned to civilian life.

One group of these engineers, under Maurice Wilkes at the University of Cambridge's Mathematical Laboratory, set about building what would become the Electronic Delay Storage Automatic Calculator, or EDSAC. When it first became operational in 1949, it boasted a 500kHz clock speed, 32 mercury delay lines in two temperature-controlled water baths for a total of 2 kilobytes of volatile storage. Programs and data could be read from, and written to, paper tape. Many institutions in the U.S. and UK can advance narrow claims to having produced the first general-purpose digital computer, for a particular value of "first". Claims have been made that EDSAC was the first computer to see widespread use outside the team that developed it; academics in other disciplines could request time on the machine to run their own programs, introducing the concept of computing as a service. EDSAC was followed by EDSAC II, and then Titan. It was only in the mid-1960s that the University stopped building its own computers from scratch and started buying them from commercial vendors. This practical emphasis is even reflected in the current name of the computer department: Cambridge doesn't have a computer science faculty; it has a computer laboratory, the direct descendant of Wilkes' original mathematical laboratory.

This focus on the practical elements of computer engineering has made Cambridge fertile ground for high-technology startups, many of them spun out of the computer laboratory, the engineering department or the various maths and science faculties (even our mathematicians know how to hack), and has made it a magnet for multinational firms seeking engineering talent. Variously referred to as the Cambridge Cluster, the Cambridge Phenomenon or just Silicon Fen, the network of firms that has grown up around the University represents one of the few bona fide technology clusters outside of Silicon Valley. The BBC Microcomputer that told me I should become a chip designer was a Cambridge product, as was its perennial rival, the Sinclair Spectrum. Your cell phone (and your Raspberry Pi) contains several processors designed by the Cambridge-based chip firm ARM. Seventy years after EDSAC, Cambridge remains the home of high technology in the UK.

Cut to the Chase

One of the biggest missing pieces from my haphazard computing education was an idea of how, underneath it all, my computer worked. While I'd graduated downwards from BASIC to assembly language, I'd become "stuck" at that level of abstraction. I could poke my Amiga's hardware registers to move sprites around the screen but I had no idea how I might go about building a computer of my own. It took me another decade, a couple of degrees and a move out of academia to work for Broadcom (a U.S. semiconductor company that came to Cambridge for the startups and stayed for the engineering talent) for me to get to the point where I woke up one morning with "microelectronic chip designer" (in fact the fancier equivalent, "ASIC architect") on my business card. During this time, I've had the privilege of working with, and learning from, a number of vastly more accomplished practitioners in the field, including Sophie Wilson, architect (with Steve Furber) of the BBC Micro and the original ARM processor, and Tim Mamtora of Broadcom's 3D graphics hardware engineering team, who has graciously provided the chapter on graphics processing units (GPUs) for this book.

To a great degree, my goal in writing this book was to produce the "how it works" title that I wish I'd had when I was 18. We've attempted to cover each major component of a modern computing system, from the CPU to volatile random-access storage, persistent storage, networking and interfacing, at a level that should be accessible to an interested secondary school student or first-year undergraduate. Alongside a discussion of the current state of the art, we've attempted to provide a little historical context; it's remarkable that most of the topics covered (though not, obviously, the fine technical details) would have been of relevance to Wilkes' EDSAC engineering team in 1949. You should reach the end with at least a little understanding of the principles that underpin the operation of your computer. I firmly believe that you will find this understanding valuable even if you're destined for a career as a software engineer and never plan to design a computer of your own. If you don't know what a cache is, you'll be surprised that your program's performance drops off a cliff when your working set ends up larger than your cache, or when you align your buffers so that they exhaust the cache's associativity. If you don't know a little about how Ethernet works, you'll struggle to build a performant network for your datacentre.

It's worth dwelling for a moment on what this book isn't, and what it won't tell you. It isn't a comprehensive technical reference for any of the topics covered. You could write (and people have written) whole volumes on the design of caches, CPU pipelines, compilers and network stacks. Instead, we try to provide a primer for each topic, and some suggestions for further study. It is concerned primarily with the architecture of conventional general-purpose computers (in essence, PCs). There is limited coverage of topics like digital signal processing (DSP) and field-programmable gate arrays (FPGAs), which are primarily of interest in special purpose, application-specific domains. Finally, there is little coverage of the quantitative decision-making process that is the heart of good computer architecture: how do you trade off the size of your cache against access time, or decide whether to allow one subsystem coherent access to a cache that forms part of another component? We can't teach you to think like an architect. For the advanced reader, Hennessy and Patterson's *Computer Architecture: A Quantitative Approach* remains an indispensable reference on this front.

The Knee in the Curve

With that last disclaimer in mind, I'd like to share a couple of guiding principles that I have found useful over the years.

In computer architecture, as in many things, there is a law of diminishing returns. There are, of course, hard limits to what can be accomplished at any given moment, whether in terms of raw CPU performance, CPU performance normalised to power consumption, storage density, transistor size, or network bandwidth over a medium. But it is often the case that well before we reach these theoretical limits we encounter diminishing returns to the application of engineering effort: each incremental improvement is increasingly hard won and exacts a growing toll in terms of cost and, critically, schedule. If you were to graph development effort, system complexity (and thus vulnerability to bugs) or cash spent against performance, the curve would bend sharply upward at some point. To the left of this "knee", performance would respond in a predictable (even linear!) fashion to increasing expenditure of effort; to the right, performance would increase only slowly with added effort, asymptotically approaching the "wall" imposed by fundamental technical limitations.

Sometimes there is no substitute for performance. The Apollo lunar project, for example, was an amazing example of engineering that was so far to the right of the "knee" (powered by the expenditure of several percent of the GDP of the world's largest economy) that it fundamentally misled onlookers about the maturity of aerospace technology. It is only now—after 50 years of incremental advances in rocketry, avionics and material science—that the knee has moved far enough to permit access to space, and maybe even a return to the Moon, at reasonable cost. Nonetheless, I have observed that teams that have the humility to accurately locate the knee bring simple, conservatively engineered systems to market in a timely fashion and then iterate rapidly, tend to win over moon-shot engineering.

Conservatism and iteration are at the heart of my own approach to architecture. The three generations of Raspberry Pi chips that we've produced to date use *exactly* the same system infrastructure, memory controller and multimedia, with changes confined to the ARM core complex, a small number of critical bug fixes and an increase in clock speed. There is a tension here: engineers (myself included) are enthusiasts and want to push the boundaries. The job of a good architect is to accurately assign a cost to the risks associated with radical change, and to weigh this against the purported benefits.

Forward the Foundation

We founded the Raspberry Pi Foundation in 2008, initially with the simple aim of addressing a collapse in the number of students applying to study Computer Science at Cambridge. We're seeing encouraging signs of recovery, both at Cambridge and elsewhere, and applicant numbers are now higher than they were at the height of the dotcom boom in the late 1990s.

Perhaps the most striking aspect of the change we've witnessed is that the new generation of young people is far more interested in hardware than we were in the 1980s. Writing an assembly language routine to move a sprite around on the screen clearly isn't quite as much fun as it used to be, but moving a robot around the floor is much more exciting. We see 12-year-olds today building control and sensing projects that I would have been proud of in my mid-20s. My hope is that when some of these young people sit down in front of the distant descendants of the BBC Micro careers program of my childhood, some of them will be told that they'd make great microelectronic chip designers, and that this book might help one or two of them make that journey.

—Eben Upton, Cambridge, May 2016

Chapter 1
The Shape of a Computer Phenomenon

THAT OLD SAYING about good things coming in small packages describes the Raspberry Pi perfectly. It also highlights an advance in computer architecture—the system-on-a-chip (SoC), a tiny package with a rather large collection of ready-to-use features. The SoC isn't so new—it's been around a long time—but the Raspberry Pi's designers have put it into a small, powerful package that is readily available to students and adults alike. All for a very low price.

A tiny piece of electronics about the size of a credit card, the Raspberry Pi single-board computer packs very respectable computing power into a small space. It provides tons of fun and many, many possibilities for building and controlling all sorts of fascinating gizmos. When something is small, after all, it fits just about anywhere. The Raspberry Pi does things conventional computers just can't do in terms of both portability and connectivity. Things you will find inspire your creativity—fun things!

What's not to like? Get ready for some truly exciting computer architecture.

In this chapter introducing the truly phenomenal Raspberry Pi line of computer boards, we look first at the Raspberry Pi's goals and history. We include the history of the Raspberry Pi's development and the visionary people at the Raspberry Pi Foundation who dreamed up the concept and achieved the reality, and we look at the advantages this tiny one-board computer has over much larger computers. We then take a tour of the Raspberry Pi board.

Growing Delicious, Juicy Raspberries

As significant advances in computing go, the Raspberry Pi's primary innovation was the lowering of the entry barrier into the world of embedded Linux. The barrier was twofold—price and complexity. The Raspberry Pi's low price solved the price problem (cheap is good!) and the SoC reduced circuit complexity rather dramatically, making a much smaller package possible.

The road to the development of the Raspberry Pi originated at a surprising point—through a registered charity in the UK, which continues to operate today.

The Raspberry Pi Foundation, registered with the Charity Commission for England and Wales, first opened its doors in 2009 in Caldecote, Cambridgeshire. It was founded for the express purpose of promoting the study of computer science in schools. A major impetus for its creation came from a team consisting of Eben Upton, Rob Mullins, Jack Lang and Alan Mycroft. At the University of Cambridge's Computer Laboratory, they had noted the declining numbers and low-level skills of student applicants. They came to the conclusion that a small, affordable computer was needed to teach basic skills in schools and to instill enthusiasm for computing and programming.

Major support for the Foundation's goals came from the University of Cambridge Computer Laboratory and Broadcom, which is the company that manufactures the SoC—the Broadcom 2835 or 2836, depending on the model—that enables the Raspberry Pi's power and success. Later in this chapter you will read more on that component, which is the heart and soul of the Raspberry Pi.

The founders of the Raspberry Pi had identified and acted on the perceived need for a tiny, affordable computer. By 2012, the Model B had been released at a price of about £25. The fact that this represented great value for money was recognised immediately, and first-day sales blasted over 100,000 units. In less than two years of production, more than two million boards were sold.

The Raspberry Pi continued to enjoy good sales and wide acceptance following the highly successful release of the Model B+ (in late 2014). And in 2015, the fast, data-crunching Raspberry Pi 2 Model B with its four-core ARM processor and additional onboard memory sold more than 500,000 units in its first two weeks of release. Most recently, the Raspberry Pi Zero, a complete computer system on a board for £4—yes, £4—was released. It's an awesome deal if you can get one—the first batch sold out almost immediately.

In 2016, the Raspberry Pi Model 3 Model B arrived. It sports a 1.2GHz 64-bit quad-core ARMv8 CPU, 1 GB RAM, and built-in wireless and Bluetooth! All for the same low price.

The original founders of the Raspberry Pi Foundation included:

- Eben Upton
- Rob Mullins

- Jack Lang

- Alan Mycroft

- Pete Lomas

- David Braben

The organisation now consists of two parts:

- Raspberry Pi (Trading) Ltd. performs engineering and sales, with Eben Upton as CEO.

- The Raspberry Pi Foundation is the charitable and educational part.

The Raspberry Pi Foundation's website at `www.raspberrypi.org` (see Figure 1-1) presents the impetus that resulted in the Raspberry Pi. This is what they say on the About Us page:

FIGURE 1-1: The Raspberry Pi official website

The idea behind a tiny and affordable computer for kids came in 2006, when Eben Upton, Rob Mullins, Jack Lang and Alan Mycroft, based at the University of Cambridge's Computer Laboratory, became concerned about the year-on-year decline in the numbers and skills levels of the A Level students applying to read Computer Science. From a situation in the 1990s

where most of the kids applying were coming to interview as experienced hobbyist program-
mers, the landscape in the 2000s was very different; a typical applicant might only have done
a little web design.

As a result, the founders' stated goal was "to advance the education of adults and children, particularly in the field of computers, computer science and related subjects".

Their answer to the problem, of course, was the Raspberry Pi, which was designed to emulate in concept the hands-on appeal of computers from the previous decade (the 1990s). The intention behind the Raspberry Pi was to be a "catalyst" to inspire students by providing affordable, programmable computers everywhere.

The Raspberry Pi is well on its way to achieving the Foundation's goal in bettering computer education for students. However, another significant thing has happened; a lot of us older people have found the Raspberry Pi exciting. It's been adopted by generations of hobbyists, experimenters and many others, which has driven sales into new millions of units.

While the sheer compactness of the Raspberry Pi excites, resonates and inspires adults as well as youngsters, what truly prompted its success was its low price and scope of develop-ment. Embedded Linux has always been a painful subject to learn, but the Pi makes it simple and inexpensive. Continuing education in computers gets just as big a boost as initial educa-tion in schools.

System-on-a-Chip

An SoC or system-on-a-chip is an integrated circuit (IC) that has the major components of a computer or any other electronic system on a single chip. The components include a central processing unit (CPU), a graphics processing unit (GPU) and various digital, analogue and mixed signal circuits on just one chip.

This SoC component makes highly dense computing possible, such as all the power that is shoehorned into the Raspberry Pi. Figure 1-2 shows the Broadcom chip on the Raspberry Pi 2 Model B. It's a game-changing advance in computer architecture, enabling single-card com-puters that rival and often exceed the capabilities of machines that are many times their size. Chapter 8, "Operating Systems", covers these small but mighty chips in detail.

The Raspberry Pi features chips that are developed and manufactured by Broadcom Limited. Specifically, the older models as well as the latest (the £4 Raspberry Pi Zero) come with the Broadcom BCN2835 and the Raspberry Pi 2 has the Broadcom BCM2836, and the new Model 3 uses the Broadcom BCM2837. The biggest difference between these two SoC ICs is the replacement of the single-core CPU in the BCM2835 with a four-core processor in the BCM2836. Otherwise, they have essentially the same architecture.

FIGURE 1-2: Broadcom chip on the Raspberry Pi 2 Model B

Here's a taste of the low-level components, peripherals and protocols provided by the Broadcom SoCs:

- **CPU:** Performs data processing under control of the operating system (a CPU with a single core on most of the Raspberry Pi models and a CPU with four cores on the Raspberry Pi 2 and Raspberry Pi 3).

- **GPU:** Provides the operating system desktop.

- **Memory:** Permanent memory used as registers for CPU and GPU operation, storage for bootstrap software, the small program which starts the process of loading the operating system and activating it.

- **Timers:** Allow software to be time-dependent for scheduling, synchronising and so on.

- **Interrupt controller:** Interrupts allow the operating system to control all the computer resources, know when the CPU is ready for new instructions and much more (this is covered in Chapter 8).

- **General purpose input output (GPIO):** Provides layout and enables control of connections, input, output and alternative modes for the GPIO pins that enable the Raspberry Pi to manage circuits, devices, machines and so on. In short, it turns the Raspberry Pi into an embeddable control system.

- **USB:** Controls the USB services and provides the Universal Serial Bus protocols for input and output, thus allowing peripherals of all types to connect to the Raspberry Pi's USB receptacles.

- **PCM/I²S:** Provides pulse code modulation (PCM, which converts digital sound to analogue sound such as speakers and headphones require) and known as Inter-IC Sound, Integrated Interchip Sound, or IIS, a high-level standard for connecting audio devices).

- **Direct memory access (DMA) controller:** Direct memory access control that allows an input/output device to bypass the CPU and send or receive data directory to the main memory for purposes of speed and efficiency.

- **I²C master:** Inter-integrated circuit often employed for connecting lower-speed peripheral chips to control processors and microcontrollers.

- **I²C/SPI (Serial Peripheral Interface) slave:** The reverse of the preceding bullet point. Allows outside chips and sensors to control or cause the Raspberry Pi to respond in certain ways; for example, a sensor in a motor detects it's running hot and the controller chip causes the Raspberry Pi to make a decision on whether to reduce the motor's speed or stop it.

- **SPI Interface:** Serial interfaces, accessed via the GPIO pins and allowing the daisy chaining of several compatible devices by the use of different chip-select pins.

- **Pulse width modulation (PWM):** A method of generating an analogue waveform from a digital signal.

- **Universal asynchronous receiver/transmitter (UART0, UART1):** Used for serial communication between different devices.

An Exciting Credit Card-Sized Computer

Just how powerful is the Raspberry Pi compared to a desktop PC? Certainly, it has far more computational ability, memory and storage than the first personal computers. That said, the Raspberry Pi cannot match the speed, high-end displays, built-in power supplies and hard-drive capacity of the desktop boxes and laptops of today.

However, you can easily overcome any disadvantages by hanging the appropriate peripherals on your Raspberry Pi. You can add large hard drives, 42-inch HDMI screens, high-level sound systems and much more. Simply plug your peripherals into the USB receptacles on the board or via other interfaces that are provided, and you're good to go. Finish it off by clicking an Ethernet cable into the jack on the Raspberry Pi or sliding in a wireless USB dongle, and worldwide connectivity goes live.

You can duplicate most features of conventional computers when you attach peripherals to a Raspberry Pi, such as in Figure 1-3, and you also gain some distinct advantages over large computers, including:

- The Raspberry Pi is *really* cheap—£25 retail or just £4 for the Raspberry Pi Zero.

- It's *really* small—all models are credit-card sized or smaller.

- You can replace the operating system in seconds simply by inserting a new SD or microSD card for almost instant reconfiguration.

- The Broadcom SoC gives the Raspberry Pi more interfaces, communications protocols and other features out of the box than conventional computers that sell for many times the price.

- The GPIO pins (see Figure 1-4) allow the Raspberry Pi to control real-world devices that have no other method of computer input/output.

FIGURE 1-3: Peripherals attached to a Raspberry Pi 2 Model B

FIGURE 1-4: GPIO pins enable control of real world devices.

What Does the Raspberry Pi Do?

The Raspberry Pi excels as the brains for all sorts of projects. Here are some examples randomly picked from the many thousands of documented projects on the Internet. This list may inspire you in choosing some projects of your own:

- Home automation
- Home security
- Media centre
- Weather station
- Wearable computer
- Robot controller
- Quadcopter (drone) controller
- Web server
- Email server
- GPS tracker
- Web camera controller
- Coffee maker
- Ham radio EchoLink server and JT65 terminal
- Electric motor controller
- Time-lapse photography manager
- Game controller
- Bitcoin mining
- Automotive onboard computer

This list just scratches the surface of possible uses for the Raspberry Pi. There's not enough room to list everything you could do, but this book gives you the information you need to come up with your own ideas. Let your own desires, interests and imagination guide you. The Raspberry Pi does the rest.

Meeting and Greeting the Raspberry Pi Board

This section begins with an introduction to the features, components and layout of the Raspberry Pi board. We show contrasts between the various models but with an emphasis on the Raspberry Pi 2. Reading this section and examining the Raspberry Pi board is like looking at a map before setting off on a journey—it gives you the lay of the land. If you know where the various important parts of the board are and how they work, it makes imagining and creating projects a lot easier because you understand the board better.

We begin with the Raspberry Pi 2 Model B (there was no Model A in the 2 series or the new 3 series). After introducing you to the Raspberry Pi 2, we'll look at the other versions, including the Raspberry Pi 3 Model, which includes more processor speed, onboard Wi-Fi and Bluetooth.

If you want to follow along with your own board, orient it as shown in Figure 1-5, with the two rows of GPIO pins at the upper left.

GPIO Pins

The GPIO pins—the row of pins at the top of the board as it's oriented in Figure 1-5—perform magic in tying the Raspberry Pi to the real world. Through these pins, you program the Raspberry Pi to control all sorts of devices. Chapter 12, "Input/Output", looks at programming the Raspberry Pi and helps you understand inputs and outputs and shows methods of controlling various devices. Let's examine these pins and get an understanding of how simple and powerful they are.

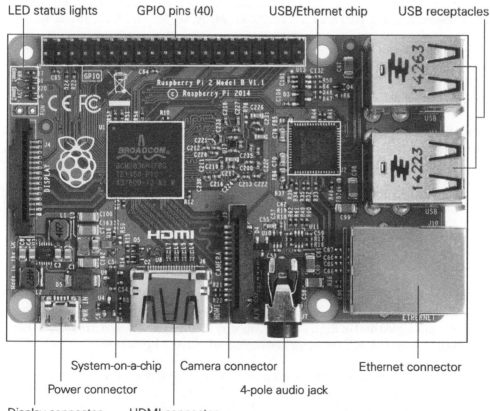

FIGURE 1-5: The Raspberry Pi 2 board with the GPIO pins at the upper left

Real-world devices—doorbells, light bulbs, model aircraft controls, lawn mowers, robots, thermostats, electric coffeepots and motors of all sorts, to name a few things—cannot normally connect to a computer or follow its orders. Through GPIO, the Raspberry Pi can do neat stuff with these real-world objects! That's why we're emphasising the GPIO pins; the pins enable you to do things with the Raspberry Pi that you can't do with conventional computers.

> **NOTE** Being able to interface with real-world devices is not a distinction that's unique to the Raspberry Pi; embedded computers are able to bridge this gap whereas conventional computers can't.

We have 40 pins—two rows of 20. The bottom row of pins (left to right) consists of odd numbers: 1, 3, 5, 7, 9, 11, 13, 15, 17, 19, 21, 23, 25, 27, 29, 31, 33, 35, 37 and 39. The top are numbered 2, 4, 6, 8, 10, 12, 14, 16, 18, 20, 22, 24, 26, 28, 30, 32, 34, 36, 38 and 40.

These pins are programmable; you can even change the layout of most of the pins! The power pins cannot be rerouted.

When you add simple external circuits, it becomes possible for the Raspberry Pi to switch all sorts of things on or off. It can also sense input from devices and respond accordingly. Thanks to the Raspberry Pi's ability to communicate in various ways—such as by wireless, by Bluetooth or on the Internet—inputs and outputs do not even have to be local. With some additional hardware, you can control devices, programs and so forth from anywhere in the world.

> **NOTE** Read Chapter 12 to learn about the several modes of operation for GPIO pins. The majority of the pins can be input, output or one of six special modes.

Status LEDs

The status light-emitting diodes (LEDs) are to the lower left of the GPIO pins. These tiny babies put out a good deal of light. On the Raspberry Pi 2, they are labelled (from top to bottom) PWR (power) and ACT (activity); PWR lights red and ACT lights green.

Whenever power is present to the board (that is, a micro USB plug provides 5 volts direct current (VDC) from a USB source or a wall adapter), the PWR light glows red. The ACT LED indicates that a microSD card is available, and only lights up when the Raspberry Pi accesses the card.

The Model B+ has the same arrangement as on the Model B except that the LED status lights are located on the opposite side of the board, and there are five LEDs:

- **ACT** (activity, green): Indicates an SD card is plugged in and accessible

- **PWR** (power, red): Indicates power is present

- **FDX** (full duplex, green): Indicates a full duplex local area network (LAN) is connected

- **LNK** (link, flashing green): Indicates activity is happening on the LAN

- **100** (yellow): Indicates a 100-Mbit/s LAN is connected (as opposed to a 10-Mbit network)

With the Model B+, the last three LEDs functions were moved to the Ethernet jack, with the FDX and 100 being combined into one LED. So flashing green on the jack shows network activity on the right LED and either solid green or yellow on the left, showing a 10-Mbits/s (megabits per second) or 100-Mbits/s network connections, respectively.

> All the Raspberry Pi models actually have five status lights; it's just that on the B+ and Raspberry Pi 2 there are two LEDs (PWR and ACT) on one side of the board, and the network indicators are on the other side as part of the Ethernet jack. **NOTE**

The status LEDs give you a quick picture of what transpires on your Raspberry Pi board, especially during the boot-up process. It goes like this:

1. When you plug in the microUSB connector (there's no on/off switch), the PWR LED lights red to show that power is present. The PWR LED stays lit so long as power is flowing to the board.

2. The ACT LED flashes green a couple of times or so, indicating an SD card is present and readable. After boot-up, this green light flashes whenever SD card access occurs.

3. As the powering-up process continues, the green light on the right of the Ethernet jack (Model B+ and later) come on if a network is present. The light flashes whenever there is traffic on the network. The left LED flashes green for a slow network and is solid yellow if you are connected to a 100Mbit/s network.

So, at a glance, the status LEDs tell us the board has power, the SD card is working and the network is active.

USB Receptacles

On the right-hand side of the board are the Raspberry PI 2 Model B's four USB 2.0 ports, as shown in Figure 1-6.

Ethernet socket

USB receptacles

FIGURE 1-6: USB 2.0 ports and Ethernet port

> **NOTE** The ports appear in the same way on the Model B+ but the older Model B provides only two USB receptacles.

USB receptacles—or ports, as some people incorrectly call them—allow you to plug in and run a keyboard, mouse and all sorts of other devices—even big hard drives!

Ethernet Connection

All sorts of Raspberry Pi tasks require a connection to both your local network and the Internet itself. Upgrading the operating system and the Raspberry Pi's firmware requires Internet access. Networking is a necessity for downloading and installing programs, web surfing, using the Raspberry Pi as a media centre to deliver movies to your humungous flat-screen TV and many more reasons.

Fortunately, you have two ways of achieving network connectivity with the Raspberry Pi. The first is a wired connection using the Ethernet socket on the lower-right corner (as the board is oriented in Figure 1-5). Refer to Figure 1-6 to see what this socket looks like.

The second way of connecting involves the USB receptacles. You can use a wireless USB dongle (a dongle being a plug-in device) or a USB-to-Ethernet adapter. If you use the latter method, you can connect the Raspberry Pi to more than one network. One reason for doing this would be a typical server setup where the Raspberry Pi connects to both the Internet and a more secure local network. Using Raspbian, for example, you can turn your Raspberry Pi into a classic LAMP (standing for Linux, Apache, mySQL, PHP) server. The Raspberry Pi serves up websites with database back ends and so on, just like on much larger servers using the same software.

Using a wireless USB dongle comes in handy if you want your Raspberry Pi to be portable. With an external battery power supply and wireless access, you can carry it anywhere! Or at least anywhere with wireless access, which is true of more and more places these days.

Audio Out

On the bottom of the board is the 3.5 millimetre (mm) audio input/output jack (see Figure 1-7). Here you can plug in headphones, a computer sound card, speakers or anything thing else that takes and plays audio input.

The Model A and Model B did not have this feature but instead had separate connectors for video and audio.   **NOTE**

FIGURE 1-7: The audio output socket

The plug that goes into the socket on the Raspberry Pi board is a four-pole plug—in this case, a tip with three rings. However, it also accepts and works with a standard three-pole mini plug like those often found on headphones and computer speakers.

> **NOTE** Poles are the tip and rings of conductors. Four-pole had a tip and three rings; three-pole a tip and two rings.

Figure 1-7 shows how the connector appears on the Model B+ and later, and Figure 1-8 shows the connector's wiring.

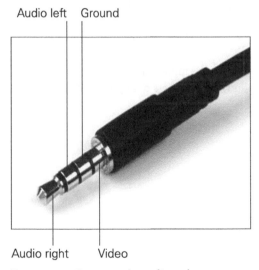

FIGURE 1-8: Connector for audio socket

Another of the Raspberry Pi limitations concerns quality of sound. The audio out from this connector is 11-bit (for truly good sounding music you'd want 16-bit). The High-Definition Multimedia Interface (HDMI) connector, which is described later in this chapter, has better audio but, of course, you have to have an HDMI device (like a big-screen TV) that has good speakers attached.

No worries, folks—like the limitations in Raspberry Pi power, solutions abound. For example, Adafruit sells a USB audio adapter, which works on the Raspberry Pi, for a very low price. It puts out better sound and allows for microphone input as well. This lets you use the Pi as a voice or music recorder or teach it to work via voice commands. Various computer soundboards designed specifically for the Raspberry Pi are also available

Even better, you can obtain high-quality sound using the I²S interface into an external digital-to-analogue convertor (DAC). Chapter 11, "Audio", covers all that good stuff.

Composite Video

Using the same 3.5mm socket described in the last section, old-style composite video is also available.

When it boots up and finds a composite video device attached, the Raspberry Pi attempts to select the right resolution. Mostly it gives a usable display but sometimes it gets things wrong.

Having video composite output may seem old school in light of the modern era's profusion of HDMI devices hanging off every wall, but it fits in with the design philosophy Raspberry Pi Foundation co-founder Eben Upton recently described. He said, "It's a very cheap Linux PC device in the spirit of the 1980s, a device which turns your TV into a computer; plug in to TV, plug a mouse and a keyboard in, give it some power and some kind of storage, an operating system and you've got a PC".

CSI Camera Module Connector

Camera modules for the Raspberry Pi give you 5-megapixel stills and 1080 high-definition video for about £16. The Camera Serial Interface (CSI) connector shown in Figure 1-9 (located between the HDMI socket and the 3.5mm audio socket) provides a place to plug the camera module into the Pi.

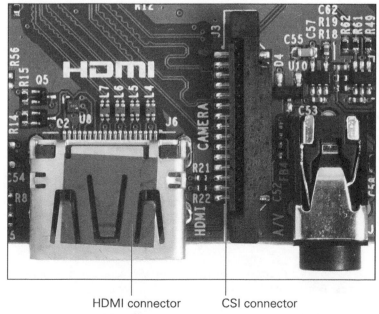

HDMI connector   CSI connector

FIGURE 1-9: CSI and HDMI connectors

CSI connects the camera module via a 15-conductor flat flex cable. Getting this cable connected and the camera module working is a bit tricky sometimes. You can find a how-to video on the Raspberry Pi website at `https://www.raspberrypi.org/help/camera-module-setup/`.

However, after the cable sits in the socket properly, the camera works great. You can program it to do all sorts of neat stuff, such as take time-lapse photos and motion-triggered shots or record video footage.

HDMI

There's nothing as fine as a nice big display showing the colourful graphical user interface (GUI) of the Raspberry Pi. A display enables you to surf the web, watch videos, play games— all the stuff you expect a computer to do. The best solution for that involves HDMI.

High-Definition Multimedia Interface (HDMI) allows the transfer of video and audio from an HDMI-compliant display controller (in our case, the Raspberry Pi) to compatible computer monitors, projectors, digital TVs or digital audio devices.

HDMI's higher quality provides a marked advantage over composite video (such as what comes out of the audio socket on the Raspberry Pi board). It's much easier on the eyes and provides higher resolution instead of composite video's noisy and sometimes distorted video.

The HDMI connector on the Raspberry Pi Model B is approximately centred on the lower edge of the Raspberry Pi board (as we have it positioned in Figure 1-5). See Figure 1-9 for what it looks like.

Micro USB Power

The micro USB power connector is on the bottom left edge of the Raspberry Pi, as shown in Figure 1-10.

The micro USB adapter brings power into the Raspberry Pi board. You might know that most smartphones use this connector type, which means you can find usable cables and wall adapters all over the place. (This is one example of how the Raspberry Pi Foundation takes users' need for inexpensive operation into consideration.)

NOTE You can also get a mobile version of a micro USB charging cable with an automotive power adaptor so you can power your Raspberry Pi in a car, using the built-in car power socket.

FIGURE 1-10: Micro USB connector used for obtaining power

The micro USB cable supplies 5VDC to the Raspberry Pi at about 1 ampere (1A) of current for the model B. Some recommendations for the B+ mention 1.5A, but if you're pushing heavy current through the USB ports (remember, four instead of two on the B+ and later), a 2A supply is smarter. For the Raspberry Pi 2, get at least a 2.4A supply.

Remember, there's no switch for turning the Raspberry Pi on and off (another saving to keep the price down). You just plug and unplug the micro USB connector. Of course, with a bit of tinkering and soldering, you could add a switch to the power cable easily enough.

Storage Card

Applying power to the Raspberry Pi causes a bit of computer code stored on the board, the bootloader, to check for the presence of the SD or (in newer Raspberry Pi versions) microSD card in its slot (see Figure 1-11) and look for code on the card telling it how to start and what to load into its RAM. If no card is there or that card has no information on it (because it's blank or corrupted) the Raspberry Pi does not start. Read more on the boot process in Chapter 8.

Do not insert or remove an SD card while the Raspberry Pi has power attached. Doing so has a very good chance of corrupting the SD card, causing you to lose the data and programs on it.   **WARNING**

The usual minimum size recommended for earlier editions of the Raspberry Pi was 8 gigabytes (8GB), although the original recommendation was 4GB. However, a number of people on the Internet report using 32GB cards, and at least one person even boasted of using a 128GB card. It seems, though, that any card larger than 32GB, under Raspbian at least, requires partitioning (using a software to specially format the SD).

Of course, you can hang just about any size of USB drive from one of the USB receptacles, if you use an external power supply. A terabyte would be a good start. The SD card is still needed to boot.

FIGURE 1-11: The micro SD slot on the bottom side of the Raspberry Pi 2

DSI Display Connection

Just right of the SD card slot but on top of the board is the Display Serial Interface (DSI) display connector. The DSI connector's design accommodates a flat 15-conductor cable that drives liquid crystal display (LCD) screens. Figure 1-12 shows the connector.

FIGURE 1-12: DSI display connection

Mounting Holes

It might seem minor, but the Model B+ and later models have four mounting holes—those reinforced holes in the board. The Model B only has two. Mounting holes come in handy when you want to secure the Raspberry Pi inside a box or case with other devices.

When you add four standoff insulators, you can use these insulted holes for fastening the board with screws to the standoffs to have a nice, safe installation.

The Chips

There are two large chips situated roughly on the centre of the left of the board (when the board is oriented with the GPIO pins at the top left; see Figure 1-13). The larger one shown is the Broadcom BCM2835 or BCM2836 on the Raspberry Pi 2 or BCM2037 on the Raspberry Pi 3. The other chip provides the Ethernet protocols for networking. You'll find more information about the what these systems-on-a-chip do in Chapter 12.

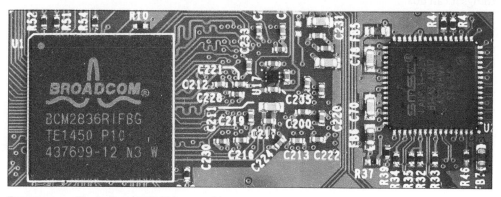

FIGURE 1-13: The SoC and USB/Ethernet chips

The Future

From its inception, the guiding principle of the Raspberry Pi was to enable and revolutionise the teaching of computer science by providing affordable, accessible hardware. It is certainly achieving this goal successfully through the widespread adoption of the Raspberry Pi as a teaching tool in schools worldwide.

The inspiration and excitement young people find, the lessons they learn and the experiments and projects they complete are significant. We are seeing the birth of a new generation of computer experts.

Something else has also happened. Those of us from prior generations—sometimes called "adults" and sometimes not—discovered the Raspberry Pi. Millions of us enthusiastically explore its incredible power and build various projects using its control functions. We, too, are learning things from this tiny computer, which takes the term "microcomputer" to a much smaller scale than those now-huge old desktops. Consequently, we are setting an example for our children. If adults can have so much fun with the Raspberry Pi, younger people realise they can as well, and so they do.

So the Raspberry Pi not only inspires the younger, student generation; it makes older generations better and more computer literate. That's quite a gift.

What happens next? The next great movement, already in progress, is the Internet of Things. Using the Raspberry Pi, your refrigerator, your car—just about every device you can think of—can become wireless and be controlled by small, easily embedded computerised controls. More and more people will continue to adopt and adapt the means of making this automation a reality. With every new release, demand grows for the Raspberry Pi and the things it can do.

In the next few years, computer architecture will continue to shrink while it grows more capable. We yearn for a thumb drive–sized device that has a 24-core CPU running at 15GHz with 10GB of fast memory and a terabyte solid state drive, all on an SoC.

We anticipate that such a device will sport a purple Raspberry logo. It won't be long now. The future rushes toward us.

Chapter 2
Recapping Computing

NOTE: YOU MAY *already know the material in this chapter. Anyone who's taken any coursework in computing, or played around with computers and programming on their own, has at least a modest grasp of what we present here. This chapter is a broad and very high-level overview of what computers do and what parts of the computer are used to do it. You'll know within a few pages whether it's useful for you or not. If it isn't, feel free to skip directly to Chapter 3.*

Although we created computers to do calculations, computers are not calculators. We've had calculators for a very long time. The abacus is known to have been used by the Persians as early as 600 BCE, and it was probably in use earlier than that. The precursor to the slide rule, called "Napier's Bones", was invented by John Napier in 1617. The very first mechanical calculator, the Pascaline, was invented by Blaise Pascal in 1642—when he was only 19! Better and more elaborate mechanical calculators were devised over the years until very recently, when digital calculators shoved mechanical and analogue calculators onto history's high shelf.

Charles Babbage is usually credited with the idea of programmability in calculation. He was too poor and his "analytical engine" too complex for him to construct it in 1837, but his son built and demonstrated a more modest version of the machine in 1888. However, it wasn't until the 1930s that the ideas underlying modern computing began to be understood fully. Alan Turing laid the theoretical groundwork for fully programmable computers in 1936. In 1941, Konrad Zuse built a programmable electromechanical computer, called the Z3 machine, that understood binary encoding and floating point numbers. Zuse's machine was later proven to be "Turing complete"—that is, capable of implementing Turing's principles of general-purpose computing.

Zuse's Z3 had been created to perform statistical analysis of the German air force's wing designs. World War II accelerated the development of digital computers on many fronts, driven first by the need to calculate artillery trajectories, and later to handle the complex mathematics used by the developers of the nuclear bomb. By 1944, the Colossus computers at Bletchley Park were in daily service aiding the cryptanalysis of German, Italian and Japanese wartime ciphers.

Not all calculation is done in a single step, as are basic arithmetic operations like addition and multiplication. Some calculation requires iterative operations that run in sequence until some limiting condition is reached. There are calculations so complex that the calculator must inspect its own operations and results as it goes along, to determine whether it has completed its job or must repeat some tasks or take up new ones. This is where programmability comes in, and where a calculator takes the fateful step away from calculation into true computing.

It's this simple: computers are not calculators. Computers follow recipes.

The Cook as Computer

In some respects, we've been computing since long before we were calculating. Homo sapiens broke away from the rest of the primate pack through the ability to pass along knowledge verbally from one generation to the next. Much of this transmitted knowledge was "how-to" in nature, such as how to shape an axe head from a piece of stone. Following step-by-step instructions is now such a pervasive part of life that, most of the time, we don't even realize we're doing it. Watch yourself work the next time you cook anything more complex than a toasted cheese sandwich. You're not just cooking. You're computing.

Ingredients as Data

All recipes begin with a list of ingredients. The list is very specific, in terms of both the ingredients and their quantities: For example, the ingredients for *carré d'agneau dordonnaise* are:

2 racks of lamb

½ cup shelled walnuts

1 small onion

1 3 oz can of liver pâté

½ cup bread crumbs

2 tablespoons parsley

1 tsp salt

2 tbsp lemon juice

½ tsp finely ground black pepper

The goal in cooking is to combine and process these ingredients to make something that doesn't already exist in your refrigerator. In computing, there are also ingredients: text, numbers, images, symbols, photos, videos and so on. A computer program can take these ingredients and combine and process them into something new: a PDF document, a web page, an e-book or a PowerPoint presentation.

Recipes are step-by-step instructions for going from the ingredients to *carré d'agneau dordonnaise*. Some recipes may be absurdly simple, but most are very explicit and usually done in a specified order:

1. Remove the bones from both racks.

2. Trim the fat off the meat.

3. Finely chop the walnuts.

4. Grate the onion.

5. Stir the liver pâté until smooth.

6. Beat the walnuts and onion into the pâté.

7. Mix the breadcrumbs and parsley together.

8. Season the stuffing mix with salt, lemon juice and pepper.

. . .and so on. Granted, you could grate the onion before you chopped the walnuts; in many cases order doesn't matter. However, it does matter sometimes—you can't beat the chopped walnuts into the pâté before you've chopped the walnuts.

Just like recipes, computer programs are sequences of steps that start at the beginning, do something with the data and then pause or stop after all the steps have been performed. You can see simple programs called scripts running in a terminal window on the Raspberry Pi as they do exactly that: they start, they run and they stop when their job is completed. You can see each step in the "recipe" scroll by as it is performed.

With more complex programs, like word processors, the recipe isn't as linear and the steps aren't reported onscreen. A word processor is a little like a cook in a café. At the counter you ask for a lunch special, the cook nods and then disappears into the heart of the kitchen to put your meal together. When it's done, the cook hands the lunch special over the counter to you through the window and waits for another order. When you're not typing or selecting commands from the menu, a word processor is like the cook waiting at the counter. When you type a character, the word processor takes the character and integrates it with the current document, then waits for another. Regardless of whether you can see the steps happen, each time you type a character, a whole long list of things happen in order, for example, to display the letter "y" at the end of the word "Raspberry".

Basic Actions

In both recipes and computer programs, individual steps may contain lists of other steps. The step of grating the onion, for example, is performed in several, smaller steps: first you have to grab the onion in one hand, then pick up the grater with the other hand, and then rub the onion against the face of the grater while allowing the grated onion to fall into a bowl.

In recipes, these internal steps are not called out every time. Most people who have done some cooking know how to grate an onion, and providing detailed directions for grating an onion is unnecessary. However, you follow steps when you grate an onion, whether the steps are spelled out explicitly in the recipe or not. This can happen only because you, the cook, already knew how to grate an onion.

That's an important point. Cooks use a large number of specific, named actions to complete a recipe. Expert cooks know them all and they can use them without explanation: peel, grate, mix, fold, zest, chop, dice, sift, skim, simmer, bake and so on. Some of these actions are commoner than others, while some—like acidulate—are used so rarely that recipes typically do spell them out in simpler terms, in this case, "Add vinegar or lemon juice to make the sauce more acidic".

Computers, like cooks, understand a moderate list of fairly simple actions. These simple actions are combined into larger and more complex actions, which in turn are combined into complete operational programs. The simple, basic steps that a computer understands are called *machine instructions*. Machine instructions can be combined into more complex actions called *subprograms*, *functions* or *procedures*. Here's an example of a machine instruction:

```
MOV PlaceB, PlaceA
```

The MOV instruction moves a single piece of data from one place to another place inside the computer. Machine instructions may be combined into functions that do a great deal more. Here, for example, is a function:

```
capitalize(streetname)
```

The capitalize() function does what you probably expect: the name of a street is a short string of text characters, which the previous statement in the program placed in a named data item called streetname. The function capitalizes the words within the street name according to standard rules for capitalization. This is how a computer turns the text "garden of the gods road" into "Garden of the Gods Road." Inside the capitalize() function may be dozens or hundreds of machine instructions, just as in a cooking task the instruction to "reduce" involves a fair bit of fussy adding, simmering, stirring and testing.

The Box That Follows a Plan

That's about as far as we can take the recipe metaphor, and perhaps a little further than we should. Computers are indeed a little like cooks following recipes. Cooks also improvise, try weird things and sometimes make a mess. Computers don't improvise unless we tell them to, and when they make a mess it's because we have made some kind of mistake, not them. A metaphor that is closer to reality is author Ted Nelson's description of a computer as "a box that follows a plan". A computer is a box, and inside the box are the plan, the machinery that follows the plan and the data upon which the plan acts.

Doing and Knowing

One more metaphor and we'll let it rest: programs are what a computer *does* and data are what a computer *knows*. (This description is credited to computer author Tom Swan.) The part that "does" is called the *central processing unit* (CPU). The part that "knows" is called *memory*. This "knowing" is done by encoding numbers, characters and logical states using the binary numeric notation discovered by Gottfried Leibniz in 1679. It wasn't until 1937 that Claude Shannon systematized the use of binary numbers into the maths and logic that computers use to this day. A *bit* is a binary digit, an irreducible atom of meaning that expresses either 1 or 0. As we explain a little later, bits are represented in computers by on/off electrical states.

Today, both the CPU and memory are made out of large numbers of transistors etched onto silicon chips. (A transistor is simply an electrical switch made out of exotic metals called semiconductors.) This wasn't always the case; before silicon chips, computers were built out of individual transistors and even vacuum tubes. (Zuse's seminal Z3 machine used electro-mechanical relays.)

Whatever they were made of, early computers followed the general plan shown in Figure 2-1. A central control console monitored several different subsystems, each of which was generally in its own cabinet or cabinets. There was the CPU, a punched tape or magnetic tape storage unit and two different memory units. One of the memory units held a series of machine instructions that comprised a computer program. The other memory unit held the data that the program manipulated. This is sometimes called the Harvard architecture, because the Mark I, a very early electromechanical computer developed at Harvard University in 1944, stored data and instructions separately.

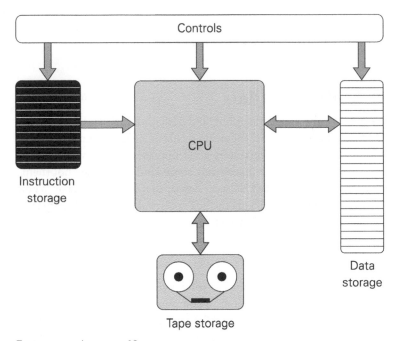

FIGURE 2-1: A pre-von Neumann computer

Not only were the data memory and the instruction memory of the Mark I physically separate, but they were also, generally, nothing like one another. Data memory might consist of vacuum tubes, dots on a phosphor screen or even sound pulses traveling through columns of mercury. (You can read more on the evolution of memory in Chapter 3.) Early instruction memory consisted of rows of mechanical switches and wire jumpers that could be moved from one point on a terminal bar to another. Technicians had to set each individual machine instruction by hand, using switches or jumpers, before the program could be run. (As you might imagine, there weren't a lot of machine instructions in early programs.)

Programs Are Data

The protean genius John von Neumann worked in many different fields, from mathematics to fluid dynamics, but computer people remember him for a remarkable insight: that *programs are data* and should be stored in the same memory system as data, using the same memory address space as data. It took some work to redesign computers to read machine instructions from data memory but once it was done, computing was changed forever. Instructions could be entered through a single panel of switches and stored in data memory, one-by-one. Later they could be written out from memory onto lengths of tape punched with patterns of holes, so that they wouldn't have to be entered by hand every time they were run.

Von Neumann's insight simplified computing greatly, and led straight to the explosion of computer power that occurred during the 1950s. Figure 2-2 is a highly simplified schematic of how modern computers operate. The figure shows no particular model or family of computer, and omits many of the more advanced features that we explain in later chapters.

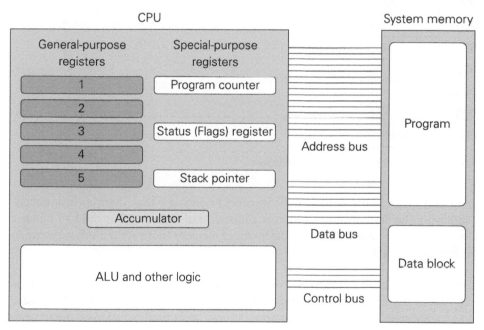

FIGURE 2-2: A simplified modern computer

Memory

In the simplest possible terms, *system memory* is a long row of storage compartments for data. Each location in the row has a unique numeric *address*. All locations are the same size; in modern computers this is generally the 8-bit byte (see Figure 2-3). However, computers read data from system memory in multi-byte chunks. Thirty-two-bit systems like the Raspberry Pi access memory 32 bits (4 bytes, generally called a *word*) at a time, and perform most of their internal operations on 32-bit quantities. In larger 64-bit desktops and laptops, system memory is accessed 64-bits (8 bytes) at a time. Note that nearly all modern computers allow operations to be performed on single bytes or 2-byte *halfwords*, though there is sometimes a speed penalty for doing so. However, the "bitness" of a computer is the size of its internal data word and operations, *not* the size of individual memory locations.

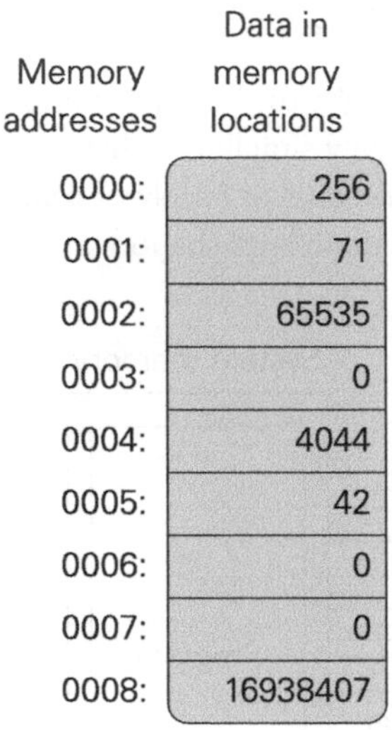

Memory addresses	Data in memory locations
0000:	256
0001:	71
0002:	65535
0003:	0
0004:	4044
0005:	42
0006:	0
0007:	0
0008:	16938407

FIGURE 2-3: Memory locations and their addresses

Memory addresses are ordered in numeric sequence beginning with 0. There is a little disconnect in having the first memory location at address 0 rather than 1, but think of number lines in mathematics, which start at 0. The maths of memory addresses is much easier when the addresses begin at 0.

The CPU locates its data for reading and writing by using memory addresses. It uses machine instructions to fetch data words from specified addresses in the system memory and place them in its registers for calculation or testing. It uses other machine instructions to write values stored in its registers to the system memory.

As mentioned earlier, computer programs themselves are stored in system memory, as sequences of machine instructions, each of which is (usually) a single data word. The difference between a program file and a data file lies almost entirely in how the CPU interprets the data in the file.

Memory is a very complicated business, and we treat it in depth in Chapter 3.

Registers

All CPUs contain a certain limited number of storage locations called *registers*. Registers are right on the silicon of the CPU, and the digital logic that executes machine instructions is not only near them but literally all around them. Each register holds a single value. Some registers have no single job and can be put to many different kinds of work. These *general-purpose registers* are named or numbered. Other registers have special jobs within the CPU. A few registers fall somewhere in between, in that they have specific jobs to do when certain machine instructions are executed, but in other cases may be used, like general- purpose registers, as a sort of silicon shirt pocket where the CPU can tuck values that will be needed again soon. Writing to registers and reading from them is fast—faster than accessing any other type of memory, especially system memory that lies outside the silicon on some other part of the computer's main circuit board.

There are many kinds of special-purpose registers. Some of the most common are:

- **Program counter:** A program counter register holds the address of the next machine instruction to be brought in from memory for execution. It "keeps the place" in a computer program.

- **Status:** A status register (sometimes called a flags register) holds a value divided into single bits or groups of bits. Each bit or group is updated with the status of something the CPU has just done. When the CPU compares the values in two registers, a single-bit "equal" flag will be set to either 1 (if the values were equal) or 0 (if the values were not equal). This allows an instruction that follows the comparison to know which way the comparison went.

- **Stack pointer:** A stack pointer holds an address in memory where a data structure called a last-in-first-out stack is stored. Stacks are fundamental to CPU operation; we describe them in more detail in Chapter 4 in the section "Inside the CPU".

- **Accumulator:** The accumulator is a register that holds the result of arithmetic and logical operations. (It is so named because it was used to accumulate intermediate values during calculations in very early computers.) In modern computers, no single register is the sole location for arithmetic results, and the accumulator's job has been redistributed to some or all of the general-purpose registers. However, some older machine instructions assume that a single register will hold the results of their operations, which is why the term has survived.

The ARM11 processor at the heart of the original Raspberry Pi has a total of 16 registers available to ordinary programs, of which three have special jobs. An additional two registers act as status registers. We have more to say about this in Chapter 3.

Registers are "valuable" because they are inside the CPU itself and therefore extremely fast. The more registers a CPU has, the less it must access system memory to store intermediate results. A universal rule in computing is that memory access is slow. A great deal of engineering has been done in recent years to reduce the number of times system memory must be accessed in order to get a given amount of work done.

The System Bus

One of the fundamental challenges of computing is getting values between system memory and the CPU as quickly as possible. Data values are stored in memory at locations that have specific numeric addresses. To access a value in the memory, the CPU must present the value's address in the memory to the memory system. The value will then be copied from memory and sent back to the CPU.

There is a pathway between the CPU and memory called the *system bus*. The system bus is a side-by-side group of electrical conductors called *lines*, each of which carries one bit of information. The number of bus lines varies depending on the type of computer and the chips it uses. The system bus carries three things:

- Memory addresses
- Data values
- Control signals that allow the CPU and system memory to coordinate traffic over the bus

In simple terms, the CPU places the address of a memory location on the bus. It also places one or more signals on the control lines, to tell the memory electronics whether the address is to be read from or written to. The CPU then either places a value on the bus to be written to the specified memory location, or waits for the system memory to place the value at the specified address on the bus to be sent back to the CPU.

Computer programs and program data are stored in different locations in memory but, except for how the CPU interprets them, there is no difference between a data word and a machine instruction. For this reason, the term "data values" embraces both data and instructions. We'll have more to say about this in the next two chapters.

Instruction Sets

There are a host of different CPU models in the world. Each has its own way of talking to memory and to other parts of the computer system. What sets the models apart most clearly are the individual operations that the CPU can perform. These are the machine instructions and, taken as a group, they are called an *instruction set*.

An instruction set is specific to a specific family of CPUs. Intel's CPUs represent one such family; ARM is another. Most individual CPUs understand only a single instruction set. The original Raspberry Pi's ARM11 processor actually has two instruction sets, though only one of them is actually used by the Raspberry Pi software. (There will be more on this in Chapter 4.)

The machine instructions in an instruction set are grouped by their general function: instructions that move data from or to memory and between registers; instructions that perform arithmetic calculations; instructions that perform logical operations; instructions that read status bits or set control bits; and so on. Early CPUs might have had as few as a dozen machine instructions. Modern CPUs can have a hundred or more.

Although it's useful to have a big-picture view of CPU instruction sets, you don't need to memorize them. Programmers rarely write programs by stringing together machine instructions. (This is done sometimes, but it's slow, specialized work.) Instead, programmers write lists of action statements that read more like human languages. These lists of action statements are then given to programs that translate them into lists of machine instructions. The translator programs are called *compilers* or *interpreters*, depending on how they operate. We cover these in much more detail in Chapter 5.

Voltages, Numbers and Meaning

It's common to say that computers don't really deal with text; they deal with numbers. Strictly speaking, even that isn't true. Down inside the silicon of the CPU where things happen, computers deal only with electrical voltage levels. The actual operation of computer chips entails a constant storm of electrical activity in which voltage levels change back and forth between two—and only two—values. One level is no voltage at all (0 volts) and the other is a single higher voltage level that may vary from computer to computer. It could be 5V or 3V or 3.6V or (on many mobile computers, as well as the Raspberry Pi) 1.2V or less. It could be some other value entirely, as long as it's always the same inside any given computer. We use 3V in the following discussion.

Computers do deal with numbers, but those numbers are encoded as voltage levels. By convention we say that a voltage level of 0V means the number 0 and a voltage level of 3V (or whatever level it is in the computer being discussed) means the number 1. Only two voltage levels are used in computer chip circuitry, so computers really only understand the two numeric digits, 0 and 1. That's all, and it doesn't sound like much. What can you do with only 0 and 1?

Everything.

Binary: Counting in 1s and 0s

Humans understand just 10 numeric digits: 0, 1, 2, 3, 4, 5, 6, 7, 8 and 9. Yet with those 10 digits we perform mind-bogglingly complex mathematical operations and express numbers that literally have no maximum value. We can express very large numbers with only a couple of different digits: a good approximation of the number of atoms in the entire observable universe can be stated as 1 followed by eighty 0s. Obviously, it's not about the number of numeric digits we have; it's about how we arrange them and (more to the point) the meaning that we assign to them.

The decimal notation that we just call numbers, which we learned when we were little, is less about numeric digits than columns. Multidigit numbers are digits arranged in columns, with each column having a value 10 times that of the column to its right. In a decimal number like 72,905, each column has a value and a digit in the column to tell us how many times that value is present in the number as a whole. In 72,905, there are 7 ten-thousands, 2 thousands, 9 hundreds, 0 tens and 5 ones.

This concept is easier to understand as a picture; see Figure 2-4.

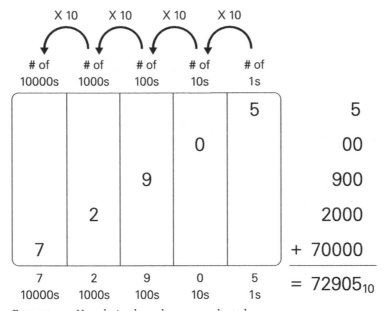

FIGURE 2-4: How decimal numbers are evaluated

We're so used to thinking in terms of powers of ten that it seems odd to imagine column values other than powers of ten. However, it doesn't just work; columnar notation using other column values is essential to understanding computing. So consider what numbers would look like if each column had a value *two* times the value of the column on its right, rather than ten. Instead of columns of ones, tens, hundreds, thousands and ten thousands, we would have columns of ones, twos, fours, eights, sixteens and so on. How many different digits would such a columnar system need?

Two: 0 and 1. In other words, instead of decimal notation with columnar multiples of ten, we have a *binary* notation with columnar multiples of two. See Figure 2-5, which dissects the binary number 11010. In 11010, there is 1 sixteen, 1 eight, 0 fours, 1 two and 0 ones. (Commas are not used in binary columnar notation.)

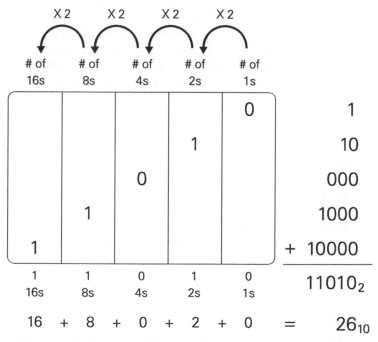

FIGURE 2-5: How binary numbers are evaluated

There is an alien look about numbers without the digits 2 to 9, but the numbers are real. To see what the binary number's value actually is in decimal terms we have to add up the values represented by all the columns: $16 + 8 + 0 + 2 + 0 = 26$. The two numbers 11010 and 26 have the same value. They're expressed in different notation, but the numbers are precisely equal. To recast a (very) old joke: there are only 10 kinds of people in the world: those who understand binary and those who don't.

The value of column multiples in a system of numeric notation is the base of the system. If the columnar multiple is 10, the system is *base 10*. If the columnar multiple is two, the system is base 2. (The small subscript numbers in the figures specify the number bases of the numbers beside them.) Theoretically, column multiples may be any integer value at all: base 3, base 4, base 8, base 11, base 16, anything. There's only one problem, which is explained in the next section.

The Digit Shortage

Our ingrained decimal notation is called base 10, and uses 10 digits. Base 2 uses two digits. Base 8 uses eight digits. Base 16 uses 16 digits—except that there are only ten digits. Zero to 9 is all we have. What about the other six digits? If we had evolved with eight fingers on each hand, there would doubtless be 16 digits, each a single, distinct symbol. Any symbols will do, as long as we agree on what each symbol means. We could use the symbols @, %, *, &, # and $. However, there is an ordering problem. These symbols have no universally understood order. Does * come before &? Only when they're typed in that order. Confusion would result without an agreed-upon ordering. So let's use six symbols that *do* have an agreed-upon order: A, B, C, D, E and F. Counting to 10 in our familiar decimal notation and symbols looks like this:

```
1, 2, 3, 4, 5, 6, 7, 8, 9, 10.
```

To count to 16 with an expanded digit set, we could say:

```
1, 2, 3, 4, 5, 6, 7 8, 9, A, B, C, D, E, F, 10.
```

In a scheme like this, the digit A represents decimal 10, B represents decimal 11, C represents decimal 12 and so on. A value is a value, irrespective of base. The differences between number bases is one of notation, not value. Base 16 is called *hexadecimal* notation, and it is crucial in understanding modern computers.

Counting and Numbering and 0

Before we go on, it's worth exploring a famous little weirdness from the computer world. Counting to 10, as we learned as kids, we begin with the digit 1. In computer technology, however, we start counting with the digit 0. When a computer person is counting memory locations, he or she starts at the first memory location and says, "0, 1, 2, 3, 4, 5. . .". What's going on here? It's actually a misunderstanding. Counting memory locations like this really isn't counting them. It's numbering them. And just as a number line from mathematics begins at 0, numbering entities in computer science begins with 0. A person would say, "There are six memory locations, numbered 0 to 5". A count (here, six) is how many entities are out there. Numbering them gives them both names and an order. The first memory location can be called "location 0". Having given that first memory location the name "location 0", it's clear that the name of the second location is "location 1" and so on.

When memory locations are numbered in this way, counting from 0, the numbers we give them are called *addresses*. The first address in an address space is always 0.

Hexadecimal as a Shorthand for Binary

Hexadecimal notation is a columnar notation, just as decimal and binary notations are. Each column has a value 16 times the value of the column to its right. The numbers look odd because the 16-digit symbols are a mixture of letters and numbers, but the notation works the same way as decimal and binary. The values of the columns mount up fast: by the fifth column, the value of the column is 65,536.

Figure 2-6 shows this. The hexadecimal number 3C0A9 is equivalent to the decimal number 245,929. Both numbers are equivalent to the binary value 111100000010101001. This is a clue as to why hexadecimal notation is important.

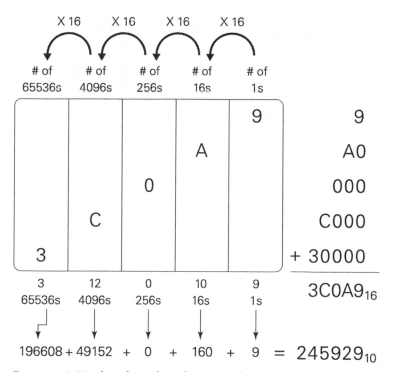

FIGURE 2-6: How hexadecimal numbers are evaluated

So why does hexadecimal notation even exist? Computers don't really use hexadecimal numbers. They use binary numbers, period, encoded as electrical voltage levels. "Hex" (as we say informally) is used by all of us who have trouble interpreting long strings of 1s and 0s. It's a sort of shorthand, allowing us to express binary numbers in a much more accessible form. 111100000010101001 is the same value as 3C0A9. Which would you prefer to work with?

Figure 2-7 summarizes the use of hexadecimal as shorthand and also binary numbers are represented by a series of different voltage levels on electrical conductors like the system bus. The system bus shown is 16 bits wide. Each line in the system bus might be a copper trace on a circuit board or a microscopic wire inside a chip, with one of either two voltages on each of the copper traces. The digit 1 represents a 3V reading on a bus line. The digit "0" represents a 0V reading on a bus line.

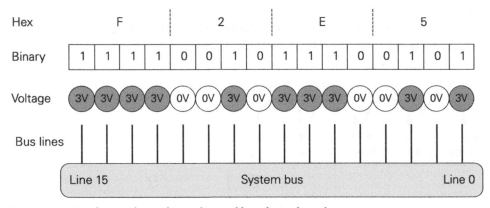

FIGURE 2-7: Bus lines, voltages, binary bits and hexadecimal numbers

Each digit in a hexadecimal number can represent values from 0 to 15. It takes four bits to represent values up to 15. This is why each digit in a hexadecimal number represents four binary digits of either 1 or 0.

It's possible to lose track of which base a given value is written in. The number 11 is a binary number. It's also a decimal number, and a hexadecimal number as well. The three values are of course different, but the two digits—11—look precisely the same. Different typographical conventions are used to explicitly specify the number base of a given number:

- For binary, the letter b or B is often used after the number; for example, 011010B.

- For binary, the prefix 0b is often used, as in 0b011010.

- You may also sometimes see the prefix % in front of binary numbers; for example, %011010.

- For hexadecimal, use the letter h or H after the number; for example, F2E5H.

- The prefixes $ and 0x are also used to designate hexadecimal notation; for example, $F2E5 and 0xF2E5.

In printed material, such as books and documentation, a subscript suffix is sometimes used to indicate the number base, as in $F2E5_{16}$. Subscripts are difficult to do in editors used for programming, so even in printed work, one of the previously mentioned conventions is used.

Doing Binary and Hexadecimal Arithmetic

Binary and hexadecimal are simply different forms of notation. All the laws of arithmetic still apply. It's possible to do addition, subtraction, multiplication and division on paper in either binary or hexadecimal. The methods are identical; you simply have to remember things like the fact that, in binary, 1 + 1 = 10. In hex, A + 2 = C and A + C = 16 (just not the 16 you're used to—16H is 22 decimal). Carries and borrows work the same way irrespective of base. Performing long division on paper in hex is a little surreal, but it can be done.

Yes, it can be done, and it may be good practice, but with a software calculator app on virtually every computer with a graphical shell it may not be the best use of your time. We're not going to explain how to do manual binary or hex maths here. Instead, we suggest you become familiar with a software calculator capable of number bases other than decimal. On the Raspberry Pi under the Raspbian operating system, the calculator is called Galculator. It's listed in the start menu in the Accessories group. If you haven't yet used any operating system (Raspbian is only one of many, as are Windows and OS X), hold that thought; we'll cover operating systems in the next section.

By default, Galculator works in decimal only, in Basic mode. To use Galculator for calculation in other number bases, first select View and then Scientific mode. The keys for hex digits A–F are greyed out. To change the number base used, select Calculator from the main menu, then Number bases from the pull-down (see Figure 2-8). Click the radio button for the base of your choice. (Galculator also supports octal, which is base 8, but octal is increasingly uncommon and we don't mention it further here.) For binary, all digits except 0 and 1 are greyed out. For hex, all digits become active.

When you're in scientific mode with your base of choice selected, Galculator works just as a calculator works in decimal.

Here's a tip: to convert a value from one base to another, enter the value in its original base and then select Calculator ⇨ Number bases and click the button for the base to which you want to convert the value. The conversion is done instantly, just by changing the base.

TIP

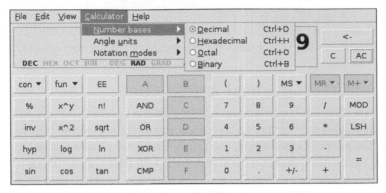

FIGURE 2-8: Changing number bases in Galculator

Operating Systems: The Boss of the Box

There is a great deal of digital machinery baked into the silicon of modern CPUs. They do not, however, run completely by themselves. Factories need managers and if a CPU and its memory system represent a factory, the factory manager is called an *operating system* (OS). There have been thousands of operating systems throughout computer history, but at the time of writing only a handful have any significant market share: Windows, GNU/ Linux, Android, OS X and iOS. None of these arose in a vacuum. Windows has its roots in IBM's OS/2, as well as an older "big iron" operating system called VAX VMS. All the others have deep roots in Unix, another big-system OS created by Bell Labs in the late 1960s.

Operating systems are programs, and like all programs they're ultimately sequences of machine instructions. Unlike word processors and video games, operating systems have special powers that enable them to manage a computer system. Many of these powers depend on special machine instructions that are designed to be used only by operating systems. Operating systems are loaded and run first, through a boot-up process controlled by a computer's bootloader, which is a special program tasked with getting the operating system from storage into memory and then running it. Once an OS has loaded and configured itself, the computer is "open for business" and the OS can begin management of the machine.

What an Operating System Does

A high-level definition of an operating system is that it stands between a computer user and the computer hardware, enabling the user to use the computer's various resources without interfering with other users or with computer operation itself. Its major jobs can be broken down this way:

- **Process management:** The OS launches individual threads of execution for its own needs and the needs of users. It allocates execution time on the CPU among executing threads. If the CPU has multiple cores, it distributes processes among the cores. (More on this later.)

- **Memory management:** The OS allocates memory to running processes, in most cases as separate memory spaces that are protected from interference by other processes. Through a technology called virtual memory, the OS allows the computer literally to use more memory than it actually has, by writing the least-used process memory out to disk when more memory is needed. (Much more on this in Chapter 3.)

- **File management:** The OS maintains one or more file systems, which allocate file storage space on disks and other mass-storage devices and manage the reading of data from files and the writing to and deletion of files.

- **Peripheral management:** The OS manages access to system peripherals like keyboards, mice, printers, scanners, graphics coprocessors and (in cooperation with file systems) mass storage devices. This is generally done through specialised software interfaces called device drivers, which are written for specific peripherals and may be installed separately, much like user applications.

- **Network management:** The OS manages the computer's access to external networks (like local area networks and the Internet) through a collection of standard methods called networking protocols. The protocols are implemented in one or more pieces of software that, taken together, are called the network stack.

- **User account management:** All modern operating systems allow different users to have their own accounts on the computer. An account includes a unique login, a set of security rules called privileges and a private file space protected from manipulation by other users.

- **Security:** Scattered throughout an OS are mechanisms to keep running processes from interfering with one another and with the OS itself. Much of OS security is done by defining rules that specify what processes and users can and cannot do. Certain users called administrators or super users have powers that ordinary users do not have, in order to control the way the OS does its work.

- **User interface management:** The OS manages user interaction with the computer through software mechanisms called shells. A shell may be as simple as a text command line in a terminal window, or it can be a full-blown windowed graphical environment like those used in Windows, Mac OS X and desktop implementations of Linux, including Raspbian on the Raspberry Pi.

Saluting the Kernel

The issue of user shells highlights the question of what is and what is not actually a part of the operating system. We're used to Microsoft Windows, in which the user interface is tightly bound to the operating system as a whole and cannot be changed except in small ways via configuration options. In Linux (including the Raspbian OS) the user interface is an installable module, not much different in nature from a pure application like a word processor. There are textual shells like bash and ksh, and many different graphical shells, including GNOME, KDE, Xfce, Cinnamon and others. These shells can be installed and uninstalled by users with administrator privileges.

Linux has a long history of modular design. Many of its elements may be changed, within certain limitations. At its heart, however, is a monolithic block of code called a kernel. The Linux kernel has full control over the computer's hardware. It adapts to differences in hardware through *loadable kernel modules* (LKMs) that extend the kernel with device-specific code. LKMs include things like device drivers and file systems.

Multiple Cores

Modern CPUs often have more than a single execution core. A *core* is a separate and almost entirely independent engine that executes machine instructions. (In silicon design circles, core has a broader meaning, as we explain in Chapter 4.) At the time of writing, CPUs with two, four and six cores are common in the personal computing world, and units with eight cores are beginning to appear. Each core executes processes independently, but all cores share system resources like memory. The operating system controls the use of all cores in a system, just as it controls everything else. The OS typically runs in one core, and parcels processes out to the other core(s) as needed.

The ARM11 CPU in the Raspberry Pi has only one core. Other ARM processors have as many as four. However, the nature of ARM hardware allows chip designers to create custom CPUs, and the latest ARM CPU—Cortex-A15—supports arbitrary numbers of cores in clusters of four if designers want them.

We'll have more to say about how ARM CPUs and ARM-based single-chip systems are created in Chapter 3.

Chapter 3

Electronic Memory

COMPUTING AS WE know it today is a wild dance between the central processing unit (CPU) and memory. Instructions in memory are fetched, and the CPU executes them. In executing instructions, the CPU reads data from memory, changes it and then writes it back. Data and instructions that are used a lot are pulled in closer, via cache. Data and instructions that aren't needed for the time being are swapped out of virtual memory onto disk.

To understand this dance you need an understanding of both the CPU and memory. Which, then, to study first? In most cases, the CPU is considered the star of the show and always begins the parade. That's a mistake. There are multitudes of CPU designs out there, all of them different and all stuffed to the gills with tricks to make their own parts of the dance move more quickly. Memory, on the other hand, is a simpler and less diverse technology. Its moves in the dance are fairly simple: store data from the CPU and hand it back when requested, as quickly as possible. To a great extent, memory dictates the speed at which the dance proceeds. The designs of our CPUs are heavily influenced by the speed limitations of system memory.

That being the case, it makes sense to study memory first. If you understand memory technology thoroughly, you're halfway to understanding anything else in a modern computer system.

There Was Memory Before
There Were Computers

For a long time, computers were really special-purpose haywire calculators. What passed for programs were lashed up by hand with switches and jumper wires representing 1s and 0s. Then John von Neumann and others proposed that programs be stored as digital patterns on the machine, right in with the data that the programs were written to process. The first generation of these stored-program computers used single-bit storage circuits (colloquially called *flip-flops*) constructed from vacuum tubes to store programs and data. Imagine for a moment storing a 1 or a 0 in something the size of your fist! Apart from being enormous, hot and power-hungry, vacuum tube data storage was *volatile*—when the computer was powered down, the electronic states of the vacuum tubes vanished as the tubes went dark.

To keep programs and data permanently, vacuum-tube data was written to strips of paper tape or cardboard Hollerith punch cards. (Hollerith cards were used in mechanical tabulation of census data. They predate digital computers by 50 years.) The machines to read tape or cards into a computer were electromechanical and very slow. Sending intermediate results out to electromechanical paper storage was even slower and wasted most of the speed that electronic computing offered. A better way to record code on data than punching holes in pulped trees was desperately needed.

Rotating Magnetic Memory

In those early, crazy days of computing, many things were tried. Mercury-based delay-line memory units stored bits as mechanical pulses—sound waves, basically—travelling through linear columns of mercury in sealed tubes. Like modern dynamic computer memory, delay-line memory had to be refreshed every time a bit (encoded as a pulse) arrived at the far end of the tube. Strings of pulses representing code and data marched endlessly through the mercury, read and written by quartz piezoelectric crystals as needed. Mercury memory systems were huge, hot, heavy and full of toxic heavy metal. They were also very touchy to adjust and keep in operation.

Another early memory storage scheme encoded bits as dots of light on the surface of a cathode-ray tube (CRT) with long-persistence phosphor, much like the tubes used in early radar displays. The dots, once written, would linger in the phosphor for a few seconds and could be read by a plate placed against the face of the tube. As with delay-line memory, CRT memory had to be refreshed periodically. Nonetheless, each of the tubes could store 1,024 bits in a fraction of the space required by delay-line storage. Known as Williams tubes, these were used as memory in the famous IBM 701 commercial computers, introduced in 1952. They were the first widely used *random-access memory* (RAM)—so-called because bits could be accessed at any time from anywhere on the face of the tube. The term *RAM* is still used today, even though we've mostly forgotten that there was ever any other kind of computer memory. The preferred term is read/write memory, but terms like *RAM*, *SRAM*, *DRAM* and *SDRAM* are so universally used that we use them in this book.

Both of these memory technologies, like vacuum-tube memory, were volatile. A memory technology that would retain its data even when the computer was powered down would make many things easier, and new things would be possible. Encoding information as tiny regions of magnetic alignment on a moving magnetic surface dates back to the early 1930s. The Germans invented magnetic sound recording, which wrote sound waveforms to spools of plastic tape coated with iron-oxide powder. By 1950, this technology had been adapted to store digital data instead of audio waveforms, and it was incorporated in the legendary UNIVAC machine to replace paper tape and Hollerith cards.

Magnetic tape was a faster storage medium than paper tape and cards, and it had the advantage of being rewritable. After a hole was punched in paper tape, the hole was permanent. However, magnetic pulses on tape could be written and erased again and again. Unfortunately, tape was still too slow to be used as computer system memory.

The solution was again invented by the Germans: a metal drum the size of a small wastepaper basket, coated with iron oxide powder, spun on its axis as quickly as the motor and bearing technology of the time would allow. Tiny magnetic sensor heads were attached to the drum's housing, with each head aligned over a separate narrow "stripe" on the drum's surface. The magnetic heads could write bits to a track by passing electrical pulses through the heads. A pulse aligned the magnetic poles of oxide particles on the drum surface, creating a tiny magnetised region. This magnetic region would induce a tiny current in the same head when it passed beneath the head. A bit was encoded as a 1 or a 0 by the presence or absence of magnetic alignment in a small region of oxide.

In a way similar to delay-line memory, bits written onto tracks circled endlessly beneath the read/write heads as the drum rotated. The bits could only be read or written sequentially. If a value written onto a drum track was needed by the computer, the computer had to wait until that value came around again in order to read it. This slowed access down, but the drums were being spun very quickly. Access was thus faster than any earlier memory technology except for electronic flip-flops inside the CPU itself.

Programmers learned how to finesse the sequential delays inherent in drum memory by synchronising their programs to the rotation of the drum. The programs knew when a particular sequence of values would appear under the heads, and did other things during the latency period. This sounds foolish today but in 1953 it was a mainstream technique and made drum memory the fastest computer memory technology available.

One final advance in rotating magnetic memory foreshadowed modern hard-drive technology: *fixed-head magnetic memory*, which consisted of a magnetic disk with concentric tracks, each track aligned with its own stationary magnetic read/write head. Disks could be spun much faster than drums, so although a drum could hold more code and data, a disk could provide access more quickly. Apart from the shape of the storage medium, magnetic disk memory and drum memory were the same. Magnetic disk storage units of this sort were used as fast "swap memory" for virtual memory systems until the early 1970s, when moving-head magnetic disk units replaced them.

Magnetic Core Memory

Moving parts can be bad news, and parts moving very quickly can be very bad news. Rotating magnetic memory was loud and prone to vibration. Worse, if a drum or bearing failed, the device would generally destroy itself beyond repair. So the world was ready for fast computer memory without moving parts. In 1955 it arrived. Unlike earlier memory technologies, magnetic core memory is still used in certain "legacy" (that is, ancient) computers and a small number of industrial process controllers.

Magnetic core memory systems use tiny *toroidal* (ring-shaped) magnetic beads called *cores*. The cores are made of an exotic iron oxide with high *remanance* (the ability to retain a magnetic field over time) and low *coercitivity* (the energy required to change the magnetic field). One core is capable of storing 1 bit. The state of any given bit is represented not by the presence or absence of a magnetic field but by its orientation. A core's magnetic field can exist in two different orientations, which by convention are called clockwise and counterclockwise. The state of a bit is changed by "flipping" its core's magnetic field from clockwise to counterclockwise, or vice versa.

The toroidal cores are woven into a rectangular matrix of very fine wire supported by a sheet of circuit board material. Each assembly is called a *plane*. Four wires pass through the centre hole of every core (see Figure 3-1):

- An *x* wire, which provides one dimension to select a core from a plane

- A *y* wire, which provides the second dimension to select a core from a plane

- A sense wire, which allows the system to read the magnetic state of a core

- An inhibit wire, which allows the system to set the state of a core

In Figure 3-1, the cores are shown edge-on. By sending carefully controlled electric currents through the four wires in various combinations, the magnetic field orientation in selected cores may be sensed or changed. Cores may be selected singly and at random as the computer requires. Like the earlier Williams tubes, magnetic core memory is random-access memory. It's also non-volatile, and the cores retain their magnetic fields (and thus their data) when the computer is powered down.

How Core Memory Works

Electrical conductors generate magnetic fields when current passes through them. The strength of this magnetic field is proportional to the strength of the current. If a wire running through the centre hole of a core generates a sufficiently strong magnetic field, the magnetic field in the core aligns itself with the direction of the current flowing through the wire.

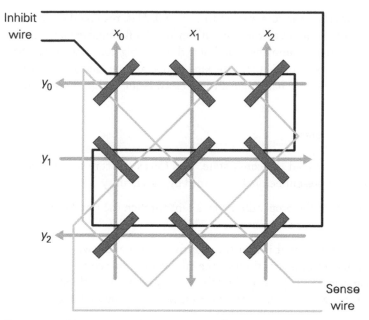

FIGURE 3-1: The structure of a core memory plane

The x and y wires are used to select one core from the grid of cores in a plane, just as x and y values select one point in a Cartesian plane from geometry. A current is passed through the x and y wires that both pass through the core to be selected. Each of the two wires carries enough current to generate half of the magnetic field required to flip the core. Thus, the core through which both wires pass is given enough of a magnetic pulse to change its orientation. The direction of the current passing through the x and y wires determines the orientation. Passing the current one way imposes a 0-state on the core. Passing the current the other way imposes a 1-state on the core.

This sounds simpler than it is. The problem is that the computer must read a core before writing to it. And reading the core involves an attempt to write to it. The process of reading a core is easier to follow as a list of steps:

1. The computer attempts to force the state of the selected core to a 0-state by sending current of the appropriate direction to the x and y wires that intersect at the core of interest.

2. If the selected core was already at the 0-state, nothing happens.

3. If the selected core was originally in the 1-state, the core state changes to 0. The state change induces a small current in the sense wire. The presence of a current on the sense wire tells the computer that the bit had originally been a 1-bit.

The computer now knows whether the core was set to 1 or to 0. Alas, reading the state of a core is like holding a match to your sweater to see if it's made of a flammable fabric. If the sweater catches fire, the material is flammable—and now there's a big hole in your sweater. By reading a core's state, the core is forced to 0. This kind of operation is called a *destructive read*. To retain the value that the core had originally expressed requires that the state read must be written back to the core.

Here's how writing to a core is done:

1. The computer attempts to read the core's state. This forces the core to the 0-state. Whatever state had been present before is discarded by the circuitry.

2. To write a 1-bit, current of the proper direction is sent through the x and y wires that intersect at the core. The core's state changes to 1.

3. To write a 0-bit, the same current is sent through the same x and y wires. However, this time, an identical current is sent through the inhibit wire. This creates a magnetic field that bucks (cancels) the field created by the x and y wires. The inhibit wire prevents (inhibits) the change to a 1-bit. Because the bit was originally a 0 bit, the 0-state remains unchanged.

It sounds a little crazy today, but it does work: to read a bit from a core, you must read it and then write it back. To write a bit to a core, you must first clear the core to 0 by reading it and then either write (1) or inhibit a write (0) by using the inhibit wire.

Memory Access Time

We've gone on about the internals of core memory at some length to make a point: electronic memory is governed by physics that may be a lot more subtle and complex than you expect. At some level, even digital devices operate by analogue physics. This complexity governs the all-important factor of memory access time. Reading memory takes time. Writing to memory takes time. From a height, progress towards increasing the speed of computers is the struggle to make memory fast enough not to slow the CPU to a crawl.

Core memory was the fastest sort of memory in existence when it was introduced, and it swept drum and fixed-head disk memory into the sea. (Disk memory evolved into hard disk mass storage as we know it today through the use of movable read/write heads.) Early core memory had an access time of 6 microseconds (μ), which fell to 600 ns nanoseconds (1 ns here is 0.001 microsecond) when the technology was mature in the mid-1970s. This was comparable to the purely electronic memory in very early personal computers like the Altair and Apple II.

Core memory was fast for its day, but it was difficult to manufacture and very expensive. This is why it was used in mainframe computers and later minicomputers, but never to any extent in personal computers. By the mid-1970s something else had appeared to change the nature of computing even more than core memory did.

Static Random Access Memory (SRAM)

You might wonder where transistors enter our story. Computer memory built from discrete (individual) transistors did exist, but it was bulkier and more expensive than magnetic core memory. It was also volatile. Although discrete transistor flip-flop memory was faster than core memory, its disadvantages kept it from being a broad commercial success.

Besides, in the late 1950s, engineers did the obvious and began placing multiple transistors on a single tiny chip of silicon. Texas Instruments (TI) engineer Jack Kilby added resistors to the same wafers, allowing all the necessary elements of computer logic gates to be integrated on one silicon wafer. The *integrated circuit* (IC) was born. The famous 7400-series of transistor-transistor logic (TTL) devices was introduced in 1966 and they were used to build new generations of computers that were faster and more compact than ever before.

Although TTL computer memory appeared along with gates and counters, it was not until 1969 that Intel's TTL 64-bit 3101 chip became the first commercial IC computer memory device. Intel's 256-bit 1101, introduced only a few months later, was slower but contained more bits and was less expensive. The 1101's use of metal-oxide semiconductor (MOS) technology was a watershed. MOS transistors are field-effect devices, in which electron flow is controlled by electric fields, as in vacuum tubes, whereas TTL chips use the older bipolar junction transistor (BJT) technology. BJTs operate by using small current flows to control larger current flows, with total current flows many times that of MOS transistors. MOS techniques could put many more transistors on a single chip while reducing power dissipation and waste heat. Except in very specialised applications, MOS soon drove TTL out of the memory market.

The 1101 and 3101 were static random access memory (SRAM) devices. They were random-access because a single bit could be accessed "at random" without any need to wait on sequential access or sift through other bits. They were static because bits written to the chips would remain in their written state as long as the chips had power—even if the computer's clock was slowed or stopped. Both chips have now been obsolete for decades, but apart from packing more bits into a package, today's SRAM chips work in very much the same way.

The basic logic element in SRAM chips is the flip-flop. A flip-flop is a logic circuit with an output that can be in one of two states, and that can be switched from one state to the other by a pulse or voltage change on an input. It will hold that state until another pulse switches it to its opposite state, or until power is removed from the circuit. Because it has two states, and because binary digits have two possible values, a flip-flop can "remember" a single bit.

SRAM bits are stored in *cells*, each of which is basically a flip-flop circuit. SRAM cells require at least four transistors. To improve speed and reliability, some designs use six transistors, at the cost of additional complexity and a smaller number of bits stored per device.

Technology has moved on quite a bit since SRAM was introduced. Except in very specialised applications that require the shortest possible access times, SRAM has been replaced by DRAM, as we'll explain shortly. But first, let's look at what SRAM and DRAM have in common: memory addressing.

NOTE   Read more about DRAM later in this chapter in the "Dynamic Random Access Memory (DRAM)" section.

Address Lines and Data Lines

As we saw with core memory, putting multiple bits in a memory device requires some way of selecting bits within the device to read or write. Core memory uses an *x/y* addressing scheme very much like a Cartesian plane in geometry to select one core from all the cores in a core memory plane. Inside an SRAM or DRAM chip, memory cells are arranged in a matrix, and they're selected using a system of *x/y* addressing. Computers don't locate cells in a memory system through *x/y* coordinates. Additional circuitry is needed to convert a binary memory address to a pair of *x/y* values that select one cell from the many.

The job of this circuitry is called *memory addressing*. Think of a computer memory system as a black box. On one side is a group of wires called address lines. On the other side is a group of wires called *data lines*. The number of wires in each group varies, depending on how much memory the system contains and how it's organised. The address lines are used to select which memory location is to be read or written to. The data lines carry data either out of the system, when a value is read, or into the system, when a value is written. There are also a smaller number of wires called *control lines*. These have various functions, the most important of which is to specify whether a selected memory location is to be read from or written to.

In reality, although memory systems may consist of a single memory chip (as the Raspberry Pi's does—more on that later) memory systems are generally put together from smaller units, either chips or groups of chips mounted on small circuit boards.

The best way to begin is to look at a very simple memory chip and how it works internally. The chip shown in Figure 3-2 doesn't actually exist, but the general principles apply to nearly all memory chips of whatever size.

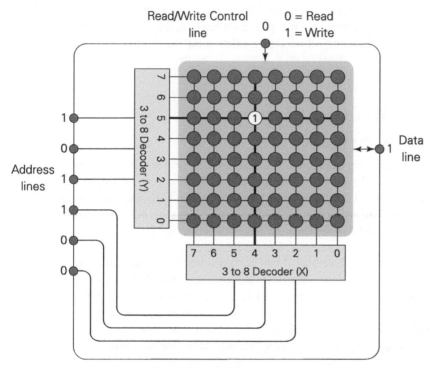

FIGURE 3-2: How a memory chip addresses cells

At the heart of the chip are 64 memory cells, arranged in a matrix of eight cells by eight cells. Each cell holds a single binary digit, which may be either a 1 or a 0. There are six address lines on the chip. Six is enough, because a six-digit binary number can express 64 different values, from 0 to 63.

Inside the chip are two decoders. A decoder is a logic element that accepts a binary number as an input value and uses it to select one, and only one, of several output lines. There is one output line for every binary value that the input lines can express. In our example, each decoder accepts a 3-bit binary number and selects one of eight output lines. A 3-bit binary number can express eight values, from 0 to 7. The decoder's output lines are numbered 0 to 7. Put the binary value 101 (equivalent to 5 in our everyday decimal notation) on the input lines, and output line 5 is selected. (In Figure 3-2, this is shown for the *y* decoder.)

Each of the two decoders handles one of the two axes (x and y) in the matrix. The 6-bit binary address is split into two 3-bit parts. One 3-bit value is applied to the x decoder and the other to the y decoder. The cell at their x,y intersection is the cell selected for reading or writing. The state of the read/write control line determines whether the selected cell will be read from or written to. When the control line is set to 0, a read is performed and whatever value is stored in the selected cell is placed on the data line. When the control line is set to 1, a write is performed and whatever value is on the data line is written to the selected cell.

Combining Memory Chips into Memory Systems

The imaginary memory chip in Figure 3-2 can store and retrieve 1 bit at a time. Since the 1972 appearance of Intel's ground-breaking 8008 CPU, however, computers use at least 8 bits at a time. Pulling an 8-bit byte out of a memory chip with a single data line can be done, but it would require eight memory-read operations to gather the whole 8 bits. A memory system like that would reduce the speed of any CPU to a crawl.

One common solution is to distribute 8 bits of data across eight physically separate chips. Figure 3-3 shows how this is done. This time, the scenario is real. The memory chips are the classic 2102 device, which was manufactured by several firms and was very popular in the 1970s. Each 2102 chip stores 1,024 bits. The 2102's 10 address lines are connected in parallel, so all 10 address lines connect to all eight chips. An address placed on the address lines will select the corresponding bit in each chip. That bit will be delivered to each chip's data pin. Because the chips work in parallel, a full 8-bit byte will be available on the row of 8 data pins with only one read from memory.

In Figure 3-3, eight chips, each containing 1,024 bits, are combined into the equivalent of a single memory chip holding 8,192 bits. But more to the point, the arrangement of bits in the memory system shown is 1,024 × 8, and not 8,192 × 1. A full 8-bit byte can be written to the memory bank with a single memory access—and read back just as quickly.

Note that the memory system has 10 address lines. To access a single byte from among the 1,024, the value placed on the address bus must be able to express values from 0 to 1,023 in binary. 1,023 in binary is 1111111111. Ten binary digits require 10 address bus lines.

A group of digital lines connecting a memory system of any kind to a computer is called a *bus*. The 10 address lines in Figure 3-3, taken together, form the address bus. The eight data lines form the data bus. However many control lines the memory system may have (the number's not important in this example) together make up the control bus.

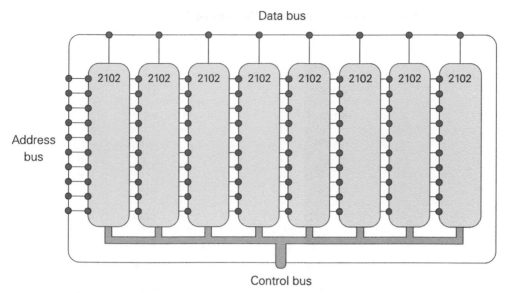

FIGURE 3-3: A 1,024 × 8 memory system

The old 2102 chip was organised as 1,024 × 1 bit. This was a common organisation for a long time, but it was far from the only one. For example, there are SRAM chips that are organised in many other ways, from 256 × 4 in ancient times, to 1,031,072 × 16 today. (There are much larger memory chips in modern systems, but they're all DRAM, which we get to shortly.)

The number of storage locations in a memory chip or system is called its *depth*. The number of bits at each storage location is a memory chip's or system's *width*. The size of a memory chip or system is the number of bits (not bytes!) that it contains. This is defined as the depth times the width.

Some examples:

- The old 2102 chip has a depth of 1,024 and a width of 1. Its size is 1,024 bits.

- The old 6116 chip has a depth of 2,048 and a width of 8. Its size is 16,384 bits.

- The modern Cypress 62167 chip has a depth of 1,048,580 and a width of 16. Its size is 16,777,280 bits.

The literal numbers describing a chip's size become ungainly beyond a certain point. Powers of 2 do not convert to round numbers in decimal notation. In talking about memory chips and systems, we use shortcuts, as shown in Table 3-1.

Table 3-1   **Conventional Terms for Powers of 2**

2^{10}	1,024	1K
2^{11}	2,048	2K
2^{12}	4,096	4K
2^{13}	8,192	8K
2^{14}	16,384	16K
2^{15}	32,768	32K
2^{16}	65,536	64K
2^{17}	131,072	128K
2^{18}	262,144	256K
2^{19}	524,288	512K
2^{20}	1,048,576	1M
2^{21}	2,097,152	2M
2^{22}	4,194,304	4M
2^{23}	8,388,608	8M
2^{24}	16,777,216	16M
2^{25}	33,554,432	32M
2^{26}	67,108,864	64M
2^{27}	134,217,728	128M
2^{28}	268,436,480	256M
2^{29}	536,870,912	512M
2^{30}	1,073,745,824	1G
2^{31}	2,147,483,648	2G
2^{32}	4,294,967,296	4G

In recent years, there's been an effort to distinguish these shortcuts (which refer to powers of 2) from the equivalent ISO prefixes (which refer to powers of 10) by introducing new shortcuts and prefixes. One kibibyte (1KiB) is the precise quantity 1,024 bytes, formerly referred to as a kilobyte (KB); under this scheme a kilobyte is now 1,000 bytes, just as a kilogram is 1,000 grams. Likewise, 1 mebibyte (1MiB) is the precise quantity 1,048,576 bytes and 1 gibibyte is the precise quantity 1,073,745,824 bytes. The new terms were defined in IEEE standard 1541, released in 2002. They are not widely used at this writing, but it's worthwhile to keep them in mind, especially when reading the scientific and engineering literature.

Dynamic Random Access Memory (DRAM)

Each SRAM memory cell is a complete flip-flop circuit that, at a minimum, consists of four transistors. SRAM is fast, certainly the fastest mass-market memory technology ever devised. It's still in use, when speed is required above all else. (We talk about how speed affects computer memory systems later in this chapter.) SRAM has two major disadvantages:

- It's big, in terms of space per bit on a silicon chip.

- It doesn't shrink well, at least past a certain point.

These limitations keep SRAM at a certain size and a certain cost per bit. This was recognised by researchers early on. In 1968, IBM fellow Robert H. Dennard proposed a radically different memory technology that did away with flip-flop data storage altogether. His memory technology stored bits as the presence or the absence of charge in a miniscule capacitor. The presence of charge represented a binary 1 and the absence of charge represented a binary 0. (This assignment of meaning is arbitrary and could be the reverse, as long the memory chip presents the proper voltage levels on its data lines.)

A Dennard memory cell consists of only one transistor and one capacitor. Even with early fabrication technologies, this was less than half as large as an SRAM cell. Dennard also had a hunch that this technology could be scaled far more easily than SRAM. He meant that the physics of a Dennard cell would allow future fabrication technology to shrink individual cells far beyond what was possible with SRAM. He was right, to an extent that no one, not even Dennard himself, could have predicted in 1968.

With metal-oxide-semiconductor (MOS) transistors designed specifically for memory cell use, Dennard's memory cells used far less power and generated far less waste heat. (This also helped with scaling—more bits could be placed on a single chip without fear of the chip "cooking" itself with its own heat.)

The trade-off lay in the physics of charge stored in a capacitor: even in the best and purest silicon chip capacitors, over time a stored charge leaks away. Large capacitors can store so much charge that they can be used as batteries sometimes. The microscopic capacitors in Dennard's scheme were so small that their charge leaked away in mere hundredths of a second. As with the ancient mercury delay-line memory systems, capacitor-based memory has to be refreshed (read and then rewritten) periodically. Thus, this memory technology is dynamic and goes by the name *dynamic random access memory* (DRAM).

How DRAM Works

Like both core memory and SRAM, DRAM memory chips are based on two-dimensional arrays of memory cells. Cells are addressed by x and y coordinates, using address decoders (look back at Figure 3-2). Each individual cell consists of a single MOS transistor and a single capacitor, as shown in Figure 3-4. The three connections to the transistor are well known to electronics hobbyists: the gate is an electrical switch toggle that either connects the source to the drain or insulates them from each other. (The source and the drain are different in minor ways that do not affect this description.)

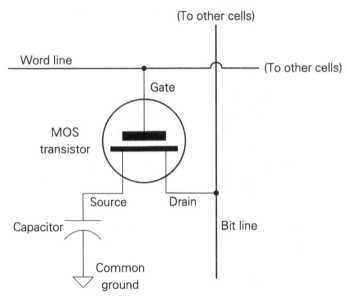

FIGURE 3-4: DRAM cells

Figure 3-4 shows four DRAM cells within a matrix of identical cells that may number into the billions. Cells are organised into rows and columns. A row (the horizontal dimension in Figure 3-4) is linked by a common connection to all cell transistor gates called a *word line*. The word line is used to select one row from all rows in the memory chip. It "flips the switch" of all the MOS transistors in a row at once, causing them to either conduct or not conduct. Cells in each column are linked by a common connection to all transistor drain leads, called a *bit line*. At the end of each column's bit line is a sense amplifier, which allows an almost unimaginably small unit of charge to be reliably interpreted as a 1 or a 0. In very general terms, the word lines are used to select cells and the bit lines are used to read and write data in cells.

An MOS transistor is a solid-state switch. When the transistor is switched on, the capacitor is electrically connected to the bit line. When a cell's transistor is switched off, the capacitor is isolated and charge (or lack of charge) is retained inside the capacitor. The charge leaks away in a fraction of a second unless the cell is refreshed. (More on that shortly.) The general idea is to select a cell and either read the state of its charge or write a charge state to the cell depending on whether a 1 or a 0 is to be written. This is not done individually, but in almost all cases to an entire row of cells at once.

DRAM operation has a familiar resemblance to the operation of core memory. DRAM, like core memory, uses destructive reads: the physics of reading the charge from the cell destroys the charge, which then has to be written back in a refresh operation. There are crucial differences; unlike core memory, which is static, DRAM needs to be refreshed regularly whether it is read or not.

These steps outline how a bit is read from a DRAM cell:

1. The cell's bit line must be given an initial voltage (a precharge) that places it precisely halfway between a full charge on the capacitor and complete discharge.

2. When the precharge is complete, the precharge circuitry is disconnected and the bit line is switched to the sense amplifier.

3. The cell's word line is selected. This turns on the MOS transistor of the selected cell (as well as all the other cells in the row) and connects the capacitor to the bit line.

4. The capacitor's charge state affects the voltage on the bit line. If the capacitor has been charged, the bit line's voltage goes up slightly. (Very slightly!) If the capacitor has been discharged, the bit's line's voltage goes down slightly. This change in voltage is exceptionally small and could amount to the difference of only one million electrons.

5. The sense amplifier converts this tiny change in voltage to a digital state of either 1 or 0.

6. The read operation destroys charge in the capacitor of the selected cell and all the other cells in the row. The state that was read must then be refreshed and written back to all cells in the row.

Writing to a DRAM cell is done this way:

1. The cell's bit line is given a voltage corresponding to the value to be written to the cell. Typically, a 1-bit is represented by full voltage and a 0-bit by no voltage.

2. The cell's word line is selected. This turns on the MOS transistor and allows the voltage applied to the bit line to pass into the cell's capacitor.

Note that DRAM cells are not accessed one at a time. Because they share a word line, an entire row of cells is accessed at once. We talk about "opening" a row (reading the values from an entire row of cells into temporary storage at the edge of the SDRAM chip) and "closing" a row (writing back any changes from the temporary storage to the cells themselves). (More on

SDRAM later.) This sounds like it might be a waste of time, but in modern computers, system memory is almost always read and written in chunks called *cache lines*, which are maintained in fast memory stores called *cache*, as we explain later in this chapter.

A row is refreshed under two circumstances:

- Any time a cell in that row is read
- Every 5 to 50 milliseconds, to prevent electron leakage from destroying cell data

Rows are refreshed simply by reading the state of the cells in the row and then immediately writing it back to the cells. This reading and writing is not done through the CPU, or in fact with any involvement of the CPU at all. A separate subsystem called a *memory controller* handles the refresh operation and a great many other housekeeping details that allow the CPU to access memory with as little delay as possible. Taken together, the memory controller and the DRAM chips that it manages are called a memory system.

The speed with which data moves between memory systems and the CPU can dominate the overall performance of the entire computer. Memory system performance is a complex business, with two different metrics that are often in tension with one another:

- **Access time:** The time it takes between the moment a memory access is requested by the CPU and the time the access is completed
- **Bandwidth:** The amount of data transferred to or from memory per unit time

Much of the rest of this chapter addresses issues related to improving the effective access time and bandwidth experienced by the CPU when accessing memory.

Synchronous vs. Asynchronous DRAM

DRAM has dominated computer memory systems since 1980 or so, and dominates them to this day. Quite apart from scaling (that is, making DRAM cells smaller), DRAM has been improved in many ways. Perhaps the most dramatic improvement was the move to synchronous DRAM (SDRAM) in the late 1990s.

Prior to that time, all DRAM was asynchronous. The operation of asynchronous DRAM is managed directly from the memory controller. The controller can open a row by presenting a row address on the unidirectional data bus and bringing the row address strobe (RAS) command line low; having done so, it can read or write cells within the open row by presenting a column address and bringing the column address strobe (CAS) command line low. A bidirectional data bus is used to transfer data to or from the DRAM; the direction of travel is determined by the write enable (WE) and output enable (OE) command lines.

An asynchronous DRAM device starts performing an operation as soon as it detects an RAS or CAS transition, but requires a finite amount of time (called *latency*) to perform each operation. The device's datasheet will typically contain timing parameters indicating how long (in nanoseconds) we must wait between, for example, opening a row and starting an access to a column in that row (the RAS to CAS latency), or starting a read access to a column and expecting to receive valid data on the data bus (the CAS to valid data out latency, or just CAS latency). The memory controller must be programmed with these timing parameters for memory operations to occur reliably.

A critical disadvantage of asynchronous DRAM is that it is only possible to perform one memory access operation at a time. While we're waiting for a row to open, the data bus is completely idle, "wasting" potential throughput. Fast page mode (FPM) DRAM, which became popular around 1995, mitigates this problem to some degree by allowing a burst of multiple accesses to an open row (multiple CAS transitions per RAS transition), but inefficiency remains when switching between rows.

The eventual solution to the wasted throughput problem was the introduction of SDRAM. The key innovation in SDRAM is the splitting of the DRAM cell matrix into multiple independent banks, which can be thought of almost as separate asynchronous DRAMs. Fine-grained control of these banks is delegated to logic inside the SDRAM itself, running off a clock (and therefore "synchronous") generated by the memory controller. The memory controller passes commands to the logic inside the SDRAM using a unidirectional control bus, which takes the place of the address bus and control signals used by asynchronous DRAM. By maintaining a short queue of upcoming memory access requests from the CPU and other bus master peripherals, the memory controller is able to schedule the commands that it issues so as to hide the latency of precharge and row-open operations, potentially keeping the data bus completely busy. For example, while receiving the results of a multi-cycle burst read from an address in bank 0, the controller might issue a command to open a row in bank 1 and then a command to close the current row in bank 2, precharging that bank so that it is ready for a future row-open command. This technique of overlapping operations on multiple banks is referred to as *pipelining* and it's the main contributor to the improved performance of SDRAM over asynchronous DRAM.

To gain more flexibility in how it pipelines memory operations, the memory controller may, under some circumstances, choose to reorder the requests in its queue. There is generally a signalling scheme between the CPU and the memory controller to help the controller understand which accesses can be reordered safely. The controller typically also reorders requests to group multiple reads and writes together, minimising the number of bus turnarounds, where the direction of flow on the data bus changes, necessitating a small amount of dead time.

Operations on the individual banks inside the SDRAM device have characteristic latencies, just as with asynchronous DRAM. Once again, these timing parameters are typically specified in the datasheet for the device; in the case of SDRAM they're generally specified as a number of clock cycles at the device's maximum supported clock frequency, rather than directly in nanoseconds. The memory controller programs these parameters into the SDRAM's internal logic at boot-up time, and relies on them to know how many cycles to wait between issuing commands on the bus and receiving data.

SDRAM Columns, Rows, Banks, Ranks and DIMMs

In the previous section you saw that an SDRAM device is composed internally of a collection of equal-sized independent banks. Each bank is structured as a matrix of a number of rows, and the bits in each row are grouped into columns of a specific width. A row in a modern SDRAM chip contains tens of thousands of bits, and a column is typically 8, 16 or 32 bits wide. A row and a column address together specify a starting point within the bank's grid of memory cells and the cells beginning at that starting point are read and written as a unit, out to the width of the column.

Typically there are 2, 4 or 8 banks on each chip. The banks themselves may be of different sizes for different chips. A common 128MB SDRAM memory chip contains 8 banks, each of which contains 16,384 rows of 1,024 columns of 8 bits. The total number of bits in the chip is thus 8 banks × 16,384 rows × 1,024 columns × 8 bits per column = 1,073,745,824 bits. It's called a 128MB chip because 1,073,745,824 bits divided by 8 bits per byte is 134,217,728 bytes. (Refer to Table 3-1 to see why that number is considered to be 128MB.)

SDRAM chips are organised as they are as a consequence of how the chips themselves are combined into memory systems. For desktop and conventional laptop computers, multiple chips are assembled onto small "stick" printed circuit modules. Until the late 1990s these were single in-line memory modules (SIMMs) because the corresponding edge connector contacts on both sides of the printed circuit board were identical and tied together. (It does not mean, as some think, that memory chips are present on only one side of the module!) SIMMs can transfer 32 bits to or from the data bus at one time.

Having the same signals on both sides of the edge connectors on SIMMs limits the number of electrical connections that can be made between the SIMM and the data bus. A SIMM typically has 72 connectors on its edge. Making the two sides of the edge connector independent at least doubles the number of connections that can be made between a module and the data bus. With this change, modules became dual in-line memory modules (DIMMs), which have dominated desktop and laptop memory systems since 2000 or so. DIMMs typically have 168 or more separate connectors, and transfer 64 bits to or from the data bus at once.

For physical compactness, many laptops and netbooks use a different, smaller type of DIMM module called a small outline DIMM (SODIMM). Seventy-two-pin SODIMMs are 32 bits wide and 144-pin SODIMMs are 64 bits wide.

On a modern DIMM, each side of the module is a separate bus-addressable memory block called a *rank*. A rank is defined as a group of memory chips sharing the same chip-select control line. A rank's chips thus appear on the data bus together. Each chip within the rank contributes 8 bits to the 64 bits that the rank reads or writes at once.

Figure 3-5 shows how a typical DIMM is organised. Precise numbers aren't stated because different modules are built from SDRAM chips of different sizes and different internal organisation.

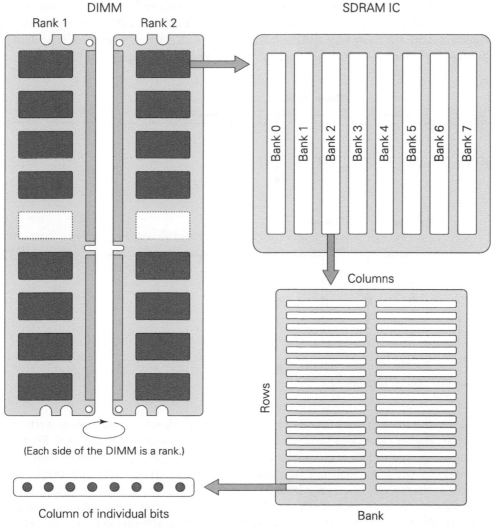

FIGURE 3-5: How a typical DDR SDRAM DIMM is organised

DDR, DDR2 DDR3 and DDR4 SDRAM

The first generation of ordinary SDRAM is today referred to as *single data rate* (SDR) SDRAM. The term only became necessary in the late 1990s, when improvements to SDRAM technology gave us *double data rate* (DDR) SDRAM. SDR SDRAM is called "single data rate" because it can transfer a single data word per clock cycle. The size of the data word depends on the design of a specific memory system (specifically the number of wires in the data bus linking the memory controller to the SDRAM). In most modern desktops and laptops, it's 64 bits. In the early Raspberry Pi models, it's 32 bits. For the Raspberry Pi 3, it's 64 bits.

In DDR SDRAM, two memory transfers occur for each clock cycle. In SDR technology, a memory transfer happens on the rising edge of each clock cycle. In DDR, memory transfers happen on both the rising edge and the falling edge of each clock cycle, essentially doubling the rate at which memory transfers happen. This is called *double pumping*. See Figure 3-6.

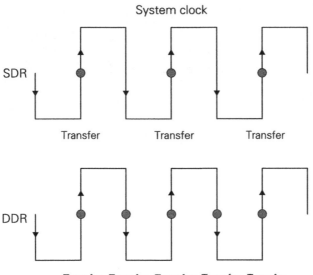

FIGURE 3-6: SDR vs. DDR timing

Increasing the memory transfer rate by increasing the clock rate causes various electrical problems. Higher clock rates for anything increase power usage and waste heat. Reliably driving a high-speed clock across a board introduces challenging signal integrity issues for chip and PCB designers; sooner or later you reach a limit in terms of edge rate; that is, the number of times a wire can change from 0 to 1 or 1 to 0 in a second. In an SDR system, the clock changes twice per cycle (from 0 to 1 and back again), whereas no data line changes more rapidly than once per cycle; in such a system you hit the wall on clock edge rate before data edge rate. By allowing the data lines to change twice per cycle, DDR signalling makes the most of a given technology's capabilities.

Moore's Law

In 1975, Intel computer engineer Gordon E. Moore observed that the number of transistors on an integrated circuit (IC) doubles every two years. It was just an observation based solely on the history of semiconductor fabrication up to that time, but the remark remained uncannily accurate for literally decades. Although some analysts had long predicted that Moore's Law would soon run into some fundamental physical limitations, it was not until 2015 that Intel confirmed that progress in shrinking circuit fabrication had slowed down. Moore himself has stated that Moore's Law would cease to apply by 2025.

At around the time of the introduction of DDR SDRAM, the internal speed at which SDRAM devices operated (as distinct from the external interface speed) stopped increasing significantly. Why? Well, the speed at which you can read a row of cells from the array is dominated by signal propagation time, which is determined by wire length and the time required for the sense amplifiers to detect the faint charge on the bit lines. Successive generations of SDRAM devices pack more storage into the same area, instead of getting smaller, and the charges stored on the capacitors in the array become smaller and harder to detect. As a result, process shrinkage, which has done so much to sustain Moore's Law for logic devices, has had little effect on the internal speed of SDRAM.

Fortunately, the internal bandwidth of SDRAM devices was incredibly high already. Recall that opening a row involves reading tens of thousands of bits simultaneously into temporary storage at the edge of the SDRAM chip. Even with a relatively slow internal speed, say one access every 10 nanoseconds (ns), that's still a lot of bandwidth, and the results end up held right where you want them, at the edge of the silicon die next to the pads. The only question is how to sensibly interface that data rate to the bus, which may support a transfer every 1ns or less.

The solution adopted by DDR, and its successors DDR2 and DDR3, is to require that memory accesses occur as short bursts running from a starting address to some number of adjacent addresses. After the internal logic in the SDRAM has read the first column, subsequent columns from the same row are available for "free" without requiring another time-consuming access to the array. This process is called *prefetching*. (See Figure 3-7.) With 32-bit SDR memory you could efficiently read a single 32-bit word, followed by another 32-bit word from another location in memory, but DDR forces you to take two adjacent 32-bit words, one on the rising edge and one on the falling edge of the clock cycle. DDR2 doubles this requirement to four adjacent words and supports data rates up to 800MHz (or equivalently clock speeds up to 400MHz). DDR3 doubles the requirement again to eight words and supports data rates of 1.6GHz or higher. In each case the faster bus is "fed" from the temporary storage at the edge of the chip, and the increasing minimum burst requirement is an acknowledgement that the array simply isn't nimble enough to keep up with full-speed demands for random access.

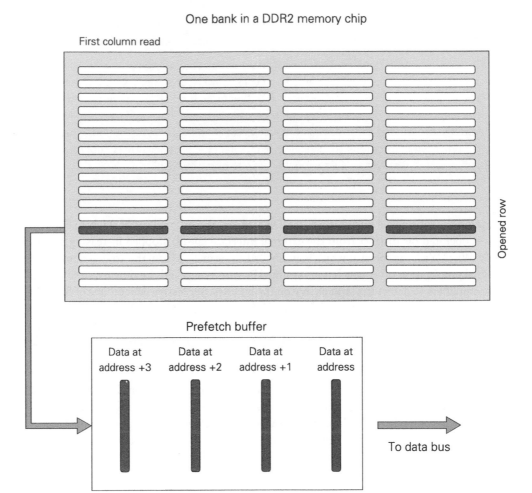

FIGURE 3-7: DDR2 prefetching

It's possible, of course, that the CPU does not need those four consecutive data words, but only the first. If the CPU reads a data word from DDR memory at some address and then immediately requests another word from an address somewhere else in memory, the last three data words are still sent over the bus, but are discarded by the memory controller. DDR memory had the ability to terminate a burst early, but this feature was dropped from DDR2 and later generations. This might seem wasteful, except that most of the time the CPU requests memory words in sequence starting at some address. This happens because in modern computers, most reads from system memory are to load cache lines into the CPU's cache. (You'll read more on cache later in this chapter.) Sequential reads are the norm, and "random" reads are an increasingly uncommon exception, as CPU cache size increases.

In addition to the protocol changes described earlier, each DDR generation has included changes to the physical signalling scheme aimed at increasing transfer speeds and a reduction in operating voltage, which reduces power draw and waste heat. The improvement is significant: DDR3 memory uses 30 percent less power than DDR2 memory.

The latest generation of SDRAM appeared in late 2014: DDR4. The operating voltage has been reduced to 1.2V (as compared to 1.5V for DDR3) enabling higher-density modules with greater transfer speeds. The range of operating frequencies increased, to 800 to 1600MHz, compared to 400 to 1067MHz for DDR3. Low-voltage versions of DDR4 memory modules operate at voltages as low as 1.05V, providing even greater power efficiency and lower waste heat. DDR4 SDRAM uses up to 40 percent less power than DDR3 modules. Module density of current devices has increased to 4GB over DDR3's 1GB.

Error-Correcting Code (ECC) Memory

If you look at modern DIMMs, particularly those intended for use in servers or other high-reliability applications, you may notice that there are sometimes nine chips on each side. Even if there are only eight chips, there will probably be an empty space with printed circuit pads for a ninth chip. The ninth chip has an optional but very useful function: error correction.

When we talk about computer memory, we generally assume that data written into memory will remain there, as written, for as long as the memory system has power. Alas, in reality, bit values in memory sometimes change "on their own", without warning. Recall that a bit in any DRAM memory chip of any type is really nothing more than a vanishingly small quantity of electrical charge in a minuscule capacitor. Unavoidable leakage causes this charge to lessen and dissipate in a very small amount of time, which is why all DRAM must be refreshed periodically.

Unfortunately, this leakage is not the only way that DRAM memory cells discharge. The charge itself is so small that subatomic particles from outside the computer can discharge a memory cell instantly. A fast neutron generated by a cosmic ray striking the memory hardware somewhere can discharge a cell and cause a memory error. This doesn't happen as often as we once thought (memory cells are small targets and cosmic rays are relatively uncommon) but when it happens, corrupt memory can bring the computer to a halt.

A technology called error-correcting code (ECC) memory was developed to prevent memory corruption from background radiation. The mechanism used in modern computer memory, called a Hamming code, was developed in 1950 by Richard Hamming. There are many ways to implement a Hamming code in memory. The scheme used today is capable of detecting two simultaneous "bad bits" in a 64-bit data word. Better still, the system can correct single-bit errors within a 64-bit data word. Because of these two functions, the scheme is called single-error correcting and double-error detecting (SECDED).

The mathematics behind SECDED Hamming codes is subtle and beyond the scope of this book. In essence, an additional 8 bits are stored for every 64-bit word in a memory system. This is the purpose of the ninth SDRAM chip on ECC memory DIMMs. Every time a new value is written to a memory location, a new Hamming code for that location is generated and written to the "extra" 8 bits. Every time a memory location is read, the memory controller hardware tests the value read against the Hamming code stored in the extra bits. If the test fails, we know that an error has occurred in that memory location since the Hamming code was last calculated. The computer can then take some sort of action, which may include logging the error, alerting the operating system or, in some cases (for single-bit errors), transparently correcting the error.

The extra DRAM chip is not free. Also, hardware that generates the codes and performs the tests imposes its own overhead, in the order of 2 percent to 3 percent. In systems where reliability is essential, the cost and overhead are well worth it. Most desktop systems do not support ECC, which is why the DIMMs used in common desktops and laptops do not include the ninth SDRAM chip in each memory rank.

The Raspberry Pi Memory System

The Raspberry Pi board is not an inherently mobile device, but it's based on parts created for use in smartphones and other portable devices like tablets. Small size and low power are the primary virtues in mobile design. Not many desktop computers can be run from small "wall wart" power adapters but Raspberry Pi can, because of its use of mobile-device parts.

The original Raspberry Pi Model B's memory system is a 400MHz LPDDR2 single-chip device containing 512MB of memory. The memory is organised as 128M × 32; that is, 134,217,728 32-bit words, or 4,294,967,296 bits. Internally, the device's 4 gigabits are divided into 8 banks, each bank containing 512 megabits in a matrix of 16,384 rows, each of which is 4,096 bytes wide. Like all LPDDR2 memory it has a minimum burst size of 4.

Power Reduction Features

The primary way to reduce power consumption on SDRAM chips is to reduce their operating voltage. The low-power LPDDR2 memory chip used in the Raspberry Pi Model B operates at 1.2V, whereas most modern DDR2 DRAM operates at 1.8V. This doesn't sound like a huge difference, but spread out over time it can have a significant effect on battery life of devices like smartphones and especially tablets.

Other power reduction features of LPDDR2 include the use of single-ended (unterminated) buses, which eliminate the power loss in the termination resistors used by "regular" DDR memory, at the cost of a reduction in achievable bus speed. Another is the provision of a self-refresh mode, which allows the memory controller to delegate the task of refreshing the arrays to the SDRAM itself when the system is idle, in turn allowing the memory controller, CPU and other system components to go into a deep-sleep mode. The memory chips used on Raspberry Pi support temperature-controlled self-refresh. When the temperature of the device falls, charge leaks away less quickly, so the device adjusts its refresh frequency according to the temperature. In normal operation the memory controller on the BCM2835 SoC (system-on-a-chip) performs a similar procedure.

Ball-Grid Array Packaging

People taking their first look at the early Raspberry Pi boards often wonder where the RAM is. There are only two ICs on the board. One of them, obviously, is the Broadcom BCM2835 SoC. The other is a combination USB and Ethernet controller from SMSC, the LAN9512. So where's the memory?

If you look carefully at the larger of the two ICs with a magnifying glass, you can see that the chip says Samsung or "Hynix" (or possibly something else) but not Broadcom. So what's going on? The DRAM chip sits right on top of the Broadcom SoC. In fact, the two are soldered together in a sort of sandwich, with the solder between them. It's deceptive because both chips are *extremely* thin. The two-chip stack is only a little more than a millimetre high.

This trick is made possible by a type of IC packaging called a *ball-grid array* (BGA). A BGA package has one or more concentric rows of connections on the package face. Some devices (like the BCM2835 itself) have connections on both faces: one face has tiny balls of solder that connect to the circuit board beneath it; the other face has almost equally tiny pads and connects to solder balls on the bottom of the memory chip piggybacked on top of it. Such a piggyback system is called *package-on-package* and is used on a great many devices where small size is paramount, especially smartphones. During assembly, the two chips are accurately aligned and then the stack is heated to the point where the solder melts, providing a conductive path between the chips. The 512MB memory chip in the first-generation Raspberry Pi has 168 connectors on its lower face; it is the equivalent of a 512MB DIMM in a chip that is smaller than a postage stamp.

More recent Raspberry Pi boards like the Raspberry Pi Zero and Raspberry Pi 3 have different ICs and still use BGA packaging. However, the RAM IC is not soldered atop the SoC IC; instead it's soldered to the circuit board itself. The method is still the same: solder balls on the lower surfaces of the ICs are melted to pads on the circuit board.

As you might imagine, the placing of the solder balls and the alignment of the two chips one atop the other calls for unforgiving precision. The entire business is done with industrial robots, as is the case for almost all other circuit-board level assembly on the Raspberry Pi board.

Cache

No matter how much faster we make our memory systems, our CPUs just seem to get faster than memory at the same time, and memory never quite catches up. Memory performance has always been a drag on overall system performance. Even with brilliant engineering like source-synchronous clocking and 8-level prefetch buffers, our CPUs always seem to want data faster than memory can provide it. As impressively as memory speed has increased over the last 30 years, system memory speed is not the primary means to speed up the overall interaction between the CPU and its data. That primary means is, and probably always will be, data caching.

A data cache is a block of fast memory lying between the CPU and system memory. The advantage of caching is that cache memory is faster—and sometimes spectacularly faster—than system memory. When the CPU first reads a block of data from memory, it is placed in the data cache. The next time the CPU needs to read something from memory, it checks first to see if what it needs is already in cache. If so, you have a cache hit. The CPU then takes the data from the cache and not from system memory. If what the CPU needs is not in cache, you have a cache miss. The requested data is moved from memory into cache and then to the CPU on the good chance that the data just fetched will soon be needed again.

Locality of Reference

How often will the CPU find that the data it needs is already in cache? The answer may surprise you: it finds what it needs in cache most of the time. There is a general principle in computer science called *locality of reference*, which states that computer operations tend to cluster together. Locality of reference has three facets:

- The same data accessed now will probably be accessed again in the near future.
- Over short spans of time, data accesses (both reads and writes) tend to cluster in the same general area of memory.
- Memory locations tend to be read from or written to in sequential order.

In essence, when the computer is performing a particular task, its memory accesses are not all over the map. They tend to be mostly side-by-side, in one general area of memory. That being the case, it makes a lot of sense to move the data in the current working area of system memory somewhere closer (in access time) to the CPU. That somewhere is cache.

Cache Hierarchy

Modern cache technology takes this to an extreme: it moves the cache all the way onto the same silicon as the CPU itself. Cache memory is our old friend static RAM (SRAM), which is a great deal faster than any generation of DRAM. So, not only is cache physically close to the CPU but it's also the fastest sort of RAM that we can make.

One reason that cache is fast is because it's small. System memory may be several gigabytes in size. Cache is miniscule by comparison and rarely stores more than 1 megabyte. Smaller is faster because there are fewer address bits to process, and also because it's easier to determine whether the data that the CPU needs is already in the cache. (More on this challenge a little later.) Make cache memory larger, and cache operations slow down.

What to do? Divide cache into more than one layer and build the layers into a hierarchy. Modern microprocessors have at least two layers of cache, and often three. The first layer, called level 1 (L1) cache, is closest to the CPU. The second layer is level 2 (L2) cache, and so on. L1 cache is faster (and smaller) than L2 cache, which in turn is faster (and smaller) than L3 cache. At the bottom of the cache hierarchy is system memory, which is the largest and also the slowest place to store data that may be directly accessed by the CPU. Of course, data in system memory may also be written out to hard disk or SSD storage, which is still slower and not available by memory address to the CPU (see Figure 3-8).

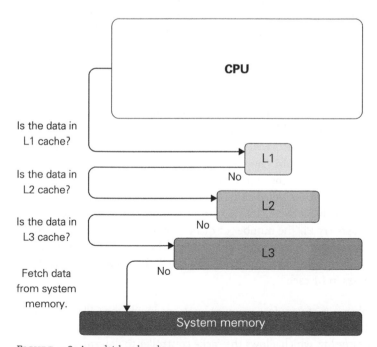

FIGURE 3-8: A multi-level cache

The number of layers of cache and the size of each layer vary depending on the microprocessor. The Intel Core i7 family has a 32KB L1 cache for each core, a 256 KB L2 cache for each core and a single L3 cache shared among all cores. The L3 cache is between 4MB and 8MB, depending on the microprocessor model. The ARM11 processor in the older Raspberry Pi models contains a pair of 16KB L1 caches: one for instructions and one for data. A 128KB L2 cache is present in the system-on-a-chip silicon surrounding the ARM11 CPU, but with a catch: the L2 cache is shared between the ARM11 CPU and the Video Core IV graphics processor, with the graphics processor given priority. The Raspberry Pi does not incorporate an L3 cache.

Cache Lines and Cache Mapping

Figure 3-8 looks a little like a programming flowchart and you might assume the process is slow, with all those decisions to make. Not so. Determining whether a given run of memory locations is already present in cache is lightning-quick, with dedicated logic built into the CPU's silicon.

There are two general mechanisms for finding out whether a given memory location is present in cache. One depends on calculation and the other depends on searching. Both have serious disadvantages. What most modern computers use is a sort of hybrid of both approaches. Whereas the "pure" approaches are rarely if ever actually implemented in silicon, you need to know how both work in order to understand the hybrid compromise that we do use.

First, here's some general technical background on caching. Caching is never done one data word at a time. In part, the reason for this is to exploit locality of reference, as explained earlier in this section. Caching also interacts well with a memory controller feature explained in detail in the previous section on SDRAM: "burst-mode" logic that can read or write multiple words from system memory in the same amount of time as a single word. Cache is read and (usually) written in fixed-size blocks called cache lines. The size of cache lines may vary, but in modern systems it is usually 32 bytes. This is true of many Intel CPUs, as well as the ARM11 processor in the Raspberry Pi. The number of cache lines capable of being stored in cache is thus the size in bytes of the cache divided by the size in bytes of the cache line. For the Raspberry Pi's L1 cache, the 16,384 bytes is divided by the 32-byte size of a cache line, giving 512 possible cache lines in L1 cache.

Cache memory is not simply a run of very fast memory locations inside the CPU. Cache has its own very specific structure. In addition to the 32 bytes of data, each location in cache has an additional field called a *cache tag*, which allows the cache controller to determine where in system memory the cache line came from. There are also two single-bit flags stored in each cache line:

- **Valid bit:** Indicates whether valid data is present in that cache line. When cache is initialised, the valid bit for all cache lines is set to false, and it only changes to true when a memory block has been read into the cache line.

- **Dirty bit:** Indicates that some of the data in the cache line has been changed by the CPU and the data needs to be written back to system memory.

The cache tag is derived from the address in system memory from which the cache line was filled. When a memory address is presented to be read or written, the address is split into three pieces:

- **Cache tag:** Identifies where in memory the cache line came from. These are the highest-order bits from the memory address, and uniquely identify a cache-line-sized and aligned block of system memory. The tag is stored with the cache line itself.

- **Index:** Identifies the cache line where the data from the system memory address would reside if it were present in cache. For a direct-mapped cache (see the next section), the number of bits is the number it takes to specify one cache line from all the lines in cache. For a 512-line direct-mapped cache, it would be 9 bits.

- **Offset:** Specifies which byte within the cache line corresponds to the byte specified by the system memory address that generated the tag. These are the lowest-order bits in the address. The number of bits is the number it takes to specify a byte from all the bytes in a line. In a 32-byte cache line, it would be 5 bits.

The block field and word field are not stored anywhere. They're used during cache access, but once a data word is read from or written to cache, they're discarded.

The structure of a cache line and how a system memory address is broken down for cache access are shown in Figure 3-9. Some of the details of cache line structure vary depending on system specifics (how large the cache is, how large the cache line is and so on) and the precise mechanism used by the system to manage caching.

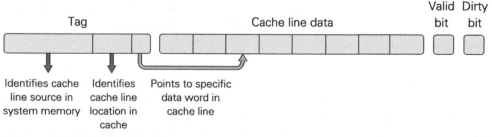

FIGURE 3-9: Cache line structure

The lynchpin issue in cache technology is where data from system memory is placed in cache. This is called *cache mapping* and it determines how the CPU knows whether a requested address is in cache. As the name suggests, cache mapping is about how the position of a cache-line-sized data block in system memory relates to its possible position in cache.

Direct Mapping

The oldest and simplest cache mapping technique, and the one that we have been implicitly assuming up to this point, is called *direct mapping*. In simplified terms: the first block of system memory can be stored only in the first cache line in cache; the second block in system memory can be stored only in the second cache line in cache; and so on. There's a lot more system memory than cache memory, of course, so when cache is full, the correspondence "wraps around" and begins again at the first location in cache.

A visual really helps you understand this, so refer to Figure 3-10 during the following discussion.

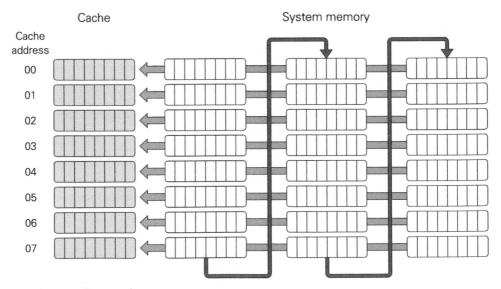

FIGURE 3-10: Direct cache mapping

In the simplified direct mapping example depicted in Figure 3-10, there are eight locations in cache, each of which stores a single cache line. (For simplicity, the cache tags are not shown.) Each cache line holds 8 bytes. The first 24 blocks of system memory are shown. Each block in system memory is the size of a cache line (that is, 8 bytes). As in all caching systems, data is read from or written to system memory in cache-line-sized chunks. The hexadecimal (base 16) numbers over each column of system memory blocks are the byte address of the start of each column. Because each column represents 64 bytes, the address of the second column is 0 + 0x40 (which is 64 in hexadecimal) and the starting address of the third column is 0x40 + 0x40, or 0x80. (128 in decimal notation.)

Any number you see beginning with "0x" is a *hexadecimal* number, meaning a number expressed in base 16 rather than our familiar decimal base 10. This is explained in some detail **NOTE** in Chapter 2. Both Windows and Linux (including Raspbian) include calculator apps that can convert hexadecimal values to decimal and back, and do arithmetic in either number base.

The mapping of system memory blocks to cache lines works like this: block 0 in system memory (starting at address 0x00) is always mapped to cache line 0; block 1 (starting at address 0x08) is always mapped to cache line 1; and so on. This is straightforward until you run out of cache lines (there are only eight lines in cache in the example in Figure 3-10). When this happens, the sequence "wraps around" and begins again: block 8 (starting at address 0x40) is mapped to cache line 0, block 9 (starting at address 0x48) is mapped to cache line 1, and so on. This is referred to as modulo *n* mapping, where *n* is the number of locations within cache. The location of any given system memory block when mapped to cache will be the memory block number modulo 8.

The term "modulo" means calculating the remainder after division. Primary school children are taught that 64 divided by 10 equals 6 with a remainder of 4. So, 64 modulo 10 is simply 4. If you need to find out which cache line system memory block 21 maps to in our example, calculate 21 modulo 8. The answer is 5 (21 ÷ by 8 = 2 with a remainder 5), and memory block 21 will always map to cache line 5. Count memory blocks in Figure 3-10 (from 0, of course) to verify that memory block 21 maps to cache line 5.

Direct mapping of system memory blocks to cache lines is mathematically precise: a given block of system memory is always stored in the same location in cache. The CPU determines whether the memory address it needs to fetch is in cache by calculating which position in cache that memory block always goes to and then comparing the value in the tag field of the cache tag with the corresponding bits in the system memory address. If it's a match, you have a cache hit. If it's not a match, you have a cache miss.

CPUs are extremely good at calculation and comparison, and direct cache mapping is the fastest cache mechanism available. However, there's a downside in that there's no flexibility whatsoever in where blocks from system memory are stored in cache. This can become an issue when the CPU is running software performing memory reads that alternate blocks. In the direct mapping example, system memory block 4 maps to the same cache location (cache line 4) as block 12, block 20, and so on, modulo 8. Suppose the software reads an address that falls in block 4; cache line 4 receives the block if it isn't there already. Then the software may need data from block 12. If block 4 is in cache, block 12 is not, because they always map to the same cache location, so block 12 is loaded, and overwrites (we say "evicts") block 4. Soon thereafter, perhaps as a program loop is executed, the software again needs data from block 4, so block 12 must be evicted. If the loop continues in this fashion, there will be thrashing (that is, repeated fetches from system memory) in cache that nullifies any of the speed gains earned by caching. In fact, because of the overhead of the caching mechanism, memory access is slower in a thrashing situation than it would be without any caching at all.

Associative Mapping

More flexibility is needed in cache mapping than direct mapping provides. Ideally, you want to have as many of the system memory blocks that software is using available in cache as possible, regardless of the addresses being accessed. If you could load a given block into any available line in cache, you could implement a replacement policy (in essence, deciding which cache line to evict when writing a new memory block to cache) that makes better use of cache space.

The job of a replacement policy is largely to avoid cache thrashing. That job is surprisingly difficult, and replacement policies are often combinations of algorithms that decide which cache line to evict when a new memory block needs to enter cache. Here are the common replacement policies:

- **First in first out (FIFO):** Once cache is full, the first cache line that was written to cache is the one evicted.

- **Least recently used (LRU):** Cache lines are given timestamps, and the system records when a cache line is used. When a new cache line must be written, the one that hasn't been accessed in the longest time is evicted. Managing the timestamp takes time and is complex.

- **Random:** It sounds counterintuitive, but one of the cheapest (in terms of logic) and most effective replacement policies picks a cache line to evict completely at random. Random eviction makes thrashing unlikely. It's also not as sensitive as FIFO and LRU to the algorithms used in software.

- **Not most recently used (NMRU):** The line to be evicted is chosen randomly, but this is tweaked so that the most recently used line is remembered and not chosen. This policy is almost as cheap to implement as the random policy and performs slightly better.

ARM processors, like the ones in the Raspberry Pi, can use either FIFO or random policies, as set by a configuration bit. In most cases, the replacement policy is random.

The most flexible way to use cache space is to allow placement of a new cache line anywhere in cache, whatever the replacement policy directs. The CPU still needs to be able to decide whether the data it needs is in cache or not and if data blocks can be stored anywhere in cache that decision can no longer be made by a single calculation and comparison. Instead, the CPU must search for a given block in cache.

Compared to calculation and comparison, searching is an extremely compute-intensive process. Searching cache lines one at a time would eat up any possible performance gains. The solution is to use a technology called associative memory. Associative memory, like all memory, stores data in a series of storage locations. What associative memory does not have is a conventional numerical addressing system. Instead, storage locations are addressed by what is stored in them.

In a fully associative cache, a memory access causes a cache tag to be generated from the system memory address just as before. However, instead of comparing this tag against the corresponding tag for one uniquely specified cache line, in this case the associative memory system compares the generated tag against every tag stored in cache in parallel. If it finds a match, you have a cache hit and the corresponding cache line is given to the CPU. If it doesn't find a match, it's a cache miss; a line must be evicted from the cache, as determined by the replacement policy, and the requested system memory block is read into the newly vacated cache line.

To people who are used to conventional addressing and sequential searches, this sounds a little bit like magic. Alas, although parallel search is fast, associative memory requires a lot of dedicated logic that takes a significant amount of die space on the CPU. For all but the smallest or most performance-critical caches, the pattern-matching logic is too expensive (in transistors, and eventually time delays) to be practical.

Die space is the area on a silicon chip (called a "die" during the fabrication process) that may be used to fabricate the transistors from which the chip's digital logic is built. There is only so much area on any given die to "spend" on transistors, so chip designers have to be very careful how they use the space that they have. The trade-off between die space and chip functionality is the oldest single challenge in large-scale chip design.

NOTE

Set-Associative Cache

At one extreme, then, is the lightning-fast and compact direct cache mapping, which is completely inflexible in terms of where data for a new cache line may be stored. At the other is the completely flexible associative cache mapping, which takes far too much on-chip logic to be implemented. The solution, as with so many difficult choices like this, lies somewhere in the middle.

This compromise is called *set-associative cache*. A set-associative caching system reorganises cache lines into sets. Each set contains 2, 4, 8 or 16 cache lines, complete with data block and tag. Figure 3-11 shows a simplified diagram of a set-associative cache with four cache lines per set. With four lines per set, a cache is known as a four-way set-associative cache. This is the cache scheme used in the Raspberry Pi, as well as a great many other laptop and desktop computers today.

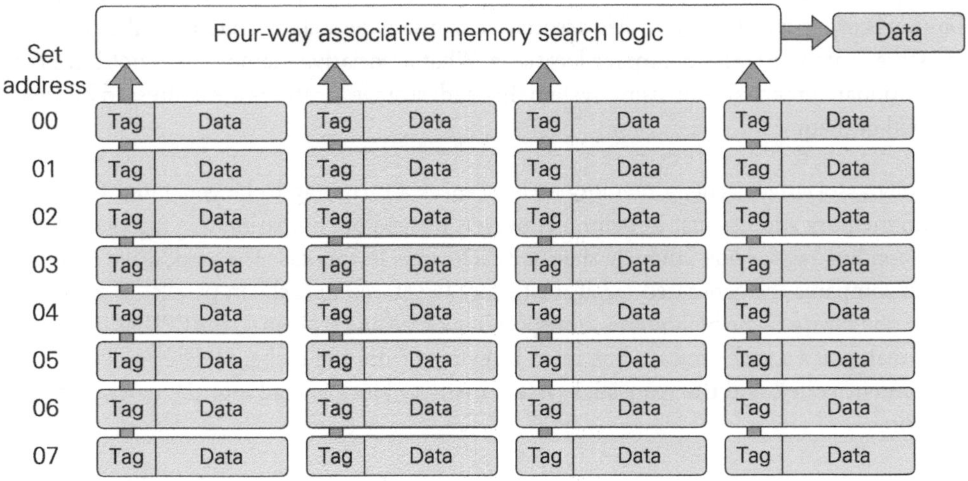

FIGURE 3-11: Set-associative cache mapping

The memory locations that map to a given set are still determined by direct mapping. This means that the modulo relationship of system memory addresses to cache positions still holds, except that now we have a little flexibility in terms of where we place an incoming block. Recall the example given earlier of an eight-line direct-mapped cache, which blocks 2, 10, 18 and 26 from system memory as they would be blocked under a pure direct-mapping scheme.

The problem remains, though: there are four system memory blocks stored in cache lines in one set. The computer can easily calculate which set any given memory address would fall into, but it cannot by simple calculation determine which cache line within a given set would contain the requested address. The CPU must search the four cache lines in a set to see which cache line's tag matches the requested address. Associative memory does this search. This is not a sequential search that looks at each cache tag in turn and stops when it finds a match. Instead, parallel comparators test the bits from the four tags in the cache line against the corresponding bits in the generated tag, all simultaneously. This logic is still complex internally, but because only four locations are being searched it can be done, and done quickly.

The process works like this: the CPU calculates which set a memory block must be in, from the system memory address. (This is done the same way as in direct cache mapping.) It then submits the address to the associative memory logic, and associative memory either tells the CPU which line in the set contains the requested block (a cache hit) or registers a cache miss. The requested block is then read from system memory and placed in one of the four lines in the set, according to a replacement policy. To summarise: set-associative cache divides a cache into sets, which in the case of the ARM11 used in the Raspberry Pi contain four cache lines. The CPU can determine which set a given address must be in through a direct mapping scheme and then it uses the pattern-matching mechanism of associative memory to go right to the matching cache line within the set—or, if the search fails, register a cache miss.

Writing Cache Back to Memory

Up to this point, we've discussed caching as though it were entirely about reading from memory. Of course, what is read is often changed. When the CPU changes a data word somewhere in a cache line, that cache line is marked as "dirty" using a single-bit flag. When a cache line's dirty bit is set, the line must be written back to the block in memory from which it was originally read. No matter what else happens, system memory blocks and their associated cache lines must be consistent. If changes to cache are not written back to system memory, those changes will be lost if the replacement policy reads in a new block to the same cache line where the changes were made.

There are two general approaches to keeping cache and memory consistent. Taken together, these are called *cache write policies*:

- **Write-through:** Means that any time a data word in a cache line is changed by the CPU, the cache line is written to memory immediately. This happens every time the line is written to, even if the writes are all entirely within the same cache line. As expected, there is time wasted writing a single cache line back to memory multiple times, but the CPU's view of memory is consistent with what is actually in memory; this is important if a peripheral such as a display controller is also accessing this memory.

- **Write-back:** Means that a "dirty" cache line is written back to memory only when the replacement policy has chosen to evict the dirty cache line from cache. Before a new system memory block is loaded into the cache line, the current contents of the line are copied back to its original block in system memory. Write-back avoids a lot of unnecessary system memory writes at the cost of a more relaxed notion of consistency.

Virtual Memory

Think of computer memory as a sort of pyramid, with the fastest, smallest blocks of memory at the top. These blocks of memory are the CPU's registers. Below the registers is the larger, slower L1 cache and beneath that, the still larger but still slower L2 cache. Beneath cache is system memory, which is much larger than cache but much slower. Next is the layer beneath system memory: virtual memory.

Virtual memory is a technology that can create truly enormous memory systems by allowing mass storage devices like hard disks to extend system memory. In a sense, virtual memory extends the cache hierarchy diagram in Figure 3-8 past system memory to a layer of storage limited only by the capacity of hard drives.

Both cache memory and virtual memory came about due to the limitations of RAM: cache because RAM is slow and virtual memory because RAM is scarce. RAM was so bulky and expensive in the mid-1960s that the seminal PDP-8 computer had a 12-bit address space that could address only 4,096 12-bit words of RAM. For machines in that era to support larger programs and multiple concurrent tasks required far larger memory spaces. Virtual memory provided them.

Virtual memory is a cooperative venture between the operating system and a hardware memory management unit (MMU) that almost always exists on the same chip as the CPU.

The Virtual Memory Big Picture

Here's what happens in virtual memory systems: a process's virtual address space (its view of memory) is divided into many small sections (often as small as 4KB in size) called *pages*. If sufficient system memory is available then the first time the process accesses an address in a given page, the operating system allocates an unused frame of system memory to back the page (that is, to store the content that the application writes to it). Later you see that the job of the MMU is to keep track of which pages are backed and to transparently route requests from the CPU for data from a page to the appropriate frame.

If there's enough memory for everybody, that's where the situation stays. However, as more processes are loaded by the operating system, and as those processes begin to access memory, you may reach a point where there are no remaining unused frames to back all of the pages that are in use in the system. In this case, the operating system must evict one or more frames, writing their contents to disk and freeing them up to back some other page. The evicted pages remain stored on disk until they are needed again. Then some other pages are evicted from system memory and the formerly evicted pages are loaded again.

This mechanism is called *paging*. The area on disk dedicated to storing pages is called a page-file. A page file may be an actual disk file, or it may be an entire dedicated disk partition that contains nothing other than pages that have been written to disk. The process of writing a page to its page file is informally called swapping out and the space on disk where pages are stored is informally called swap space. In the Raspbian operating system, swap space exists by default in the file /var/swap.

The net effect of virtual memory management is to give each process the illusion that it has its own private system memory space separate from that of all other processes, with as much memory as it requires.

Mapping Virtual to Physical

Does this sound familiar? It should. Virtual memory is indeed a kind of caching technology, albeit one driven by the need for space rather than speed. The central trick, as with caching mechanisms, is to relate addresses in the larger, virtual memory system to addresses in the smaller physical system memory, and to decide on a policy for evicting pages when system memory is exhausted.

When a process is launched, the operating system creates a structure in system memory called a page table, which describes the address space of the new process. Each entry in the table describes one page belonging to the process, including what frame (if any) backs the page in system memory and what operations (for example reading and writing data or fetching instructions) may be performed on the page. If a page has been swapped out, it is marked in the table as invalid (unavailable for any operations). An attempt to access an invalid page results in a page fault, which the operating system must handle.

Every time the process uses a memory address—for example, the address of the next machine instruction to be executed—a memory translation operation is performed. The virtual address requested is translated to the corresponding physical address in system memory. This happens in two parts:

1. The frame containing the physical address is located in memory.

2. The offset into the frame to which the physical address "points" is extracted from the virtual address. This resolves the physical address to a single data word within a frame.

The CPU then accesses the data word at the translated physical address in system memory. Figure 3-12 shows a simplified virtual memory system. The process has been given eight pages of virtual memory. Five of those pages are present in system memory frames. The other three pages have been swapped out to swap space. Each virtual memory page has a corresponding entry in the process page table. The process page table points to frames in physical memory where each process page resides. We summarise the state of the permission bits as a single valid bit, which is set to binary 0 for any process page that is not currently in memory.

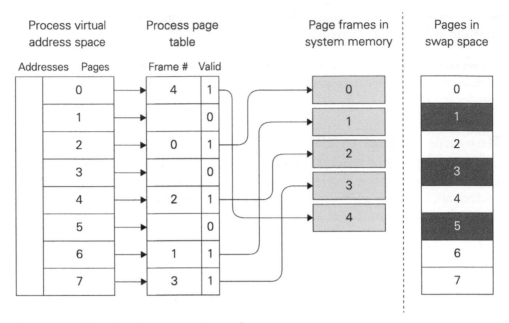

FIGURE 3-12: How virtual memory paging works

So what happens when the CPU requests an address in process page 3? That page is not in memory and the request triggers a page fault. The memory manager must then bring in page 3 from swap space. Note that the process only has five frames in physical memory and those frames are all in use. The memory manager has to make room by evicting one of the in-memory pages to swap space. Only then can the memory manager load page 3 and allow the CPU to continue on. In reality, the operating system generally attempts to schedule another independent process while the input/output (I/O) operations associated with paging occur and may speculatively write to disk pages that it expects to evict soon, thus speeding up the paging-out process.

The decision as to which page to evict to make room for page 3 involves a replacement policy, just as in cache systems, and the policies are often the very same ones. In a LRU policy, it would be the page that had not been used for the longest amount of time.

Memory Management Units: Going Deeper

That's the view from a height. The key in virtual memory systems is the memory management unit and to understand how MMUs work and what other benefits they bring to a computer, you have to dig a little deeper and see the detailed process of memory access from the eyes of a computer program.

Consider a process running on a machine that does not have an MMU. As it executes, it accesses memory to fetch instructions and to read and write data. It takes the addresses that the CPU has generated and use them directly to access memory, so if your program performs a read from address 0, this would automatically read the very first thing contained in the physical SDRAM connected to your CPU chip. Figure 3-13 shows the setup, in which the CPU directly generates physical addresses.

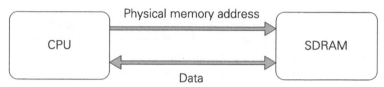

FIGURE 3-13: Direct use of physical memory addresses

This is how the earliest single-user computers, early microcomputers and some current embedded systems operate. However, several things are hard to implement in such a setup:

- **Memory protection:** One of the functions of a modern operating system is to isolate processes running in the CPU from one another. In a direct-addressing setup, stability and security suffer, because there is nothing to stop one process from reading from or writing to a section of memory owned by another process.

- **Virtual memory:** You saw in the preceding section that by allowing infrequently used areas of memory to be swapped out to disk, you can support programs that need to work on larger amounts of data than can fit in the machine's physical memory. In the simple setup (see Figure 3-13), there is no mechanism to trap accesses to parts of memory that have been swapped out.

- **Defragmentation:** When a program has been running for a long time, its view of memory often becomes fragmented, with many small memory allocations splitting free space into fragments, none of which may be large enough to support new allocations above a certain size. In this setup there is no way to compact memory to consolidate free space without forcing the application to manage its own memory.

The solution to all three of these problems is to introduce a layer of remapping between the addresses that are generated by the CPU, which we'll now refer to as *virtual addresses*, and the physical addresses that reference external memory. The component that performs this remapping is the MMU (see Figure 3-14).

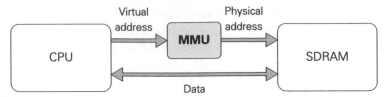

FIGURE 3-14: An MMU intermediating virtual and physical addresses

The MMU builds a contiguous virtual address space for the CPU by stitching together non-contiguous pages of physical memory (see Figure 3-15). Different CPUs support various combinations of page sizes; most support 4KB pages and this is the size most commonly used by operating systems like Linux. We assume this page size, and 32-bit virtual and physical addresses, in the following discussion.

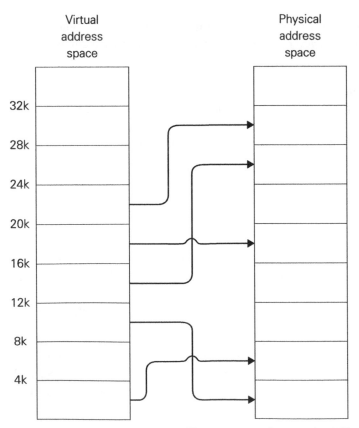

FIGURE 3-15: Stitching the virtual address space together out of 4KB blocks of physical memory

The MMU dismantles each incoming 32-bit virtual address into a 20-bit page number and a 12-bit (2^{12}; that is, 4K) page offset. The page number is looked up in the memory-resident page table, to give a 20-bit frame number and a set of permission bits. If the permission bits indicate that the requested access is valid, the frame number and page offset are re-combined to form the physical address (see Figure 3-16).

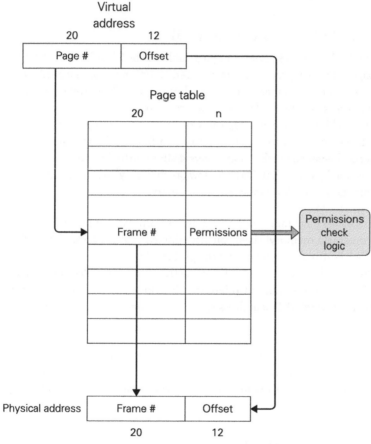

FIGURE 3-16: Converting virtual to physical addresses through lookups in the page table

This system addresses the three memory challenges described earlier:

- Fragmentation may be solved trivially by shuffling free pages behind the process's back. The application doesn't have to manage its own memory.

- By giving each process a separate table pointing to non-overlapping frames, you can enforce isolation. This requires that the process not be able to write to the page table—a requirement that lies behind the need to create processor privilege levels, which is covered in Chapter 4. You store the page table in frames that aren't mapped into the process address space and stop the process from adjusting the page table base pointer.

- Virtual memory can be implemented by marking pages that have been swapped to disk as inaccessible (using the permission bits), catching the page fault that occurs when you access the page, and triggering the paging-in process.

Multi-Level Page Tables and the TLB

Page table entries are usually 4 bytes in size, so your page table will be $2^{32} \div 2^{12} \times 4 = 4\text{MB}$ in size. If you require a page table per process (as is required to enforce isolation) this gets expensive, fast. The solution is to implement a multi-level page table. Two-level page tables save space by exploiting the sparseness of process address spaces—very few processes require a full 4GB of virtual address space. In a typical two-level system, the most significant 10 bits of the virtual address are used to select an entry in a first-level page table, which optionally points to a second-level page table that covers 4MB of virtual address space (see Figure 3-17). If there is no valid page in that 4MB window (as shown by an X in the first-level table entry) you may omit the second-level table, saving memory.

One last thing: with a two-level page table, you now must perform two additional accesses to memory every time you access memory! Have you just crippled your processor by tripling the cost of memory access? Fortunately, you can fix the problem by caching the most recent few translations in a fully or highly associative cache inside the processor, called the translation lookaside buffer (TLB). Due to locality of reference (described earlier in this chapter) and because each TLB entry "covers" 4KB of address space, even a small TLB has an excellent hit rate.

To avoid contention between accesses to the TLB from instruction fetch and data accesses, the ARM11 core actually has two small micro-TLBs, one associated with the L1 instruction cache and the other associated with the L1 data cache, along with a larger (but still relatively small) central TLB.

The Raspberry Pi Swap Problem

As good as virtual memory sounds, there is a catch: the Raspberry Pi lacks a mass storage device appropriate for swap space. There is no hard drive, as there is on laptops and desktops. SD cards were not designed for use with filesystems that write to "disk" as frequently as Raspbian's. The flash storage medium in an SD card is composed of memory cells that may be changed only a certain number of times. That number is large but it is still limited, and every time a cell is written to, it's one step closer to failure. (For more on this, see Chapter 4.) When physical memory is full, a virtual memory system begins reading and writing to its swap space a lot. To avoid killing the SD card, the Raspbian OS is configured to use swap space only when absolutely necessary. Remember that a single SD card contains not only swap space but also everything else in your Raspberry Pi system, including Raspbian and all of your installed programs and configuration data. If the SD card dies, the system could become corrupt and you would have to rebuild it from scratch on a new card.

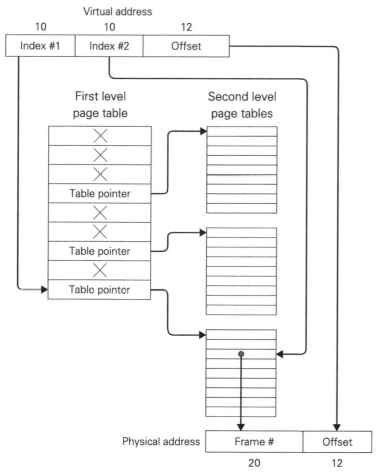

FIGURE 3-17: A two-level page table system for translating virtual addresses to physical addresses

A second, less serious problem is that SD cards are not especially fast, as flash storage devices go. Once Raspbian begins swapping, the performance of the system could slow to a crawl. Think of virtual memory on the Raspberry Pi as a safety mechanism to protect against crashes, and not performance enhancement. If you notice everything getting slow, you know that you're out of memory and need to start closing programs to make swapping unnecessary.

Watching Raspberry Pi Virtual Memory

It's possible to run a simple memory monitor utility called vmstat (for "virtual memory statistics") in a Raspbian terminal window. The vmstat utility summarises the current state of the Raspberry Pi virtual memory system and updates it, either a set number of times or at a set time interval. The vmstat utility is command-line only, and must be run from a terminal window, such as the one displayed by LXTerminal.

Open an instance of LXTerminal and type the following command:

```
vmstat
```

Launched this way, vmstat displays one line of data beneath a two-line column header. This is the state of the virtual memory system at the moment the command was issued. You can repeat the command after an elapsed time interval and limit the number of repeats to a specified count by using two optional parameters:

```
vmstat [interval] [count]
```

The interval parameter is given in seconds. If you give an interval parameter but not a count parameter, vmstat continues to post an update at each interval as long as you let it run. Output from vmstat may be redirected to a file if you'd like to keep the data for later analysis.

The meaning of the various columns displayed by vmstat is summarised in Table 3-2.

Table 3-2   vmstat's Columns

Column	Meaning
r	The number of processes currently waiting to run
b	The number of processes currently "asleep"
swpd	The number of pages that have been written out to swap space
free	The amount of unallocated memory
buff	The amount of allocated memory in use
cache	The amount of memory that could be reclaimed for use by swapping
si	The amount of memory in KB swapped in per second—usually 0
so	The amount of memory in KB swapped out per second—usually 0

Column	Meaning
bi	The number of blocks read from block devices per second
bo	The number of blocks written to block devices per second
in	The number of system interrupts per second
cs	The number of context switches per second
us	The percentage of time the CPU is spending on all non-kernel processes
sy	The percentage of time the CPU is spending on kernel processes
id	The percentage of time the CPU is idle
wa	The percentage of time the CPU is waiting for I/O operations to complete

Leave vmstat running while you open and close application windows and watch what happens to the numbers. One thing to keep in mind is that the bi and bo columns are not dedicated to swap space access. They include it, but they also include ordinary read/write access to the SD card filesystem. This includes logging and web caching, so if you see an uptick in bi and bo while using a web browser like Midori, remember that network adapters are not block devices and what you're seeing is ordinary filesystem traffic between the browser and the SD card. The swpd column reports total swap space page writes and if it remains at 0, virtual memory has not begun swapping. The si and so columns report the speed of swap space reads and writes. As with swapd, they will usually be zero. If you start to see nonzero values in si and so, the Raspberry Pi may have begun to thrash. Close some apps and see if the swap traffic goes away.

Chapter 4

ARM Processors and Systems-on-a-Chip

THIS CHAPTER IS about central processing units (CPUs), the beating hearts at the centre of all computers. A great deal of what people call "computer architecture" is the inner structure of the CPU. More specifically, this chapter is about the Advanced RISC Machine (ARM) processors, especially the ARM11 microarchitecture used in the original Raspberry Pi.

The focus on the ARM11 microprocessor architecture leads to a secondary topic in this chapter: system-on-a-chip (SoC) devices, which include not only an ARM CPU but also a graphics processor, a mass-storage controller for SD card access, a serial port controller and several other subsystems that have often been implemented as separate chips or chip sets outside the CPU.

The Incredible Shrinking CPU

Early computers were enormous because they had to be; at first, digital logic was based on high-reliability versions of what were essentially radio tubes, each of which was the size of your thumb. Whole rooms in specially engineered buildings were needed to house, power and cool thousands of radio tubes. Imagine a building the size of a modern server farm—which today would house rack upon rack of multicore blade servers—containing a *single* CPU.

The arrival of commercially manufactured transistors in 1955 ushered in the second generation of CPUs. The new developments meant that what had previously filled whole rooms could now be contained in three or four cabinets the size of refrigerators. Transistors were one-hundredth the size of the tubes that they replaced and required one-thousandth of their power. Printed-circuit technology allowed the mass production of computers, albeit for small values of "mass". IBM had made exactly 19 of their first-generation tube-based 701 systems.

Just a few years later, IBM's transistor-based 1401 sold 10,000 units. The original PDP-8 machines from Digital Equipment Corporation (DEC) were only half the size of a refrigerator and more than 50,000 units were sold.

The third generation of computer technology arrived in the mid-1960s with the development of integrated circuits. By placing first a few, and eventually many, transistors on a single silicon chip, movement was allowed in two directions: high-end computers (mainframes) stayed physically large but increased their compute power enormously; and lower-end computers (minicomputers) were smaller in size and their price meant that smaller companies and schools could afford them. By 1970, the PDP-8 CPU cabinet was half a metre wide by not quite a metre long, and only 30cm high. Its peripherals (mechanical printers, tape and disk drives, power supply and so on) made the full system fairly bulky, but the CPU itself could fit on a desktop and was only a little larger than the first personal computers. Across its lifetime, the PDP-8 series sold half a million units.

Microprocessors

As small as it was, the commercial PDP-8 minicomputer CPU was still spread out across several circuit boards crammed with individual integrated circuits. (A special-purpose single-chip version appeared in the mid-1970s, long after the PDP-8 had begun its fall to obscurity.) Silicon fabrication techniques continued to improve in the late 1960s, driven by the mainframe computer industry's insatiable demand for solid-state memory chips. By 1970 it was possible to fabricate 2,500 transistors on a single silicon chip. This was enough (barely) to cover all the necessary logic of a simple CPU. A team led by Intel's Federico Faggin designed the 4004 microprocessor, which became the first commercial mass-produced single-chip CPU.

The 4004 is considered an oddity today because of its 4-bit data word; its primary use was in desktop calculators. Nonetheless, it had the same memory addressing capability (4,096 bytes) as the PDP-8. It was the seed from which Intel grew its CPU empire. The company quickly released the 8008 in 1972 and the 8080 in 1974. The 8080 contained 4,500 transistors, and its design influenced all successful Intel CPUs from then on. In 1974, the 8080 became the heart of what is recognised as the first truly useful personal computer, the Altair 8800.

On the heels of the 8080 came dozens of microprocessors, some of which were quite successful: Motorola's 6800, Zilog's Z80, RCA's COSMAC 1802 series (which in a radiation-hardened silicon-on-sapphire variant was used in many spacecraft, including Galileo) and MOS Technology's 6502, which was used in several very popular personal computers including the Apple II and the original BBC Microcomputer, which led directly to the development of the Acorn ARM processors.

Most of those early microprocessors fell into the shadows of Motorola and Intel before 1980. The 30,000-transistor 8086 (and its budget-priced sibling, the 8088) kicked personal computing into the business world with the IBM PC. The 50,000-transistor 68000 powered the first graphical user interface (GUI) computers, including the Sun and Apollo workstations and later the Apple Lisa and Macintosh. Motorola's and Intel's microprocessor architectures were competitors as they evolved, but Motorola's 68000 architecture had a difficult time competing with Intel CPUs and fell out of use by the mid-1990s. By 2006, Apple Computer was using Intel processors in its Macintosh line, and Intel became the dominant player in personal computing. By 2016, Intel's Haswell-E CPUs contained 2.6 billion transistors, and the high-end Xeon server chips could have more than two billion. Intel's "Knight's Corner" Xeon Phi supercomputer component processor contains an astonishing seven *billion* transistors.

Transistor Budgets

These numbers aren't just mind-blowing. Transistor count has affected the evolution of microprocessor architectures in fundamental ways. For example, any CPU design begins with an engineering study to indicate how large the silicon die will be, and at what size the transistors will be fabricated. This gives a maximum transistor count for the die long before any of the actual die layout has been performed.

After the total number of transistors is known, those transistors are parcelled out to the various component functions that make up a CPU: so many transistors go to cache, so many go to the registers, so many go to implementing machine instructions and so on. Subsystem design teams guard these "transistor budgets" as jealously as governments or corporations guard their financial budgets.

The eventual CPU design is always a compromise between the features the designers want to "buy" and the limitations of the transistor budget they are given to shop with. If you ask a CPU designer why one particular desirable feature didn't make it into final silicon, the answer is almost invariably, "We didn't have the transistor budget for it".

Digital Logic Primer

Chapter 3 explained that computers store data as patterns of binary 1s and 0s, expressed as the presence or absence of a voltage on a wire. A full treatment of digital logic design is beyond the scope of this book, but we review here a few basic concepts that are helpful in understanding the internal workings of CPUs.

Logic Gates

All computation in digital computers is performed by *logic gates*, which accept one or more binary inputs and generate (usually) one binary output. The four most basic logic gates are NOT, AND, OR, and XOR. These logic gates are shown in Figure 4-1 with their truth tables, which summarise what output value is generated for every possible combination of inputs. Each type of gate is represented by a symbol, which is used in schematic diagrams of multi-gate logic circuits.

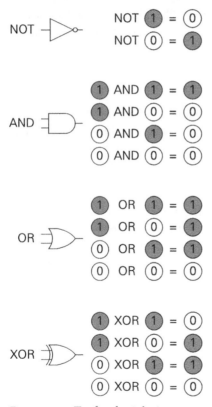

FIGURE 4-1: The four basic logic gates

A chip designer has access to a cell library with which he or she can construct larger circuits. A modern complementary metal-oxide semiconductor (CMOS) cell library has hundreds of cells computing a range of more complex functions that have several inputs, but at their hearts all of these more complex CMOS functions are constructed using NMOS (N-channel Metal Oxide Semiconductor) transistors and PMOS (P-channel Metal Oxide Semiconductor) transistors. NMOS transistors conduct when their gate input is high (that is, +V, whatever voltage is used in the design) and PMOS transistors conduct when their gate inputs are low, or 0V (often called *ground*). NMOS and PMOS transistors are thus *complementary* in how they conduct. We can use one NMOS and one PMOS transistor to form the basic CMOS NOT gate (often called an *inverter*), as shown in Figure 4-2.

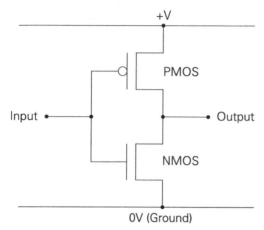

FIGURE 4-2: A CMOS NOT gate

When a high voltage level (binary 1) is placed at the input terminal, the NMOS transistor conducts, pulling the output low (binary 0). When a low voltage level (binary 0) is placed on the input terminal, the PMOS transistor conducts, pulling the output high (binary 1).

All logic gates impose a characteristic delay, which is the time required for the output or outputs to respond to a change in one or more of the inputs. If you connect simple gates together in sequence (that is, with the output of one connected to the input of the next) to compute a more complex function, the delay of the composite circuit is given by the sum of the delays on the longest path from an input to an output. This is known as the propagation delay of a logic path.

Flip-Flops and Sequential Logic

You now know how to build combinatorial functions of arbitrary inputs (that is, functions created by combining simpler logic gates), but to build a computer you need to be able to build systems that have *state* (memory) and can evolve that state over time. Chapter 3 mentioned the bi-stable flip-flop as the storage element in simple SRAM (Static Random Access Memory) cells. The D-type flip-flop is the ideal storage element for saving a state inside a computer; see Figure 4-3.

Flip-Flops: Where Bits Live

A *flip-flop* is an electronic circuit that stores a logical state, conventionally described as either 1 or 0. Once set to a particular state by a digital signal on an input (typically a voltage change from 0 volts to 5 volts or 5 to 0) the flip-flop will maintain that state until another input signal changes it. Because a flip-flop can store one of two logical states, it is sometimes described as *bistable*. There are several different types of flip-flop, but the one most used in computer logic is the *D-type*, where D stands for "data". The 1 and 0 states stored in flip-flops may be used to express computer data, hence the name.

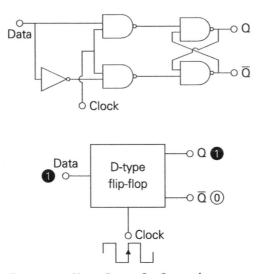

FIGURE 4-3: How a D-type flip-flop works

A D-type flip-flop takes a snapshot of the D input every time it sees a low-to-high transition on its clock input (a rising clock edge), and presents it on the Q output until the next clock edge arrives. You can build complex systems by combining D-type flip-flops that store state with a combinatorial logic circuit to compute the next state from the current state and (optionally) external inputs.

Figure 4-4 presents a simple example. Assuming you've built a piece of combinatorial logic to add 1 to a four-digit binary number, you can implement a counter that increments a four-digit value stored in four flip-flops every time the clock ticks. The maximum clock speed is determined by the longest path through the cloud of combinatorial logic: you need to respond to a change in the values in the flip-flops and get the new value ready before the next clock edge comes along.

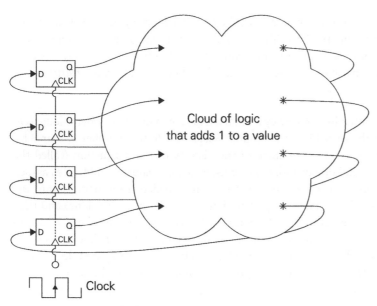

FIGURE 4-4: A counter built from four flip-flops

Another useful example is a shift register, shown in Figure 4-5. A shift register hands bits down the chain of flip-flops, advancing by one position every clock edge.

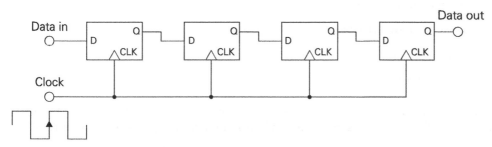

FIGURE 4-5: A shift register built from four flip-flops

Everything you see in this chapter is an elaboration of these fundamental principles: clouds of combinatorial logic and D-type edge-triggered flip-flops that store a digital state.

Inside the CPU

As explained briefly in Chapter 2, a computer program is just a long series of *very* small steps. Each of these very small steps is called a *machine instruction*, and it is an "atomic" unit of action that cannot be divided further outside of the CPU. Each family of CPUs has its own unique roster of machine instructions. They may do similar things, but, in general, the machine instructions from one family of CPUs will *not* execute on another family of CPUs. The definition of a CPU's machine instructions and what they do is called its *instruction set architecture* (ISA).

An instruction is represented in memory by a binary value some number of bytes long. (On many 32-bit CPUs like the ARM11 in the original Raspberry Pi, this number is four 8-bit bytes.) Within this binary number are encoded the identity of the instruction (called the *operation code*, or *opcode*), and one or more operands, which are values or addresses associated with the instruction. A binary machine instruction is loaded from memory into the CPU, where the CPU decodes it (takes it apart to determine what must be done) and then executes it, during which the actual work of the instruction is accomplished. When an instruction has been dispatched for execution it's said to have been issued, and after it is completely executed it's said to be retired. The next instruction in the program is loaded into the CPU for execution. (In modern CPUs, the process is more complicated than that, as we explain later in this chapter.)

From a height, program execution by the CPU works like this:

1. Fetch the first instruction in the program.

2. Decode the instruction.

3. Execute the instruction.

4. Fetch the next instruction.

5. Decode the instruction.

6. Execute the instruction.

. . .and so on, for as many instructions as are in the program. The *program counter* is a pointer inside the CPU that contains the memory address of the currently executing instruction.

Machine instructions do things like

- Add, subtract, multiply or divide

- Perform logical operations like AND, OR, XOR and NOT on binary values

- Shift a multi-bit binary value to the left or right

- Copy data from one location to another

- Compare values against constants or other values

- Perform CPU control functions

The values on which the machines operate may come from external memory or from one of a comparatively small number of registers inside the CPU itself. A *register* is a storage location that can hold multiple bits at once; typically 16, 32 or 64, depending on the CPU. Results from machine instruction operations may be stored to memory or to registers.

In modern CPUs, separate subsystems execute different groups of machine instructions:

- **Arithmetic logic unit (ALU):** Handles simple integer maths and logical operations

- **Floating point unit (FPU):** Handles floating point maths

- **Single-instruction, multiple data (SIMD) unit:** Handles vector maths that performs operations on multiple data values at once. This type of maths is essential in audio and video applications.

A modern high-performance CPU may have multiple copies of each unit to support parallel execution of instructions, as we explain a little later.

Branching and Flags

As useful as executing a linear sequence of instructions may be, the real magic of computing lies in the ability of a program to change its course of execution depending on the results of its work. This is done using *branch instructions*, which have the power to skip forward or backward in the sequence of machine instructions that make up a program. Some branch instructions—called unconditional branch instructions—tell the CPU to "just go" and load the next instruction from a memory address included in the branch instruction.

A conditional branch instruction combines a test of some sort with a branch. These tests generally involve a group of single-bit binary values called *flags* that are stored somewhere in the CPU, generally in a group called the flags register or status word. When certain machine instructions execute, they set (change to binary 1) or clear (change to binary 0) one or more flags. For example, all CPUs have instructions that compare the values of two registers. If the values are equal, a flag (generally called the zero flag) is set to 1. If the values are not equal, the flag is cleared to zero. The flag is called the "zero" flag because of the way comparisons work. To compare two registers, the CPU subtracts one of them from the other. If the result of the subtraction is zero, they are equal, and the zero flag is set. If the result of the subtraction is anything but zero, the two registers are not equal, and the zero flag is cleared.

A machine instruction is just a binary number. Although it is possible to program directly in machine code, for convenience programmers generally use an assembler to convert assembly language directly into machine instructions. Instructions in assembly language are represented by a short string called a mnemonic, and the various operands are written in human-readable form. The assembly language representation of a conditional branch machine instruction might look like this:

```
BEQ [address]
```

What the instruction does is to branch if equal (that is, if the zero flag is set) to the machine instruction stored at the specified memory address; if the zero flag is clear, execution continues to the next instruction in memory.

There may be a dozen or more flags in a CPU's architecture. Some flags reflect equality or the fact that a register's value has become zero. Some indicate whether an arithmetic carry has occurred. Some indicate whether a register has been set to a positive or negative value. Some indicate error conditions, like numeric overflow or an attempt to divide by zero. Some reflect the current state of the CPU's internal machinery. For each flag there are one or more conditional branch instructions that check the value of the flag and branch accordingly.

In addition to supporting conditional branch instructions, the ARM CPUs used by the Raspberry Pi has a more general conditional execution feature in its instruction set that is described in some detail later on.

The System Stack

There are a fair number of data structures catalogued and described by computer scientists including arrays, queues, lists, stacks, sets, rings and bags, among others. A few are used so often that some CPUs have hardwired support for them in their machine instructions. The most important of these is the stack.

A *stack* is a last-in-first-out (LIFO) data storage mechanism essential to the operation of most modern CPUs, including the Raspberry Pi's ARM11. The key characteristic of stack operation is that data items are removed from the stack in the reverse order of how they were stored.

A metaphor captures this well. If you've ever eaten in a school cafeteria, you may have seen a common mechanism for storing plates and saucers: a spring-loaded platform within a metal cylinder, adjusted to balance the weight of whatever plates it contains. When you place a plate in the cylinder the platform moves down just enough to make room for the next plate. When you need a plate, you simply take one from the top of the cylinder. With its load lightened, the platform rises just enough to bring the next plate to the top of the cylinder.

The key to the plate storage cylinder is that the first plate placed in the cylinder is all the way at the bottom. The last plate placed in the cylinder is at the top. The last plate stored is the first one taken out of storage—thus, "last in, first out".

In a computer system, a stack is an area of memory set aside for LIFO data storage and managed by machine instructions designed to implement the stack data structure. Figure 4-6 shows a simple stack.

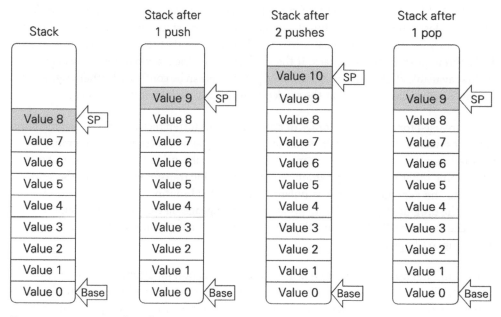

FIGURE 4-6: How a stack works

The stack begins at a location in memory specified by a *base pointer*. (A *pointer* is simply a memory address.) After it's loaded with an address, the value of the base pointer doesn't change. A second pointer, called the *stack pointer*, indicates the memory location to be accessed next. It's sometimes called the "top of the stack". In Figure 4-6, the items at the top of the stack are shaded.

To add an item to a stack, the stack pointer is first incremented so that it points to the next available memory location in the stack. The data item is then written to that location. Informally, this is called pushing an item onto the stack.

To remove an item from the stack, the item at the top of the stack is first copied to a register or some other place in memory, and then the stack pointer is decremented so that it points to what had previously been the top item on the stack. This process is called popping an item from the stack. If you follow the four stack snapshots in Figure 4-6, you can see how the stack grows or shrinks as items are pushed onto it and popped from it. The last item pushed onto the stack is the first item popped from it—remember, last in, first out.

There are some variations on how stacks are implemented in any given architecture. An *ascending stack,* as just described, grows upwards in memory with each push by incrementing the stack pointer to the next higher memory location. A *descending stack* grows downwards in memory with each push by decrementing the stack pointer to the next lower memory location. The ARM CPU stack can be configured to work either way, though by convention ARM stacks are descending. Some architectures assume that the stack pointer points to the first free memory location on the stack, whereas others assume that the stack pointer points to the last item pushed onto the stack. If the stack is empty, the stack pointer always points to the first available stack location. Again, ARM processors can be configured either way, but, by default, ARM stacks assume that the stack pointer points to the last item pushed.

Stacks are used for temporary storage of both data items (often register values) and memory addresses during subroutine calls. A *subroutine* is a sequence of actions in a program that is executed as a group and given a name. Any time the subroutine's actions need to be executed, some other part of the program can *call* it, meaning transfer execution to the subroutine until the subroutine's work is finished. Then the subroutine returns execution to the part of the program that called it. In programming languages like C and Python, subroutines are called *functions.* We'll have much more to say about subroutines and their role in programming in Chapter 5.

Many computer architectures provide a dedicated instruction for calling a subroutine, which automatically pushes the program counter value to the stack before branching to the start address of the subroutine. When the subroutine is finished, the saved program counter (referred to as the return address) may be popped back into the program counter by another dedicated instruction, and the program continues on its way. If the subroutine wants to use a CPU register (which is likely already in use by whoever called the subroutine), it can push the existing value to the stack itself, and pop it back before returning.

Note that although the ARM CPUs can choose to save subroutine return addresses on the stack manually, there is a faster way that doesn't impose the time penalty of accessing system memory. As you see a little later in this chapter, return addresses are first stored in the link register (LR), allowing some leaf functions (those functions that do not call any functions in turn) to avoid stack accesses altogether.

Stacks are useful in that they can manage nested subroutine calls (subroutine calls made from within subroutines). Each time a new nested subroutine call is made, another layer of data and return addresses is added to the stack. Assuming that the stack has room, dozens or even hundreds of nested calls may be made. If the stack becomes full and no longer has room for additional values, an attempt to push anything on the stack causes a stack overflow. If there is no protection in place, for example from a memory management unit, data stored in memory areas adjacent to the stack are then overwritten, and program malfunctions occur.

System Clocks and Execution Time

As described earlier in the "Digital Logic Primer" section, everything that goes on inside a sequential circuit like a CPU is synchronised to a pulse generator called the *clock*. Each pulse from the clock triggers a *clock cycle*, during which the CPU does some specific work. In very old CPUs, a single machine instruction might take anywhere from 4 clock cycles to 40 clock cycles to complete execution. Different instructions took different times, and some (like multiplication and division instructions) took a lot more time than others.

Why did different instructions take more time? In the early decades of computing, machine instructions were implemented within the CPU silicon as sequences of *microinstructions*, which are very simple mini-steps from which more complex instructions may be built. (Microinstructions are not accessible from outside the CPU.) Microinstructions conserved space on the CPU chip by allowing a large number of machine instructions to be implemented by combining a far smaller number of microinstructions. The digital logic that implements instructions is thus shared across many instructions, reducing the total transistor count required. The list of microinstructions required to perform each instruction is called *microcode*.

Executing machine instructions implemented as microcode adds significant time to instruction execution. Whenever possible, CPU designers hardwire instructions; that is, they implement each instruction directly with transistor logic dedicated to that single instruction. This takes more transistor budget and more room on the chip than microcode, but it produces *much* faster instructions. As more transistors could be fitted on a single chip, more and more instructions were hardwired and fewer relied on microcode. Even so, until fairly recently, the use of microcode forced some instructions to take more clock cycles to complete than others. Figure 4-7 shows how this worked on early computers that had slow instructions due to microcode.

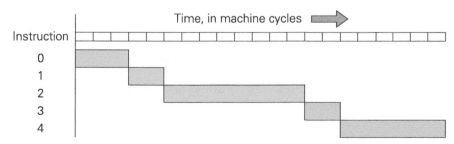

FIGURE 4-7: Machine instructions and clock cycles

Higher transistor budgets allow more hardwired instructions. At some point, there are enough transistors on a chip to hardwire even complicated operations like multiplication and division. When all machine instructions are hardwired, all instructions execute in almost the same amount of time. The Holy Grail in CPU architecture has always been to execute all machine instructions in a single clock cycle. By 2000 or so that goal had mostly been achieved, and the chart of machine instructions versus clock cycles changed to something like Figure 4-8.

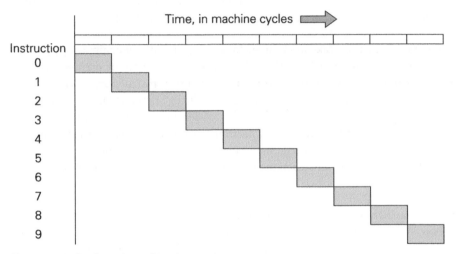

FIGURE 4-8: Single-cycle machine instructions

Figure 4-8 might make you think that instruction execution speed had hit a wall, and the only thing that could be done to get more instructions executed per second would be to increase the clock speed. You'd be wrong.

Pipelining

There's a misunderstanding about CPU operation and clock speeds: the CPU does not operate as quickly as the clock speed demands. The clock speed can only be as fast as the CPU allows. The CPU needs a certain amount of time to do what it does.

If you look closely at how a CPU executes a single machine instruction, you see that it happens in a number of relatively distinct stages:

1. Fetch the instruction from memory.

2. Decode the instruction.

3. Execute the instruction.

4. Write back any changes made by the instruction to registers or memory.

When a machine instruction is executed in a single clock cycle, all four stages happen in one wave of transistor activity. This wave propagates through the CPU from the logic that deals with fetching and decoding instructions through the execution stage to the write-back logic. It's tough to make that wave proceed more quickly, and the maximum clock speed will be determined by the time taken to get a signal down the longest path through all that logic.

However, because the four stages occur in a specific order, you can treat each stage as a separate action. If you can engineer the logic that executes machine instructions such that all four stages take roughly the same amount of time, an interesting possibility opens up: you can overlap them. See Figure 4-9.

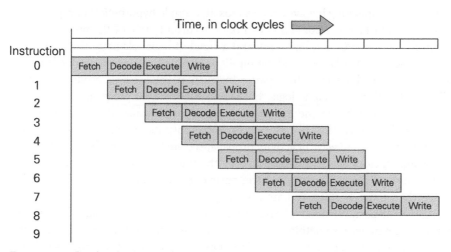

FIGURE 4-9: Overlapping instruction execution

In Figure 4-9, each stage of instruction execution takes one clock cycle. This means that the clock can be made faster, because executing an instruction now takes four ticks of the clock rather than one. This sounds like a step back in performance, even if the clock rate doubles. In fact, it sounds at first like a paradox: it takes four clock cycles to complete any single instruction, but one instruction is issued and another retires (that is, finishes its work) every clock cycle. The net result is that you still have instructions executing in a single, much faster clock cycle.

To get a sense of this, consider the sort of conveyor-belt pizza ovens that you see baking pizzas behind some pizza counters. The chef drops a raw pizza on the conveyor belt at the opening of the oven. Ten minutes later, the pizza emerges from the oven fully cooked and ready to sell. It takes 10 minutes to bake a pizza. However, there can be five pizzas making their way through the oven at any given time, and assuming that the chef keeps dropping raw pizzas on the belt, a finished pizza will emerge from the oven every two minutes. The first pizza takes 10 minutes. But once the oven is full, a pizza is finished every two minutes.

Overlapping the execution of machine instructions in this way is called *pipelining*. First implemented in supercomputers during the 1980s, pipelining is now the norm in virtually all CPUs, even Microchip Technology's low-cost PIC (Programmable Intelligent Computer) microcontrollers. Pipelining is second only to memory caching as a contributor to recent CPU performance improvements.

Pipelining in Detail

To get a feel for what pipelining involves, take a look at a simple hypothetical non-pipelined processor, as shown in Figure 4-10. Flip-flops hold the current state of the processor (the current program counter (PC) and registers), and a cloud of logic calculates the next state ready to be fed back into the D inputs of the flip-flops in time for the next clock edge. You can roughly divide this cloud into three parts: Instruction Fetch (IF), Decode (DC), and Execute (EX). In the IF part is some logic that works out the next program counter (PC) value—there are no branches in the hypothetical processor example. The registers aren't needed until the EX part. At the start of each cycle the outputs of some of the flip-flops change, and during the cycle a wave of activity propagates from left to right through the logic cloud. The maximum clock speed is determined by the time taken to traverse the longest path through the cloud's logic. During the latter parts of the cycle, the left-hand bits of the cloud have reached a steady state, and are just supplying the results to the still-changing logic in the right-hand part. Wouldn't it be nice to take a snapshot of that steady state and let the left-hand bits get on with something else, such as fetching the next instruction? A pipelined processor inserts pipeline latches (again, flip-flops) into the cloud to do precisely that.

Figure 4-11 shows a processor with pipeline latches. In the illustration, we split the logic cloud into three subclouds. The IF cloud just needs to get the instruction from memory and figure out the next PC value in time for the first set of pipeline latches to record the result. It can then get on with fetching the next instruction during the next cycle, while the DC cloud logic decodes the previous instruction using the pipeline latch data as its input. The register read/write is all done during the EX part because we weren't using the registers until the EX part of the original cloud, and we want to be able to write a value to the register file during one cycle and use it in the next cycle.

The speed of the CPU is again determined by the time required to traverse the longest path in any part of the cloud, but because we chopped up the cloud into three parts, what was once the longest path is bound to be quicker than in the non-pipelined processor shown in Figure 4-10.

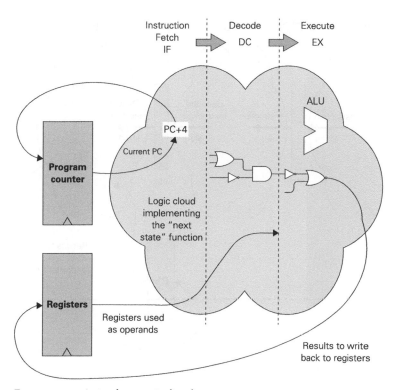

FIGURE 4-10: A simple non-pipelined processor

Looking at this, you might imagine that the EX stage is a bit "full". All the interesting stuff, in particularly the arithmetic logic unit (ALU), lives there. If so, you'd be right: in a simple pipeline like this, the EX stage tends to contain the longest path, and thus constrains the pipeline. The next logical step, which you see in the ARM11 in the next section, is to subdivide the EX cloud into multiple smaller stages. This in turn requires you to cope with the issues that arise when the register file is read from and written to in different pipeline stages.

Deeper Pipelines and Pipeline Hazards

How much overlap you can create in a given CPU depends primarily on how many stages a CPU's instruction execution can be broken down to. Early on, 3- and 4-stage pipelines were state of the art. As you will see later, the ARM11 CPU inside the original Raspberry Pi has an 8-stage instruction pipeline, and many of the current Intel processors have pipelines with 20 stages or more. A challenge for CPU designers pondering longer pipelines is that the different stages of instruction execution don't all take the same amount of time: because it takes one clock cycle to perform each stage, the length of the clock cycle governing CPU operation is the time required to complete the slowest pipeline stage.

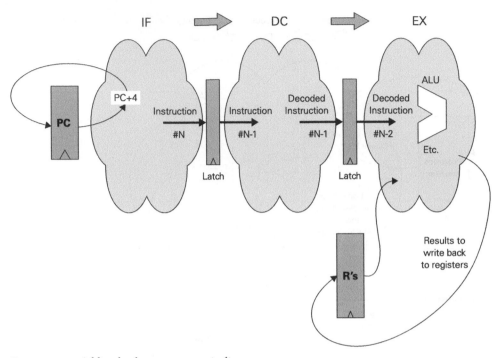

FIGURE 4-11: Adding latches to create a pipeline

Moving instructions through the pipeline at a continuous, uniform rate is crucial. Certain things can disrupt the smooth flow of instructions through a CPU pipeline. These are called pipeline hazards, and they can lead to delays in the pipeline. The delays are called pipeline stalls. There are three general categories of pipeline hazard:

- **Control hazards:** Caused by conditional branch instructions
- **Data hazards:** Caused by data dependency between instructions
- **Structural hazards:** Caused by resource conflicts

It's easy to see how a conditional branch could disrupt a pipeline. If the first instruction shown in the pipeline in Figure 4-9 is a conditional branch instruction, and if (as is generally the case) the logic that resolves whether a branch is taken is located in the EX stage, you could end up branching away from sequential instructions that are already in the pipeline and have been fetched and decoded. Those instructions would no longer be in the path of program execution. So to preserve the illusion that you're executing instructions one at a time they would need to be discarded and the pipeline would need to be refilled with instructions starting at the branch target address. Thinking back to the pizza-oven metaphor, if the order-taker submits an incorrect order to the chef, one or more pizzas already on their way through the oven may need to be discarded, and replacements placed on the belt. This leads to a pause before new, valid pizzas start to emerge from the oven—not to mention a loss of overall throughput.

One historical approach to control hazards is to abandon the illusion that you're executing instructions one at a time and to say that our branches are delayed: sequential instructions that have entered the pipeline at the time when the branch is resolved always execute, regardless of whether the branch is taken. It is then up to the assembly-language programmer or high-level language compiler to find useful work to fill these branch delay slots.

This behaviour is uncommon, however. Most architectures attempt to mitigate the impact of pipeline hazards through two interrelated mechanisms: *branch prediction* and *speculative execution*. Here, the CPU's execution logic attempts to predict which of two possible branch destinations will be taken. The prediction is based on a cumulative history of branches taken in that part of the code. The CPU fetches instructions from the more likely destination before the actual result of the branch is known, and starts executing them speculatively. Recovering from an incorrect prediction involves killing the speculatively executed instructions before they reach a stage of the pipeline that can affect the outside world, generally by replacing them with *bubbles* (no-op instructions, which do nothing). Speculative execution amounts to the CPU doing some guessing, and bad guesses are expensive. They incur a delay roughly proportional to the depth of the pipeline, which needs time to refill. A delay of 20 cycles is not unusual in a modern high-performance processor, so branch predictor improvements have become a major determinant of CPU performance.

Data dependence is more subtle. Suppose the result value from one instruction is needed as an operand by the next instruction in the pipeline. The second instruction may require the value before the first instruction has finished generating it. If you don't stop the second instruction from proceeding through the pipeline it would end up using a value that is garbage or a leftover from some earlier calculation. This doesn't happen in the simple pipelined processor described earlier, because reading the registers, computing the result and writing it back all occur in the EX stage. The registers are entirely consistent once the next instruction arrives at the EX stage. It's only once you start to break the over-full EX stage apart (as almost all modern processors, including the ARM, do) that you need to worry.

Resource conflicts happen when two instructions in the pipeline need to access some CPU resource at the same time. For example, if two instructions in different pipeline stages need to access external memory via the cache system at the same time, one of these instructions must take priority over the other. A trivial example of this can occur between the IF stage reading instructions, and some other pipeline stage (the EX stage in our simple example) reading or writing data. This particular conflict may be partially resolved by splitting the unified level 1 cache into two separate caches: one for data and one for machine instructions. This is called a *modified Harvard architecture*, after Harvard's early experimental computers that stored and accessed machine instructions and data separately. The ARM11 CPUs incorporate a modified Harvard architecture.

Detecting and resolving data dependence and resource conflict hazards takes still more transistors on the silicon to solve. The general approach is for the instruction decode logic to identify when a hazard is about to occur in the pipeline; the hardware that performs this check is referred to as an *interlock*. If a fetched instruction represents a hazard of any kind, a bubble is inserted into the pipeline ahead of the problematic instruction. This generates a delay that allows earlier instructions to finish what they're doing before they conflict with instructions coming up the pipe.

The ARM11 Pipeline

The pipeline in the ARM11 CPU is divided into eight stages, as shown in Figure 4-12. The pipeline isn't quite as simple as the one shown in Figure 4-9. In addition to the pipeline being divided into eight different stages, there are three possible paths through the pipeline. Which path the execution takes depends on what type of instruction is executing.

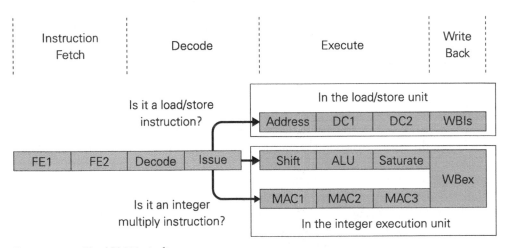

FIGURE 4-12: The ARM11 pipeline

The first four stages are identical, regardless of the instruction. However, when the instruction is issued, the decode logic chooses one of the three possible paths. Each category of instructions has its own pipeline path:

- **Integer execution path:** For most instructions that execute integer operations
- **Multiply-accumulate path:** For integer multiply instructions
- **Load/store path:** For load and store instructions

The stages shown in the figure and their abbreviations are:

- **FE1:** The first fetch stage; the address for the instruction is requested and the instruction is received.

- **FE2:** Branch prediction is done in this stage.

- **Decode:** The instruction is decoded.

- **Issue:** The registers are read and the instruction is issued.

- **Shift:** Any required shift operations are done in this stage.

- **ALU:** Any required integer operations are done in the ALU in this stage.

- **Saturate:** Integer results are saturated; that is, forced to fall within integer range.

- **MAC1:** The first stage for execution of multiply instructions.

- **MAC2:** The second stage for execution of multiply instructions.

- **MAC3:** The third stage for execution of multiply instructions.

- **WBex:** Whatever register data was changed by the instruction is written back to the registers. WBex is the last stage on both the integer execution path and the multiply-accumulate path.

- **Address:** Used to generate addresses used by the instruction to access memory.

- **DC1:** The first stage during which the address is processed by the data cache logic.

- **DC2:** The second stage during which the address is processed by the data cache logic.

- **WBls:** The final stage in the load/store path writes back any changes made to memory locations.

Making things yet more complex is the fact that the integer execution path and the multiply-accumulate path are handled by the integer execution unit, and the load/store path is handled by the separate load/store unit. An *execution unit* is a CPU subsystem that handles the "work" of an instruction—that is, integer maths or logical operations, memory access and so on. If a floating point coprocessor is present in the core, the coprocessor's own pipeline, not shown here, handles execution once the instruction is issued. (We'll explain coprocessors in more detail later on, in the section "Coprocessors.")

Superscalar Execution

As it turns out, still more performance can be wrung from the pipelining idea. A mechanism called *superscalar execution* appeared towards the end of the 1980s. A superscalar architecture has an instruction pipeline like the one described in the previous section, as nearly all CPUs do today. However, a superscalar CPU issues more than one instruction for execution at the same time. Once issued, the instructions execute simultaneously. With superscalar CPUs, the execution of instructions goes beyond overlapping, to true parallelism. A superscalar pipeline is shown in Figure 4-13.

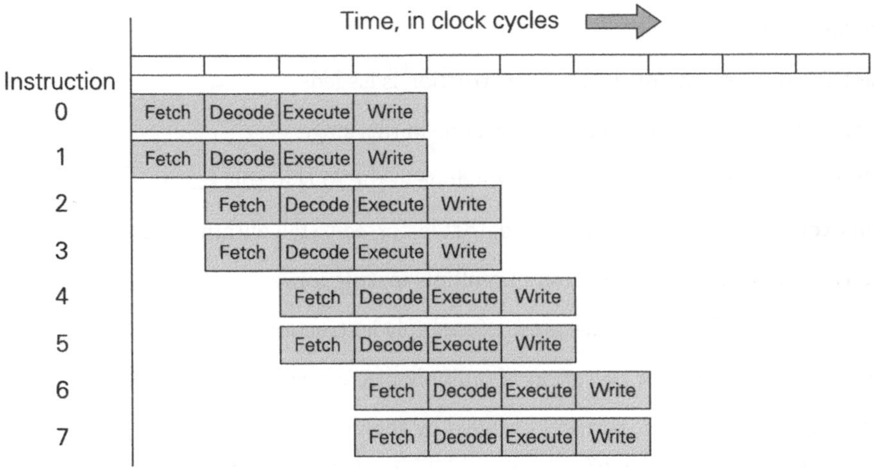

FIGURE 4-13: Superscalar execution

In a simple case like this, a superscalar CPU fetches two instructions from memory and examines them to determine whether they can be run in parallel. If so, the CPU parcels out execution of both instructions to dual execution units. The execution units are *not* complete processor cores. They handle the work of the instruction only and specialise in integer maths and logic, floating point maths and vector maths. The CPU strives to keep all the execution units busy as much of the time as possible.

The basic mechanism is the same as with pipelining: the CPU checks for data dependencies in the instruction stream, such as whether an instruction provides a data value to the instruction that follows it. If such a dependency exists, the two instructions cannot be issued at once, and a pipeline stall occurs. For example, if one instruction adds a value to Register 4, and the next instruction in sequence multiplies the contents of Register 4 by still another value, the instructions cannot be issued together to run in parallel because the second instruction depends on data calculated by the first.

As with pipelining, the compiler that generates program code has the power to look for data dependencies and rearrange instructions so that two consecutive instructions do not depend on one another in ways that would trigger an interlock; that is, a situation where one instruction gets ahead of another on which it relies for data. These optimisations have become less important lately, because recent superscalar CPUs allow *out-of-order* execution. Such CPUs have the ability to dynamically reorder the incoming instruction stream to maximise the amount of achievable parallelism and minimize data dependencies that cause interlocks.

Superscalar execution, and particularly out-of-order execution, is expensive in terms of transistor logic. In addition to the burden of providing duplicate execution units, the logic to implement dependency checks becomes increasingly complex. In theory it is possible for a CPU to issue more than four instructions at once, but at around this point designers generally reach a point of diminishing returns.

The ARM11 microarchitecture does not support superscalar execution. Superscalar capability was introduced into the ARM family with the "Cortex A" family of processors, some of which are capable of issuing four instructions at once. (More on Cortex later in this chapter.)

More Parallelism with SIMD

Superscalar execution is difficult to implement but easy to describe: multiple instructions are issued at the same time, and they execute in parallel. Modern CPUs support another type of parallelism: instructions that operate on multiple data items at once. As a class, these are called single-instruction, multiple data (SIMD) instructions. Most computer architectures have their own SIMD instructions, which are generally not identical to or even compatible with those of other architectures.

SIMD is best explained by an example. Ordinary addition instructions in a 32-bit microarchitecture like ARM11 add one 32-bit value to another 32-bit value in a single operation. Other instructions perform subtraction in the same way. Certain common tasks in computing require that a great many additions (or other arithmetic operations) be performed as quickly as possible. Adjusting colour on a display is one such challenge. If you have a 1600-×-1200 pixel display, you have to process almost two million pixels. Each pixel, furthermore, requires three or four additions or subtractions to adjust colour. That's a lot of maths, even if it's simple and repetitive maths.

With traditional machine instructions, the only way to do all those additions and subtractions is one at a time (see Figure 4-14). Adjusting the whole group of pixels requires a program loop that takes one pass to process each value. (We'll describe program loops in more detail in Chapter 5.) Such a loop requires one branch per value, as well as an instruction to load the value and another to write the changed value back.

There are tricks to minimise the number of branches required in such a loop, but tricks save only so much, and they come at the cost of additional instructions and additional memory. If you have to process two million pixels, it all adds up, and not in a good way.

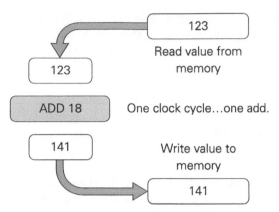

FIGURE 4-14: Processing one value at a time

SIMD instructions are designed to do the same work on more than one data value at a time. Whereas regular instructions operate on scalars (single values), we say that SIMD instructions operate on *vectors*. A vector is simply a one-dimensional array of data values arranged such that a given architecture's SIMD instructions can act on them. Vectors are typically from two to 16 data values in length, with a width (the number of bits in each value) varying from architecture to architecture.

In many computer architectures, a single SIMD instruction performs four operations (addition, subtraction multiplication and division) at once, in parallel. In some computer architectures it may be more than four operations, but the principle is the same: a vector of four values is loaded from memory into registers. A SIMD instruction performs an operation on all four values in the vector simultaneously. Then the entire vector is written back to memory. Figure 4-15 illustrates this.

What would have taken four separate additions or subtractions is now accomplished with only one, saving three clock cycles. Better yet, in most architectures there are associated SIMD instructions that load and save four memory values at once.

Why build SIMD machines instead of increasing the superscalar issue width of the processor and allowing the programmer to stick with instructions that operate on scalars? The key benefit of SIMD is that the cost, in terms of time and energy, of fetching and decoding a SIMD instruction is shared across several computations. Because the programmer explicitly declares that the computations are independent by using a SIMD instruction, there is no need for expensive interlock logic to detect and work around dependencies that now cannot occur.

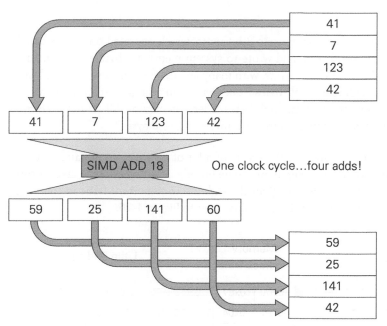

FIGURE 4-15: How SIMD instructions work

It's not immediately obvious to beginners what SIMD instructions are used for but, as it turns out, the mathematics of sound and graphics (especially 3D graphics and video) requires a lot of repetitive maths on long sequences of values. A SIMD instruction can perform mathematical operations on long sequences of values at once. SIMD instructions can radically improve the performance of code that handles tasks such as encoding and decoding sound and video and managing 3D graphics.

The ARM11 core in the original Raspberry Pi supports SIMD instruction execution in a limited way: a 32-bit data word is loaded as always, but the SIMD instructions treat each of the 4 bytes within the word as a separate value. This obviously limits the size of the values that may be processed using SIMD, though a great deal in graphics and audio processing can be done with 8-bit quantities.

In the newer ARM Cortex CPUs, there is a coprocessor called NEON, which provides SIMD instructions that operate on multiple quantities stored in special 128-bit registers. This allows throughput over twice that of the SIMD instructions in the ARMv6 instruction set. You can read more on NEON a little later, in connection with ARM Cortex.

Endianness

The first mass-market microprocessors were 8-bit units, which operated on data 8 bits (1 byte) at a time. They also read from and wrote to system memory 1 byte at a time. Later CPUs raised this to 16 bits and then 32 bits, with many architectures now reading and writing 64 bits at a time. Accessing multiple bytes from memory in a single read or write raises a non-obvious question: how are those multiple bytes ordered in memory? If a 4-byte or 8-byte quantity is read from memory, how does the CPU interpret those bytes?

This issue is called *endianness*, so named because of a bit of sly satire in Jonathan Swift's novel *Gulliver's Travels*, where the Lilliputians argue bitterly about whether to crack a soft-boiled egg on the wide ("big") or narrow ("small") end. It's an important issue in computer architectures, if not in eggs. During this discussion, refer to Figure 4-16.

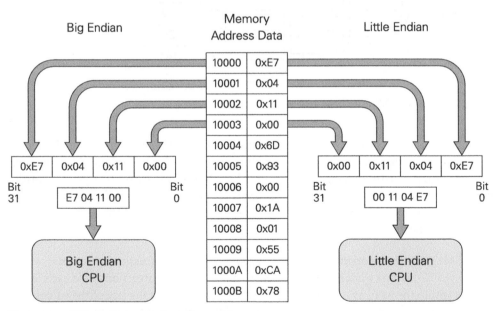

FIGURE 4-16: Big-endian vs. little-endian architectures

Figure 4-16 shows a short run of computer memory. Each location has an address and stores 1 byte of data. Address and data values are given in hexadecimal form. A modern 32-bit CPU like the ARM11 core reads or writes 4 bytes during every memory access. If those 4 bytes represent a 32-bit number, you need to know the order in which the 4 bytes appear in the number. In a columnar notation (see Chapter 2 for a recap) the least significant column of a number is by convention shown on the right, and the most significant column is shown on the left. "Most significant" here means "highest value". The rightmost column in 32-bit binary notation has the value of 2^0, or 1. The leftmost has a value of 2^{31}, or 2,147,483,648. (Refer to Table 3-1 in Chapter 3.) Order matters!

In a little-endian architecture, the least significant byte of a multi-byte value is stored at the lowest address of the four in memory. The most significant byte is stored at the highest address of the four. In Figure 4-16, the data at address 0x10000 is 0xE7. In a little-endian system, the value 0xE7 is interpreted as the least significant byte. In a big-endian system, the value 0xE7 would be the most significant byte. This changes the value of the 32-bit number radically: in a little-endian system, the hexadecimal value 0x00 11 04 E7 is 1,115,367 in decimal. In a big-endian system, the hex number changes to 0xE7 04 11 00, which in decimal form is 3,875,803,392.

Although abstruse technical issues favour little-endian architectures over big-endian ones, for the most part little-endian architecture has been a convention. Most recent microprocessor architectures, including Intel's x86, have been little endian. (Motorola's 6800 and 68000 and Sun Microsystems' SPARC are notable exceptions.) Mainframe architectures like IBM's venerable System 360 are often big endian.

By default, the ARM11 core is little endian. However, ARM architectures since ARMv3 offer an interesting feature: the endianness may be configured as either little or big as needed. This is called *bi-endianness*. Because computer networks are by convention big endian, allowing a CPU to interpret network data as big endian yields performance improvements, because the bytes of a value do not need to be re-ordered by the CPU.

The other place endianness matters crucially is in data files. Applications that operate on byte-resolution binary data in memory need to know whether a CPU has written that data to disk in big-endian or little-endian chunks. If a data file is moved to a system using a different endianness, the CPU may load the data in a different order, and an application that accesses the file may not be able to interpret its data correctly.

Rethinking the CPU: CISC vs. RISC

Around 1980, a new concept, which came to be called *reduced instruction set computing* (RISC), emerged from labs at IBM's Thomas J. Watson Research Center, the University of California at Berkeley and Stanford University. The results of these research programs would eventually be developed into the popular POWER (Performance Optimization with Enhanced RISC), SPARC (Scalable Processor Architecture) and MIPS (Microprocessor without Interlocked Pipeline Stages) architectures, respectively, and they embodied a radically different vision of how CPUs should be designed compared to the state of the art at the time. The term *complex instruction set computing* (CISC) was coined retroactively to refer to these prior architectures. The battle between RISC and CISC architectures has been one of the defining features of the computer industry over the last three decades.

By the mid-1970s, the design of high-performance CPUs for use in minicomputers and mainframes had come to focus on two key goals: increasing code density and bridging the semantic gap with the high-level programming languages of the day. Both of these goals led designers to pack more and more functionality into individual machine instructions. A look at instruction sets from the dawn of computing shows some wild and peculiar examples: one first-generation CPU had an instruction that triggered a camera aimed at an early video display; another had an instruction that raised the protective lid from the attached system printer. And remember, these weren't library routines or utility programs. These were genuine, wired-into-the-CPU machine instructions.

The requirement for increased code density was driven by the high cost and low relative speed of memory. As explained in Chapter 3, for most of the history of computing, system memory was horribly expensive. When memory was expensive, memory systems were necessarily small. The total physical address space of the DEC PDP-8 minicomputer was only 4,096 bytes. Back when the PDP-8 was designed, this was all the memory that a typical purchaser could afford. Larger programs could be run, but only after operating systems began to implement virtual memory (see Chapter 3).

Under these conditions, there was obviously an advantage in keeping programs physically short. Complex, semantically rich instructions help to reduce instruction count: a snap-the-camera machine instruction requiring 2 bytes in memory could take the place of a snap-the-camera subroutine that might require 50 or 100 bytes in memory. By the mid- to late-1970s, the availability of high-capacity DRAM chips had reduced the imperative to pursue code density at all costs. (As an aside, it was inexpensive memory, as much as inexpensive CPUs, that made the first personal computers possible: a $100 CPU chip won't help you much if memory costs $5,000 per kilobyte.)

The term "semantic gap" refers to the difference between the behaviours expressible in high-level languages (nested loops, function calls, multidimensional array indexing) and those provided by the underlying hardware (conditional and unconditional unstructured branches, the ability to load and store from addresses in memory). Microcoding allowed designers to create instructions that directly implemented high-level features at the machine language level, closing the gap. A compiler, or a careful low-level programmer, could achieve significant performance gains by using these instructions, but in practice most compilers chose to ignore them for reasons of simplicity and portability between architectures. A rough 80/20 rule was observed, in which 20% of instructions were used 80% of the time, and many were not used at all. Tantalisingly, the "reduced instruction set" used by compilers bore a close resemblance to the microinstructions provided inside the CPU.

The earliest experimental RISC machines exploited this insight by providing only a very small instruction set comprising very simple instructions; they can be thought of as CPUs that simply exposed their microinstructions to the outside world. It takes more RISC instructions to implement a program, but program performance was excellent in comparison with CISC architectures; because RISC instructions ran very quickly, their simple execution made it easier to apply techniques like pipelining, and compilers hadn't been using the more complex instructions anyway.

One distinguishing feature of RISC CPUs has always been that all or nearly all of their instructions are implemented in hardwired logic. Indeed, today microcode has been banished from the internals of even the main surviving CISC architecture—Intel x86. Since the Netburst microarchitecture was introduced in 2000, Intel processors have operated internally on RISC-like micro-ops, with legacy CISC instructions translated to independently issued micro-ops at the very front of the pipeline.

At the same time RISC processors have added instruction-set features in search of incremental performance and, ironically, code density, to the point that the once-sharp distinction between RISC and CISC has become thoroughly blurred. Much of the original motivation for simplifying instruction sets was motivated by a desire to repurpose limited transistor budgets toward new performance features, such as cache and greatly expanded register sets. As transistor budgets exploded during the 1990s, instruction set expansion became possible again. Today, many RISC architectures (including ARM) have roughly the same number of instructions as their CISC counterparts.

RISC's Legacy

Despite the blurring of the distinction between RISC and CISC, it is still possible to identify some key characteristics that the RISC movement brought to the CPU architecture table:

- Expanded register files
- Load/store architecture
- Orthogonal machine instructions
- Separate caches for instructions and data

There is a fifth RISC characteristic that not everyone understands: RISC was a fresh start. With almost 40 years of experience to draw on, computer scientists reimagined CPU architecture from scratch. Assumptions based on the limitations of 20-year-old technology were cast aside. Requirements to support "legacy" code vanished. Intel's current x86 architecture still reflects decisions made to allow easy conversion of programs for 1974's 8080 chip to 1980's 8086. RISC architectures had no such legacy to support.

Let's take a closer look at these characteristics.

Expanded Register Files

Taken as a group, a CPU's registers are called its *register file* or *register set*. Machine registers are "expensive" in terms of transistor budgets. Early CPUs had very few, and those they had were small. The 8080 had seven 8-bit registers that could be used in ordinary programming. The popular Motorola 6800 and MOS Technology 6502 had only three each. By contrast, the first ARM CPUs had 13 32-bit general-purpose registers, and the later POWER RISC processors had 32.

Registers are the fastest data storage locations in the entire computer. Reading data from memory takes much more time than processing data in registers. With enough registers to hold operands and intermediate results, a program can "stay out of memory" (and thus stay inside the far faster machinery of the CPU) as much as possible. This increases performance by avoiding round trips to memory (or at least to cache), and helps modern out-of-order superscalar processors to identify opportunities for instruction-level parallelism.

Load/Store Architecture

In most CISC architectures, machine instructions can act directly on data stored in system memory. This was done because CISC architectures are old and generally "register-starved". A typical CISC ADD instruction can add the contents of a register or an immediate value to a data word in memory:

```
ADD [memory address], 8
```

This instruction adds the literal value 8 to the memory location at the address given in the first operand. Instructions like this are slow because they require two memory accesses for a simple addition: one to fetch the original value from memory, and another to write the new value back. In a real-world program, such an addition would be part of a longer sequence of actions. If these calculations could all be done within registers, memory would be accessed much less often. Alas, when all the registers are busy, there's no alternative.

With access to a larger register file, RISC architectures generally remove memory-access powers from most instructions so that they act only on registers. Accessing memory becomes the speciality of a small cadre of machine instructions that do nothing else.

Designing a CPU this way results in a *load/store architecture*. Values are loaded from memory into registers by specialised load instructions, worked on within the registers and then written from the registers back to memory by specialised store instructions. The goal (as with almost everything in modern computer architectures) is to access memory as little as possible and to simplify the internal working of the pipeline.

Orthogonal Machine Instructions

Most CISC instructions have deep historical roots. As computer architectures evolved across the 1950s and 1960s, new instructions were added to instruction sets in response to new needs. This tended to make CISC instruction sets hodgepodges of multi-byte instructions of several lengths. They were not designed as a group; instead they "just grew".

The second problem with such ad-hoc instruction sets is that many instructions are special cases, in terms of how they access memory or registers. Early CPUs, for example, had one register called an *accumulator*, which held values acted upon by arithmetic and logical instructions. (The name comes from the fact that some very early computers and electromechanical tabulators accumulated intermediate results in a designated register.) Many early instructions had forms that treated the accumulator as a special case among registers.

Special cases make decoding and executing instructions more involved and time-consuming than they would be otherwise. So when computer scientists began designing new RISC instructions sets from scratch, they did away with special cases and made all instructions the same length. For 32-bit RISC architectures (including the original Raspberry Pi's ARM11 CPU) this length is virtually always one 32-bit word.

An instruction set designed such that instructions are all the same length and CPU resources are treated without special cases is said to be *orthogonal*. The internal structure of machine instructions is also standardised to simplify instruction decoding, as we'll explain later on.

Separate Caches for Instructions and Data

As explained in Chapter 2, the earliest computers, like Harvard University's 1944 Mark I machine, stored machine instructions and data in entirely separate memory systems. John von Neumann pointed out that machine instructions are not physically different from data, and both should reside in a single memory system.

The computer scientists who created the early RISC CPUs backed away from von Neumann's principle a little. They demonstrated that although code and data should be stored in a single memory system, there were performance advantages in having a separate instruction cache and data cache. The StrongARM microarchitecture was the first implementation of the ARM ISA to have separate code and data caches. The contribution of cache to CPU performance is shown by the fact that out of the 2.5 million transistors on the StrongARM silicon die, the designers chose to devote 60% to the two caches. The ARM11 microarchitecture also uses this "modified Harvard architecture" and has separate caches.

The reasons for the improved performance lie in the notion of locality, as explained in Chapter 3. Machine instructions are generally stored in a separate area of memory from program data. More significantly, instructions in memory are usually accessed in sequence as a program is executed. Data are arranged as blocks of memory words that may be accessed in any order as the program's needs require. Data access may not be truly random, but it's rarely sequential. Separate code and data caches allow the use of different replacement policies and potentially cache line sizes (see Chapter 3) tailored to the access patterns of each cache.

Not all RISC architectures are the same, of course. Across RISC's 35-year history, many things have been tried. It's a measure of the success of RISC design principles that most modern CISC architectures incorporate many RISC characteristics, including the dominant CISC architecture, Intel's x86.

The rest of this chapter focuses on a particular family of RISC CPUs: the ARM processors from ARM Holdings PLC, especially the ARM11 processor and the ARM CORTEX processors that followed it.

ARMs from Little Acorns Grow

In early 1981, the British Broadcasting Corporation (BBC) began working on a project to foster computer skills among its audience, especially young people. The Computer Literacy Project required a solid and reasonably inexpensive mass-market computer to serve as a basis for the program. The project put out specs and asked for bids. The only design that met their specifications was the Proton from Acorn Computers, which was based, like the Raspberry Pi Foundation, in Cambridge. The Proton was based on the same 6502 microprocessor used in the popular Apple II machine. After its adoption by the BBC, the Proton became known as the BBC Microcomputer and more than 1.5 million were sold.

Once the IBM PC legitimised personal computers for business use, Acorn decided to create a higher-end unit to sell to the office market. It evaluated all the major microprocessors of the time, including the 8086 and the 68000, and found them unsuitable for various reasons. In 1983, Acorn began an ambitious project to design its own microprocessor for use in its high-end systems.

A team led by Acorn engineers Sophie Wilson and Steve Furber drew on research that came out of the Berkeley RISC Project. First silicon for the Acorn RISC Machine (ARM) CPU came back in mid-1985. ARM1 was a prototype that was never produced commercially. Production chips appeared in 1986, as the ARM2. ARM2 microprocessors first served as coprocessors in the 6502-based BBC Microcomputer to increase machine performance, particularly in areas like graphics and computer-aided design (CAD).

The first complete ARM-based microcomputer was released in 1987, as the Acorn Archimedes. The Archimedes included something new for Acorn: Arthur, an operating system with a fully graphical user interface. Arthur was later developed into RISC OS, which still exists.

RISC OS is available as a free download for the Raspberry Pi. You can learn more about RISC OS (and obtain the release for the Raspberry Pi) at `https://www.riscosopen.org/wiki/documentation/show/Welcome to RISC OS Pi`. **NOTE**

Development of the ARM CPUs was spun off to a separate company in 1990, at which time the ARM acronym changed to Advanced RISC Machine. Advanced RISC Machines became ARM Holdings in 1998.

Microarchitectures, Cores and Families

The nomenclature ARM uses for its products can be confusing at times. The instruction set architecture (ISA) of the ARM processors has a version number. A separate version number is given to the ARM microarchitecture. The term *microarchitecture* refers to the way that a CPU designer implements an instruction set architecture in silicon. Think of it this way: the ISA defines the behaviour of a CPU, and the microarchitecture defines its structure.

ARM processors are grouped in families, each with its own microarchitecture version number. The first ARM ISA version was ARMv1, used only in the prototype ARM1 processor. The ARMv2 ISA was implemented in the ARM2 and ARM3 families of CPUs. ARMv3 was implemented in the ARM6 and ARM7 families, and so on. The original Raspberry Pi's CPU belongs to the ARM11 family, which implements the ARMv6 instruction set. Processors within an ARM family generally differ in small ways that reflect emphases rather than significant architectural differences. The ARM11 microarchitecture applies to all four cores in the ARM11 family.

You'll often hear ARM CPUs referred to as "cores". The word *core* is not a precise technical term in the computer industry. Most of the time it indicates any large independent component that may exist in a single-chip design containing multiple cores. In the ARM universe, a "core" is more specifically a CPU that may be incorporated into a custom device that includes non-CPU logic like USB and network ports, graphics processors, mass storage controllers, timers, bus controllers and so on. Such a device is called a *system-on-a-chip* (SoC).

Selling Licenses Rather Than Chips

The ARM-specific definition of "core" will start to make a little more sense once you understand the radical difference between the business models used by ARM Holdings and Intel.

Intel designs and manufactures finished chips, each one in its own plastic or ceramic integrated circuit package, ready to be plugged or soldered into a computer circuit board. ARM Holdings, by contrast, is purely a design firm. Its engineers design CPU cores and other computer logic, and then license the designs to other firms. Firms that license ARM designs may customise them or integrate them with in-house logic to create a finished SoC design. They then take the design to a firm called a *chip foundry* that manufactures integrated circuits for them.

As long as the computer industry was dominated by mature and mostly identical laptop and desktop PC designs, Intel's business model predominated. However, after smartphones and tablet computers entered the mass market, customisation became crucial not only to differentiate products but also to evolve them. Innovation in ARM-powered devices extends all the way down to the CPU silicon. Most licensees use finished and certified ARM cores, but ARM has also licensed its ISA to a number of architecture licensees who then create their own custom cores representing a non-ARM microarchitecture. The earliest example of this is the StrongARM core, which was designed by Digital Equipment Corporation in the 1990s and later sold to Intel as XScale. StrongARM/XScale implements the ARMv4 ISA in a novel microarchitecture; it was the first CPU in the ARM line to incorporate separate instruction and data caches. More recent architecture licensees include Apple, with their Swift cores, and Qualcomm, with their Scorpion and later Krait cores.

The Raspberry Pi computers all use SoCs designed by Broadcom. The first generation boards contain a single ARM11 core. The second and third generation boards each contain four Cortex family cores. At this point we'll turn to a more detailed description of the ARM11 microarchitecture. Later in this chapter, we will explore the Raspberry Pi's SoC device and how SoCs are designed.

ARM11

The ARM11 microarchitecture, announced in 2002, was the first, and so far the only, ARM family to implement the ARMv6 ISA. It's a 32-bit microarchitecture, meaning that all machine instructions are 32 bits wide and that memory is accessed in 32-bit words. Some ARM machine instructions are designed to operate on smaller operands, of which there are two types: 16-bit halfwords and 8-bit bytes.

The ARM Instruction Set

The ARMv6 ISA includes three separate instruction sets: ARM, Jazelle, and Thumb. Of these, the ARM instruction set is the most frequently used.

ARM

You'll see an occasional ARM machine instruction in this chapter (and elsewhere in this book, including a complete program in Chapter 5) so it would be good to take a quick look at how machine instructions are built. Let's look at a few examples.

We say "built" advisedly, because ARM machine instructions allow various options to make them work in different ways, as needed.

NOTE

The easiest machine instructions to understand are those that perform arithmetic operations on data. Remember from our earlier discussion that RISC machine instructions don't access memory directly. All work to be done on data is done with data stored in registers. Consider the ADD instruction, which adds the contents of two registers and places the sum in a third register. The general assembly-language form of an ADD instruction looks like this:

```
ADD{<condition code>} {S} <Rd>, <Rn>, <Rm>
```

Instructions are summarised this way in most ARM instruction references. The notation works like this:

- Anything enclosed by curly brackets ({ }) is optional. Anything not inside curly brackets is required.

- Anything within angle brackets (< >) is a placeholder for a symbol or a value.

- Rd means destination register. When an instruction has a destination register operand, the destination operand is the first after the mnemonic. Rn and Rm name the source register operands. The m and n don't stand for anything specific.

Nearly all ARM instructions may be executed conditionally. (We cover this in some detail later in this chapter.) The optional <condition code> specifies 1 of 15 conditions that must be met before the instruction's action takes place. If the condition code is not met, the instruction works its way through the pipeline but does not take any other action. If no condition code is specified, the default is "always", meaning unconditional execution.

The optional S suffix directs the ADD instruction to modify the condition flags based on the result of the addition; these flags then control any subsequent conditionally executed instructions. Without the S suffix, a machine instruction does its work without changing the values of the flags. This means that a series of instructions can perform their work conditionally, based on an initial operation that sets the flags.

The following instruction handles adding the contents of register 1 (R1) to register 2 (R2) and placing the sum in register 5 (R5):

```
ADD R5, R1, R2
```

To build the instruction such that it only executes if the Zero flag is set, you'd add the condition code EQ to the mnemonic:

```
ADDEQ R5, R1, R2
```

Subtraction works in much the same way. An instruction to subtract R3 from R4 and place the difference in R2 would look like this, assuming the programmer wants the subtraction to set the flags:

```
SUBS R2, R4, R3
```

Not all instructions take three operands. The MOV instruction copies a value stored in one register to another, or places a literal value into a register:

```
MOV R5, R3
MOV R5, #42
```

The first instruction copies whatever is in R3 into R5. The second stores the literal value 42 into R5.

Although it's no longer generally available, the *ARM Architecture Reference Manual* is very useful as an introduction to the several ARM instruction sets. (You can sometimes find available downloads by performing a Google search on the title.) Writing short assembly language programs and then inspecting their execution in a debugger is a good way to see what various instructions do. The GNU Compiler Collection, which is included with the Raspbian operating system, has a very good assembler. Chapter 5 explains how to assemble and run short assembly language test programs.

Jazelle

The Jazelle instruction set allows an ARM11 core to execute Java bytecodes directly, without software interpretation. (Chapter 5 explains bytecode languages like Java and Python.) ARM Holdings deprecated Jazelle in 2011, which means that the company will not be evolving the technology any further and recommends that it is not used in new projects.

> Computer manufacturers sometimes *deprecate* a feature or a product line once they feel it has reached the end of its useful life. This does not mean that they disable it but rather that they advise strongly against its future use. Many manufacturers add that a deprecated product or feature may well be withdrawn at some time in the future, or that support for it will be eliminated in various ways. Deprecated features and products should not be used in new designs for those reasons. **NOTE**

Thumb

The Thumb instruction set is a 16-bit implementation of the 32-bit ARM instruction set. Thumb instructions are 16 bits wide instead of 32 bits wide. This allows greater *code density*, meaning that more instructions (and thus more functionality) may be stored in a given quantity of memory. Some low-end devices have limited memory, and they access that memory 16 bits at a time over a 16-bit system bus. Thumb instructions are designed to make more efficient use of such a bus. Thumb instructions still process 32-bit quantities in registers. Not all registers are fully available to Thumb instructions, and certain other hardware resources are available in only limited ways.

The Thumb instruction set is interesting for another reason: after Thumb instructions are fetched from memory or cache, they're expanded to ordinary ARMv6 instructions by dedicated logic inside the CPU. After they enter the instruction pipeline, they're no longer Thumb instructions at all. Thumb instructions are thus a sort of shorthand that allows more instructions to fit in a given amount of memory. The Thumb instruction set is generally used in programming *embedded systems*, which are devices that incorporate microprocessors and software to do their work but are not general-purpose computers themselves. The line is not sharp: the Raspberry Pi is often used for embedded systems, even though it has enough memory and CPU power to function as a conventional desktop computer.

> When the ARM11 core is executing Thumb instructions, it's said to be in the Thumb state. Similarly, the core is in the Jazelle state while executing Jazelle instructions. In virtually all cases, the Raspberry Pi operates in the ARM state, using the full 32-bit ARM instruction set. **NOTE**

Don't confuse the processor *state* with the processor *mode*. Read on.

Processor Modes

Early desktop operating systems did little or nothing to prevent applications from misbehaving. CP/M-80 systems, in fact, had so little memory that much of CP/M-80 basically removed itself from memory after launching an application and then reloaded itself when the application terminated. PC-DOS remained in memory, but Windows was a user interface running over PC-DOS rather than an operating system until Windows NT was first released in 1993. CP/M-80 and PC-DOS are more correctly considered system monitors than operating systems.

NOTE   A *monitor* is system software that loads and runs applications but does little in terms of managing system resources.

Part of the problem was a shortage of memory, but a greater part was that the CPU chips at the time had no ability to protect system software from application software. In 1985, Intel's 386 CPUs were the first Intel chips to offer a practical *protected mode*, which provides the operating system kernel with privileged access to system resources denied to applications (which run in real or User mode) and was a prerequisite for implementing a true operating system on Intel processors. All modern CPUs intended for use in general-purpose computers contain logic to manage system resources and prevent applications from interfering with the operating system and other applications.

ARM11 processors provide several different modes to support operating system management of user apps and the computer's hardware. These are summarised in Table 4-1. All but User mode are considered *privileged* modes, meaning that they have full access to system resources. Supervisor mode is specifically for use by operating system kernels and other protected code connected with operating systems. System mode is basically User mode with full privileges and access to all the hardware. It is not used much, except in low-end embedded work; it's considered obsolete.

Table 4-1   ARM11 Processor Modes

Mode	Abbreviation	Mode bits	Description
User	usr	10000	For user application execution
Supervisor	svc	10011	For the operating system kernel
System	Sys	11111	Now obsolete
Secure monitor	mon	10110	Used in TrustZone applications
FIQ	fiq	10001	For "fast interrupt" servicing
IRQ	irq	10010	For general-purpose interrupt servicing
Abort	abt	10111	For virtual memory and other memory management
Undefined	und	11011	For software emulation of undefined machine instructions, as in coprocessors or newer ISAs

The FIQ, IRQ, Abort and Undefined modes support interrupts and exceptions. *Interrupts* are signals from hardware devices outside the CPU indicating that the device requires attention. *Exceptions* are anomalous events within the CPU that require special handling by the CPU, generally in cooperation with the operating system. These include virtual memory page faults and arithmetic errors like divide-by-zero. We mention these again in connection with registers.

The System Monitor mode is used with an ARMv6 feature called TrustZone, which creates isolated memory regions called *worlds* and manages data transfers between them. TrustZone is used primarily in content digital rights management (DRM) to prevent programs from "sniffing" decrypted content in memory and writing it out to storage. TrustZone is not implemented in all ARM11 processors, and requires special changes to behaviour of the system data bus used in SoC designs. TrustZone is not available in the BCM2835 SoC in the Raspberry Pi.

ARM's Supervisor mode is the mode used by the operating system kernel. The kernel and the memory it runs in are often called *kernel space*. When an ARM system is reset, the CPU is placed in Supervisor mode and the kernel begins executing. In Unix/Linux jargon, *userland* is the memory and software environment where user applications run. Some operating systems place noncritical device drivers in userland, along with software libraries that provide an interface to the OS and certain hardware resources.

Most of the differences between the several processor modes have to do with the use of the ARM register file. Let's take a closer look at the ARM family's register riches.

Modes and Registers

One of the fundamental decisions behind RISC CPU design is to put as many registers as is practical within the CPU. The more registers a CPU has, the less often it has to access instruction operands in memory or save intermediate results out to memory. The more that a CPU can execute its instructions without accessing memory, the faster that execution will be.

Compared to almost any non-RISC ISA, ARMv6 has a lot of registers. All are 32 bits in size. There are 40 registers in all: 33 general-purpose registers plus 7 status registers. Not all of these registers are available at all times in all modes. Furthermore, some of the registers have special functions that place limits on how they may be used.

Untangling ARM register usage requires a chart indicating which registers are available in which modes. Refer to Figure 4-17 during the following discussion.

Processor Modes

User & System	Fast Interrupt	Interrupt	Supervisor	Abort	Undefined	System Monitor
R0	R0	R0	R0	R0	R0	R0
R1	R1	R1	R1	R1	R1	R1
R2	R2	R2	R2	R2	R2	R2
R3	R3	R3	R3	R3	R3	R3
R4	R4	R4	R4	R4	R4	R4
R5	R5	R5	R5	R5	R5	R5
R6	R6	R6	R6	R6	R6	R6
R7	R7	R7	R7	R7	R7	R7
R8	R8 R8_fiq	R8	R8	R8	R8	R8
R9	R9 R9_fiq	R9	R9	R9	R9	R9
R10	R10 R10_fiq	R10	R10	R10	R10	R10
R11	R11 R11_fiq	R11	R11	R11	R11	R11
R12	R12 R12_fiq	R12	R12	R12	R12	R12
R13	R13 R13_fiq	R13 R13_irq	R13 R13_svc	R13 R13_abt	R13 R13_und	R13 R13_mon
R14	R14 R14_fiq	R14 R14_irq	R14 R14_svc	R14 R14_abt	R14 R14_und	R14 R14_mon
R15 (PC)	R15 (PC)	R15 (PC)	R15 (PC)	R15 (PC)	R15 (PC)	R15 (PC)

ARM State General-Purpose Registers

CPSR	CPSR	CPSR	CPSR	CPSR	CPSR	CPSR
	SPSR_fiq	SPSR_irq	SPSR_svc	SPSR_abt	SPSR_und	SPSR_mon

ARM State Program Status Registers

FIGURE 4-17: The ARM11 register file

Of the 16 ARM general-purpose registers, only the first 13 are truly general purpose. Registers R13, R14 and R15 play special roles in program execution. R15 acts as the program counter (PC), which always contains the address of the next instruction to be executed. Unlike some other processor architectures, the ARM program counter may be freely read and written to even in User mode. Simply writing a new address to R15 effectively implements an unconditional branch, but doing so is considered bad programming practice. Hard-coding addresses in software makes it impossible for operating systems to decide where in memory to load and run the code, and such code is very likely to malfunction.

R14 is called the *link register* (LR). The LR is used to execute fast subroutine calls using one of a group of instructions called Branch with Link. When a BL or BLX instruction is executed, the CPU stores the return address in the LR and then branches to the subroutine address. When the subroutine finishes executing, the return address stored in LR is copied back to the program counter. The program then continues on its main line of execution, having "ducked out" to execute the subroutine.

R13 is by convention used as the stack pointer (SP). The ARM SP works the way SPs work in nearly all CPU architectures. (Refer to Figure 4-6 and the associated text earlier in this chapter if you don't understand how stacks work.) Most ARM instructions allow you to use R13 as a general-purpose register, but ARM Holdings has deprecated this use, and for a very good reason: nearly all operating systems make intensive use of the stack, and without extreme care, using SP as a general-purpose register can cause crashes.

Banked Registers

Figure 4-17 suggests that there are a lot more ARM registers than there actually are. Read the figure carefully: each column represents a processor mode, and beneath the mode is a list of registers available while the CPU is operating in that mode. All modes can access registers R0 to R7, and it's the *same* R0 to R7 irrespective of mode. There is not a separate group of registers from R0 to R7 for each mode.

After that it becomes complicated. In Fast Interrupt mode, registers R8 to R14 are private and have their own mode-specific names: R8_fiq, R9_fiq, and so on. Machine instructions that specify one of the R8 to R14 registers while the CPU is in Fast Interrupt mode access registers in Fast Interrupt mode's private bank. Registers R8_fiq to R14_fiq are *banked registers*. There's more information about Fast Interrupt mode later in this chapter.

In Figure 4-17, all shaded registers are banked registers. Fast Interrupt mode has a lot of them; the other modes have either two or, in the case of User and System modes, none at all.

Note that the description of processor modes and registers in Figure 4-17 applies only to ARMv6 and earlier ISAs.

The Current Program Status Registers

Most ARM registers are general-purpose, or almost general-purpose. One register is definitely not: the current program status register (CPSR) is a single 32-bit value divided into bits and groups of bits. Each bit or group stores some information about what the CPU is doing (or has recently done) at any particular instant.

Figure 4-18 shows what's inside the CPSR. Explaining all of it in detail is beyond the scope of this book, and in any case much of it is mainly of use to compilers and assemblers who build executable programs. (Read more on this in Chapter 5.) The shaded areas represent bits that are undefined and reserved for use in newer ARM microarchitectures.

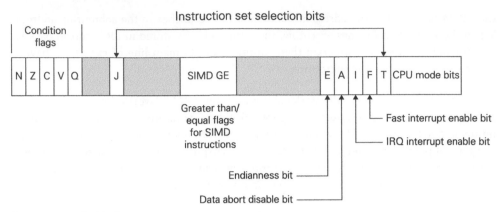

FIGURE 4-18: Inside the current program status register

The part of the CPSR that sees the most use is the group of five bits called the *condition flags*. Each of the five bits in the group may be tested by conditional branch instructions. The N, Z, C, and V bits may also be tested by a conditional execution mechanism that can be used to "turn an instruction off" if one or more of the condition flags match the corresponding flags inside the instruction itself. (More on this in the section entitled "Conditional Instruction Execution".)

- **N (Negative) flag:** Set when the result of a calculation is considered negative.

- **Z (Zero) flag:** Set when the result operand of an instruction is 0. Because of the way that comparisons are calculated, the Z flag is also set when two compared operands are equal.

- **C (Carry) flag:** Set when an addition generates a carry or when a subtraction generates a borrow. C is also changed by shift instructions (which shuffle the bits in a 32-bit value left or right) to the value (1 or 0) of the last bit shifted out of the operand.

- **V (Overflow) flag:** Set when a signed overflow occurs in the destination operand.

- **Q (Saturation) flag:** Used with saturated integer arithmetic instructions to indicate that the result of a saturated addition or subtraction was corrected to place it within the range of the destination operand. Saturated arithmetic is frequently used by digital signal processing (DSP) algorithms and is outside the scope of this book.

With the exception of the Q flag, the ARM processor condition flags work very much as condition flags do in other architectures, including Intel's.

The T and J bits select which of the three ARMv6 instruction sets is active. If the T bit is set, the CPU is in the Thumb state. If the J bit is set, the CPU is in the Jazelle state. If neither is set, the CPU is in the ARM state.

The CPU mode bits indicate which mode the CPU is currently using. The binary values for each mode are included in Table 4-1.

Four bits are used as flags indicating a greater than or equal to (GE) result after the execution of certain SIMD instructions.

The E bit specifies the "endianness" of current CPU operations. When set to 1, it indicates little-endian operation. When cleared to 0, it indicates big-endian operations. The E bit must be set by two machine instructions specifically for that purpose, SETEND LE and SETEND BE.

The A bit allows system software to discriminate between a virtual memory page fault and an actual external memory error.

The I bit and F bit are interrupt masks. More on this in the next section.

Interrupts, Exceptions, Registers and the Vector Table

Understanding banked registers requires an understanding of the nature of interrupts and exceptions. These are events that require CPU attention, irrespective of what the CPU is doing when the event occurs. When a virtual memory page fault occurs, the CPU *must* handle it to continue running. When the CPU encounters a machine instruction that it doesn't understand, it must "switch gears" for a moment and figure out what to do next. When one of the computer's peripherals has data ready or needs data, the CPU must service the request, often within a short time frame if correct operation is to be assured.

In every case, when an event happens, the CPU responds by running a special block of code known as a *handler*. Handlers are not part of user applications. They're typically installed and configured by the operating system. There are several different classes of interrupt and exception, each with its own processor mode and banked registers. When an interrupt or exception occurs, the CPU immediately changes the processor mode, stores the current program counter in the new mode's banked version of the link register and the CPSR in the new mode's saved program status register (SPSR), and sets the program counter to one of a small number of addresses within the vector table; the mode and address chosen depends on the type of event that has occurred. The vector table is eight 32-bit words in length and resides either at the very bottom or nearly at the very top of the address map. Each entry is generally a single 32-bit unconditional branch instruction that directs the CPU to the appropriate handler elsewhere in memory (see Figure 4-19).

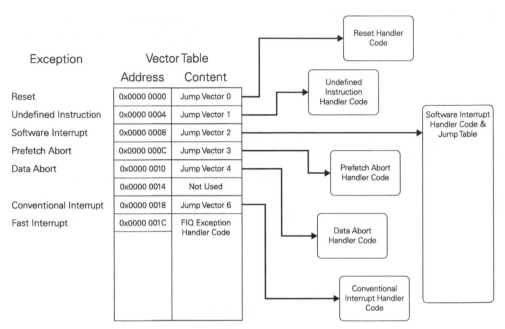

FIGURE 4-19: The ARM exception vector table

You can now see the value of the banked registers. Interrupts and exceptions can happen at any time, and the CPU must have room to store the bare minimum amount of state required to resume the user-mode program where it left off. It can't rely on being able to store the program counter in the user-mode LR, as it would normally do with a branch with link instruction. What if the interrupted program has just made a function call and needs the value in LR to know where to return to? It can't even rely on being able to push values to the user-mode stack. What if the stack is nearly full, or the program is using R13 as a general-purpose register? The sudden appearance of banked copies of LR (R14) and SP (R13) provides room to store the return address, and a pointer (generally pre-initialised by the operating system) to a stack that is guaranteed to be valid and have enough space.

The branch from the vector table takes execution into the appropriate handler, where the code does what it has to do to satisfy the exception. Typically the handler will first save some registers to the (known valid) stack to free up some registers with which to work. Once the handler is complete, it must explicitly restore these registers from the stack, and the CPSR from the copy in the SPSR, before returning to User mode and resuming execution at the address stored in the mode's banked copy of LR.

Fast Interrupts

There are two separate types of interrupt, which we'll call regular (IRQ; from Interrupt Request) and fast (FIQ; from Fast Interrupt Request), corresponding to two physical signals entering the ARM11 from outside SoC, and two entries in the vector table. Fast interrupts have two useful properties that help to minimise interrupt servicing latency compared to regular interrupts.

The FIQ vector table entry is located at the end of the table. Although it's perfectly permissible to insert a branch instruction to a handler in this table entry, as we must do for the IRQ entry and the various exceptions, it is more common to simply append the handler to the table, with the first instruction inside the table itself, so that the flow of control passes smoothly into the handler with no possibility of pipeline stalls.

While all other processor modes have only banked copies of SP (R13) and LR (R14), FIQ mode also has banked copies of R8 to R12. FIQ handlers therefore have five dedicated scratch registers that they can use without corrupting the registers of the interrupted program or incurring the time penalty of pushing registers to the stack.

Response to FIQ events is faster and more deterministic than the IRQ case because we minimise memory access. Indeed, if the exception handler code is present in cache (see Chapter 3), the exception begins and ends without accessing system memory at all. Under Linux on Raspberry Pi, we use FIQ to service high-frequency interrupts from the USB core, and IRQ to service all other system peripherals.

Software Interrupts

One further type of event deserves mention at this point. Unlike all the other interrupts and exceptions, a software interrupt (SWI) doesn't interrupt what the CPU is doing at some unplanned moment. Instead, it can be seen as a kind of subroutine call that's used to enter supervisor mode in a carefully managed way, generally for the purpose of communicating with the operating system kernel. The SWI doesn't include the address of the subroutine in the call; instead, software interrupts are numbered, and the number of the software interrupt is included as an operand to the software interrupt machine instruction, which would be written like this in ARM assembly language:

SWI 0x21

When an SWI instruction is executed, the CPU executes the branch instruction stored at address 0x0000 0008 in the vector table (refer to Figure 4-19). This branch takes execution to the SWI handler. The interrupt number included as the operand to the SWI instruction is generally used by the exception handler to select yet another branch, to the block of code that handles the specific software interrupt given in the operand. There may be dozens or more software interrupts, each with its own number and each with a subhandler corresponding to that number.

The value of SWIs is that they allow user programs to make managed calls into the operating system. As mentioned in Chapter 8, the operating system kernel comprises code for accessing peripherals, providing a virtual machine abstraction to individual processes and guaranteeing security properties, including isolation between processes. The limitations on what applications can do when in User mode, particularly with respect to configuring the MMU (see Chapter 3), underpin the notion of process isolation. An SWI is the only way to switch from User to Supervisor mode; forcing this transition to happen via the vector table prevents applications from running arbitrary code in a privileged mode.

Interrupt Priority

So what happens when a second interrupt or exception occurs while an earlier one is still being handled? Handlers are special in a number of ways but they're still code, and they take time to run. Having an exception occur while an exception handler is running is not only possible but likely. Sorting this out is done in two general ways:

- Both kinds of interrupt (IRQ and FIQ) may be disabled independently while an exception handler is executing. This is done with two disable bits in the CPSR: F and I. Setting F to 1 disables fast interrupts. Setting I to 1 disables conventional interrupts. Interrupts may be disabled within all or part of an exception handler.

- Each of the various classes of exception has a priority (see Table 4-2). Priorities work like this: a handler for an interrupt or exception of a given priority may be interrupted by one of higher priority, but not by one of lower priority. For example, the handler for the Reset exception is of Priority 0 and may not be interrupted by anything. An IRQ handler may be interrupted by an FIQ exception, but not vice versa.

Table 4-2   ARM11 Interrupt Priorities

Exception	Priority
Reset	1
Data abort	2
Fast interrupt (FIQ)	3
Conventional interrupt (IRQ)	4
Prefetch abort	5
Software interrupt	6
Undefined instruction	6

When an interrupt handler begins executing, all interrupts of the same priority are automatically disabled. Thus an IRQ handler cannot be interrupted by another IRQ exception unless the IRQ handler has the intelligence to sort out simultaneous interrupts and re-enables IRQ exceptions.

Interrupts may not be disabled by software running in User mode, because this would undermine the operating system's ability to schedule other processes. Software interrupts may be issued by userland programs, but because software interrupts have the lowest priority, all other kinds of exceptions may occur during a software interrupt handler, unless interrupts are specifically disabled.

The software interrupt exception has the same priority as the undefined instruction exception because the two cannot occur together. All software interrupts are generated by the SWI instruction, which is present in all ARM processors and is thus always defined.

Conditional Instruction Execution

In most instruction set architectures, conditional branch instructions are used to alter the flow of program execution. The ARM CPUs have conditional branch instructions, but they also offer something that in many cases is even better: conditional instruction execution. All 32-bit ARM instructions have a 4-bit field inside them expressing condition codes. The ARM architecture provides 15 condition codes, for conditions like equal, not equal, greater than, less than, overflow, and so on. (Four bits are capable of expressing 16 conditions codes, but one of the values is reserved and not used.) The condition code field is evaluated while the instruction is being decoded by the CPU.

The codes correspond to various combinations of the four condition flags maintained in the CPSR: N, Z, C, and V. If conditional execution is enabled for an instruction then that instruction executes *only* if its condition code agrees with the current state of the condition flags. Note that this is *not* a bit-by-bit comparison of the condition codes to the four CPSR flags. Each four-bit binary value has an assigned meaning—for example:

- %0000 means that the instruction executes if the Z flag is set.
- %0001 means that the instruction executes if the Z flag is cleared.
- %1000 means the instruction executes if the C flag is set and the Z flag is cleared.
- %1100 means that the instruction executes if the Z flag is cleared, and the N flag is equal to the V flag.

One of the codes, %1110, means that the flags will be ignored and that the instruction will always execute. (Recall that the "%" prefix means that the value shown is in binary notation.)

Condition codes are built into machine instructions by the assembler or compiler that creates an executable program. For assembly language, condition codes are specified with a two-character suffix appended to the mnemonic indicating the condition or conditions under which the instruction will execute. For example:

MOV R0, #4	No suffix; always executes
MOVEQ R0, #4	Executes if Z=1 (Equal)
MOVNE R0, #4	Executes if Z=0 (Not Equal)
MOVMI R0, #4	Executes if N=1 (Negative)

All of these instructions copy the value 4 into R0. The first form lacks a suffix, and so it executes unconditionally; that is, always. The second form executes only if the Z flag in CPSR is set to 1, indicating that an earlier comparison (or other operation) generated a result of 0; for comparisons, a result of 0 indicates that the two values compared were equal. The third form executes only if an earlier operation cleared the Z flag to 0; for comparisons, this means that the values compared were not equal. The fourth form executes only if the N flag is set to 1, meaning that a comparison or other operation generated a negative value. There are 15 possible condition codes, including a code meaning "execute always".

Why is conditional execution such a useful feature? Figure 4-20 shows two ways of doing the same thing in ARM assembly language. The algorithm is a simple IF/THEN construct: If R0 = R4, then execute the code in Block A; otherwise, execute the code in Block B. What the code in Block A and Block B actually does is not important for the example, and the instruction boxes in those blocks have been deliberately left blank.

The first machine instruction is a comparison that checks to see if two registers (R0 and R4) are equal. The CMP (compare) instruction does that. If the two registers are found to be equal, CMP sets the Z flag to 1. If they are not equal, CMP sets the Z flag to 0.

The traditional way of coding this, in ARM or any other architecture, is on the right. After CMP, a conditional branch instruction tests the Z flag for inequality using the NE (Not Equal) suffix. If the two registers are not equal, execution branches to a location labelled BlockB. If the two registers are equal, the conditional branch lets execution continue into Block A. At the end of Block A, an unconditional branch takes execution to whatever code lies after the IF/THEN construct. Block B begins at the label BlockB, and continues to the end of the IF/THEN construct.

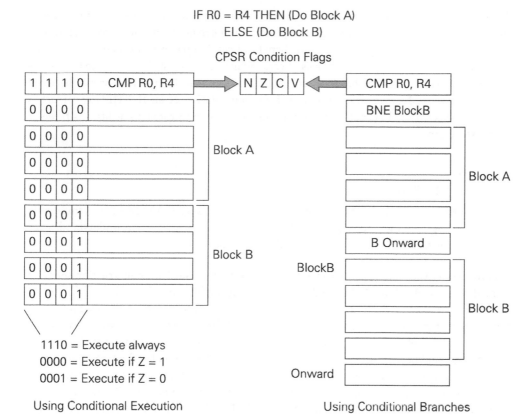

FIGURE 4-20: ARM conditional execution

The sequence of instructions on the left does the very same thing. This time, however, all of the instructions are subject to conditional execution. The instructions in Block A have been set to execute only if the Z flag is 1 (condition code set to %0000). The instructions in Block B have been set to execute only if the Z flag is 0 (condition code set to %0001). The other flags are not involved in this example. In terms of which blocks execute, you can see that it's either/or: if Block A is executed, Block B will not be, and vice versa. No branches are required.

Conditional execution makes two instructions unnecessary: the BNE conditional branch, and the B unconditional branch. That's valuable all by itself. The real win, however, is that mispredicted branches can disrupt the instruction pipeline and slow down execution. Anything that can be done to avoid branches will speed up execution.

It's important to remember that instructions are not "skipped" when their condition codes are not met. They still move through the pipeline and consume one clock cycle. However, they do no work and change nothing. The benefit of conditional execution derives from the avoidance of branches over small blocks of code, which can cost much more time than reading (but not executing) the block. There is a block size threshold (which varies between microarchitectures) above which the branch implementation of an IF/THEN construct is preferred. This threshold is not large, and in most microarchitectures it's as little as three or four instructions.

Coprocessors

There's nothing new about coprocessors, and they are not specific to the ARM architecture. Understanding how they operate in an ARM11 context does require an understanding of CPU exceptions, so this is a good point to take them up.

A *coprocessor* is a separate, specialised execution unit that usually has an instruction set of its own, distinct from that of the CPU. It generally has additional registers to support its machine instructions. Early in microprocessor history, coprocessors were separate chips, connected to the CPU through an external bus. One of the earliest and best-known coprocessors was Intel's 1980-era 8087, which lived in a separate 40-pin Dual Inline Package (DIP) socket and could be installed by a careful end user. The 8087 provided floating point maths instructions to the integer-only 8086 and 8088. It implemented 60 new instructions and several numeric concepts previously unavailable in microcomputers, like denormals to express underflow values, and the not-a-number (NaN) value to hold the results of undefined operations like divide-by-zero or values outside the domain of real numbers, like imaginary numbers.

Underflow and Denormal Values

Problems arise in computer maths when software has only a limited number of bits to express very, very large or very, very small values. When a value is too large to express in 80 bits (the largest common real-number format) that value "overflows" the number meant to receive it, and an error is generated. Less obviously, the reverse is possible: a value so small (that is, so close to 0) that it cannot be accurately expressed in 80 bits. This is called *underflow*. A special kind of number called a *denormal* is used to express values resulting from underflows at lower precision, allowing them to be expressed in 80 bits, and used in further calculations without generating an error.

Later on, another reason for using coprocessors arose when customisable CPU architectures like those offered by ARM became popular. If the coprocessor is relatively independent of the CPU, it can be included or excluded from custom designs as needed.

The ARM Coprocessor Interface

The ARM family of CPUs supports several different types of closely coupled coprocessors, including floating point, SIMD, and system control and cache maintenance. Modern transistor budgets have allowed all of these to be included on the same silicon with the CPU, sometimes as optional elements of custom designs. The ARM11 CPUs have a generalised coprocessor interface allowing as many as 16 coprocessors to cooperate with the CPU. The CPU uses a dedicated set of coprocessor interface instructions to communicate with coprocessors. Coprocessor instructions are compiled or assembled into the stored executable program file on disk or (in the Raspberry Pi) the SD card. They are part of the ordinary ARM instruction stream coming in from memory. They aren't set apart in a separate memory area or specially treated by the ARM core.

Each coprocessor present in an ARM system has a unique 4-bit ID code. Coprocessor instructions contain a field for the ID code of the coprocessor on which they will execute. If the CPU core fetches a coprocessor instruction that doesn't match the ID code of any existing coprocessor, it triggers an undefined instruction exception. (More on this shortly.)

One of the primary goals of the ARM coprocessor interface is not to slow down the CPU core. Beyond checking to see if a coprocessor instruction is coded for an existing coprocessor, the core does not spend time sorting out coprocessor instructions within its own pipeline. The core sends all the instructions it fetches from memory directly to all coprocessors. The coprocessor decodes all incoming instructions, which include both ordinary ARM instructions as well as coprocessor instructions. During the decoding stage, the coprocessor rejects any instructions that are not recognised as its own. This includes both ARM instructions and instructions coded for other coprocessors. The coprocessor recognises its own instructions, and adds only those to its internal execution pipeline. The coprocessor then sends a signal back to the core indicating that it has accepted an instruction.

The first-generation Raspberry Pi's ARM1176JZF-S CPU includes two coprocessors—the System Control Coprocessor and the Vector Floating Point (VFP) coprocessor—which are described in the next sections.

The System Control Coprocessor

The ARM11 System Control Coprocessor exposes a large suite of registers that are used to configure and control the operation of ARM core mechanisms like cache, direct memory access (DMA), the memory management unit (MMU), the TrustZone security system, exception handling and system performance, among others. Where tightly coupled memory (TCM) is present, it is managed by the system control coprocessor. (TCM is optional, and is not implemented in the Raspberry Pi's BCM2835 silicon.)

Two ARM instructions handle communication with the system control coprocessor: the MCR instruction (from "move from coprocessor to register") is used to read data from a coprocessor register; and the MRC instruction (from "move from register to coprocessor") is used to write data from the core to a coprocessor register. MCR and MRC instructions can be used to communication with any coprocessor, but they represent the sole means of access to the system control coprocessor as it does not define any data processing operations of its own.

The Vector Floating Point (VFP) Coprocessor

There are excellent reasons for gathering *floating point operations* (that is, computer mathematics operating on fractional values) into a dedicated coprocessor. Floating point maths isn't used much in a large number of software categories, but scientific and engineering applications, and games, use it a lot. CPUs designed for certain kinds of embedded systems work do not necessarily need a full maths coprocessor. Floating point operations, when required, can be implemented in library subroutines. Furthermore, floating point maths must be able to express values that have many significant figures, which requires registers larger than 32 bits to express.

The ARM11 core includes an extensive floating point maths coprocessor, the VFP11 Vector Floating Point Coprocessor. As with the ARM core itself, there is an ARM architecture for floating point machine instructions, which has evolved over time and has its own version numbering. VFP11 implements the VFPv2 instruction set architecture, which in turn implements a large subset of the IEEE 754 standard for binary floating point arithmetic. VFP11 is accessed by the ARM11 core through the ARM coprocessor interface, using two dedicated coprocessor numbers: 10 for single-precision instructions and 11 for double-precision instructions. Single precision as used in an ARM11 context means values represented in 32 bits. Double-precision values are represented in 64 bits.

The term *vector* as used here denotes a one-dimensional array (that is, a series) of same-type data items. (There is more on arrays and other data structures in Chapter 5.) This may sound familiar: vector maths is what SIMD instructions were designed to perform. The vector-processing features of VFP are relatively slow and limited and, starting with the Cortex group of ARM architectures, VFP vector maths has been deprecated in favour of the more powerful NEON SIMD coprocessor. (More on NEON later on, in connection with ARM Cortex.)

The VFP architecture provides single- and double-precision add, subtract, multiply, divide and square root operations, plus multiply-and-accumulate. This last is a specialised operation often used in digital signal processing (DSP). Given the importance of DSP in media software, optimised instructions for use in DSP work are a big win, performance-wise. Instructions are also provided for conversions between numeric types, and load/store instructions for moving floating point data directly between memory and VFP coprocessor registers. The VFPv2 architecture provides four banks of eight 32-bit registers. Two consecutive registers may be used to hold 64-bit double-precision values.

The IEEE 754 standard makes recommendations on how computer logic should implement transcendental functions (the exponential function, logarithms and trigonometry) but with VFPv2 these are not implemented in machine instructions and must be implemented as subroutines in libraries.

Emulating Coprocessors

Nearly all architectures that support coprocessors provide a way to handle coprocessor instructions when the coprocessor in question isn't present in a system. This is called *instruction emulation*. On the ARM processors, it's handled by way of the undefined instruction exception.

Instruction emulation requires one subroutine in memory to perform the work of each emulated instruction. The core checks each coprocessor instruction that it fetches to see if the required coprocessor exists on the system. If not, the core triggers an undefined instruction exception. The exception handler contains a jump table with branches to emulation subroutines for all instructions coded for the missing coprocessor. The exception handler inspects the coprocessor instruction that triggered the exception, and branches to the appropriate emulation subroutine. The subroutine does the work that would ordinarily be done inside the coprocessor, and then returns control to the next instruction in the core pipeline.

Each instruction coded for a non-existent coprocessor triggers a separate exception into an emulation subroutine. As you might imagine, emulating a single-cycle instruction with a subroutine that might require dozens or hundreds of cycles is very slow. However, it's certainly better than halting the current program.

ARM Cortex

The ARM11 family was followed by a new group of ARM microarchitectures in 2006: Cortex. Unlike ARM11, which emcompassed only four cores based on the same microarchitecture, the Cortex brand encompasses many different core designs, each optimised for a particular application domain and area/performance/energy trade-off point. The Cortex processors fall into several categories called *profiles*, denoting broad emphasis:

- **Cortex-R:** Cores optimised for real-time embedded system service in automotive and industrial control devices

- **Cortex-M:** Small, inexpensive, low-power cores optimised for use in microcontroller applications

- **Cortex-A:** Cores optimised for use in devices like smartphones, tablets, e-book readers, digital TV appliances and other applications where a full operating system is necessary

- **SecureCore:** Cores optimised for use in high-security financial and communication devices like ATMs, mass transit ticketing, pay-per-view media controllers, e-voting and ID systems

For space reasons, we're confining this discussion to the A profile and sticking to the high points in the evolution of ARM CPUs.

Multiple-Issue and Out-Of-Order Execution

The ARM11 core is a single-issue processor, which means that it loads one machine instruction into the pipeline at a time. The Cortex A8 introduced superscalar execution to ARM, and issues two instructions into its pipeline at once. This is often called dual issue. (See the "Superscalar Execution" section earlier in this chapter.) The Cortex A9 core can issue two instructions at once, and the A15 three.

The Cortex A9 adds yet another performance trick new to ARM: out-of-order execution (OOE). In simple terms, OOE allows the CPU to determine when a machine instruction has to wait for its operands to be available and sets it aside until it's ready to be issued to the execution units. Other instructions, taken from later in the instruction stream, can be issued during this time, provided their operands are available. When the operands of an instruction waiting in the dispatch queue arrive, the instruction is then issued to the pipeline.

Pre-OOE, the terms dispatch and issue meant the same thing: allowing an instruction to enter the execution pipeline. With OOE, an instruction can be dispatched to a queue after it's been decoded, but the instruction is not issued to the execution units until its data is known to be available.

As you might expect, OOE requires yet more smarts (and lots more transistors) to avoid hazards and perform correctly. Before the instructions are retired, the CPU must ensure that OOE did not affect the results of the task being executed. This is a larger version of the challenge facing pipelined execution generally and superscalar execution in particular.

Thumb 2

The Cortex A8 core introduced the Thumb 2 instruction set enhancements. In simplest terms, Thumb 2 augments the original 16-bit Thumb instruction set with a selection of 32-bit instructions, with the result that the Thumb 2 instruction set is nearly feature-equivalent to the full 32-bit ARM one, and the instruction-count penalty associated with Thumb is largely absent. Even with the new 32-bit instructions, 16-bit instructions can be used frequently enough to yield a useful increase in code density (especially on low-cost embedded systems with limited memory).

One shortcoming of the Thumb instruction set is the lack of conditional execution. Thumb 2 provides a partial fix for 16-bit Thumb instructions using the new IT (IF/THEN) instruction. IT provides a condition code that governs a block of up to four subsequent 16-bit instructions. Each instruction in the block can be tagged with either the condition code specified by the IT instruction or its complement, and it executes only if the condition is satisfied.

Thumb EE

The Cortex A8 core introduced the Thumb-EE execution environment. Thumb-EE is an instruction architecture incorporating Thumb 2 instructions with features optimised for use with just-in-time (JIT) compilation of high-level languages like Java, Python, C# and Perl. Faster cores, larger memory spaces and better JIT compilers have made Jazelle and Thumb EE less necessary, and ARM Holdings deprecated Thumb EE in 2011.

big.LITTLE

Power consumption is a critical issue in mobile computing, and much of the innovation in new ARM generations has gone to increasing performance without sacrificing ARM's traditional advantage in energy efficiency. One technique introduced with the Cortex family goes by the trademark big.LITTLE. In devices implementing big.LITTLE there are two ARM cores (or clusters of cores) working together: a high-performance (out of order, multi-issue) core like the A15 that emphasises performance over energy per instruction, and a lower-performance (in order, single-issue) core like the A7 optimised for much lower energy used per instruction. The operating system can move individual processes between high- and low-energy cores on demand, and shut down unused cores, providing a much broader dynamic range in both processing capability and energy usage than would be available from a single mid-performance core.

The big.LITTLE technology was intended for use in custom SoC parts. The paired cores must be architecturally compatible and support multi-cluster cache coherence for the system to work. The A7/A15 pair was the first; the latest is the A53/A57 pair, which implements the new ARMv8 instruction set architecture.

The NEON Coprocessor for SIMD

The Cortex family of processors introduced a major new coprocessor: NEON. Prior to the ARMv7 instruction set architecture, SIMD support on ARM was handled by ARMv6 instructions on the ARM core, and acted on four 8-bit quantities held in ARM general-purpose registers. NEON moves SIMD instruction execution out to the coprocessor, and adds more than 100 SIMD instructions to ARMv7. This removes dependence on ARM general-purpose registers, and allows a 128-bit wide SIMD-specific register set. Each of the 16 128-bit NEON registers is interpreted as containing multiple values of the same type. Four data types are supported:

- Sixteen 8-bit quantities

- Eight 16-bit quantities

- Four 32-bit quantities

- Two 64-bit quantities

Which data type is used depends on the form of the SIMD machine instruction being executed. Underneath it all, the register is just a block of 128 bits. The instruction divides the source and destination registers into *lanes*, which are logical groupings of bits that are treated as separate quantities during SIMD maths (see Figure 4-21).

The 16 128-bit registers may be accessed as 32 64-bit registers. If calculations don't require lanes wider than 64 bits, this allows more calculations to be done in registers without additional load/store operations.

ARMv8 and 64-Bit Computing

The Cortex family introduced the ARMv7 instruction set architecture. The new (at the time of writing) Cortex A50 family introduces a new ISA, ARMv8. The primary purpose of ARMv8 is to implement 64-bit computation and memory addressing for the ARM core family. In fact, ARMv8 provides three different instruction sets:

- **A32:** The 32-bit ARM instruction set, essentially unchanged from ARMv6 and ARMv7

- **T32:** The Thumb 2 instruction set, essentially unchanged from ARMv7

- **A64:** The new 64-bit instruction set

A NEON SIMD add using 16-bit lanes

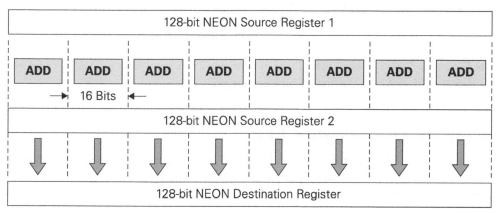

A NEON SIMD add using 32-bit lanes

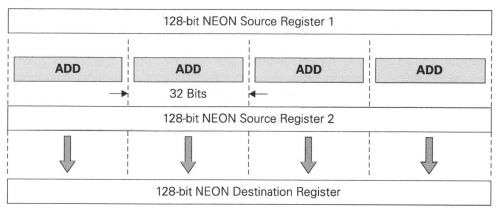

FIGURE 4-21: How NEON SIMD lanes divide 128-bit registers into logical quantities

A64 makes significant changes to the Cortex architecture:

- The general-purpose registers are 64 bits wide instead of 32.
- Machine instructions remain 32 bits in size to retain A32 code density.
- Instructions may take either 32-bit or 64-bit operands.
- The stack pointer and program counter are no longer general-purpose registers.
- An improved exception mechanism makes banked registers unnecessary.

- New optional instructions implement AES (Advanced Encryption Standard) encryption and both the SHA-1 and SHA-256 hashing algorithms in hardware.

- New features support hardware-assisted virtual machine management.

The Raspberry Pi 3 computer, introduced in February 2016, incorporates an ARMv8 64-bit quad-core CPU. It is thus the first 64-bit Raspberry Pi.

Systems on a Single Chip

It's easier to describe the architecture of an Intel chip than an ARM-based chip, simply because there are so many more different varieties of the latter "in the wild". ARM-based chips are custom jobs, in two senses:

- The CPU itself may be easily customised in terms of cache size, installed coprocessors and other significant features like TrustZone security.

- The CPU very often shares silicon with peripherals like network controllers, graphics processors and even blocks of system memory, to form SoC devices.

Some ARM-based SoC parts (for example, the Apple A6X) are custom-designed and manufactured by a specific firm for its own mobile device products. Semiconductor manufacturers offer SoC parts of their own design to device manufacturers that don't have the in-house resources to create a custom SoC from scratch.

The Broadcom BCM2835 SoC

The first-generation Raspberry Pi computers are based on the BCM2835 SoC chip, designed and sold by Broadcom to manufacturers that want to field mobile devices like smartphones, tablets and e-book readers. The BCM2835 contains nearly all the digital logic necessary to create a standalone, graphics-intensive mobile computer. This logic falls into three broad categories:

- A single ARM core, the ARM1176JZF-S, licensed from ARM Holdings

- A 1080p30-capable graphics processor, the VideoCore IV, developed and owned by Broadcom

- 128KB of Level 2 cache, shared with the CPU but used primarily by the VideoCore IV processor

- A suite of peripherals for the use of the ARM11 core, including:

  - An interrupt controller

  - Timers

  - A pulse-width modulator (PWM)

  - Two universal asynchronous receiver-transmitters (UARTs)

  - A general-purpose I/O (GPIO) system providing 54 I/O lines

  - An inter-IC sound (IIS or I2S) system and bus

  - A serial peripheral interface (SPI) master/slave bus mechanism

The BCM2835 does not contain system memory. As described in Chapter 3, the single SDRAM memory device piggybacks on top of the BCM2835 device, using package-on-package (POP) ball-grid array (BGA) packaging.

Broadcom's Second- and Third-Generation SoC Devices

The Raspberry Pi 2's release in February 2015 ushered in the second generation of Raspberry Pi computers. At the heart of the Raspberry Pi 2 is the BCM2836 SoC, which differs from the BCM2835 primarily in the CPU and Level 2 (L2) cache. The CPU is a quad-core ARM Cortex A-7 running at 900 MHz. Level 2 cache is 256KB, shared with the VideoCore IV graphics processor. The Raspberry Pi 2 board has 1 GB RAM, and the higher-capacity RAM IC is not mounted atop the SoC as in the Raspberry Pi 1 computers, but elsewhere on the printed circuit board.

The Raspberry Pi 3 computer, released in February 2016, is based on the BCM2837 SoC, again with a 1GB RAM IC mounted directly to the printed circuit board and not atop the SoC device itself. The BCM2837 contains a quad-core 64-bit ARM Cortex A-53 CPU, with 512KB shared L2 cache. The dual-core VideoCore IV processor now runs at 400 MHz (300 MHz for 3D graphics) rather than the 250 MHz of the earlier SoCs. Beyond that, it is almost identical to the original BCM2835.

How VLSI Chips Happen

It's beyond the scope of this book to explain very large scale integration (VLSI) semiconductor fabrication in detail, but some understanding is necessary so that the jargon and the design challenge make sense.

VLSI chips are fabricated with a photolithography process, which uses short-wavelength ultraviolet (UV) light and a set of photographic masks to chemically impose patterns on a silicon wafer. These patterns are applied in layers that eventually combine to form individual transistors, resistors, diodes and capacitors. People who have made their own printed circuits at home by etching away copper to form patterns of conductive traces on fibreglass boards will have a sense for what's going on. The difference, of course, is that VLSI fabrication involves patterns that are mere nanometres (billionths of a metre) in size.

A single masking operation works like this:

1. A coating of a photosensitive chemical called *resist* is applied to the wafer.

2. The mask is positioned over the wafer.

3. UV light is allowed to shine through the mask, hardening areas exposed to the UV.

4. The mask is removed, and the portions of the resist coating that were not exposed to UV are washed from the wafer.

5. A chemical process is applied to the wafer. Only where the unexposed resist was washed away can the chemicals reach the wafer.

6. The hardened resist is removed chemically in preparation for the next operation.

The chemical process in step 5 can be a number of things. An etchant may be applied to remove silicon. The wafer may be exposed to various chemicals for *doping* the silicon—that is, infusing small quantities of elements like boron and phosphorus to alter the electrical properties of the silicon. This was originally done by exposing the wafer to dopant chemicals in gaseous or liquid form. These days, to achieve the precision required by increasingly smaller chip features, doping is often done by bombarding the wafer with dopant ions accelerated electromagnetically. Copper or some other metal (generally aluminium) may be applied to resist-free areas of the wafer, creating conductive paths.

Depending on the complexity of the integrated circuit (IC) being fabricated, there can be 20 or 30 separate masks, and as many as 50 masking steps. Masking must be done with a mind-boggling level of precision. If even one masking step is performed out of alignment, the entire wafer will be faulty and must be discarded.

Processes, Geometries and Masks

The fabrication process described in the preceding section is a very touchy one. All the elements interact, and none can be changed without affecting the others. The sizes and shapes of the regions in the masks dictate the electrical properties of the silicon regions that the masks are used to create. At the sizes specified in modern IC designs, a difference of just a few million atoms in a P-N junction (a region where P-type and N-type semiconductor material are in contact, creating one or more transistors) can make the difference between a junction that works and one that works poorly or not at all. Leakage across junctions increases as the junction size decreases. Waste heat generated per unit area also increases as the sizes of the devices (transistors, resistors) decrease. All these factors must be taken into account.

For these reasons, it's impossible to shrink an IC design just by optically shrinking the mask patterns used in fabrication. Creating a chip with smaller circuit elements means re-engineering the entire fabrication process from scratch. In fact, engineers use the word *process* to mean a very specific sequence of steps that cannot be changed in any way. The defining parameter of a fabrication process is the size of the smallest components created on the silicon die. This is called the *process geometry*. At the time of writing, the cutting-edge geometry is 14 nanometres. To put this in perspective, the *lattice constant* of silicon—the distance between silicon atoms on a smooth crystalline surface—is .54 nanometres. This means that a 14-nanometre feature on a silicon die is about 30 to 35 *atoms* wide.

Because the size of the features drawn on a mask dictates their electrical properties, masks for fabricating a device are process and geometry specific.

IP: Cells, Macrocells and Cores

Modern ICs, of whatever function, are almost never created from whole cloth. In other words, design engineers do not sit down at a CAD workstation and begin drawing individual transistors and other components. With hundreds of millions of devices on modern silicon dies, that would take a very long time. Fortunately, it's also unnecessary.

Just as program code can be designed as a library of standard subroutines, digital logic expressed in silicon can be designed as libraries of standard cells. In a custom IC design context, a *cell* is a single logic element (for example, a gate, an inverter, a flip-flop and so on) that has been laid out in mask form and verified for proper operation. Larger blocks of digital logic (registers, adders, memory blocks and so on) are called *macrocells*. When designers get to a subsystem level (processors, caches, coprocessors) the designs are generally called *cores*.

Libraries of standard cells and macrocells, along with complete and tested cores, are often sold by design houses and fabricators to groups wanting to create their own custom designs. The libraries and cores are licensed as intellectual property (IP), and IC design engineers idiomatically refer to any licensed digital logic block as "an IP".

Hard and Soft IP

Design houses sometimes license logic blocks that have already been tested and laid out for masks to be used in a specific fabrication process and geometry. These are called hard IPs, macrocells or cores, and are basically maps of polygons that may be integrated into CAD designs for process masks. Hard IPs are compact and reliable, but they can't be used in processes other than the ones they were designed for.

Modern IPs are most often delivered as soft cores. These are descriptions of the logic and electrical behaviour of the IP, but not the physical layout on silicon. Soft IP is licensed in the form of source files written in a hardware description language (HDL) expressing the logic in an abstract form called register-transfer level (RTL). RTL is a way of describing hardware in terms of registers formed of flip-flops and combinatorial logic using simple logic gates. The description is of logic states transferred through clouds of flip-flops and gates, hence the term. RTL descriptions may be written in any of several HDLs, the most popular being Verilog and VHDL.

With a description of a design's RTL logic written in an HDL, an IP may be synthesised to a matrix of individual gates called a netlist, and then placed (laid out in two dimensions) and routed (connected to one another) for a particular process. This essentially converts a soft IP to a hard IP, and is referred to as hardening an IP. Most IPs today are delivered as RTL files, and the synthesis and routing are done during the synthesis and routing of the SoC as a whole.

Floorplanning, Layout and Routing

The actual physical creation of an SoC begins with a finished netlist that defines the entire device both logically and electrically. The challenge of creating SoC parts from a netlist lies in arranging cells and macrocells on a silicon die and connecting them as the netlist requires. Creating a tentative layout for an SoC is called *floorplanning*, and the metaphor is apt: engineers have to parcel out the area of a silicon die into regions big enough to hold all the parts of the design, just as architects divide the floor of a building into offices, lift-shafts, hallways and so on. Floorplanning must be done within a number of constraints:

- There is only so much area on the die.
- Many macrocells (especially hard IPs licensed from design firms) have a fixed size, shape and orientation and thus no "wiggle room" for fitting into a layout.
- There may be a maximum number of connection pads on the device package.

- Some logic blocks (such as line drivers) must be physically close to the connection pads that they serve.

- Data paths must not introduce timing problems or *crosstalk,* which is electrical interference between adjacent conductors caused by capacitive or inductive effects.

Within such constraints, engineers strive to make the layout as small as possible, not only to maximise the number of devices per wafer, but also to minimise signal propagation delays. Floorplanning is a sort of intuitive "first cut" at a layout, to make the later job of the CAD software tools as easy as possible. With a floorplan in hand, engineers turn to placement, during which the precise position of elements in the layout is done using CAD tools. Placement may demand iterative changes in the floorplan, including the size and aspect ratio, which defines the proportions of the rectangle embracing the layout.

The final step is *routing*, which encompasses the crucial job of creating data paths, clock distribution paths and power distribution paths. Routing is where issues with crosstalk and capacitive coupling are actually modelled and the resulting timing violations (cases in which signals arrive at a flip flop too late, or too soon) are corrected when found. Towards the end of the chip design process, the team enters what is termed the timing closure loop: violations are fixed by adjusting transistor sizes or inserting buffers, which in turn creates a (hopefully) smaller number of new violations, which are then fixed in turn until none remain. With routing finished for the desired process, the SoC design may be "taped out" (written to files in a final version) and sent to a chip foundry for mask creation and the eventual fabrication of "first silicon".

Standards for On-Chip Communication: AMBA

Integration of IP cores from multiple sources and the construction of a bus fabric to tie them together into a coherent whole comprise one of the most challenging steps in the design of any IC. The scale of the challenge grows with the complexity of the design, the clock rates at which it operates and the reduction of the size of the process geometry. Standards can help to simplify the design process by abstracting away the details of bus implementation, allowing IP cores and infrastructure components to be reused elsewhere on the chip, or in new projects.

In 1996, ARM Holdings introduced the Advanced Microcontroller Bus Architecture (AMBA) to do precisely that: provide standards for creating and reusing IP. ARM later released actual soft IP implementing AMBA-compliant on-chip data buses for SoCs. In the 20 years since its introduction, AMBA has gone through four generations; today it's the de facto standard for on-chip buses, especially for SoCs that incorporate ARM processor cores. The AMBA standard is public and may be used without payment of royalties to ARM Holdings.

The AMBA spec includes several different bus architecture definitions, which are informally called *protocols*. Each protocol includes specs for both the physical connections between cores and the logic that governs data movement over the connections. The protocol used in the BCM2835 SoC is the Advanced Extensible Interface (AXI), which is part of the AMBA 3 specification. The version of AXI used in the Raspberry Pi is thus referred to as AXI 3. An AXI bus may be configured at design time to be from 8 to 1024 bits wide, in powers of two. The internal buses in the BCM2835 are between 32 and 256 bits wide, depending on the bandwidth required.

An AXI bus may be imagined (roughly) as an interconnected network of utility trenches dug between several buildings in a corporate campus. Builders lay pipes in the trenches to carry water, electricity, natural gas, wastewater or steam. The pipes are run side-by-side in the trenches but are not interconnected. An AXI bus incorporates five channels that carry data along paths on the SoC silicon, around and between the various cores on the SoC. Each channel is *unidirectional*, meaning that data passes only one way through the channel, just as water or natural gas flows only one way through the pipes that carry it. The flow of data over each bus is controlled using ready-valid signalling: the upstream end asserts (sets to high, or logic 1) a valid signal if it has data to transmit, the downstream end asserts a ready signal if it is able to accept data, and data is transferred during a clock cycle if, and only if, both signals are high.

Channels conduct data between two kinds of endpoints: master and slave. These are roughly equivalent to client and server in the network world. The master (which could, for example, be a CPU, graphics processor or video decode engine) requests a transaction, and the slave (which could be an SDRAM controller or a peripheral such as a UART) complies with the master's request. The master may request either a data read or data write transaction, but in either case the transaction is requested and controlled by the master.

The five AXI3 channels are:

- **Read address channel:** Carries address and control information from a master to a slave endpoint that acts as a data source

- **Read data channel:** Carries the requested data back from the slave to the master

- **Write address channel:** Carries address and control information from a master to a slave endpoint that stores or otherwise uses data

- **Write data channel:** Carries one or more pieces of data associated with a write address from the master to the slave that needs the data

- **Write response channel:** Carries acknowledgment signals from the slave to the master, indicating that the data had been successfully received

Using these five channels, data may be moved very quickly around the bus (see Figure 4-22).

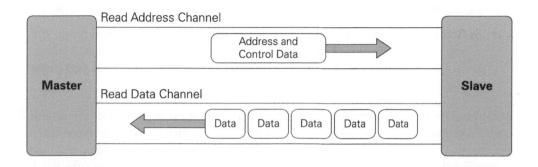

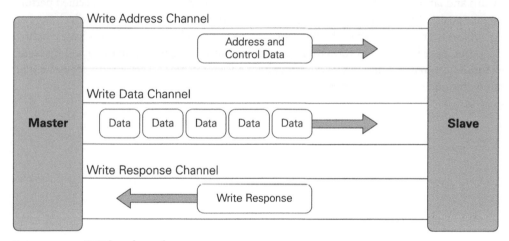

FIGURE 4-22: AXI3 bus channels

Three general types of bus component may be inserted into AXI3 channels:

- **Register slices:** "Latch" data moving through a bus channel into temporary memory. This allows timing conflicts to be resolved by breaking long paths into shorter ones. Metaphorically, a register slice is a way to place a "slice" of the bus onto a shelf, where it can wait until the other end of the channel signals the register slice that it can accept the slice data. Register slices can be combined to allow pipelining of data passing along the bus, in a way similar to how pipelining works for machine instructions in CPUs.

- **Arbiters:** These merge multiple upstream buses into a single downstream bus. This allows multiple masters to interchange data with a single slave. The arbiter manages control information to ensure that the proper upstream bus receives read data and write responses intended for it. As an example, an arbiter is used to allow the ARM, the graphics processor and the video decode engine inside BCM2835 to share access to main memory.

- **Splitters:** These divide a single upstream bus into multiple downstream buses. This allows a single master to exchange data with multiple slaves. As an example, a splitter is used to allow the ARM11 to access both main memory and the various peripherals on the SoC.

With these three components, an on-chip bus fabric can be made to connect the various cores making up an SoC in almost any useful combination. Much of the effort expended in designing an SoC is devoted to constructing a fabric that is capable of providing real-time masters, such as camera and display interfaces and video decode engines, with the bandwidth and latency quality-of-service (QoS) guarantees they require to meet specified performance goals. This in turn requires us to come up with policies that determine which port of an arbiter is granted access to the downstream bus if multiple upstream buses have pending requests, based on static information (the identity of the requesting master) and dynamic information (recent traffic history). QoS system design remains an active area of research in academic and commercial circles.

Chapter 5
Programming

COMPUTER HARDWARE AND computer software are traditionally considered two separate continents on Planet Computing. The term "computer architecture" usually means hardware architecture, to the extent that a great many university-level computer architecture books don't cover programming at all, much less cover the higher level discipline of software architecture and design.

This may be a mistake, especially for pre-university students who have had no formal instruction in either hardware or programming. Separating the study of hardware and software into two disciplines is a convenience only. Anyone who has a serious interest in computing needs to study both. It's too glib to say that software wouldn't exist without hardware. The truth is that modern hardware requires software to design and manufacture it, and, more to the point, all computers (which are hardware) require software to make them operative and useful.

Keep in mind that this book is primarily about hardware. Teaching programming using specific languages and tools is best done in separate books, many of which already exist, especially for Python, which is in some sense the "default" language for the Raspberry Pi. What we're going to do in this chapter is present a broad picture of the *idea* of programming, with an eye towards giving you a head start on choosing a programming language and an overall approach to the challenge of building your own software.

Programming from a Height

By now you should understand that computers do what they do by performing a very large number of very small steps in carefully arranged sequences. (Flip back to Chapter 2, "Recapping Computing," if this isn't clear to you.) The steps are called *machine instructions*, and we've spoken of them informally all along. They are the "atoms" of a computer program, and cannot be broken down into smaller units of action (see Chapter 4).

What we call *computer programming* is the process of writing and arranging these steps, verifying that they do what we need them to do, and keeping them current over time as those needs evolve. These three components of the programming process are called *coding*, *testing* and *maintenance*.

Prior to coding, there has to be a design stage. Writing program code off the top of your head (and observing the consequent error messages) is useful while you're learning a new programming language, but long-term it's a losing strategy for writing any sort of software that must do a real job over a period of time. Computer programs of any significant size must be designed before the programmer writes the first of those many steps. Different people or groups may do the design work versus the programming work, especially for large software systems that span different computers across networks.

Software design is a separate, necessary discipline on which programming depends. For the sort of simple programs you may write while you're first learning programming, the design step may seem almost trivial. For larger systems, design may become the toughest challenge you'll face during the entire project, and inadequate design will likely doom the project to failure.

The Software Development Process

Irrespective of what programming language or tools you use, the process of software development follows a pretty consistent map, which is shown in Figure 5-1. It begins with an idea that solves some sort of problem. An idea is just an idea; once you begin fleshing it out and taking notes you've already stepped off square one and have begun designing your program.

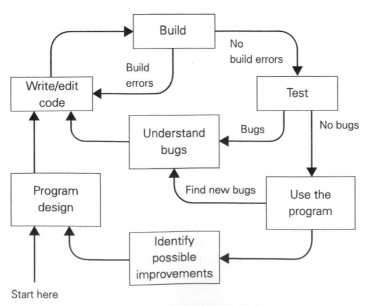

FIGURE 5-1: A map of the software development process

With some sort of design in hand (and there are a multitude of ways of performing software design) you sit down in front of your programming tools, open an editor window and begin writing actual program code. Although purists frown on the notion, it's true that the design and coding stages are not completely distinct. It's in the nature of the creative process that making an idea concrete generates not only insights about the idea but also new ideas. Especially while you're still building your programming skills, coding may cause you to realise that something in your design won't work or doesn't serve the mission of the project. Going back to the design process temporarily isn't exactly "following the map" but it may keep the entire project from going off the rails later on, leaving you with hundreds, thousands or (yes, it happens!) tens of thousands of lines of essentially useless code.

At some point you'll have one or more files containing program code that represent a working program. This is called your *source code*. The next step is to turn your programming language loose on it as you build an executable program from the textual code files that you've written in your editor. The term "build" contains one or more steps that depend on the programming language and toolset that you're using. For some languages, like Python, much of the build process happens "behind the scenes", whereas for others, like C, you are required to explicitly invoke tools such as compilers and linkers (which are described later in the "High-Level Languages" section). For now, think of it this way: the build process crunches your code and either gives it a (qualified) clean bill of health or presents you with a list of compile-time errors.

A *compile-time error* is something in your code that prevents your toolset from creating an executable program. All programming languages have *syntax*; that is, a set of rules about what program elements are called and how they're put together in your source code files. Violate that syntax, and you get an error. In statically typed languages, some errors will be type mismatches, which means a conflict between the type of data you've defined (text, numbers, etc.) and what your code is trying to do with it. Dynamically typed languages give you more leeway at compile time: type mismatches make themselves known at runtime, when the offending statement is executed. This is called a *runtime error*.

NOTE

Error messages provide hints as to what you did wrong, and a line in a source code text file represents the point at which your toolset noticed the error. This is not necessarily where the error itself lies! You'll have to think a little about what you wrote and how it adheres to or violates your language's syntax or type rules. While you're learning, you'll doubtless spend time digging through a syntax chart or reference on your chosen language. Once you've internalised the language, it will take a lot less time and effort to spot errors.

Fixing errors requires you to return to the text editor, change the problem source code and save a new version of the file or files. After that, you build the program again (and probably again, for several or many more iterations) until your toolset no longer gives you a list of errors. Done!

Well, not exactly done. Not even close. Once you have a program that can be run, you have to run it and see what it does. With that you move to the testing stage, during which you evaluate your program's behaviour against what you've set out in your design. The program may run but then crash, and if you're fortunate your toolset will give you a run-time error providing some hints as to why. Even if it runs, the program may do unexpected things. This sort of problem is known as a *bug*.

NOTE   The first person to use the term bug in the context of computing was Admiral Grace Hopper of the United States Navy, who found a dead moth stuck in a relay of an early electromechanical computer in 1947. Although technically a hardware rather than a software problem, Admiral Hopper's moth kept her program from running correctly, and she said she had to "debug" the computer to make things work again. She taped the moth itself to her log book, where it remains to this day at the Smithsonian Institution. Since then, anything that keeps a program from running correctly is called a bug.

Debugging software is an art and a discipline all to itself. Identifying a bug does not imply understanding what you actually did wrong in your source code. Working out how to fix a bug takes some study and sometimes a walk around the block to clear your head. Once you've figured out the problem (or *think* you've figured out the problem) you again return to your code editor, make your changes and then rebuild the program.

Getting the bugs out of a program can take longer than writing the program itself, especially while you're still learning the game. There will come a time when you realise that your list of bugs has all been repaired, and the program is finally doing useful things in the ways that you had planned. Now you're done!

Waterfall vs. Spiral vs. Agile

But you're still not really done. One of the tenets of modern software development is that software is rarely if ever "done" in the sense that nothing more needs to be changed, now or ever. The programming process is inherently *iterative*—that is, it's a series of feedback loops that take into account a program's design goals, its bug list, and new insights about how what needs to be done could be done better.

Programming wasn't always like this. In its early years, the software development process was often conceptualised as a sort of construction task like erecting an office building, in which the entire blueprint must be complete, fully understood and costed before the first shovel of dirt is thrown. In this world, user requirements are gathered and a detailed design document for a piece of software that meets these requirements is produced; the design is implemented in code and tested; all known bugs are fixed; and then the implementation phase is deemed complete and the project is placed into an ongoing maintenance mode.

This linear sequence of steps is now called the *waterfall model* because it proceeds inexorably from the top to the bottom. In the model's purest incarnation, user requirements cannot be changed after the design document is underway, and the design document cannot be changed after coding has begun. If the users do not understand their own needs, or if they cannot communicate their needs to the designers, what they get in the end might not help them or, in some cases, can be worse than nothing at all.

After recognising the shortcomings of the waterfall model, software designers began to explore something a little more like what's shown in Figure 5-1. The insight was that, realistically, many projects cannot be fully understood by *anyone* before at least some code has been written. Programmers take the user requirements and create a simple, feature-limited prototype and let the users play with it. Based on user feedback, the programmers then expand the prototype or in some cases scrap it entirely and begin again, correcting initial misunderstandings even if they were fundamental to the design. After users see their requirements implemented in software, they will as often as not update their requirements to reflect the insights that playing with a prototype have triggered. The requirements, design and coding steps are visited not once but many times, going around in a loop much like that in Figure 5-1. The prototype grows by increments; these development methodologies, of which Barry Boehm's spiral model is the best-known example, are therefore known as *incremental models*. Figure 5-2 shows the waterfall and spiral models side by side.

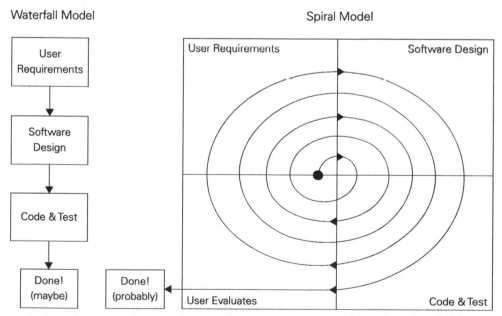

FIGURE 5-2: Waterfall model vs. spiral model

Although traditional incremental models generally represent an improvement on the waterfall, they are heavyweight, with an emphasis on up-front planning and top-down management of the development process. From the mid-1990s onwards, a variety of lightweight incremental models emerged, which emphasised flexibility and responsiveness. These approaches came to be known as *agile software development*, or simply *agile*. The (commendably brief) Agile Manifesto, issued in 2001, summarises the goals of agile software development:

We are uncovering better ways of developing software by doing it and helping others do it. Through this work we have come to value:

- **Individuals and interactions** over processes and tools

- **Working software** over comprehensive documentation

- **Customer collaboration** over contract negotiation

- **Responding to change** over following a plan

That is, while there is value in the items on the right, we value the items on the left [the bolded items] more.

Kent Beck	James Grenning	Robert C. Martin
Mike Beedle	Jim Highsmith	Steve Mellor
Arie van Bennekum	Andrew Hunt	Ken Schwaber
Alistair Cockburn	Ron Jeffries	Jeff Sutherland
Ward Cunningham	Jon Kern	Dave Thomas
Martin Fowler	Brian Marick	

© 2001, the above authors. This declaration may be freely copied in any form, but only in its entirety through this notice.

Agile development is a "big picture" strategy, and the fine details of how the work is actually done may vary between teams and projects. Common agile practices include:

- **Timeboxing:** A large project is divided into discrete smaller projects of fixed duration, each with its own schedule and deliverables, simplifying short-term time management.

- **Test-driven development:** A developer first produces a unit test for a new feature, and then writes the simplest good-quality implementation that passes the test.

- **Pair programming:** Two programmers (the driver and the observer) work together at a single terminal, providing continuous code review and a separation between the strategic and tactical aspects of programming.

- **Frequent or continuous integration:** Developers regularly commit their changes to the shared code base, avoiding "integration hell".

- **Frequent stakeholder interaction:** Regular releases are made and feedback sought, providing early notice of requirement changes.

- **Scrum meetings:** Short daily team meetings promote team cohesion and provide a forum for team members to share progress, plans and impediments.

The following are two of the best-known agile methodologies:

- **Scrum:** A framework in which development proceeds as a sequence of sprints, each allocated a certain limited amount of time. (This is called *timeboxing*.) At the start of each sprint, outstanding tasks from the project backlog are prioritised, and a subset is selected to form the sprint backlog. Daily scrum meetings are held during the sprint. At the end of each sprint, the product should be releasable (albeit incomplete if there are tasks remaining on the project backlog).

- **Extreme programming:** A variety of practices—including pair programming, and continuous integration, testing and deployment—that are, in a sense, "extreme" variants of accepted best practices. The development process consists of four mutually supporting activities: coding, testing, listening (that is, gathering user feedback) and designing. The overriding goal is to remain responsive to requirement changes.

One way to think about agile development is that it does not so much design software as evolve it, through continuous feedback from users triggering continuous improvement by programmers. In a way, the design emerges from experience. Although old-school programmers sometimes consider the agile process chaotic, across a range of problem domains it appears to produce better software faster than either the waterfall or traditional incremental models.

Programming in Binary

Programming is an old, hard game. In the very beginning, there were no tools, and programmers wrote sequences of machine instructions as binary numbers. These could then be loaded from paper tape or punch cards or, particularly in the case of "bootstrap" startup code, written into memory manually through toggle switches on the CPU cabinet front panel. An "up" toggle indicated a binary 1, and a "down" toggle indicated a binary 0. Programmers would flip the row of toggles until it reflected a binary machine instruction, and then push a button to store the binary pattern in memory. Then they did it again, flipping switches and storing the next instruction, and so on. The rows of switches you may have seen in movies on the control panels of gigantic old computers were for exactly this purpose. Front panel switches lingered until the late 1970s, particularly on cost-sensitive hobbyist computer systems like the Altair 8800, but better tools have long since made them unnecessary.

Writing a program in binary was done by first writing a description of a machine instruction, and then looking up the binary pattern for that instruction. For simple programs on machines with simple instructions sets, this was time-consuming but not terribly difficult. The manufacturers of early single-chip central processing units (CPUs) like the Motorola 6800 and Zilog Z80 would publish reference cards with tables showing the hex encoding for all instructions in common forms. The need to write more complex programs, on CPUs with more complex instruction sets, quickly turned binary programming into slow, painful drudgery that cost far more in time and trouble than it was worth.

Assembly Language and Mnemonics

As early computers came to be used by a broader audience of academic and commercial users, simple tools were developed to automate the mechanical aspects of the programming process. As described in Chapter 4, a typical machine instruction consists of an *opcode* (literally an operation code, describing what sort of operation the instruction performs) and zero or more *operands* (which define where a data processing instruction finds its input data and stores its result, or where a branch instruction branches to). If you assign a short, notionally meaningful name called a *mnemonic* to each opcode, and come up with a textual convention for specifying the operands, code becomes much easier to write. For example, a machine instruction that moves data from one place in the computer to another might use "mov" as the mnemonic for its opcode.

Following is a short sequence of machine instructions expressed as human-readable opcode mnemonics and operands. The mnemonics are on the left, and the operands are to the right of the mnemonics. There are several kinds of operands, including numbers, memory addresses, register names and qualifiers of various sorts. Any single opcode may have more than one operand, or none at all.

```
mov edx,edi
cld
repne scasb
jnz Error
mov byte [edi-1],10
sub edi,edx
```

A software utility can translate the mnemonics and operand descriptions directly into binary, saving the programmer the work of doing the translation manually. This utility is called an *assembler*, as it does the work of assembling a binary machine instruction from information given in the mnemonic and operand descriptions; the textual description of a machine code program is called *assembly language*. (Chapter 4 briefly mentioned assembly language.)

Although nominally human-readable, assembly language is terse and reveals little about what the instructions are intended to accomplish. Programmers often include comments in their assembly language source code files to describe briefly an instruction's purpose:

```
mov edx,edi           ;Copy starting address into EDX
cld                   ;Set search direction to up-memory
repne scasb           ;Search for null (0 char) in string at EDI
jnz Error             ;REPNE SCASB ended without finding null
mov byte [edi-1],10   ;Store an EOL where the NUL used to be
sub edi,edx           ;Subtract position of NUL from start address
```

Note that comments describe not only the instruction but also its role within the program. In spite of any marketing hype, *no computer language is self-explanatory*. All computer languages allow comments, and you will always need comments to remind yourself what a given line of code is doing in the larger scheme of things. This is especially true after you've set a program aside long enough that its details are no longer fresh in your mind.

High-Level Languages

Assembly language still exists, and you can write assembly language programs for the Raspberry Pi with the GNU tools that come free with the Raspbian operating system and all other flavours of Linux. We'll have more on this tool set later on, in the section entitled "A Tour of the GNU Compiler Collection Toolset." Unless you're trying to eke every last drop of performance out of a system, however, it's a lot more work than it needs to be. Assembly language describes the behaviour of a program at a low level of abstraction: one line of assembly language is translated by the assembler directly to one single machine instruction. Early on, computer scientists developed more sophisticated, expressive languages in which one textual command (generally called a *statement*) corresponded to a sequence of machine instructions. Such languages were called high-level languages because they allowed the programmer to describe the desired behaviour of a program at a higher level of abstraction than the very literal assembly language could.

The term GNU refers to a large group of free and open-source software (FOSS) products, from assemblers to compilers to the Linux operating system itself, which is formally named GNU Linux. The Term "GNU" is an acronym, for "GNU's Not Unix," which is how the computer scientist Richard Stallman meant to indicate that he was writing an operating system called GNU that was similar to Unix, but not a literal clone.

NOTE

The earliest high-level language to see wide use was FORTRAN, developed at IBM by a team led by John Backus in the early 1950s, and made available to IBM's customers in 1957. FORTRAN (from FORmula TRANslator) reduced the number of statements necessary in a program by a factor of 20. The classic "Hello, world" program written in early FORTRAN was simplicity itself:

```
PRINT *, "Hello, world!"
END
```

In addition to the obvious benefit of reducing the textual size of a program's source code and making it easier to read, FORTRAN hid the details of the workings of the computer from the programmer. Programmers did not need to know how the CPU controlled the various mechanisms of the system printer, if all they wanted to do was print a line of text. The word PRINT was translated into a middling number of machine instructions that moved text across a cable to the printer and told the printer to print that text to paper. Furthermore, if the machine instructions for printing text to paper were always the same, it was a waste of effort to include them in every single program. The machine instructions for printing were necessary, but they were stored in a separate file. The utility that translated FORTRAN statements to machine instructions compiled the machine instructions from several sources (some of which would later be called libraries) to form the final executable program. The translator program was thus called a compiler.

FORTRAN was developed and used primarily for mathematical and scientific computing. It was quickly followed by COBOL, created by a group led by Admiral Grace Hopper (of "bug" fame) in 1960. Hopper's COmmon Business Oriented Language went on to become one of the most-used languages in the history of computing. The minimal "Hello, world!" in COBOL is a little more complex than in FORTRAN:

```
IDENTIFICATION DIVISION.
PROGRAM-ID.HELLO-WORLD.
PROCEDURE DIVISION.
DISPLAY "Hello, world!"
    STOP RUN.
```

One of COBOL's goals was to make program source code easier to read. It strove to put everything right there in front of the programmer in plain language. Why? A fair bit of long-horizon thinking went into COBOL, including the insight that long-term use of COBOL programs would require maintenance by different programmers over time, each of whom would have to learn how a program worked so it could be fixed or extended. There was thus value in making COBOL programs as easy to understand as possible. Long-horizon thinking definitely worked, and COBOL remained in common use on mainframe computers (that is, large systems designed for centralised use) for almost 40 years. COBOL still sees occasional use on legacy mainframe systems.

Prior to the mid-1960s, computers were *batch-oriented* systems. This means that programmers wrote their programs on paper, entered them to a stack of Hollerith punch cards, and handed the cards to the technicians who operated the mainframe systems in that era. (Figure 5-3 shows a punch card containing a FORTRAN statement.) The technicians would queue up stacks of cards, and drop them into card readers when a stack's turn came. The card readers would read the cards and submit the code they contained to be compiled and then executed on the mainframe. The mainframe would either print a list of compiler errors or (if the program had compiled correctly) the program's results. The printout would be stored with the stack of punch cards and handed back to the programmer some time later, depending on how busy the mainframe was and how many stacks were waiting their turn.

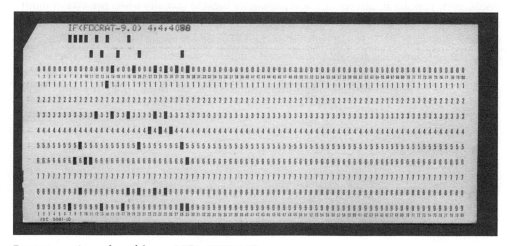

FIGURE 5-3: A punch card from a 1970s FORTRAN program

By the mid-1960s, the price of computers, printers and card punches was falling to the point where universities and even the occasional secondary school could afford them. Terminals could be placed outside the "glass walls" of the computer room itself, allowing people other than technicians to submit programs. At first, these terminals were Teletype machines or IBM terminals incorporating their Selectric printing technology. The Teletypes could punch and read paper tape, and many of the IBM Selectric terminals had card readers attached. Dozens of terminals could be attached to a single mainframe computer through a mechanism called *time sharing*, in which the mainframe would give each terminal a little slice of time to work in round-robin style. Each slice might be a fraction of a second, but that was enough time to read a keystroke or print a character. Unless the system got too busy, programmers sitting at the terminals had a convincing illusion that they had the entire machine to themselves.

Selectric terminals with card readers were still used mostly for submitting batch jobs to mainframes, but the presence of keyboards allowed something new: interactive computing. A programmer could type a sequence of lines comprising a simple program, and then submit them for immediate compilation and execution, without having to use punch cards. On a good time-sharing system the response time was almost immediate.

In 1964, two researchers at Dartmouth College, John Kemeny and Thomas Kurtz, designed a programming language specifically for use by students at interactive terminals. Their Beginner's All-Purpose Symbolic Instruction Code (BASIC) language owed a lot to FORTRAN and could be used for many of the same things. A BASIC program could consist of a single line, which reduced the "Hello, world!" test program to something close to a minimum:

```
10 PRINT "HELLO, WORLD!"
```

BASIC grew popular at universities, and popularity became ubiquity when personal computers appeared in the mid-1970s. BASIC was easy to implement, even on very simple computers, and easy to learn. Through the end of the 1970s and into the early 1980s, BASIC was often the only language available to personal computer owners. IBM even put a version of BASIC in read-only memory (ROM) on its seminal IBM PC in 1981. It may still be true that more people have been introduced to programming through BASIC than any other single language.

Après BASIC, Le Deluge

FORTRAN, COBOL and BASIC represent the deep roots of three cultures within computing: scientific, business and educational. They were not the only programming languages within those cultures. Thousands of programming languages have been designed and tried, nearly all of them now forgotten or used only by small groups of diehard enthusiasts and preservationists.

These were not wasted efforts. Most languages are designed around a specific idea, often a new take on an existing idea and sometimes a new idea entirely. Here are a few early examples:

- Lisp (from LISt Processor) appeared at MIT in 1958, to explore the use of lambda calculus (a mathematical mechanism for expressing computation in terms of functions), recursion and tree-structured data.
- Pascal was created by Swiss researcher Niklaus Wirth in 1970 to explore structured programming and data structures. Wirth later created the similar languages Modula-2 and Oberon to explore his take on modular programming.

- In 1972, Bell Labs computer scientist Dennis Ritchie defined the C language (so named because it replaced the now-vanished B language, which in turn was based on Martin Richards' BCPL, which happily is available on the Raspberry Pi) as a sort of CPU-independent higher-level assembly language. A key motivator for C was to allow easy implementation of the Unix operating system on different hardware architectures, and it remains a popular language for system-level programming. The Linux kernel used on the Raspberry Pi is written almost entirely in C.

- Researchers at Xerox's PARC research lab developed the Smalltalk language during their exploration of object-oriented programming (OOP) concepts. (Read more about OOP in the section entitled "Object-Oriented Programming".) First released in 1980, Smalltalk lives on today mostly through an open-source implementation called Squeak. Squeak may be run on the Raspberry Pi.

The insight to be taken from this is that different challenges require different approaches and, more fundamentally, that you have to try things to see what works. Computer science, like all science, builds on and sometimes abandons earlier knowledge. All languages in use today descend from earlier languages and earlier, simpler versions of themselves. C++ and Objective C are very nearly supersets of C. Pascal in 2014 draws on Wirth's later languages, as well as FORTRAN and C. Ada was developed as a rigorously robust version of Pascal.

If you intend to be a programming enthusiast, develop the habit of experimenting with as many different computer languages as you can. Being multilingual in programming languages has another, more subtle benefit: you'll be better able to identify the common ideas used across languages, which makes learning new languages in the future even easier.

Programming Terminology

Before we go on, it may be helpful to sketch out what a typical program looks like conceptually. We can't cover all current terminology in one chapter in one book, just as we can't explain any particular programming language in detail. Instead, our goal is to define a few terms that we're going to use for the rest of this chapter (and elsewhere in this book). A word of caution: much of what we present here relates specifically to imperative programming languages such as C and Python, which model computation as a sequence of discrete steps that modify state. Functional programming languages, such as Haskell, model computation in terms of functions, and are beyond the scope of this chapter. In Figure 5-4 we've sketched out a simple and very generic computer program and its most important components. There are a lot of details that will have to wait until later. Objects, for example, are vital in modern programming, but they don't summarise well in 25 words or less.

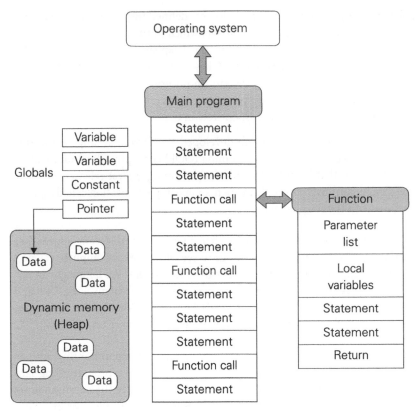

FIGURE 5-4: Fundamental programming terminology

Here are the concepts you need to be familiar with right now:

- **Variable:** A named storage location whose value may change during execution. In contrast, a constant is a named or unnamed value that cannot be changed during execution.

- **Expressions:** These combine the values of one or more variables and constants using operators to compute a result. In the expression a+b*4, a and b may be either variables or constants (depending on context), 4 is a constant, and + and * are operators.

- **Statements:** Sequential units of action. The simplest example in most languages is an assignment of the result of an expression to a variable; more complex statements can be built by concatenating together simpler statements, or by using conditional and looping constructs like if and while.

- **Functions (sometimes called procedures or subroutines):** Named blocks of code that may or may not return a value. Variables that are defined within a function are only accessible from inside the function and are said to be *local* to it. Local variables are generally stored in the CPU register file or on a stack; the stack also stores function return addresses and preserves values for which there is no room in the register file. A function can call another function, meaning that the flow of control takes a temporary detour into the function, returning when it has finished its work.

Variables that are defined outside any function are said to be *global* and are accessible from (almost) anywhere.

Some languages, including C, require all statements to be inside a function. The `main` function, which is called by the system when execution starts, marks the entry point to the program. Other languages, including Python, allow statements outside functions; execution starts with the first such statement in the program file.

- **Arguments:** Values passed to a function from its caller. Parameters are special-purpose local variables that receive the argument values when execution of the function begins. In this Python example:

```
def foo(a, b, c):

    return a*b+c

print foo(1, 2, 3)
```

a, b and c are parameters, whereas 1, 2 and 3 are arguments.

- **Heap:** A pool of memory where programs may allocate memory to store arbitrary-sized data items. *Pointers* are values that describe the location of data in the heap, generally as a memory address.

How Native-Code Compilers Work

The job of a native-code compiler is to take a source code file written in a high-level language and generate an equivalent object code file composed of binary machine instructions. (Do not confuse the terms "object code" and "object," as used in OOP. The two are unrelated.)

Compilers process their input in several steps or passes. Although object code is the ultimate goal, the compiler may write one or more other files to disk along the way, and may delete such temporary files when they're no longer needed.

The compilation process can be broken down into the following steps:

- Preprocessing (optional)
- Lexical analysis

- Parsing

- Semantic analysis

- Intermediate code generation

- Optimisation

- Target code generation

NOTE Many of the preceding steps (particularly the first few) are common to both native-code and bytecode compilers, which are covered later in this chapter in the "Bytecode Interpreted Languages" section and the sections that follow it; we'll refer back to this section during that discussion.

Let's look at each step in a little more detail. As we do, keep in mind that we're not describing any single compiler product, and all compilers handle compilation a little differently. Some compilers simplify the process by combining two or more passes into a single pass.

Preprocessing

Languages that incorporate a preprocessing pass, including C, perform a stage of text-based manipulation of the incoming source code before presenting it to the compiler proper. The C preprocessor performs several tasks:

- **Removing comments:** All text enclosed by comment delimiters (or in some other way marked as comments) is removed because it's for the sake of humans reading the source code and is of no use to the compiler. There are some exceptions in certain languages that place instructions to the compiler within specially marked comment blocks. How those are handled is both language and compiler dependent.

- **Defining and expanding macros:** Object-like macros provide a way to define constants. You might define a macro called `PI` to be `3.14159`; the preprocessor replaces each occurrence of `PI` in the source code with the literal `3.14159`. Function-like macros provide a way to define simple inline functions. You might define a macro called `RADTODEG(x)` to be `((x)*180/PI)`. The preprocessor replaces an occurrence of `RADTODEG(a+b)` in the source code with `((a+b)*180/3.14159)`.

- **Conditional compiling:** Sections of code can be conditionally excluded from compilation. This is often used to remove debugging code from release builds of software or to change behaviour depending on the target platform.

- **Including files:** The contents of other files can be incorporated wholesale into the source code. A C example is the `stdio.h` include file, which defines commonly used C input and output functions.

Lexical Analysis

During the lexical analysis stage, a part of the compiler called the *lexer* scans the stream of characters making up the preprocessed source code and identifies all the various language features in the text. These include reserved words (also called keywords) like break, begin, and typedef, identifiers like foo and bar, symbols like + and <<, string literals like "foo" and numeric literals like 5 or 3.14159. The lexer emits a stream of tokens, one for each keyword, identifier, symbol or literal. Any text that can't be identified as a token understood by the compiler is flagged as a compilation error.

You will see the identifiers "foo," "bar," "bas," and perhaps a few others come up in code examples within programming tutorials. These are called *metasyntactic* identifiers because they're used while describing programming language syntax in tutorials and demonstrations of language features. Metasyntactic identifiers are not treated specially by compilers and are used by convention among programmers, specifically programmers with roots in Unix and C.

NOTE

The stream of tokens from the lexer is then scanned by the parser, which checks to see if the tokens follow the structural rules of the language. The lexer identifies tokens individually; the parser makes sure the tokens are arranged in a legal fashion. A do keyword must have a matching while keyword. An opening brace must have a closing brace, and so on, for the full description of a language's syntax. Any deviation from that syntax is flagged as a compilation error. The output of the parser is a structure called an *abstract syntax tree* (AST), which represents the structure of the program. The AST is directly analogous to a sentence diagram for a natural language that identifies a sentence's subject, verb, object and so on.

Semantic Analysis

During semantic analysis, the compiler checks the AST to be sure that the syntactically correct program is meaningful. Much of this work involves creating a symbol table of named items in the program, and then checking whether variables and constants of supported data types (numeric, text, Boolean, and so on) are used together in ways that make sense. A statement written in a statically typed language that adds a Boolean value to a character might well be correct in terms of syntax:

```
junk = true + 'a';
```

However, what does it mean to add true to 'a'? Nothing, of course! Although syntactically correct, the statement is semantically meaningless, and the compiler will flag it as a type mismatch error. Syntactically correct but semantically meaningless sentences appear in natural languages too: Noam Chomsky famously offered "Colourless green ideas sleep furiously" as an example of a syntactically valid English sentence that is semantically meaningless.

Keep it straight in your head: Syntax is about *structure*. Semantics is about *meaning*.

Intermediate Code Generation

After the compiler verifies that the program is both syntactically correct and semantically meaningful, it is able to begin generating intermediate code. Using the parse tree as a guide, the compiler creates a linear sequence of instructions that expresses the logic of the program. These instructions are not generally the native machine instructions of the target CPU architecture. Instead, they are a sort of "artificial" instruction set belonging to a *virtual machine* (VM) that acts as an "ideal" CPU that is a notch higher in abstraction than a real, silicon CPU. For example, a VM may have a great many registers in its definition—and sometimes, as many registers as the logic of the program calls for. No CPU has hundreds of registers, so a later pass has to rewrite the intermediate code to attempt to fit those "virtual registers" into the limited register set of the real CPU, spilling those that don't fit to memory. This process is known as *register allocation*.

Optimisation

The intermediate code's primary role is to simplify the implementation of one or more *optimisation* passes. During optimisation, the compiler looks for ways to eliminate code duplication and rearrange intermediate code instructions to make the program more compact and faster to execute. The development of optimisation techniques is an area of ongoing research in both the academic and commercial domains.

Target Code Generation

With the creation of an optimised intermediate code file, we reach a fork in the road. Up to this point, the compilation process is close to the same, whether the compiler is a native code compiler or a bytecode compiler, and we'll pick up the discussion again in the next section on bytecode languages. The next, and final, step in native code compilation is *target code generation*. During this step, the intermediate code is converted to a sequence of native machine instructions that can execute on a specific CPU.

But which CPU? A compiler is not limited to creating code for the machine on which the compiler is running: a compiler running on an Intel CPU can be configured to generate code for the one of the ARM instruction set architectures (ISAs), and vice versa. This is called *cross-compilation*. A compiler is hosted on a specific CPU, which means that it is a native-code program compiled to run on that CPU. However, it may generate code that targets any CPU for which the compiler incorporates a code generator. Cross-compilation is especially useful for the creation of software to run on low-power embedded systems that don't contain enough memory or disk storage to run the compiler itself. In your early work with the Raspberry Pi you'll probably write programs and compile them right on the Raspberry Pi system itself. Many people who use the board as an embedded system develop code on Intel PCs by using a compiler that is hosted on Intel-based Windows or Linux and targets the

ARMv6 ISA, which includes the ARM11 CPU . The generated code is almost always operating system-specific as well.

With the creation of a native code object file, the compilation process is complete.

A *platform* is the combination of a specific CPU running a specific operating system. An Intel CPU running Microsoft Windows is a platform. (It's commonly called "Wintel.") An Intel CPU running Linux is an entirely separate platform, as is an ARMv6 CPU running Linux. The output of a cross-compilation operation is generally specified as being for a specific platform. **NOTE**

Compiling C: A Concrete Example

Let's take a look at the various stages involved in compiling a simple function, written in C. This section requires close attention, and perhaps a little experience in the C language itself.

The example function takes three integer arguments a, b and c, and a pointer to an area of memory, d. It writes the ten integers b*c, a+b*c, 2*a+b*c . . . 9*a+b*c into memory, starting at address d. The number of integers written can be changed at compile time by adjusting the constant COUNT, which is set using the C preprocessor directive #define:

```
#define COUNT 10

void foo(int a, int b, int c, int *d)
{
  int i = 0;
  do {
   d[i++] = i * a + b * c; // fill in table
  } while (i < COUNT);
}
```

Preprocessor

The preprocessor discards the comments, and replaces the use of the macro COUNT with its value, 10. Few modern languages have preprocessors; in this case, constants and inline functions take the place of macros, and comments would be discarded by the lexer:

```
void foo(int a, int b, int c, int *d)
{
  int i = 0;
  do {
   d[i++] = i * a + b * c;
  } while (i < 10);
}
```

Lexer

The lexer analyses the character stream that makes up the program, and groups characters into tokens. Each token may be one or more characters in length, and represents a reserved word, an identifier (shown as a double-outlined box in Figure 5-5), a symbol or a literal. Whitespace is not syntactically meaningful in C, and so is discarded from the token stream at this stage.

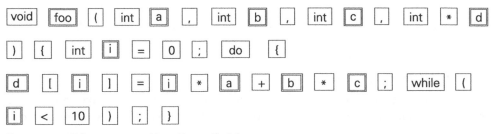

FIGURE 5-5: Tokens generated by a C compiler's lexer

Parser

The parser attempts to build an AST out of the stream of tokens from the lexer. It is powered by a set of rules, often expressed in a descriptive notation called Backus-Naur Form (BNF). BNF is perhaps the most-used metasyntactic notation system in computer science. It abstracts the structure of a programming language into a set of rules called a *grammar*. A grammar precisely describes the syntax of a programming language and can be used to determine if a given program is syntactically correct. The standard GNU utility, bison (derived from the older UNIX tool yacc—bison is GNU yacc), can automatically generate a parser for a programming language, given a BNF description. A selection of BNF grammars for various common programming languages may be found here: www.thefreecountry.com/sourcecode/grammars.shtml.

As an example, imagine a simple language that consists only of expressions containing multiplication, addition and identifiers. This language would have three rules, which might appear in the input file to bison in roughly this form, using BNF:

```
add_expr   : mul_expr             { $$ = $0; }
    | add_expr '+' mul_expr;    { $$ = ADD_EXPR($0, $2); }
    ;
mul_expr   : identifier           { $$ = $0; }
    | mul_expr '*' identifier;  { $$ = MUL_EXPR($0, $2); }
    ;
identifier : ID                   { $$ = $0; }
    ;
```

Each rule has three parts:

- A *name* (in this case `add_expr`, `mul_expr` or `identifier`).

- One or more *productions*. A production describes something you might see in the token stream that this rule will match.

- For each production, an *action*; this is often used to create a node in the AST as a result of matching a rule. In a yacc grammar, actions can return values by assigning to the pseudovariable `$$`, and make use of values returned by the rule's children (represented by pseudovariables `$0`, `$1` and so on).

A *pseudovariable* is a sort of placeholder in a grammar rule. It tells us where a value may be substituted for the pseudovariable. Pseudovariables keep a rule abstract and independent of any particular type, value or values.

NOTE

Our language description says that a valid `mul_expr` can be either an identifier, like "a", or another (shorter) valid `mul_expr` followed by a "*", followed by an identifier. So "a" (being an identifier) is a valid `mul_expr`, and so is "a*b" (because "a" (being an identifier) is a valid `mul_expr`, and "b" is an identifier), and so is "a*b*c" (because "a*b" is a valid `mul_expr` and "c" is an identifier). As the parser recognises "a*b*c", the actions first build a `MUL_EXPR` node for "a*b", and then a `MUL_EXPR` node that refers to the first node and represents "(a*b)*c". The final AST could be written as:

```
MUL_EXPR(MUL_EXPR(a, b), c)
```

Satisfy yourself that the rule for `add_expr` successfully recognises the expression "a*b+c*d" and produces the following tree:

```
ADD_EXPR(MUL_EXPR(a, b), MUL_EXPR(c, d))
```

A pleasing side effect of the way that these rules have been written is that multiplication is more "sticky" (or, more formally, it has higher precedence) than addition, so `a*b` and `c*d` have been correctly grouped together according to the precedence rules you remember from school. Applying a simplified version of the full C grammar to the earlier token string might yield the following AST:

```
FUNC_DEF (
        name: foo
        params: [(a, INT), (b, INT), (c, INT), (d, INT*)]
        returns: VOID
```

```
body: SEQ_STMT (
        stmt[0]: AUTO_DECL (
                name: I
                type: INT
                initialize: 0
        )
        stmt[1]: DO_LOOP_STMT (
                body: EXPR_STMT (
                        expr: ASSIGN_EXPR (
                                lhs: INDEX_EXPR (
                                        array: d
                                        index: i
                                )
                                rhs: ADD_EXPR (
                                        lhs: MUL_EXPR (
                                                lhs: i
                                                rhs: a
                                        )
                                        rhs: MUL_EXPR (
                                                lhs: b
                                                rhs: c
                                        )
                                )
                        )
                )
                test: LESS_THAN_EXPR (
                        lhs: i
                        rhs: 10
                )
        )
)
)
```

Semantic Analysis

Armed with the AST, the compiler can construct a symbol table that describes the type of each formal parameter and local variable within function foo:

```
a: int
b: int
c: int
d: int*
i: int
```

From this, it can determine that both d[i] and i * a + b * c have type int, and that d[i] is an lvalue. An *lvalue* is a suitable target for an assignment: a and d[i] are lvalues, whereas b * c is not. The assignment d[i] = i * a + b * c is therefore determined to be semantically valid.

Intermediate Code Generation

When we have a semantically valid AST, we can set about converting it into intermediate code. The intermediate code generator knows how to convert each type of AST node into one or more intermediate code instructions, and these rules are applied recursively. For example, to convert an ADD_EXPR node we first convert its left and right children (called lhs and rhs in the example from the "Parser" section), and then emit an ADD instruction to combine the results. To convert a DO_LOOP_STMT we emit a label, then convert the body of the loop and the loop test expression (called body and test in the example), and finally emit a conditional branch back to the start of the loop, which is predicated on the result of the test:

```
FUNCTION foo(p0, p1, p2, p3)
MOV          t0, #0                ; temporary 0 stores count
label:
    MUL          t1, t0, p0            ; calculate i * a
    MUL          t2, p1, p2            ; calculate b * c
    ADD          t3, t1, t2            ; calculate i * a + b * c
    MUL          t4, t0, #4            ; index = count * sizeof(int)
    ADD          t5, p3, t4            ; calculate address
    STW          [t5], t3              ; store i * a + b * c in d[i]
    ADD          t0, t0, #1            ; increment loop count
    BRANCHLT     t0, #10, label        ; branch if count < 10
```

Simple Optimisation

Notice that b * c is calculated each time around the loop, when it's only dependent on the formal parameters b and c, which don't change. We say that b * c is *loop invariant*, and apply loop-invariant code motion to hoist the computation out of the loop, saving nine cycles. As we only need one register to store b * c, rather than two registers to store the separate values, we've also usefully reduced *register pressure* (the number of values that need to be remembered at any given point in the program) by one, which improves the chances of fitting all the values we need into the target CPU architecture's registers. If we had needed b and c on their own as well as b * c then this optimisation would have required more registers than might be available, and the compiler would need to apply a heuristic (that is, a mechanism used to solve a particular code-generation case that might not apply to all cases) to see whether the trade-off was worth making.

```
FUNCTION foo(p0, p1, p2, p3)
  MOV           t0, #0
  MUL           t2, p1, p2      ; hoist loop-invariant calculation
label:
  MUL           t1, t0, p0
  ADD           t3, t1, t2
  MUL           t4, t0, #4
  ADD           t5, p3, t4
  STW           [t5], t3
  ADD           t0, t0, #1
  BRANCHLT      t0, #10, label
  RET
```

More Aggressive Optimisation

A more aggressive optimiser might be able to detect that both the address, which we'll denote a(i), and the value stored, which we'll denote v(i), change by a fixed amount each time we go around the loop:

```
a(0) = d          a(i+1) = a(i) + 4
v(0) = b*c        v(i+1) = v(i) + a
```

Also we leave the loop just before we write to address a(10) = d + 40. It can therefore eliminate the potentially costly multiplication instructions, which can be hard to schedule due to their long pipeline depth, instead keeping a running value of a(i) and v(i), and replace the test i < 10 with the test a(i) < a(10). This class of optimisation is known as *induction variable elimination*:

```
FUNCTION foo(p0, p1, p2, p3)
  MUL           t1, p1, p2
  MOV           t2, p3
  ADD           t3, t2, #40
label:
  STW           [t2], t1
  ADD           t1, t1, p0
  ADD           t2, t2, #4
  BRANCHLT      t2, t3, label
  RET
```

Target Code Generation (Register Allocation, Instruction Scheduling)

Now we have an optimised program represented in intermediate code; the final step is to convert that program into assembly language for our target platform. The key challenges are finding a machine register to store each value computed by the program between the point it is defined and the last point at which it is used (this is called *register allocation*), implementing each intermediate instruction by using one or more machine instructions, and ordering those machine instructions so as to avoid triggering interlocks inside the CPU pipeline (this is called *instruction scheduling*):

```
; In the ARM EABI calling convention, the first four
; arguments are in provided r0-r3

; r0-r3 may also be used as scratch registers without
; saving to the stack

foo::
  mul         r1, r1, r2     ; r1 = b * c (reuse r1)
  add         r2, r3, #40    ; r2 = d + 40 (reuse r2)
label:
  stw         [r3], r1       ; store v(i) at a(i)
  add         r3, r3, #4     ; a(i+1) = a(i) + 4
  add         r1, r1, r0     ; v(i+1) = v(i) + a
  cmp         r3, r2         ; have we reached a(10) yet?
  Blt         label          ; if not, loop
  B           lr             ; return to link address
```

Linking Object Code Files to Executable Files

When the compilation process is done and the smoke clears, what you have is not quite an executable program file. Most modern compilers generate an object code file that requires one additional step before you can run it: *linking*. The key to understanding linking lies in these two points:

- Nearly all workaday programs (as opposed to simple test or learning programs) are written in several pieces, each of which is compiled separately to an object code file.

- Nearly all programs make use of code libraries that are object code files containing useful functions and data definitions that may be considered "standard parts" in software development.

Of course, the simple programs you write as you learn a programming language or toolset will be small enough to create in one piece. However, whether you realise it or not, even your simple test programs probably make use of existing code libraries. Nearly all high-level languages have a runtime library containing standard functions implementing support for text strings, higher maths, date and time manipulation, and so on; the runtime library also contains startup code, which runs before your main function and initialises data structures used by other library functions. Other libraries may contain code specific to a particular operating system, for access to displays, printers and file systems.

What a linker does is combine multiple object code files and functions from statically linked libraries into a single executable code file that may be run on the target computer. This requires more than just writing out the object code files nose-to-tail. Code in one object code file may call functions, or use data definitions, from libraries and other object code files. Calling a function requires the memory address of the function. There's no way to specify a memory address in another object code file stored somewhere else on disk or solid-state drive (SSD.) Instead, the compiler puts a placeholder into the spot where such an external address needs to go. The placeholder says, in effect, "address to be determined".

While the linker is combining separate object code files into a single executable file, it looks for such placeholders and calculates addresses that, in most cases, are offsets from the beginning of the executable file. The long and winding road from source code files to a finished executable program file is shown in Figure 5-6. Note the way that references to identifiers in one object code file "plug in" to the actual functions or variables in another object code file.

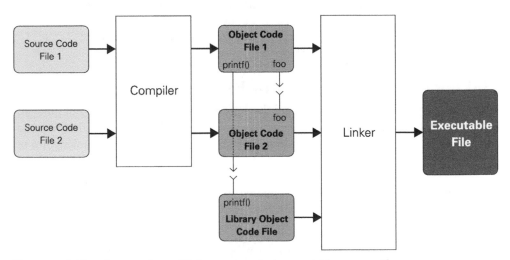

FIGURE 5-6: How the compiler and linker create a single executable program file

Pure Text Interpreters

In the preceding section, we briefly mentioned the concept of bytecode compilation. Before we elaborate on this, it is helpful to take a brief detour back into programming history. Early versions of the BASIC language were modelled on FORTRAN and were compiled on mainframes and minicomputers just as FORTRAN was. In the mid-1970s, the first personal computers often had too little memory for a real operating system, much less a compiler.

To enable users to learn programming and write their own software, a different kind of BASIC language system appeared: the *text interpreter*.

In a text interpreter system, a program is written in the form of a textual source code file, just as with native code compilation. However, there is no compilation step at all; when a program is run, the source code file is opened by a piece of software called an *interpreter*. The interpreter reads the first line from the source code file and then performs whatever work that line specifies. When the first line is done, the interpreter reads the next line, performs the work it specifies and so on, through the source code file. The key characteristic of text interpreters is that they process a single line of program source code at a time. Figure 5-7 illustrates this process.

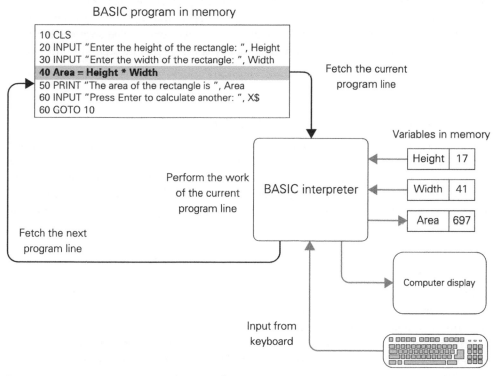

FIGURE 5-7: A text interpreter for the BASIC language

A text interpreter takes each line of source code apart after it's read from the file. It then calls subroutines to evaluate arithmetic expressions like `Height * Width` and process keywords like `INPUT` and `PRINT`. The text interpreter creates variables in memory as the source code introduces them, and manages them while the program runs. Values are read from variables as needed in calculations, and new values are given to variables when a program line assigns or recalculates a variable's value. The text interpreter handles displaying the program's output on the computer monitor, and the reading of text input from the computer keyboard.

Text interpreters for simple dialects of BASIC were comparatively straightforward to write and (more importantly) were compact. An interpreter consisted of a simple line lexer and parser, and then a collection of functions to execute the various keywords and features of BASIC. Many early personal computers, from the Commodore VIC-20 up to the original IBM PC, had a BASIC interpreter stored on read-only memory (ROM) chips soldered to the motherboard. In many cases, the BASIC interpreter stood in for a simple operating system, and allowed single commands to be entered to an interactive command line.

Pure text interpreters for programming languages like BASIC were everywhere in the 1970s and 1980s, but are nearly extinct today. Where text interpreters are still used, it is for creating command files for operating systems, database managers and large, complex applications that allow commands to be "batched" in text files. This was once called *scripting*, but that term has broadened to include programming for any language that incorporates interpretation at any level.

Bytecode Interpreted Languages

One useful characteristic of text interpreters is that they insulate a running program from the fine details of the underlying platform. A BASIC program's PRINT keyword does the same thing, whether it's running on DOS, Linux or any other operating system. The interpreter itself is a native-code machine-language program, and deals with hardware and operating system specifics, but a BASIC program will run identically on any text interpreter, on any platform, that understands the appropriate dialect of BASIC.

This attribute of BASIC programs is called *portability*; the portability of applications became an important consideration once computers grew cheap enough to be commodities, with hundreds and later thousands of different and often incompatible designs up and down the market. There were hundreds of different ways to write characters to a display, to send text to a printer, and to read and write data to storage devices. Programs had to be written in a slightly different way on each system, in order to take advantage of that system's features. The portability problem plagues us to this day, and the best solution we now have centres on an evolved form of interpretation.

P-Code

In the mid-1970s, researchers at the University of California, San Diego developed a new kind of compiler for the Pascal programming language. The UCSD Pascal compiler operated in much the same way as the native-code compilers we described earlier. The resemblance stopped at the point where UCSD Pascal generated intermediate code. Native code compilers take their intermediate code and use it as a guide for generating native code. The UCSD compiler's intermediate code was written to a file, and then that file of intermediate code was executed by an interpreter installed on a computer. As with BASIC's text interpreter, the UCSD interpreter insulated the program from the details of the underlying computer. A program written in the UCSD Pascal syntax could theoretically be compiled once, and then the intermediate code could be run in an identical manner on any machine for which an interpreter had been written. The code was thus extremely portable between otherwise incompatible computers.

This technology was dubbed the P-System, where the "P" originally stood for "pseudocode" and later "portability code". (Both are now-obsolete terms for "bytecode", which we will discuss in the next paragraph.) The intermediate code (p-code) generated by the UCSD compiler was not textual. It was a sequence of binary instructions that resembled machine instructions but were actually instructions understood and executed by the interpreter program. These instructions represented an instruction set for a virtual machine; that is, a CPU that did not exist in silicon, but was emulated using a p-code interpreter.

The P-System was the first technology of its kind to win wide acceptance. The notion of p-code was soon taken up by other researchers for other languages. The underlying idea of a virtual instruction set for a virtual machine does not depend on Pascal or any other specific programming language, and the P-System was later expanded with support for languages including Modula-2, BASIC, and FORTRAN. The term p-code was eventually abandoned in favour of bytecode, but the meaning is the same: bytecodes are synthetic machine instructions generated by a bytecode compiler and intended to be executed by a bytecode interpreter. The term comes from the fact that most bytecode systems use 8-bit (1 byte) instructions. However, there is nothing inherent in the bytecode concept limiting instructions to a single byte. For example, the Dalvik bytecode technology, which forms part of the Android operating system, uses 16-bit instructions in its bytecode.

The firm Western Digital introduced an interesting product line in 1979: the Pascal MicroEngine, which was a custom microprocessor that executed UCSD p-code as its native instruction set. P-code ran much more quickly as native code without an interpreter between itself and the CPU, but the MicroEngine was eclipsed by the release of the IBM PC in 1981 and never hit critical mass. The concept of "hardware assist" for bytecode execution is a recurring theme: several vendors have released microprocessors that directly execute Java bytecode, and some members of the ARM family of CPUs include special features to execute Java language bytecode in hardware efficiently. (Chapter 4 touches on this briefly.)

Java

Bytecode never went entirely out of use after the P-System was released, but it was uncommon until the early 1990s, when James Gosling at Sun Microsystems (now a subsidiary of Oracle) developed the Java programming language and virtual machine as a bytecode system.

The overriding goal with Java was portability: programs compiled to Java bytecode would run identically on any computer supporting the Java Runtime Environment (JRE). Sun popularised the slogan, "Write Once, Run Anywhere" to emphasise Java's big selling point.

Even in its first release, the Java system was much more sophisticated than the P-System ever was. The JRE includes the Java Virtual Machine (JVM), which implements the Java bytecode interpreter, as well as the Java runtime code libraries and various software tools that allow Java code to run inside web browsers and from web servers. Programmers who want to write Java programs need the Java Development Kit (JDK), which in addition to the JRE includes the Java language compiler and a number of other tools supporting software development.

The JVM does more than simply execute Java bytecode. It manages an area of memory reserved for the use of Java programs, in which data items are created, used and then destroyed when no longer needed, with their memory space automatically reclaimed by a utility called a *garbage collector*. The JVM also monitors data manipulation and watches for program code that attempts to do undefined things with data that might potentially crash a program and damage the JRE or other software outside the JRE, like the operating system. The JRE became a model for similar bytecode systems created by others, and today such a system is more generally called a *managed runtime environment* (MRE). The way bytecode programs are compiled and run in an MRE is shown in Figure 5-8.

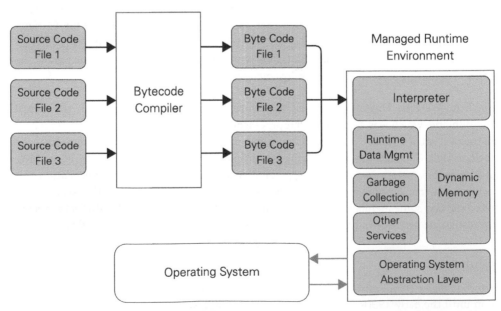

FIGURE 5-8: Bytecode executed in an MRE

An MRE is not by itself an operating system, and there is an operating system running underneath every MRE. The operating system manages the physical hardware of the computer on which it runs. To make itself operating-system independent, the MRE includes an operating system abstraction layer that gives the bytecode programs executed in the MRE a standard "view" of the operating system that is always the same, regardless of what operating system exists below the MRE.

Java was a spectacular success almost immediately. Microsoft soon saw the value in the Java idea and released its .NET Framework system in 2002 as a competitor. Architected by Anders Hejlsberg (the creator of Turbo Pascal) it included a new Java-like language, C#, which compiles to bytecode called the Common Intermediate Language (CIL), which in turn runs on the Common Language Runtime (CLR) VM.

Many books have been published on programming Java with the JDK. One of the most popular is *The Java Tutorial: A Short Course on the Basics*, 5th edition, by Sharon Zakhour, Sowmya Kannan and Raymond Gallardo (Addison-Wesley, 2013). For younger students (aged 10 and up) *Java for Kids* by Philip Conrod and Lou Tylee (Kidware Software, 2013) may be more accessible.

Just-In-Time (JIT) Compilation

Portability and security are the big value-adds in bytecode systems like Java and .NET, but they come at a cost: execution speed. Interpreted bytecode, while faster than interpreted source code text in languages like BASIC (largely due to the elimination of repeated lexing and parsing) is still significantly slower than native code. One solution to this problem came out of research involving the Smalltalk language, and was first widely implemented for Java: *just-in-time* (JIT) compilation.

The idea behind JIT compilation is fairly simple: instead of having the system interpret bytecode, a JIT compiler (informally called a *jitter*) compiles bytecode to native code "on the fly", as it is needed. The whole file isn't compiled at once and, on most systems, bytecode that is never executed isn't compiled at all. Compilation is usually done in blocks; a block may be anything from a few consecutive bytecode instructions to an entire function. Once a block of bytecode is compiled to a block of native code, the MRE can branch directly to the native code rather than interpreting the bytecode for the block instruction by instruction. Because blocks of code are often executed multiple times during a program session, the native code blocks generated by the jitter are not discarded, but are stored in a software-managed cache (see Figure 5-9).

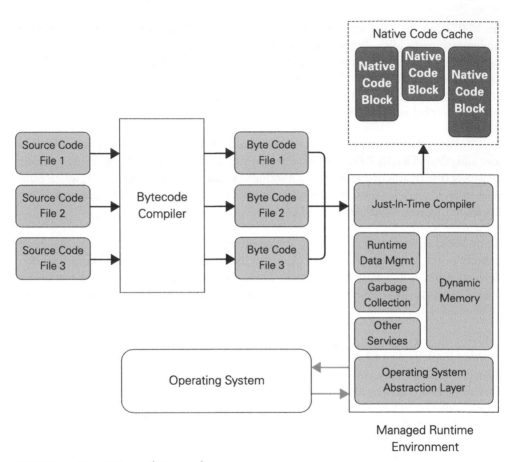

FIGURE 5-9: How JIT compilation works

Due to the initial overhead of JIT compilation, execution of a bytecode program is slow when the program is first run. As blocks of native code accumulate in the cache, execution occurs in native code more often, and performance improves. In general, the performance is never quite as good as a well-written program compiled with an optimising native-code compiler, but because much of the work of compilation is done when the program is first compiled from source code to bytecode, JIT compilation can be done with surprising speed.

There is a sort of 80/20 effect in code execution, meaning that a relatively small proportion of program code ends up running the majority of the time. Newer versions of the Java JIT compiler contain logic that analyses a compiled Java program to determine where these "hotspots" are. It then focuses its attention on optimising those hotspots. The JIT's analysis is *heuristic*—that is, it compiles statistics on what elements of a program impact code performance (this is called *tracing*) and "learns" as execution continues. Such a JIT compiler is called a tracing JIT. As the JIT accumulates trace data, it applies progressively more sophisticated optimisations to those code paths that execute most often.

A sophisticated tracing JIT can learn enough about a program during execution to actually rewrite portions of the code based on the types and even the values of function arguments. In certain circumstances these optimisations are so good that hotspots can run faster than an equivalent native program, which cannot typically be rewritten at runtime.

Bytecode and JIT Compilation Beyond Java

Java remains the single most common use of bytecode technology. Since Java's appearance, many other languages have either been designed to use bytecode or converted from pure text interpretation to bytecode, sometimes with a JIT compiler. Here's a list of a few of the most popular:

- Ruby, inspired by Smalltalk, is commonly used with a web-application framework called Rails. Ruby and Rails are both available for the Raspberry Pi.

- JavaScript is a browser-based language supported by all modern web browsers. The current release of Mozilla Firefox includes the IonMonkey JIT compiler for JavaScript.

- Lua is a scripting language for control scripts within operating systems and applications, especially game engines. A separate implementation of the Lua language called LuaJIT uses a trace JIT compiler and achieves much higher performance than Lua 5.2. Both Lua 5.2 and LuaJIT are now distributed with Raspbian.

- Python is a bytecode language, and a JIT compiler implementation of Python called PyPy is now part of the standard Raspbian image.

Android, Java and Dalvik

Oddly enough, one of the biggest uses of the Java programming language is not for the JRE at all. The Android operating system for smartphones and tablets is integrated with and depends on a bytecode MRE called Dalvik. Native code applications may be run on Android, but the Dalvik MRE is available on every Android device, without exception. An application that runs on any instance of Dalvik should run on all of them.

The recommended way to write applications for Android is first to write them in Java, and compile them to Java bytecode. The Android Software Development Kit (SDK) then takes the Java bytecode and compiles it to the completely different bytecode understood by the Dalvik MRE. Dalvik contains a JIT compiler that converts Dalvik bytecode to blocks of native code for whatever CPU the system runs on.

Data Building Blocks

Earlier in this chapter, Figure 5-4 showed a simple program in diagram form to define some common terms. Chapters 3 and 4 described the physical mechanisms by which data are stored (memory) and instructions are executed (the CPU). Now we take a closer look at some of the features that high-level languages provide to enable programmers to describe data and code.

The emphasis here is on understanding fundamental concepts, rather than on the syntax of any one specific language. The same concepts can be expressed in very different ways in different languages, but a solid grasp of the underlying principles will be of use regardless of which language you end up using.

Identifiers, Reserved Words, Symbols and Operators

In a programming language, an *identifier* is a human-readable name given to something in the program. Most modern languages share a common lexical form for identifiers: a sequence of alphanumeric characters and underscores, where the first character is not a digit. `DelaySinceMidnight`, `Error17`, and `radius` are all identifiers. `2.746` and `42fish` are not. Some sequences of characters that would otherwise be valid identifiers may be considered *reserved words* or *keywords*, which have special meaning to the compiler and can be used only in certain ways within the rules of the language's syntax. The words `while` and `if` are reserved words in most languages, whereas `otherwise` is a reserved word in some languages but not others. The only way to be sure whether a word is reserved for a given language is to look in a language reference manual for that language.

Certain non-alphanumeric characters may have special meaning in a language. Characters or short groups of characters with special meaning are called *symbols.* In C, the group `//` is a symbol called a *comment delimiter.* Anything from the `//` group to the end of a source code line is a comment that is ignored by the compiler at the preprocessing stage. (Comments, again, are meant to be read by programmers and not compilers.) In Pascal, pairs of curly braces enclose comments. In C, pairs of curly braces group statements and variable declarations to form compound statements. In C the semicolon character is a symbol called a *statement terminator*; it tells the compiler where a statement ends.

Some symbols are used as *operators*, which combine values to generate new values, exactly as familiar symbols like + and – do in an algebraic expression. There are operators in most languages: for familiar operations like addition, subtraction, multiplication, division and raising to a power; for bitwise and logical operations like AND, OR and XOR; for manipulation of character strings and sets; and a few odds and ends like address extraction and modulo maths. Unary operators like negation (-x in C) and bitwise NOT (~x) take one operand; binary operators like addition (x+y) and multiplication (x*y) take two operands; some languages have ternary operators, which take three operands.

Values, Literals and Named Constants

A *value* is a single piece of data used by a program. The numbers 42 and 7.63, and the string "foo" and the Boolean values true and false (which implement Boolean logic in computer languages) are all values. Operators operate on values to create new values. In the expression 42+23, 42 and 23 are both values (in this case they are referred to as *literal values* or *literals* because they appear literally in the expression), as is the result 65, which is created by the + operator at runtime.

It's often useful to give names to literals. Many languages provide a mechanism to define *named constants*, which allow an identifier to be used in place of a literal for more readable code. For example, you may be writing a program that compresses its database after more than 10,000 records are written to the database. You can define a named constant called CompressionThreshold with the value 10,000. This allows you to write a statement like this:

```
If RecordCount > CompressionThreshold:
    CompressDatabase()
```

Named constants allow you to name a value *once* in your program, and use the named value everywhere in your program (which might be hundreds or thousands of places) in place of a literal. That way, if necessary, you can change the definition of the named constant at one place in your program and the compiler will "plug in" the changed literal value consistently everywhere you've used the constant's name. It's either that or change a literal value at all the necessary spots in your source code and just hope you don't miss any!

Variables, Expressions and Assignment

Literals and named constants are values, and by definition are constant at runtime. If you need to change one, you must change its definition in the source code and rebuild. In contrast, *variables* are not values but containers for values. Your program must fill them at runtime with either values given as constants or values computed by an expression. This is called *assigning* a value to a variable, and it's done with an assignment statement, as in the following examples:

- C, C++, Java: TheAnswer = 42;

- Python: TheAnswer = 42

- Pascal: TheAnswer := 42

Although these examples look very similar, there is a little subtlety here. In Python and Pascal the assignment statement is a fundamental syntactic element of the language, whereas in C, C++ and Java assignment is performed as a side effect of the = operator in an expression.

An *expression* is a formula for the runtime calculation of a value using a language's operators and syntax. Expressions may contain literals, named constants and variables that already contain values. If variable R contains the radius of a circle, the circle's area may be computed by using the mathematical formula pi × radius^2. When expressed in a programming language, such a formula becomes an expression. Precisely how it's written depends on a language's syntax. Some languages, including Python, have a separate exponentiation operator. C, C++, Java, and Pascal do not:

- C, C++, Java, Pascal, and many others : `Pi * (R * R)`
- FORTRAN, Python, Ada, and others : `Pi * R**2`

In most languages, parentheses are used to set order of evaluation in expressions, just as they are in mathematical formulae.

Types and Type Definitions

Each data item that a program uses is represented in memory as one or more binary numbers. The meaning of a particular binary number is context-dependent: the byte 00000001_2 might represent the number 1, or the Boolean value `true`; the byte 01000001_2 might represent the number 65, or the character "A" in ASCII encoding. Most high-level languages have a type system, which associates a type with each value. The type allows the compiler or runtime to perform the appropriate operations when values are used, and to detect operations that are semantically meaningless (such as adding a Boolean to a character in many languages, or adding two pointers together in C).

Primitive types are the building blocks of a language's type system. Common primitive types include:

- **Booleans:** These take two values, true and false. A Boolean value can occupy as little as a single bit of storage, though for convenience at least 8 bits (1 byte) are generally used. Although not a requirement, it is common to use zero to represent false, and any non-zero number to represent true.

- **Integers:** Whole numbers, like 42 and –12. Unsigned integers must be positive, and can be represented as straight binary numbers; signed integers may be positive or negative, and are generally stored in two's complement format (which is discussed in more detail in the "Two's Complement and IEEE 754" section). The range of representable integer values depends on the number of bits allocated to the number. C compilers for

32-bit architectures generally allocate 32 bits (4 bytes) to store an integer, giving a range of 0 to 4,294,967,295 for unsigned values.

- **Floats** (floating-point numbers): Can take on fractional values, like 3.4 and –10.77. Floats are often represented in memory as 32 or 64 bits of data, into which are packed a sign bit s, an exponent (the magnitude of the value) e and a mantissa (the value's significant digits) m. The value represented is given by the formula:

m * 2e if s == 0 or

-m * 2e if s == 1

The IEEE 754 standard (which is covered in more detail later in the "Two's Complement and IEEE 754" section) specifies ways of packing s, e and m into words of various lengths, and rules for performing arithmetic operations on numbers stored in this form. Most modern architectures conform to this standard.

- **Characters:** Small (generally 8- or 16-bit) integers, each of which represents a character of printed text.

- **Strings:** Sequences of characters. Some languages provide strings as primitive types, whereas others implement strings as arrays of characters. C strings are null-terminated: the end of the string is marked by placing a special null character (with binary representation zero) in memory. Other languages store the length of the string separately alongside the array of character data or, in the case of Java, define a special class of object to represent strings. Even if strings are not primitive types, it is common to provide language features to make them appear to be. For example, in Java, where each string is represented by an instance of the system class `java.lang.String` (we will cover objects, instances and methods at the end of this chapter), it is legal to write:

String s = "foo" + "bar";

and the compiler silently translates this into a series of calls to methods of the `String` class.

In addition to providing primitive types, most languages provide ways of progressively building up more complex composite types by combining multiple primitive types or simpler composite types. Common varieties of composite types include:

- **Arrays:** Ordered sequences of variables, treated as a unit. Individual elements of an array are selected by an index, often specified using square brackets as index delimiters; for example, `GradeArray[42]`. Arrays may have more than one dimension, and each dimension may be a different size.

- **Structs** (also called *records* or *tuples*, depending on the language): Groups of non-ordered named variables. Each variable in a struct is called a *member* or a *field*. Fields within a struct are selected by name, often using the dot (`.`) field selection operator.

Suppose you have a struct type named ContactStruct that includes a field named LastNameField, and a variable with type ContactStruct called contact. You would then refer to that field of contact using the syntax contact.LastNameField.

- **Sets:** Unordered collections of values, with the property that any value may not be present more than once. The internal implementation of a set is generally optimised to make testing for the presence of a particular value cheap, and facilities are provided to compute the union, intersection and differences of sets efficiently.

- **Maps or dictionaries:** Provide a mechanism for storing a collection of values, each of which is indexed by a key. This can be a seen as a generalisation of the array composite type, often using the same square bracket notation, but allowing keys of (nearly) arbitrary types rather than just integers and eliminating the requirement to specify a maximum size when the array is created.

- **Enumerations:** Unordered collections of values, each given an arbitrary name by the programmer; the value chosen to represent each member is generally chosen automatically by the compiler. They can be used as a type-safe alternative to named constants if we have, for example, a parameter that controls the behaviour of a function and can take one of a small number of distinct values.

- **Pointers:** These specify the location of another value in memory and are generally defined to point to an instance of a specific type. When we have a pointer, we can dereference (follow) it to manipulate the underlying value. Careless use of pointers can lead to hard-to-debug crashes and security exploits, which is one reason that some languages, especially Java, do not include unrestricted pointer types but instead provide runtime-checked, type-safe references to objects or arrays.

Static and Dynamic Typing

Programming languages can be broadly divided into statically and dynamically typed languages based on how they treat types. In *statically typed* languages such as C, types are associated with variables when the code is written, and the type of a value stored in a variable is implicitly that of the variable itself; the compiler is able to allocate storage for variables, and for the intermediate results generated when evaluating expressions, ahead of time, which is efficient, and can perform semantic analysis (as we saw in the section on compilers) to detect and flag operations between incompatible operands at compile time.

In the following fragment of C code, the variable foo has type int, and the variable bar has type float. The compiler knows it can allocate either a single machine register or a 4-byte section of stack to hold each value (on a typical 32-bit machine), and that when adding them together it must (according to the C type rules) emit an instruction to convert or cast foo into a floating-point value, followed by a floating-point add instruction:

```
int foo = 42;
float bar = 98.2;
...
float baz = foo + bar;
```

Throughout the lifetime of a variable in a statically typed language, only compatible values may be assigned to a variable, so the following C example will result in a compilation error:

```
int foo = 42;              // foo has type int
char *bar = "hello world"; // bar has type "pointer to char"
foo = bar;                 // error!
```

By contrast, in *dynamically typed* languages such as Python and JavaScript, types are associated with values at runtime. Variables have no type: they merely contain a reference to a typed value; in a naïve implementation, storage for the value (and a description of its type) will be allocated on the heap and recovered when it is no longer needed by a process of garbage collection. Semantic checks on the types of operands occur at runtime; this is potentially expensive, though the development of tracing JIT's for dynamically typed languages has reduced the cost substantially.

In the following fragment of Python code, the function add() is invoked three times. On the first invocation, x and y refer to two values of type int, so the + operator is deemed to represent integer addition. On the second, x and y refer to two values of type string, so the + operator is deemed to represent concatenation. On the third, x and y have different types, so the attempt to add them causes a TypeError to be thrown. A tracing JIT, such as that found in PyPy, would potentially compile two versions of this function and invoke the appropriate one based on the operand types:

```
def add(x, y):
   return x + y

print add(1, 2)                # prints "3"
print add("hello ", "world")   # prints "hello world"
print add("foo", 1)            # gives TypeError
```

As you will see shortly, statically typed object-oriented languages such as C++ and Java provide some dynamic features through the use of subtype polymorphism. Programmers can declare several types B, C or D, which are derived from type A and rely on dynamic dispatch to do different things depending on which type a particular value is an instance of. Polymorphism comes into play through object-oriented programming, which we'll cover later in the section "Object-Oriented Programming".

Two's Complement and IEEE 754

There are a number of possible ways of representing signed integers as strings of binary digits. Perhaps the most obvious is *sign and magnitude* notation, in which we have a single bit that is set to one if the number represented is negative and a string of digits that represents the unsigned version of the number (its magnitude). Although this is simple to understand, it is unsatisfying that zero has two representations (+0 and –0), and arithmetic operations are somewhat difficult to implement: when we add two signed numbers, we must inspect the sign bits, decide whether to add or subtract the unsigned magnitudes, and then perform conversions to get the result back into sign and magnitude format.

The vast majority of architectures represent numbers using *two's complement* notation. To compute the two's complement representation of a negative number, we write the regular binary representation of the positive number and then invert every bit and add one. For example, the 8-bit binary representation of five is:

$5 = 00000101_2$

To find the representation of -5, we invert each bit:

11111010_2

and add one:

$11111011_2 = -5$

Table 5-1 shows the 8-bit binary and hexadecimal representations of the numbers from 3 down through 0 to -3.

Table 5-1   **A Two's Complement Countdown**

Binary	Hexadecimal	Signed decimal
00000011	03	3
00000010	02	2
00000001	01	1
00000000	00	0
11111111	FF	-1
11111110	FE	-2
11111101	FD	-3

The useful property of two's complement notation is that regular unsigned addition now works to calculate the sum of signed values, regardless of whether they are positive or negative. So, for example:

$1 + -3 = 00000001_2 + 11111101_2 = 11111110_2 = -2$

$-1 + -2 = 1111111_2 + 11111110_2 = 11111101_2$ (with 1 carried out) $= -3$

The situation for real numbers (values that may have decimal parts) is more complex. One possibility is to multiply the real number by a large constant (often a power of two), and then round the result to an integer, which can then be represented using two's-complement notation. We might choose the constant $256 = 2^8$, so the number 1.0 would be represented as 256, and 2.125 would be represented as 544. This is referred to as a *fixed-point* representation, because a fixed number of bits in the representation (in this case 8) are allocated to storing the fractional part of the number, with the rest allocated to storing the integer part.

In most applications, the operations that are performed on real numbers involve values of widely varying magnitude; this can make it hard to choose an appropriate multiplier for a fixed-point representation. It is therefore customary to use a floating-point representation for real numbers, in which there is no fixed number of digits to the right of the decimal point. Floating-point numbers consist of a mantissa (the significant bits of the value), an exponent (the magnitude of the value) and a sign, positive or negative, packed into a single binary word. The representation and range of floating-point values, and the exact results of floating-point operations, were compiler-dependent until the IEEE 754 floating-point number standard appeared in 1985. IEEE 754 defines several floating-point formats that may be used as types in programming languages. The range of some is breathtaking: the 128-bit floating-point number can express positive values as high as 10^{6144}. (To put this number into perspective, consider that there are "only" about 10^{80} atoms in the entire observable universe.) Figure 5-10 shows how the three elements of a floating-point value (the sign, the mantissa and the exponent) are packed into an IEEE 754 64-bit value.

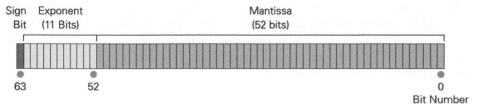

FIGURE 5-10: Inside a 64-bit floating-point number

Code Building Blocks

A single-threaded program in an imperative programming language is a description of a series of steps required to perform an operation. A *statement* is a complete description of one of those steps. It's the equivalent of a sentence in a language spoken by humans. Put some number of statements in sequence, and you have a program. In broad terms, there are really only four kinds of statements:

- **Assignment statements:** These give a value to a variable or an element of a compound variable, as explained a little earlier in this section.

- **Function calls:** These are invocations of functions defined in a library or elsewhere in the program; for example, `print()` or `factorial()`. A function call is typically made simply by naming the function and providing zero or more arguments.

- **Control statements:** These alter the sequence of execution within the current function.

- **Compound statements:** These are sequences of statements treated as a group within some sort of control statement.

Control statements and compounds statements are inextricably connected, and we'll treat them together.

Control Statements and Compound Statements

Being able to change the course of execution of a program at runtime is fundamental to the programming idea. Some statements must be executed under some circumstances but not others. This is called *conditional execution*. Some statements must be executed not once but multiple times. This is called *looping*. An imperative programming language provides varieties of control statement to implement each of these behaviours.

Compound statements are written as sequences of statements between delimiters. In C, C++, C#, Java, and languages descended from them, these delimiters are generally curly braces (`{` and `}`). In Pascal and Ada, the delimiters are the keywords `begin` and `end`. Python is rare among languages in that it lacks delimiters completely. Compound statements in Python are delimited by indentation in the source code. We'll show you how this works in the examples for the control statements.

If/Then/Else

The most fundamental control statement is the `if/then/else` statement, which exists in some form in all programming languages. The general structure of the statement is illustrated in Figure 5-11.

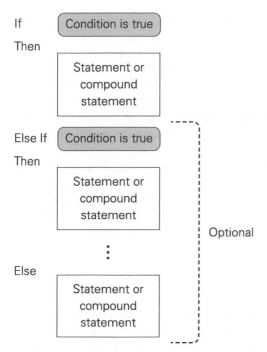

FIGURE 5-11: The if/then/else statement

The simplest form of if statement tests a condition and executes a statement if the condition evaluates to true. If the condition is not true, execution falls through and continues with the statement immediately following the if statement.

To reiterate: *don't obsess on syntax.* You can always look up syntax in a language reference. Focus on the logic. A simple example will give you a sense of the different ways that programming languages express the same logic:

```
if (I > 99) FieldOverflow(Fieldnum, I);       C and its descendants

if I > 99 then FieldOverflow(Fieldnum, I)      Pascal

if I > 99:                                     Python
    FieldOverflow(Fieldnum, I)
```

Note from the examples above that the C family of languages lacks the keyword then, and in Python the colon, line break and indentation are an essential part of the syntax. If you're coming to Python from some other language (especially C or its relatives) it's crucial to remember: Python considers whitespace (line breaks, spaces, and tabs) significant. Very few other programming languages do.

If statements may contain an optional else part, which specifies a statement or compound statement to execute when the tested condition is not true. This is the last portion of the diagram in Figure 5-11. In between then and else you have the opportunity to insert additional tests, each governing execution of a statement or a compound statement. There may be any reasonable number of such nested tests, which are called else/if structures.

What are multiple else/ifs good for? One metaphor would be sorting categories out of a disordered pile. If you have a jar full of coins and want to bag them up for deposit at the bank, you first sit down at the table and sort them. Is the coin a penny? If so, slide it to the penny pile; otherwise, is it two pence? If so, slide it to the two-pence pile; otherwise, is it five pence? If so, slide it to the five-pence pile, and so on, up to the two-pound denomination. This form of logic is called a *multi-way branch*.

Switch and Case

Multi-way branches are so common in programming that in many languages a special type of control statement is provided to implement them. Different languages implement multi-way branch logic in different ways, using different keywords. The C family calls it a switch statement and uses the keyword switch. Pascal and Ada call it a case statement and use the keyword case. (A few languages, including FORTRAN and some versions of BASIC, use select case.)

Unfortunately, the logic behind C's switch is not quite the same as the logic behind Ada's and Pascal's case. The two are different enough, in fact, so that they should be mapped out separately. The general form of a case statement is shown in Figure 5-12. The general form of a switch statement is shown in Figure 5-13.

The case statement is the simpler of the two. In a case statement, a variable is tested against a list of cases. Each case contains an individual value or list of values, generally expressed as constants. If the variable's value matches one of the cases, the statement or compound statement belonging to that case is executed. In the coin metaphor, the case values on the left would literally be the values of each denomination. The statement associated with the penny case would increment a counter that tallies pennies, and so on. In a case statement, once a match is found and the case's action is taken, the case statement is done, and execution continues with the next statement in the program. If no match is found, an optional otherwise case can be used to take a "none of the above" action. In our metaphor, this might be the action taken when a foreign coin like an American quarter or Mexican peso is found in the coin pile.

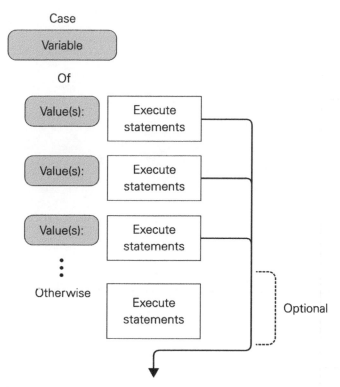

FIGURE 5-12: The case statement

The switch statement is similar, but with a very important twist: once a value is found, the case containing that value is executed, as are all the cases that follow it. If only one case is to be executed, a break statement must be placed at the end of the statements present in that case. A break statement ends the switch statement, and causes execution to continue with the next statement in the program. As with case, an optional "none of the above" case (this time referred to as the default case) can be defined.

This may seem bizarre to beginners, especially if they've used languages with the simpler case statement. The reason for case-action fall-through in switch is historical; it's descended from a FORTRAN statement called a computed goto. In modern practice, there's a break statement at the end of every case except in rare circumstances. When every case ends with a break statement, switch works the same way as case. We'll see the break statement appear again shortly, in connection with loops.

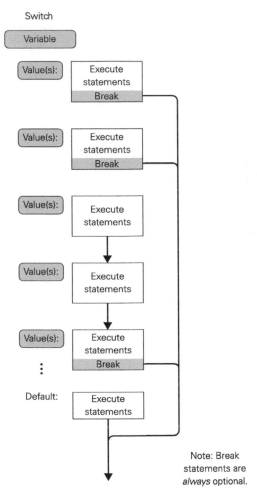

FIGURE 5-13: The switch statement

Python offers neither switch nor case, and multi-way branches must be written either as else/if sequences or by using Python dictionaries and functions, as in the following example:

```
def case_penny():
  print "Got a penny!"
def case_tuppence():
  print "Got a tuppence!"
def case_fivepence():
  print "Got a five pence!"
def default():
  print "Got something else!"
```

```
Coincases = {"1": case_penny, "2": case_tuppence, "5": case_
  fivepence}

x = raw_input("Coin value? ")

if (x) in Coincases:
  Coincases[x]()
else:
  default()
```

Repeat Loops

When a statement or compound statement must be executed multiple times, it's done within a framework called a *loop*. There are three general types of loop in programming:

- **repeat loops:** These take some action and then test a condition. If the condition evaluates to `true`, the loop ends. Otherwise, the action is repeated.

- **while loops:** These test a condition first. If the condition evaluates to `true`, some action is taken. Otherwise, the loop ends.

- **for loops:** These take action once for every value in a collection of values. In computer science this is called *iteration*.

The `repeat` loop is the simplest to understand. It's illustrated in Figure 5-14. The sense of the logic is that some action is repeated until a condition becomes `true`. At that point the loop ends. If the test at the end of the loop turns up `false`, execution returns to the top of the loop and begins again. What's important to remember is that a `repeat` loop's action is always performed at least once.

The `repeat` statement uses the `repeat` and `until` keywords in Pascal and languages descended from Pascal. In C and other C-like languages, `repeat` loops are implemented with the keywords `do` at the beginning of the loop and `while` at the end. The flow of control is the same, but the sense of the test is reversed, so the loop terminates when the test returns `false`.

While Loops

The `while` loop is like a `repeat` loop upside-down: The test is made at the *beginning* of the loop rather than at the end. The condition is tested, and if the test returns `true`, the loop's action is performed. After each pass through the loop, the condition is again tested at the top. When the condition returns `false`, the loop ends. If the condition is initially found to be `false`, the loop ends immediately and its action is never taken at all. See Figure 5-15.

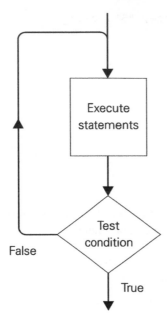

FIGURE 5-14: The repeat statement

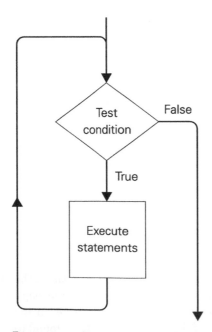

FIGURE 5-15: The while statement

For Loops

There are times when you need to perform an operation once for each element in a collection of values, rather than looping until a condition becomes `true` or `false`. This is called a `for` loop. Some languages restrict `for` loops to iterate over a sequence of monotonically increasing or decreasing integers that differ by a fixed step. So, for example, in Pascal we might write:

```
FOR i := 10 TO 20 DO  { Display every integer from 10 to 20 }
  WRITELN(i);
```

or in some dialects of BASIC it would look like this. (The REM means that the line is a remark; that is, a comment):

```
REM PRINT 0, 2, 4, 6, 8, 10

FOR I = 0 TO 10 STEP 2
  PRINT I
NEXT
```

The variable that takes on the integer value for the current iteration is referred to as the *loop counter*. It's possible that the loop counter is used simply as a counter and takes no part in the work done by the loop statements other than to dictate the number of times that the statements in the loop are executed. Most of the time, however, the loop counter is used to access elements in an array or to take part in some calculation.

Python supports iteration over arbitrary collections of values, so we might write the following. (In Python, a line beginning with "#" is a comment):

```
# print "foo", "bar", "baz"
for s in ["foo", "bar", "baz"]:
  print s
```

A BASIC-like `for` loop can be implemented in Python using the built-in function `range()`, which generates the sequence of integers between a start and an end value with an optional step value. We could write the preceding BASIC example like this:

```
# print 0, 2, 4, 6, 8, 10
for i in range(0, 12, 2):   # ranges do not include the end value
  print i
```

C provides a very flexible for loop construct that behaves like a generalised while loop. It allows the user to specify an initialisation operation to occur before the loop, a loop test that is evaluated before each iteration and must be non-zero for the loop to proceed, and an operation to perform to move to the next element. So we might write the following to iterate over and print every element in a linked list:

```
LINK_T *link;
for (link = start; link != NULL; link = link->next)
  printf ("%d\n", link->payload);
```

Figure 5-16 shows the logic of for loops.

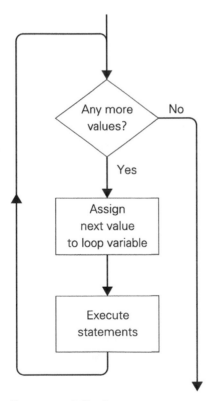

FIGURE 5-16: The for statement

The Break and Continue Statements

Many languages provide two special-purpose control statements that are used almost exclusively in loops. A break statement ends the loop unconditionally. Execution continues with the next statement after the innermost enclosing loop. break may be placed anywhere in the loop, usually under the control of an if/then/else statement inside the loop. (As we saw earlier, the break statement is also used in switch statements.)

The continue statement may also be placed anywhere inside the loop, generally under the control of an if/then/else statement. When executed, continue jumps immediately to the test that governs the loop, so that the test is made again. In a sense, continue "short-circuits" the current pass through the loop. See Figure 5-17 to see the operation of break and continue shown side by side.

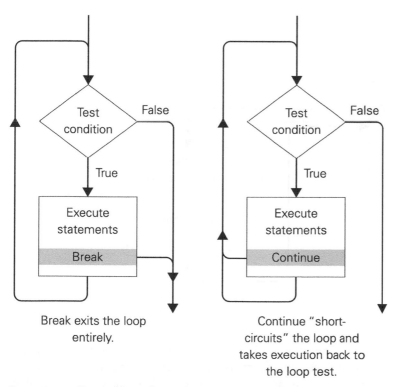

FIGURE 5-17: The break and continue statements

The example shown in Figure 5-17 is a while loop, but break and continue work in all loop types.

NOTE

It's worth remembering that break and continue are not necessarily present in all programming languages. Some languages support one or both under different keywords; for example, continue is implemented in Ruby as the next keyword.

Functions

In an imperative programming language, a *function* is a named sequence of statements. When the function is called from elsewhere in the program, its statements are executed until execution reaches the end of the function or a `return` statement, at which point the function ends and execution continues at the statement following the call to the function (see Figure 5-18). Functions allow common tasks to be defined in one place and used whenever necessary, keeping duplication of code to a minimum.

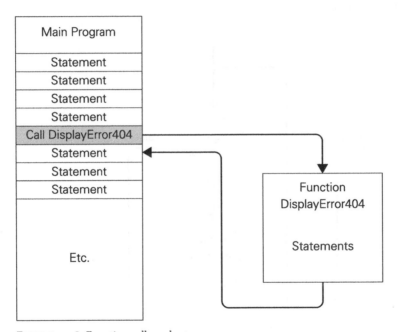

FIGURE 5-18: Function calls and returns

That's how functions operate from an execution standpoint. They have another very important trick: you can pass data values into a function. The function, having made use of those data values, can return one (or in some languages more than one) new value to the code that calls it. Because functions may return values, they can be used in expressions as well as statements. Figure 5-19 shows how this works. The `CalculateArea` function accepts a numeric value representing the radius of a circle, and returns a value calculated as the area of a circle. Radius in, area out.

A function can take zero or more *parameters*, which are special-purpose variables that "carry" values across the gap between the function and the code that calls it. The names and (for statically typed languages) types of a function's parameters are given when the function is defined in your source code. In Figure 5-19, `CalculateArea` has a single parameter, R.

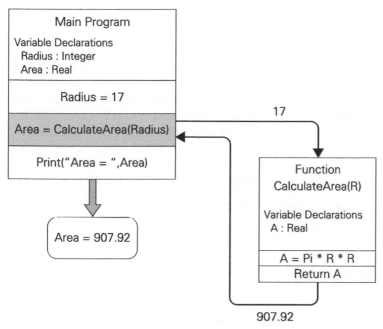

FIGURE 5-19: Passing values to and from functions

When a function is called, we must specify an argument corresponding to each of the function's parameters. An *argument* may be a literal or named constant, or a variable, or the result of an expression. In Figure 5-19, the main program declares a variable named Radius. Radius is assigned the value 17, and is then used as the argument to CalculateArea, providing the initial value of the parameter R. CalculateArea can use R as a variable during calculations. It defines its own variable A, and assigns the calculated area value to it. A is then specified as the function's return value. The function takes the value from A and carries it back to the statement that called it. The main program's variable Area accepts the value from the function and can display it or use it anywhere else a value may be used.

Locality and Scope

A function may define its own constants, variables, types, and even (in many languages) its own functions, like Russian nested dolls. If you're perceptive, the question will soon arise: what if the identifiers that a function defines conflict with those defined elsewhere in the program? If a function defines a variable called Area, and there is already a variable called Area defined outside the function, which variable is accessed when you use the Area identifier?

This problem involves the *scope* of an identifier, which may be simply defined as the places in a program where a given identifier may be "seen" by the code. In most languages, identifiers that are defined within a function are local to that function. Anything defined outside a function is not local to anything so its scope is said to be *global*.

Figure 5-20 illustrates global scope. The example program defines two functions: CalculateArea and CalculatePerimeter. It also defines the constant pi and two variables: Area and Radius. All of these definitions are global. Each of the two functions has its own local definitions. Both define a named constant: TheAnswer. CalculateArea defines a local variable called Area. Each function defines TheAnswer with a different value. Several questions arise:

- If the main program references TheAnswer, which value does it get: 17 or 42?

- Can the CalculateArea function call CalculatePerimeter?

- Can one of the functions redefine pi as 3.0?

- If CalculateArea assigns a value to its local variable Area, is the global variable Area affected? How about vice versa?

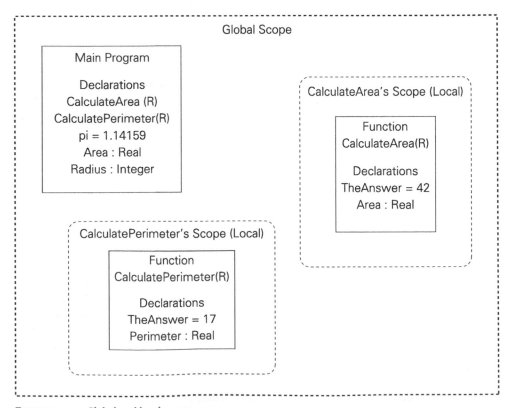

FIGURE 5-20: Global and local scope

These questions can be answered by applying four general rules:

- Local can see global.

- Global can't see local.

- Local can't see other local.

- Local can define a local item under the same identifier as a global item, and thus hide global.

Let's use these rules to answer the four questions:

- The main program can't reference either local definition of `TheAnswer`. Global can't see local.

- `CalculateArea` can call `CalculatePerimeter`. Both functions were defined at global scope, and local can see global.

- Either function could define an identifier called `pi`, giving it the value 3.0, 17.76 or anything else. In doing so it would hide the global constant `pi`: subsequent uses inside the function would see the new identifier, whereas uses elsewhere in the program would continue to see the original one.

- Nothing the main program does to its variable `Area` affects the local variable `Area` defined by `CalculateArea`. Global can't see local. Nor can `CalculateArea` change the main program's global variable `Area`. But wait. . . can't local see global? Of course. But in this case, `CalculateArea` has defined a local variable with the same identifier as a global variable. From `CalculateArea`'s perspective, the global variable `Area` is now hidden because `CalculateArea` used the identifier `Area` to define its own local variable `Area`. The global `Area` is hidden by the local `Area`.

The rules are not there solely to impose order. In most languages (including C, C++, Java, Ada and Pascal) a function's arguments and local variables literally do not exist unless the function has been called and is running. A function's arguments and local variables are set up on the system stack (which is explained in Chapter 4) by the code that calls the function. When the function returns, those arguments and local variables are removed from the stack and no longer exist. Languages like Python still use the idea of scope, even though functions are handled in an entirely different way "under the skin". Scope is a subtle business, and as with almost everything else in programming, the details vary widely from language to language. Worse, there are occasional language implementations that permit certain tricks allowing code to violate the rules of scope. This is always a bad idea.

Scope will come up again in the next section of this chapter.

Object-Oriented Programming

Up to this point, we've drawn a hard distinction between code and the data that code operates upon. For the first three decades of digital computing, tools and development methodologies largely reflected this separation. A programmer would define a collection of functions to perform the operations required of the program, and a collection of concrete data structures (arrays, structs or records and so on) to contain the program's state. For large applications, the choice of functions and structures is typically informed by a *domain modelling process* during the design phase; this aims to capture the relevant real-world entities (perhaps vehicles and people for a government vehicle licensing application), constraints (every vehicle has a single owner) and operations (transferring ownership of a vehicle, applying for a driving licence) in the domain where the program will be used.

In the 1970s, computer science researchers at a number of institutions began to experiment with a new conceptual model for programming, which became known as *object-oriented programming* (OOP). OOP attempts to reduce the semantic gap between the design and implementation phases of the development process by providing facilities at the language level to describe entities and the operations that can be performed on them. A new species of data structure was born—the *object*—which expands on the notion of a struct or record (see the section in this chapter entitled "Types and Type Definitions") by also incorporating the functions that act on its internal data.

The jargon changed, as jargon often does when new concepts appear. Programmers define *classes* of object, which often correspond closely to the entities identified during domain modelling; in the case of our vehicle licensing example the programmer might define a class `Car` and another class `Person`. As the program runs, individual objects will be created in memory, each of which is an *instance* of some class; we might have millions of instances of class `Car`, of which one represents my car, and millions of instances of class `Person`, one of which represents me. A class definition describes the data elements (variously called fields, attributes or properties), which each instance of that class will possess, and a function (generally called a method) for each operation that can be performed on an instance. An instance of `Car` might have a string field `license_plate`, and a field `owner` that refers to the instance of `Person` that corresponds to the car's current owner, and a method `change_owner` to change the current owner. Figure 5-21 provides a summary of this terminology.

Don't get the terms class and object mixed up. A class is a type definition; it exists in your source code. An object is an instance of a class, and is a real data item in memory at runtime, allocated and initialised according to the specifications of its class and the particulars of the language you're using.

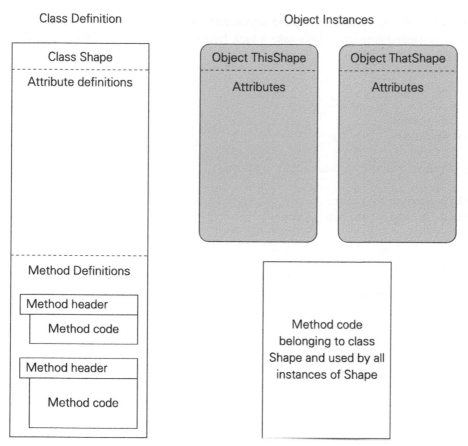

FIGURE 5-21: Classes and objects

In most languages, new objects are initialised by a special constructor method defined in the class definition. When an object is no longer needed, it may be explicitly destroyed (in languages like C++), or removed by automatic garbage collection (in languages that offer it, like Java). Any cleanup required is handled by a special destructor or finaliser method. In most cases, objects are referred to via references, which are effectively pointers to the location in memory where the object's data is stored; when a new object is created, and the constructor has been executed, a reference is returned that can be used to access the object's fields and call its methods.

The syntax for defining classes, for creating objects and for accessing their fields and records varies widely among languages. Let's take a look how a simple version of Car might be defined and used, first in C++:

```cpp
class Car
{
  Person *owner;
  char *plate;

  Car(Person *owner, const char *plate)
  {
    this->owner = owner;
    this->plate = strdup(plate);
  }

  ~Car()
  {
    free(this->plate);
  }

  void set_owner(Person *owner)
  {
    this->owner = owner;
  }
};

Car *my_car = new Car(me, "RN04 KDK");

printf("%s\n", my_car->plate);
my_car->set_owner(you);
```

and now in Python:

```python
class Car:
  def __init__(self, owner, plate):
    self.owner = owner
    self.plate = plate
  def set_owner(self, owner):
    self.owner = owner

my_car = Car(me, "RN04 KDK")

print my_car.plate
my_car.set_owner(you)
```

Most object-oriented languages are share three basic language features:

- **Encapsulation:** Classes define both the data elements (fields) that will be associated with each instance and the code (methods) that operate on them.

- **Inheritance:** A class may be a *subclass* of another class, meaning that it inherits the fields and methods of its *superclass*, to which it adds its own.

- **Polymorphism:** An instance of a subclass may be used in a context where an instance of a superclass is expected.

The next sections look at each of these features in a little more detail.

Encapsulation

The binding together of data with the code that manipulates it is called *encapsulation*. But what is it good for? After all, even in a language that lacks object-oriented (OO) features, nothing stops us from declaring a struct or record type, and writing a function that takes a reference to an instance of that type and performs operations on its elements.

The key distinction is that encapsulation usually implies a mechanism for *data hiding*, which is when the programmer has full control over which fields or methods are visible from outside the object. You can allow code from other parts of the program to "reach in" and directly read or write a field, or call a method, or you can declare the field *private*, which means it can only be accessed by the object's methods. The methods then act as a sort of controlled interface to an object's data. In C++ we might write:

```
class MyClass
{
private:
  int my_attribute;

public:
  int get_attribute();
  void set_attribute(int new_value);
};

MyClass *c = new MyClass();

// these lines will give compile-time errors

int a = c->my_attribute;

c->my_attribute = 42;
```

```
// use the accessor methods instead

int a = c->get_attribute();

c->set_attribute(42);
```

The my_attribute field is declared private (using the access qualifier private), and so is only accessible to the get_attribute() and set_attribute() methods. The compiler can detect and reject attempts to access my_attribute directly.

A brief example may help to explain the importance of data hiding. Suppose you want to create a class that models a child's piggy bank. A piggy bank contains coins of various denominations. The coins have a total value, but it might be interesting to record which denominations are present in the bank, and how many of each are there. The different coins are referred to by an enumerated type CoinConstant, with elements like FivePence, TwentyPence and OnePound. The interface to the object's data will consist of methods to add a coin, remove a coin, report the number of coins of a given denomination and report the total value of all coins. In C++, the skeleton of our class might look like this:

```
class PiggyBank
{
  // some internal state here

public:
  void add_coin(CoinConstant c) { ... }
  void remove_coin(CoinConstant c) { ... }
  int how_many_of(CoinConstant c) { ... }
  int total_value(){ ... }
};
```

The four methods represent the only access that the outside world has to the coin bank object's data. The outside world cannot see the data's internal representation at all.

There are a number of obvious ways to implement the piggy bank class. You could define a private counter field for each coin denomination. Or you could look around and see if there are any predefined library data types that would work as well or better. Most programming languages offer predefined data types called *collections* that include arrays, lists and so on. A *bag* is a collection data type that can tell you whether a particular value is present (in a way similar to the set data type) and also how many times that value is present in the bag. One bag collection inside your object would do almost the entire job of modelling the coin bank.

Whether you define the data yourself or use a "canned" data type instead doesn't matter. The point is that the internal representation of the data remains hidden. If the data inside the coin bank object could be accessed directly from outside the object, outside code could make assumptions about the structure of the data, or change data in ways that have unintended consequences. By limiting data access to a small number of methods, access is controlled completely by the object itself, and you can change the internal representation of the data at any time without fear of breaking outside code that depends on the object's internals.

Taken together, the definitions of a class's methods (and any public data items, if they exist) are called the class's *interface*.

Inheritance

If encapsulation were the sole advantage of OOP, it would still be well worthwhile. OOP has other significant tricks up its sleeve, however, and the next one up for discussion is called inheritance.

Most languages allow new types to be defined in terms of existing types. This is routine and done in various ways, for example an array of real numbers, a set of characters or a struct containing members of several other types. A struct, in fact, may include another struct as one of its members.

This comes close to what *inheritance* is: a class is defined as a child or subclass of an existing class. The child class inherits everything defined in its parent or superclass: all fields and methods defined in the parent class are available in the child class. The child class may add its own fields and methods that did not exist in its parent class; this extends the parent class but does not change the behaviour inherited from the parent class. Inheritance allows that too: a child class may redefine fields and methods belonging to a parent class. We say that the child class *overrides* inherited elements.

Figure 5-22 illustrates how inheritance works. The base class Shape is used to model two-dimensional shapes as might be drawn in a flowcharting program. There's not much in Shape: a constructor, a destructor and the fields x, y and line_width, which define where a shape is located on the screen and how bold a line the shape will use. A child class Circle is later defined as inheriting from Shape. The Circle class gets everything in Shape and adds a new property, Radius. It also defines a new method, Redraw, and defines its own constructor and destructor.

Now, why do it this way? The key to understanding inheritance is to think of classes in a hierarchy that moves from an abstract base class at the top to specific child classes at the bottom. An ellipse is a specific kind of shape. A polygon is another kind of shape. If you're writing a flowcharting program, you would probably define an Ellipse child class and a Polygon child class below Shape. Drawing a rectangle is different from drawing a pentagon, so under Polygon you would then create child classes like Rectangle, Pentagon, Hexagon and so on. Such a hierarchy is shown in Figure 5-23.

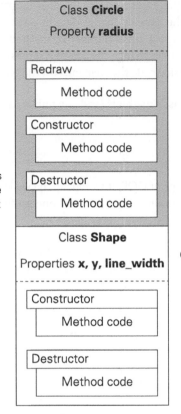

Class **Circle** adds the **radius** property and method **Redraw.**

With class **Shape** as its base class, class **Circle** inherits everything that **Shape** has.

Class **Circle** inherits the **x** and **y** properties.

Class **Shape**'s constructor and destructor are overridden by those of class **Circle.**

FIGURE 5-22: How inheritance works

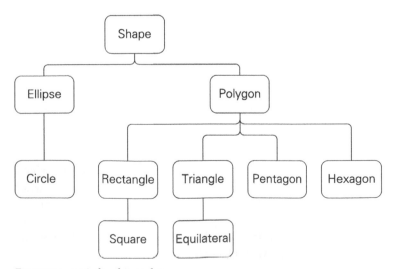

FIGURE 5-23: A class hierarchy

A circle is a special case of an ellipse, and a square is a special case of a rectangle. This is why `Circle` is a child class of `Ellipse`, and `Square` is a child class of `Rectangle`. Classes are generally created as belonging to this kind of hierarchy, with an abstract base class providing the methods and fields that all child classes have. Child classes add specificity, either by defining new methods and fields, or by overriding those that they inherit.

You may already be experienced in this kind of thinking. Consider text styles in a word processor or desktop publishing program. A generic paragraph style might specify the font and the type size and nothing else. You can then define more specific paragraph styles that add first line indents, space before and after, margin insets, bullets and numbering and so on. This is key: *the generic paragraph style contains only those style items that all paragraphs have.* This provides a default font and type size for all paragraphs—and also allows you to change the font in all paragraph styles by changing it only once in the basic paragraph style. Because the more specific paragraph styles are, in a sense, child classes of the basic paragraph style, they inherit the font and type size and can override it to whatever they need for the specific types of paragraph that they are.

If you have some grounding in OOP, it may occur to you that the example shown in Figure 5-22 isn't optimal. You're right, it isn't—but to explain why, we first have to explain the third leg in OOP's three-legged stool: polymorphism.

Polymorphism

Key to the idea of object-oriented programming is that objects know what to do. If we want to draw a shape object, we call its `Redraw()` method. The object knows what sort of shape it is, and its `Redraw()` method allows it to redraw itself on the screen according to its class. The redrawing itself is done in class-specific ways, but the method name is the same for all shapes.

It sounds odd at first, but in OOP, you don't always have to know the precise class of an object in order to call one of its methods. This feature goes by the heavy-duty word *polymorphism*, from the Greek for "many shapes". Because objects know what to do, you simply have to tell them to go do it. You don't have to tell them how.

A good metaphor for polymorphism is the humble farmer. There are many kinds of farmer who grow many different kinds of crops. However, all farmers have certain tasks in common: they prepare the ground, plant, tend and harvest. Each of these tasks is done in a different way for different crops; harvesting tomatoes is nothing like harvesting wheat. Tomato farmers know how to harvest tomatoes, and wheat farmers know how to harvest wheat. If a government weather office predicts that an early killer frost is coming later in the week, it would be enough to call or text all the farmers in the frost area with a simple message: "Harvest your crops now". The weather office people don't need to tell the farmers how to do their harvesting. The farmers know how. Telling them to start harvesting is enough.

In the programming world, polymorphism acts on classes in a hierarchy. If the base class in the hierarchy defines a method, then all classes that descend from it have that method. Each class may override the method with class specifics, but all classes in the hierarchy respond to a call to that particular method.

How does this work in practice? Let's go back to our shapes example, and the scenario illustrated in Figure 5-24. A number of shape objects have been created, and all have been added to a collection. (We described the idea of collections earlier in this chapter in the section entitled "Types and Type Definitions".) Here, the collection is defined as a list of class Shape. Inside, the list is really a list of pointers to objects of class Shape. We can step through the list and perform an operation on each object in the list. In this case, for each object in the list, we call Redraw(). It works because all classes descending from class Shape contain everything that Shape contains. If class Shape contains the Redraw() method, so do all of its descendants.

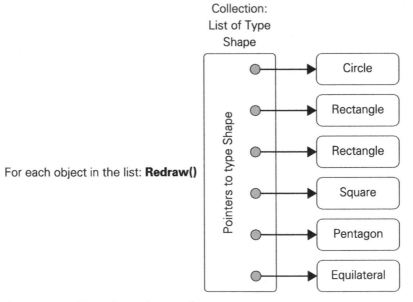

FIGURE 5-24: How polymorphism works

This is why the example as originally configured in Figure 5-22 isn't ideal. The Redraw() method wasn't present in class Shape because Shape is so generic that there's nothing to draw. However, if we intend to use polymorphism to call a method, that method must be present throughout the hierarchy. The proper place for the Redraw() method is in the hierarchy's base class Shape, from which all other shape classes descend. This is true even if the Redraw() method is empty. A class like Shape that is not intended to be instantiated is called an *abstract class*. The whole purpose of an abstract class is to ensure that particular methods are defined in all classes that descend from the abstract class.

Polymorphism comes free in dynamically typed languages like Python and Smalltalk, because an association between an identifier and an object may be changed at any time, and every object carries with it type information that can be used to resolve which version of the method to call. In C++, however, the type of an identifier is determined at compile time, which can cause problems. Consider the following code:

```
class Rectangle
{
  void name()
  {
    printf("Rectangle!\n");
  }
};

class Square : public Rectangle
{
  void name()
  {
    printf("Square!\n");
  }
};

Rectangle *r = new Rectangle();
r->name();              // prints "Rectangle"

Square *s = new Square();
s->name();              // prints "Square!"

Rectangle *r = new Square();
r->name();              // prints "Rectangle!" even though r
                        // points to an instance of Square
```

This defines a class `Rectangle`, with a method `name()` that prints "`Rectangle!`", and a subclass `Square`, which overrides `name()` to print "`Square!`". We instantiate a `Rectangle`, and call its `name()` method, which prints "`Rectangle!`", as expected. Next we instantiate a `Square`, and call its `name()` method, which prints "`Square!`", again as expected. The third example is more perplexing at first glance. We instantiate a `Square`, but store the pointer in an identifier that has type `Rectangle *` (pointer to `Rectangle`); this is semantically legal, as `Square` is a child of `Rectangle`, so every `Square` is also a `Rectangle`. However, when we call `name()`, the program prints "`Rectangle!`" rather than "`Square!`".

The reason for this is that the compiler decides which version of the `name()` method to call based on the type of the pointer `r`, rather than on the type of the object it points to.

The fix for statically typed languages is called *dynamic dispatch*, which looks at the object itself to determine the appropriate method body to invoke. A common mechanism for implementing dynamic dispatch is to have each object carry around a pointer to its class's virtual method table, which points to the appropriate implementation of each method. In C++ methods must be explicitly tagged as `virtual` to be included in the virtual method table and thus be available for polymorphic calls; methods that are not flagged as virtual are subject to static dispatch.

OOP Wrapup

OOP is both a programming technology and a way of thinking about structuring code and data. The basic idea is that data should be defined along with the code that manipulates it. A data type defining code and data together is a class. An object is an instance of a class; that is, a data item created in memory according to its class definition. Three basic principles define OOP:

- **Encapsulation:** Combines code and data into classes, and allows the programmer to control access to a class's code and data through the use of access qualifiers and class functions called methods which have privileged access to fields.

- **Inheritance:** Allows us to define a class as an extension of another class. Everything the parent class defines is inherited by the child class. This allows related classes to be combined into a hierarchy of classes moving from a generic parent at the root to specific descendant classes at the leaves.

- **Polymorphism:** Allows related classes in a hierarchy to respond to method calls in cases where the caller does not know the precise type of the object on which is it calling the method. Metaphorically, the caller tells an object, "Do X: you know how", and relies on dynamic dispatch to ensure that the correct implementation is called.

The details of how OOP is implemented vary significantly by language, and especially by whether a language is statically typed (C++, Object Pascal) or dynamically typed (Python, Smalltalk) but many of the principles are the same.

A Tour of the GNU Compiler Collection Toolset

If you want to try native code programming on the Raspberry Pi, the easiest way involves a set of compilers and tools that predates Linux itself. Linux is written in C (with a very small amount of assembly language) and the GNU Compiler Collection (GCC) is the toolset used to build Linux from its source code files. The GCC is preinstalled in Raspbian Linux. This section takes you on a quick tour of the GCC toolset, with a test program in C.

gcc as Both Compiler and Builder

The gcc is more than a set of compilers and utilities. The gcc program itself (always written in lowercase) is nominally the C compiler of the collection. However, in addition to being a compiler it's also a sort of build supervisor. When you launch gcc to build a C program, gcc in turn launches several other tools present in the collection to complete the build. The gcc build process includes these four steps:

- **Preprocessing:** Expands macros and include files. To accomplish this step, gcc launches a preprocessor utility called cpp.

- **Compiling:** Translates a preprocessed C file into its intermediate code, which for gcc is assembly language source code. The gcc program does the compilation itself.

- **Assembly:** Translates the assembly language source code into native object code. The gcc program launches the GNU assembler, as, to perform this step.

- **Linking:** Converts and binds together one or more object code files into a single native code executable file. The gcc program launches the GNU linker, ld, to perform this step.

All four of these steps may be accomplished by a single invocation of the gcc program. To see how it works, let's build the classic "Hello, World!" program in C, using the gcc.

To begin, open the Raspbian file manager and create a work folder somewhere under the pi folder. It doesn't matter what the folder is called; tests will work fine. Next, open a text editor window and enter the following short program:

```
#include <stdio.h>

int main (void)
{
printf ("Hello, world!\n");
return 0;
}
```

Save the C source code to a file named hello.c in your work folder. Navigate to your work folder with the file manager to be sure the file was saved. Then press the F4 key to open your work folder in a terminal window. (If F4 doesn't launch a terminal window in the editing environment you're using, you will have to launch one manually.) Enter the following command at the terminal command line:

```
gcc hello.c -o hello
```

This command turns gcc loose on your source code file, and uses the -o option to direct it to generate an executable file named hello. (In general, Linux executable files don't have file extensions.) Assuming you entered the source code correctly, gcc will do its work and return to the command-line prompt. In your work directory will now be the files hello.c and hello.

To run the executable, enter this command:

```
./hello
```

The message will appear in the terminal window:

```
Hello, world!
```

Now, let's do it again, one piece at a time. Erase the executable file hello, and then execute this command in the terminal window:

```
cpp hello.c -o hello.i
```

The program cpp is the preprocessor utility. The -o command tells it to create an output file named hello.i. You'll see the file appear in the file manager window. You can open hello.i in a text editor, but unless you've had some experience in C, it won't make much sense to you. Basically, your test program is at the end, and the bulk of the rest consists of external function headers (in place of that #include preprocessor directive at the top of the original source) that allow your program to call functions in the standard C library.

The next step is to compile the preprocessed source code to intermediate code. Enter this command:

```
gcc -S hello.i
```

Compilation is something that gcc itself does. The output in this case is hello.s, which is the program compiled into assembly language source code. The -S (uppercase) command tells gcc to create assembly source code and then stop. You can open hello.s in a text editor to see the assembly source code, and it's an interesting exercise to see if you can follow the logic. Even if you're writing in pure C on the Raspberry Pi, studying ARM assembly language may come in handy if you ever have to debug a peculiar problem. If you're feeling really ambitious, or intend to pursue assembly language systematically, try invoking gcc with the options -O1, -O2, and -O3 and then examining the code in the generated .s files. These three options (which use the letter "O" and not the digit "0," by the way) instruct the compiler to apply increasingly sophisticated levels of optimization to the generated code.

That said, there's a caution here: don't try to learn how to write assembly language by using the assembly language source output of gcc as a model. A .s file produced by gcc contains all kinds of things that are necessary to generate machine code from a program originally written in C. Writing assembly language is a separate discipline, and you should learn it by reading books on assembly language.

If you're not convinced, take a look at hello.s in a text editor. Then compare it to the "Hello, World!" program as written from scratch in assembly language:

```
.data

message:
.asciz "\nHello, World!\n"

.text

.global main

main:
push {lr}    @ Save return address on stack
ldr r0, message_address    @ Load message address into R0
bl puts  @ Call puts() function in clib
pop {pc} @ Return by popping return address into PC

message_address: .word message

.global puts
```

In C work, it's best simply to let assembly language be an intermediate language.

The third step is to assemble hello.s to an object-code file. Enter this command:

```
as -o hello.o hello.s
```

This time, we're using as, the GNU assembler. It will produce the object code file hello.o. Object code files contain binary machine instructions, and you can't open them in a text editor to examine them in any useful way.

You can't execute them either. That takes one last step, which is linking hello.o with a fair number of other things in the C runtime library. Unfortunately, linking a C program manually by invoking the linker ld at the command line is a very complicated business, and it is where gcc's skills as a build manager really come in handy. Instead of having you type in hundreds of characters, we'll run gcc again in *verbose mode*, during which it will display every command it issues to cpp, as, and ld. Enter this command:

```
gcc -v hello.c -o hello
```

The –v command puts gcc in verbose mode. As you'll see, while your terminal screen fills up and scrolls, it's verbose with a vengeance. There's a lesson here too: building a program is often complex even when the program itself is trivially simple. Unless you have a very good reason not to, let gcc do the heavily lifting on C projects.

Using Linux Make

The gcc compiler is actually very good at managing the complexity of the build process, but it has limits. Once you go beyond simple test programs like "Hello, World!" you should study Linux make. In general terms, a *make utility* is a software mechanism that coordinates the compilation and linking of multiple source code files into a single executable file. Make utilities pay special attention to two things:

- **Dependencies:** What source code files depend on what other files to provide functions, data definitions, constants and so on.

- **Timestamps:** When a source code file was last changed, and when object code files and executables were last built.

When we say that File X *depends* on File Y, we mean that we need File Y to build File X. Furthermore, a change in File Y requires that File X be rebuilt, otherwise File X may make assumptions about code or data defined in File Y that are no longer true. That can cause several kinds of error. For example, if a variable called Distance is defined in File Y as an integer, code in File X will use integer maths to manipulate the Distance variable. If we change Distance to a floating-point number in File Y, the integer maths code in File X may no longer work correctly. We then have to modify and rebuild File X to match the changes we made earlier in File Y.

Files may depend upon files that in turn depend upon other files. This is called a *dependency chain*. We saw this on our quick tour of gcc: an executable file depends upon one or more object files, which in turn depend upon one or more source files (see Figure 5-25).

In Figure 5-25, a dependency chain begins at any block and follows the arrows to the executable file. All object files depend on their source files. The Library A object file depends on the Library A source file, and so on. Application Modules 2 and 3 both make calls into Library A, so both depend on Library A. Neither depends on Library B. Application Module 1 makes calls only into Library B, so it depends on Library B but not Library A. All chains end at the executable. This means that the executable file depends on everything.

The brute-force way to avoid problems when building the application executable is to rebuild *everything* whenever *anything* changes anywhere in the chart. That may work for simple projects, but once there are eight or 10 source code files, lots of time will be wasted rebuilding code that doesn't depend on anything that has changed since the last build.

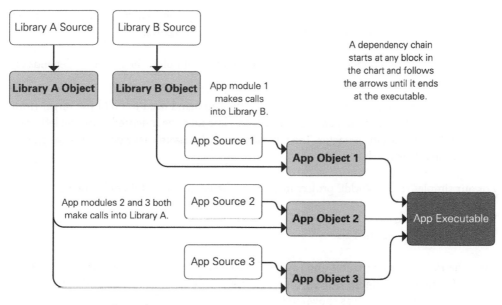

FIGURE 5-25: Dependency chains

The make utility automates the build process. It uses file timestamps to determine what has to be rebuilt and what doesn't. If an object file is newer than its source file, it means that any changes made to the source file are already reflected in the object file. Once edits are made to the source code, the source file will be newer than the object file. The make utility then invokes whatever tools are necessary to rebuild the object file.

The same is true of object code files that make use of code or data in other object code files. In Figure 5-25, the App 1 object code file calls functions in Library B. So when the Library B source code changes, Library B has to be rebuilt. However, because Application Module 1 calls functions in Library B, any changes to Library B will require that Application Module 1 be rebuilt as well. Because the application executable depends on everything, it must be newer than everything. Once some part of a dependency chain becomes newer than the application, the whole chain starting at the newer file must be rebuilt.

How does the make utility know what depends on what? It needs a road map, and on Linux operating systems, the road map is called a *makefile*. The makefile is a simple text file that describes dependencies among files, and how files are to be rebuilt. Its default name is `makefile`. If you define a project folder and all project files are present in that folder, you can use the default name. Once you have a makefile that describes your project, you can kick off a build by simply executing the program `make` in a terminal window. Even if there's only a single source code file in your project, it's less keyboarding to simply type `make` than, for example, `gcc hello.c -o hello`.

In its simplest form (as you'll encounter it while learning a new language or programming generally) a makefile is a sequence of rules. Each rule has two parts:

- A line defining a target file and one or more component files. The target file depends on the component files.

- A line immediately beneath it specifying the command used to build the target from its components. In Linux make, this second line must be indented from the left margin by a single tab character. The tab character helps make easily determine which line in the rule is which.

For our simple "Hello, World!" project in C, the makefile would contain only one rule:

```
hello: hello.c
  gcc hello.c -o hello
```

Type the rule into a text editor and save it as makefile, with no file extension. Then type make. If your executable file is older than your source file, hello.c, make will rebuild your executable by running gcc as shown in the second line of the rule.

As explained earlier, gcc hides some of the complexity of a build by automatically executing the preprocessor, assembler and linker as needed. If you're not using compilers in gcc, you may have to spell out the steps separately in your makefile. Here's an example makefile that invokes a non-gcc assembler and the gcc linker separately to create an executable:

```
hellosyscall: hellosyscall.o
  ld -o hellosyscall.o hellosyscall
hellosyscall.o: hellosyscall.asm
  nasm -f elf -g -F stabs hellosyscall.asm
```

Rules generally begin with the executable file and work back from there. The preceding make-file begins with the rule defining the dependency of the executable file on its object file, and how the executable is created with the linker ld. The second rule defines the dependency of the object file hellosyscall.o on hellosyscall.asm, and how the object file is built from the source file with a non-gcc assembler called nasm.

If your project has libraries or multiple modules with separate source code files, those rules would be included after rules building the executable. As a rule of thumb: the file that depends on everything (generally the executable) has the first rule in the makefile. The file or files that depend upon nothing but their own source would be last. Look back at Figure 5-25 and trace out its dependency chains if this isn't clear to you.

Chapter 6
Non-Volatile Storage

NON-VOLATILE DATA STORAGE has been available since long before anyone ever dreamed about computers. Human memory has a limited lifespan, but spoken language allows information to cross the gap between individuals, allowing that information to live longer than any single person. Human memory, however, is prone to errors and data loss. The development of written language means that information can be placed somewhere independent of human memory, at least as long as there is someone who knows how to interpret the language it's written in. Books, for example, have been called "software that runs in the mind"—an apt metaphor. More to the point, books are data storage that serves the human computer inside our skulls. They address permanence and the imprecision of memory. Interpretation is up to us.

Understanding archaic written languages, and ancient scripts such as Mycenaean Linear A, has been a problem in archaeology. Archaeologists have discovered good examples of characters arranged in groups, which may be words; but sadly, the language they express has been forgotten for at least 3,000 years. **NOTE**

This chapter looks at computer data storage that falls outside the computer-memory partnership. (In Chapter 3, we discussed computer memory in detail.) Data storage outside the CPU and electronic memory is often called *mass storage* because its capacity far exceeds that of conventional computer memory. A more precise term is non-volatile storage, which expresses the primary value of mass storage: its contents remain intact even when the computer powers down or the storage medium is disconnected from the computer. With the short-lived exceptions of magnetic disk and drum memory and later magnetic core memory, computer main memory has been *volatile*, which means its data vanishes when the power drops or the computer malfunctions in other ways.

Punched Cards and Tape

The earliest mass-storage technologies had a lot in common with books: they were composed of paper. Also, they were developed to serve technologies that were not computers, and not, in fact, electronic at all. In the same ways that computers were built on the shoulders of calculators, paper-based storage drew on early communications and tabulation machinery.

Punched Cards

Just as writing might be considered "meaningful ink markings applied to paper", paper-based mass storage is basically meaningful holes punched in paper or pasteboard. What many call the "IBM card" or "computer punched card" is older than IBM and much older than computers. Although the idea of a punched card goes back to Charles Babbage, and before him to the Jacquard Loom, widespread use of data stored on punched cards began with Herman Hollerith, who created a card-based system to tabulate data from the American census of 1890. The original Hollerith card placed round holes at standardised locations on the card, for the sake of mechanical tabulators, but the meaning of each hole was defined by whoever was using the cards. The first-generation tabulator machines were purely mechanical and simply counted holes in a given position on the card. Later machines incorporated electro-mechanical counters that could do limited cross-tabulation on the cards—for example, tabulating how many instances there were of cards containing punches at several specific locations at once. This allowed the Census Bureau to count easily the number of women aged 18 to 35 or the number of men in a household working in agriculture, and so on.

The Hollerith technology was wildly successful. Hollerith's 1896 Tabulating Machine Company later merged with three other similar firms, and under the leadership of Thomas Watson the company became International Business Machines (IBM). The punched card format of 80 columns of 12 rectangular holes on a card measuring 7 ⅜" × 3 ¼" with a cropped corner to define orientation was standardised in 1929; it remained basically the same until the technology went out of broad use in the 1980s. (A picture of a late-era IBM card is shown in the previous chapter, Figure 5-3.) The meaning of holes adhered to no single standard and remained application-specific for many years. Extended Binary Coded Decimal Interchange Code (EBCDIC), the first strong standard for encoding characters on IBM cards, did not appear until 1964 and was introduced with the System/360 mainframe.

Tape Data Storage

As papermaking technology grew good enough to manufacture continuous lengths of paper tape, inventors began using it for data storage. Scottish inventor Alexander Bain incorporated a crude punched tape system to feed his 1846 experimental "chemical teletype", which used an electric current to print marks on chemically treated paper. Although electrome-chanical teleprinters were used sporadically from the 1850s on, the Teletype machine as we know it today did not really become a force until it was standardised and given a typewriter-style keyboard in the first quarter of the twentieth century. Messages were encoded by punching hole patterns in a length of paper tape, and the tape was queued up to be fed into the telegraph system as time allowed. The first standardised encoding system for teleprinter paper tape was originally devised by Emile Baudot in the 1870s and later adapted for tele-printer use by Donald Murray around 1900. The Baudot-Murray code (generally abbreviated to "Baudot") used combinations of holes in five columns. The 5-bit Baudot code remained the standard for teleprinters for more than 60 years, until the 7-bit American Standard for Code Information Interchange (ASCII) system was introduced in 1963.

The use of teleprinter paper tape in computing was almost accidental. The 1930 Model 15 Teletype console was the mainstay of the world's teleprinter network for almost 30 years. It was rugged and highly configurable, and it could be operated by someone who hadn't had extensive training. However, it had serious shortcomings: the machine's 5-bit Baudot code could only express 60 different values in two groups of 30, which were selected by two shift codes. This was enough to express upper-case characters, numeric digits and common punc-tuation, plus a handful of control codes like bell and carriage return. Lower-case characters did not become possible on teleprinter hardware until the mid-1960s.

A committee was convened by the American Standards Association in 1960 to establish a modernised standard for communications data encoding. Among other goals, the X3.2 com-mittee wanted to expand encoding to allow lower-case characters and more punctuation. This required at least 7 bits, and when the ASCII standard was released in 1964, it was a 7-bit code. Eight-row paper tape systems were being deployed at that time, which allowed ASCII encoding plus a single parity bit on each row to help detect characters that had been garbled in transmission. The ASCII character codes are shown in Figure 6-1. Each entry in the chart shows the character plus its hexadecimal and decimal numeric equivalents.

Eight-row tape allowed something else: binary encoding of 8-bit quantities. Minicomputer manufacturers designed their interfaces to allow the use of inexpensive Teletype consoles like the mid-1960s Model 33 ASR. They were mass-produced and thus much less expensive than IBM's computer line printers. In addition to acting as operator consoles, the Model 33 eight-row tape punches and readers could store and read binary data, one byte per row. Given the high cost of IBM's magnetic tape systems (more on this shortly), the use of paper tape in minicomputer shops was a natural, and it continued until minicomputers themselves passed out of broad use in the 1980s. A sample of 8-bit paper tape is shown in Figure 6-2.

Late in the paper tape era, tapes made of Mylar became available, which made the tape much more resistant to wear and damage. Using any sort of punched tape for archiving was a slow process, but it was by far the least expensive archiving technology available for small systems until the advent of floppy diskettes.

Hex	Dec	Char	Hex	Dec	Char	Hex	Dec	Char	Hex	Dec	Char	Hex	Dec	Char	Hex	Dec	Char	Hex	Dec	Char	Hex	Dec	Char
00	0	NUL	10	16	DLE	20	32		30	48	0	40	64	@	50	80	P	60	96	`	70	112	p
01	1	SOH	11	17	DC1	21	33	!	31	49	1	41	65	A	51	81	Q	61	97	a	71	113	q
02	2	STX	12	18	DC2	22	34	"	32	50	2	42	66	B	52	82	R	62	98	b	72	114	r
03	3	ETX	13	19	DC3	23	35	#	33	51	3	43	67	C	53	83	S	63	99	c	73	115	s
04	4	EOT	14	20	DC4	24	36	$	34	52	4	44	68	D	54	84	T	64	100	d	74	116	t
05	5	ENQ	15	21	NAK	25	37	%	35	53	5	45	69	E	55	85	U	65	101	e	75	117	u
06	6	ACK	16	22	SYN	26	38	&	36	54	6	46	70	F	56	86	V	66	102	f	76	118	v
07	7	BEL	17	23	ETB	27	39	'	37	55	7	47	71	G	57	87	W	67	103	g	77	119	w
08	8	BS	18	24	CAN	28	40	(	38	56	8	48	72	H	58	88	X	68	104	h	78	120	x
09	9	TAB	19	25	EM	29	41	)	39	57	9	49	73	I	59	89	Y	69	105	i	79	121	y
0A	10	LF	1A	26	SUB	2A	42	*	3A	58	:	4A	74	J	5A	90	Z	6A	106	j	7A	122	z
0B	11	VT	1B	27	ESC	2B	43	+	3B	59	;	4B	75	K	5B	91	[	6B	107	k	7B	123	{
0C	12	FF	1C	28	FS	2C	44	,	3C	60	<	4C	76	L	5C	92	\	6C	108	l	7C	124		
0D	13	CR	1D	29	GS	2D	45	-	3D	61	=	4D	77	M	5D	93	]	6D	109	m	7D	125	}
0E	14	NUL	1E	30	RS	2E	46	.	3E	62	>	4E	78	N	5E	94	^	6E	110	n	7E	126	~
0F	15	SI	1F	31	US	2F	47	/	3F	63	?	4F	79	O	5F	95	_	6F	111	o	7F	127	

FIGURE 6-1: ASCII character encoding

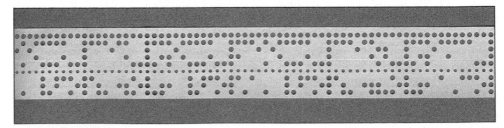

FIGURE 6-2: 8-bit paper tape

One of the key attributes of both punched card and paper tape storage is that it was purely *sequential*. Cards ran through the reader one at a time, in order. Data was read from the tape, one 5- or 8-bit row at a time. It was not just sequential, it was sequential in one direction: forward. Theoretically paper tape could be run backwards through a reader, but in practice commercial tape readers ran tape in only one direction. This meant that random access to data on cards or tape was simply impossible. Something approaching tape random access became possible only when IBM developed 9-track bidirectional magnetic tape decks in 1964. After that innovation appeared, paper tape's days were numbered, and it was increasingly confined to low-end minicomputers like those from Digital Equipment Corporation.

The Dawn of Magnetic Storage

Paper tape is important in the history of computing mostly because it brought the ASCII character encoding system out of telecommunications and made it the standard in non-mainframe computing. As mainframes themselves were traded in for server farms, ASCII eventually dominated the computer industry from top to bottom.

Paper tape was nowhere near the most popular tape storage ever created. In 1953, IBM introduced its vacuum-tube 701 series of mainframe computers. Mass storage for the 701 series consisted of IBM punched cards and a new technology for IBM: magnetic tape. The 727 tape drive was not the first magnetic tape deck (Univac had one by 1951) but it was the drive that brought magnetic tape storage into the mainstream. A single 2,400ft reel of ½" cellulose acetate (later Mylar) tape could hold roughly 6 megabytes (MB) and transfer data from tape to the central processing unit (CPU) at a speed of 15,000 characters per second. The 727's successor, the IBM 729, could store 11MB on a similar reel and had a peak transfer rate of 90,000 characters per second. By the end of the mainframe magnetic tape era, the typical IBM magnetic tape deck could write 140MB on a 2,400ft reel, and transfer data at 1,250,000 8-bit characters or binary bytes per second.

After the introduction of IBM's System/360 in 1964, tapes stored data on 9-track reels, with 8 data bits written in parallel across eight of the tracks and a parity bit in the ninth track for checking data integrity. The System/360 line also introduced the EBCDIC character-encoding standard, which IBM had created in 1963 to bring order to character encoding across its very broad product line. EBCDIC was an 8-bit standard that could express 256 different characters. It included lower-case characters from the outset, as well as a significant number of unassigned codes that were used in local applications for non-English characters and special-purpose symbols. These local variations made EBCDIC harder to use than 7-bit ASCII, and although EBCDIC was a universal encoding standard on IBM hardware until nearly the end of the mainframe era, ASCII eventually replaced it, even on IBM hardware. The general problem of non-English character encoding was eventually solved by the Unicode system, which established standards for expressing more than 100,000 distinct characters (at the time of writing) using both 8-bit and 16-bit encodings.

Magnetic tape outlasted mainframes and remains in limited use to this day. Early low-end microcomputers used off-the-shelf consumer audio cassette decks for non-volatile storage of programs and data. Even after floppy diskettes became common, audio cassettes were used for archival backup due to their low cost. Information was typically encoded using a simple modulation scheme such as frequency-shift keying (FSK), in which zeros and ones are sent as pure tones of different frequencies, and an ordinary 90-minute cassette could contain about 650 kilobytes (KB) per side.

Since the 1980s, nearly all magnetic tape-based mass storage systems have used tape completely enclosed in cartridges. This eliminates any need for the user to hand-thread the tape, and allows the rapid removal and replacement of one tape data set with another by unskilled operators. High-capacity tape cartridges are still in use for archival backup, although cloud-based backup on remote servers is gradually replacing tape as the primary commercial archiving technology, with tape surviving mostly on "legacy" (older) hardware.

Let's take a much closer look at how magnetic recording works.

Magnetic Recording and Encoding Schemes

Digital magnetic tape technology was adapted from analog audio tape systems perfected by German firms (especially BASF) before and during World War II. The fundamental mechanism is the same irrespective of the shape of the underlying storage medium. In truth, it hasn't changed radically since IBM's early magnetic tape systems.

In simple terms, it works like this: a very small electromagnet with a microscopic gap between its poles is positioned above a moving magnetic medium, such that the gap is closest to the medium. The electromagnet is called a *head*. Early systems used the same coil and core for both reading and writing. Modern systems use separate heads for reading and writing, but they're mounted together and move together.

For many years the separate read heads were smaller versions of the inductive write heads, but still used the same basic electromagnet-centred design. In the early 1990s, IBM created magnetoresistive (MR) read heads, which were smaller and more sensitive than was possible with inductive read heads. MR heads use a minute length of magnetoresistive material, which changes its resistance in response to changes in the magnetic flux beneath it. MR heads are much more sensitive than inductive heads, which makes it possible for the variations in magnetisation of the magnetic medium to be smaller, allowing more bits to be recorded in the same area. In 2000, IBM took MR head technology further still, using a related physical effect called giant magnetoresistance (GMR) to increase head sensitivity significantly over that of MR heads. GMR read heads and perpendicular write heads together triggered the explosion in hard drive capacity that today gives us multi-terabyte storage on a single drive.

The magnetic coating applied to tape or disk platters consists of minute grains of some magnetic material. Early tape and disk systems used red iron oxide; later systems used chromium oxide. Modern hard drives use exotic cobalt-nickel alloys. Even though the grains are roughly spherical, each can act as a separate magnet, complete with distinct north and south magnetic poles. Recording data involves aligning the magnetisation of a number of adjacent grains to form a single *magnetic domain*. This magnetisation is accomplished by sending a controlled electric current through the write head. The direction of alignment of the domains that pass under the head's gap depends on the direction of an electric current through the head's write coil.

Flux Transitions

The boundary between two magnetic domains is referred to as a ***flux transition***. It turns out that the read head, whether of a conventional inductive design, or using MR or GMR, can more accurately sense the magnetic field associated with a flux transition than the field associated with the domains themselves. Rather than using the domains to directly represent binary data (with one orientation representing a 0-bit, and the opposite orientation a 1-bit), the control electronics use an encoding scheme to impose a pattern of flux transitions on the medium to represent the data. Numerous schemes have been used over the history of magnetic recording; the trend has been towards more sophisticated schemes that make more efficient use of the medium (that is, they require fewer flux transitions on average to represent each bit). As well as representing the data, a scheme must generally meet two further criteria, regardless of the data written:

- **Timing recovery:** The pattern written to the medium must contain reasonably frequent flux transitions to allow the control electronics to synchronise the position of the head.

- **Low digital sum:** There should be an approximately equal number of domains of each orientation, so that the medium as a whole has no magnetic field.

One of the simplest (and earliest) encoding schemes is *frequency modulation* (FM), in which the difference between a 0-bit and a 1-bit is in the frequency with which flux transitions appear on the magnetic medium, as shown in Figure 6-3. A *bit cell* is a region on the medium in which a single bit is encoded. Bit cells are all the same physical length. A bit cell with a single flux transition at the beginning is interpreted as a 0-bit. A bit cell with a flux transition at the beginning and another in the middle is interpreted as a 1-bit.

FM encoding wastes space on the magnetic medium because it requires room for two flux reversals per bit. Modern encoding techniques make much better use of space through mechanisms like run-length limited (RLL) coding; these encoding schemes process several input bits at once and are thereby able to reduce the average number of flux reversals per bit while still meeting timing and digital sum requirements.

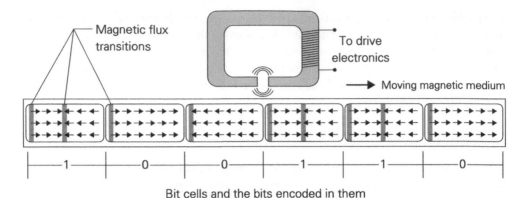

Bit cells and the bits encoded in them

FIGURE 6-3: Magnetic recording of data bits

Pay close attention to the direction of the arrows in Figure 6-3. After a flux transition, the magnetic orientation of the medium doesn't change until the next flux transition. The actual direction of magnetic orientation doesn't matter, as you can see if you compare the direction shown in the several regions expressing 0-bits. What matters is how many orientation changes (that is, flux reversals) occur per bit cell.

Perpendicular Recording

The mechanism shown in Figure 6-3 is called *longitudinal recording*. This means that the magnetic domains in the medium are magnetised in a direction parallel to the moving magnetic medium. Key to longitudinal recording is the position of the read/write head over the moving medium. The two poles of the head and the gap between them are parallel to the medium, resulting in parallel orientation of the magnetic domains within the grains.

Longitudinal recording techniques used in hard drives began to reach density limits in the late 1990s. The orientation of a magnetic domain can spontaneously flip due to thermal effects, with the result that magnetic recordings tend to degrade over time; this process is semi-affectionately known as "bit rot". The stability of a domain is strongly influenced by its size, and by the coercivity of the storage medium. As longitudinal recording grew denser, the typical lifetime of the magnetic domain orientation in the medium grew shorter until error rates made the technology unworkable.

> **NOTE** Not all magnetised materials are equally good at keeping their magnetism. The degree to which a magnetised material can resist demagnetisation is called its *coercivity*. Materials with high coercivity are difficult to demagnetise, and are used for permanent magnets. Materials with low coercivity can be magnetised and demagnetised with relative ease. Low-coercivity materials are used in magnetic storage media like magnetic tapes and disks, where bits are encoded as magnetic regions that may be changed as data is written and rewritten.

The solution appeared in the mid-2000s when perpendicular recording was developed. Magnetising the grains in a direction perpendicular to the plane of the drive platter, as opposed to in the plane for longitudinal recording, delivered improved long-term stability. This in turn permitted a further increase in density. Two innovations made this possible:

- The write head was redesigned so that the magnetic lines of force were concentrated at one of the head's magnetic poles and spread out at the opposite magnetic pole. The flux density at the narrow pole was concentrated enough to cause flux transitions, whereas the same flux at the wide pole was not. Only one pole was effective, and for that reason the head came to be called a monopole. The high field strength near the monopole allows the use of a magnetic medium with higher coercivity, which directly increased domain stability.

- To draw the magnetic flux down from the write head in a vertical direction, a magnetic layer was deposited on the hard drive platter beneath the magnetic medium. The material in this layer was engineered to easily conduct magnetic flux without becoming magnetised. It pulls the flux down from the narrow pole and conducts it beneath the magnetic medium until the wide pole draws it back up into the head.

Figure 6-4 illustrates this scheme, which is called *perpendicular recording*. The mechanism is rarely used in tape storage because the mechanical instability of tape makes the desired densities difficult to attain. The huge density increases in hard drives in the last five years are almost entirely due to the change from longitudinal to perpendicular recording. Without it, today's inexpensive multi-terabyte drives would be impossible.

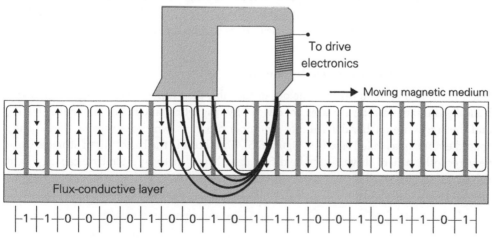

FIGURE 6-4: Perpendicular recording

Magnetic Disk Storage

The first rotating magnetic disk storage was non-volatile but it was not mass storage; it was main memory, and the short-lived successor of the short-lived magnetic drum. (See Chapter 3 for more on early magnetic disk and drum memory.) Magnetic disks were not used for mass storage until IBM's Model 305 Random Access Memory Accounting Machine (RAMAC) was introduced in 1956. The key difference between early head-per-track rotating disk main memory and RAMAC's disk storage was that RAMAC's drive used multiple platters and moving read/write heads. The unit stored about 5MB on fifty 24-inch magnetic platters. Access time was between 600 and 750 milliseconds. The disk unit alone weighed about a metric tonne and had to be moved by forklift.

The great challenge with early hard drive technology was that the platters were not sealed, and even with aggressive air filtering, smoke and dust particles got between the platters and the read/write heads and caused disk crashes. The amount of space between the heads and the platters had to be larger than the size of typical dust particles, which limited the density of storage on the platters. In 1973, the IBM 3340 Winchester drive subsystem introduced a sealed disk mechanism in which the read/write heads, positioner arms and servos, and the platters themselves, were a fully enclosed unit. This reduced head crashes and allowed other economies that assumed a clean operating environment. Heads could be moved closer to the platter surfaces, and used aerodynamic principles (flying heads) to maintain a specified distance from the platters with great precision.

Hard drives were too expensive for use on desktop computers until Alan Shugart's company Seagate Technology introduced the ST-506 5 ½" hard drive in 1980. It stored 5MB and was deliberately made to be the same physical size as full-height 5 ¼" floppy drives so it could fit in personal computer floppy drive bays. It originally cost £1,000. Mass production, and the entry of other firms into the market, caused prices to drop rapidly during the 1980s.

Cylinders, Tracks and Sectors

From the time that hard drives came out of the labs, their lowest level of organisation was basically the same: platter surfaces are divided by magnetic markers into concentric tracks, and the tracks are further divided into a number of *sectors*, which are separated by equally spaced empty areas called *gaps* (see Figure 6-5). The sector is the basic unit of storage. Until very recently, a hard drive sector held 512 data bytes. In today's terabyte-capacity hard drives, using such small sectors wastes drive space. Since 2012, most new hard drive designs use a standard called Advanced Format, which increases sector size to 4,096 data bytes.

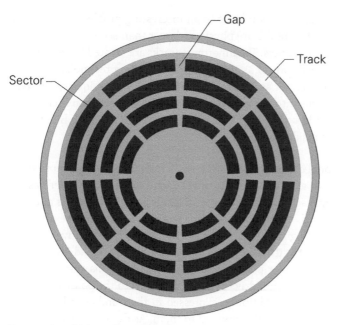

FIGURE 6-5: Disk tracks and sectors

A sector contains more than data bytes alone. Sectors are divided into fields:

- **Sync field:** Marks the beginning of a sector and also acts as a timing marker that allows drive electronics to make sure that the read/write heads are synchronised to the platter.

- **Address mark field:** Contains the sector's number, its position on the disk and some status information.

- **Data field:** Contains the sector's actual data. As mentioned earlier, this is generally either 512 bytes or 4,096 bytes.

- **Error Correction Code (ECC) field:** Contains about 50 bytes of parity information on a 512-byte sector for error detection and correction. (See Chapter 3 for more about ECC technology.)

The Advanced Format consolidates eight 512-byte sectors into a single 4,096 sector, and saves about 10 percent of disk space by consolidating eight gaps, sync fields and address fields into one. The ECC field must be larger for error handling on longer sectors. However, the ECC field for an Advanced Format sector is only twice the length of the ECC field for a 512 byte sector, rather than eight times the length, so space gains can be made there as well.

The geometry of track and sector organisation leads to an interesting problem: the sectors towards the rim of drive platter in Figure 6-5 are physically larger than sectors closer to the hub, and yet store the same number of bytes. The innermost tracks are created to be as dense (in terms of bits per unit of linear distance) as the magnetic recording technology allows, which means that the outer tracks are not as dense as they could be. A technique called *zone bit recording* divides a platter's tracks into zones and places more sectors in zones closer to the rim. This keeps the number of bits per linear unit roughly constant from the hub to the rim and allows the disk to store considerably more data.

From the beginning of the personal computer hard drive era, drives incorporated more than one platter, and used both sides of all platters in the drive. Each side of each platter has its own read and write heads. A single actuator arm moves all heads across all platters at once. At any given time, all heads access the same track on their respective platters. The set of all tracks that lie under the heads at any given time is called a *cylinder*. Early hard drive controllers specified the location of data on the drive in terms of cylinder number, head number (to indicate a particular side of one particular platter) and sector number. This system, called *cylinder-head-sector* (CHS), worked well until drive capacity increased to the point where the number of heads, cylinders or sectors could not be expressed in the number of bits that a computer's Basic Input/Output System (BIOS) allocated to them. As drive controller intelligence moved from external controllers to integrated (on-drive) controllers, a new system called *logical block addressing* (LBA) was used to locate data within a drive. In a drive equipped with LBA (as all drives have been since 1996), sectors are identified as logical blocks, each with a single logical block number counted from 0. The on-drive controller translates between the LBA and whatever combination of cylinders, tracks and sectors that the drive contains. Neither the BIOS nor the operating system (OS) is explicitly aware of the internal arrangement of any given drive. However, logical blocks are in general numbered in the same physical order as they exist on the disk. Some OS disk access scheduling algorithms make use of this fact to ensure efficient use of the disk.

Low-Level Formatting

Before a hard drive can be used, magnetic markers defining tracks and sectors must be laid down on all its platter surfaces. This process is called *low-level formatting*. The broader term "formatting" really encompasses three things, all of which must be done before a drive can be put into service:

- **Low-level formatting:** Defines the actual physical tracks and sectors on disk platters.
- **Partitioning:** Divides a drive into separate logical regions, each of which can operate independently of all the others, almost as though all partitions were separate hard drives.

- **High-level formatting:** Sets up a mechanism for organising a drive's sectors into folders and files. This is done according to the requirements of OS components called *file systems*.

Read more about partitioning and high-level formatting later in this chapter in the "Partitions and File Systems" section.   **NOTE**

Until about the mid-1990s, low-level formatting was done after a hard drive was physically installed inside the end user's computer. The formatting was accomplished either by a separate software utility or by routines in the machine's BIOS. As the density of hard drive recording increased, the precision of the sync markers (also called *servo markers*, because they were used in a servo feedback system controlling head position) became difficult for the drive's physical mechanisms to achieve. To achieve the precision that drive reliability required, manufacturers began performing low-level formatting on drive platters before they were installed in the drive. This is handled with a machine called a *servo writer*, which is capable of higher precision than the drive's inexpensive arm and head positioning system.

In current drives, low-level formatting cannot be completed after the drive is assembled. Manufacturers have recognised a need for repurposing drives and have provided users with utilities to perform drive reinitialisation. The utilities do two major things:

- The drive's platter surfaces are scanned for sectors that cannot be read from or written to. Such bad sectors are marked so that they will not be used after reinitialisation.

- All data stored on the drive is overwritten with some binary pattern, which may be one or more bytes in length. This removes user data, as well as partitions and file systems, and basically returns the drive to the empty state it had when it was first installed.

There is some question as to whether data can be recovered from a drive after reinitialisation. If the utility really does write a pattern over every byte in every sector (and especially if it does this more than once) it becomes extremely difficult to recover data. To save time, some reinitialisation utilities eliminate partitions and file systems but do not try to overwrite every sector. In many cases there is a separate utility or menu option called secure erase that must be executed separately and might take many hours to wipe a drive with a capacity beyond one terabyte.

Because magnetic recording basically uses analog magnetic marks to encode digital data, it may be possible to dismantle a drive and examine the platters using special equipment that detects traces of older recording around the edges of new recording. Such traces are called *data remanence*. The limited precision of the drive's head-positioning mechanism makes this possible. In applications where data simply cannot be allowed to remain on a drive, such as in the military, the drive itself is physically destroyed, generally by dismantling the drive and grinding the coating off the platters or shattering platters made of glass. Ordinary users can achieve levels of security suitable for home use by hitting a drive several times with a 10-kilo sledgehammer.

Interfaces and Controllers

Alan Shugart's seminal ST-506 drive was "dumb"; its electronics could only move the heads to a requested position and impose or recover data bits using the heads. The intelligence was all in its external controller board, which was installed on the computer's expansion bus and connected to the drive with three separate cables: drive control, drive data and power. The controller accepted requests from the OS for a particular sector, and translated those requests into head motion commands that the drive could execute directly. This ST-506 interface and its higher-performance successor, ST-412, dominated small computer systems until the late 1980s.

The evolution of hard drive storage involved more than packing ever-denser data storage onto the platters. A good bit of it lay in migrating disk control from the external controller board into the disk drive itself. In the 1980s, the Small Computer Systems Interface (SCSI) provided a high-speed interface to arbitrary storage devices, which could include tape, disk, optical disk or almost anything else that stored data. SCSI moved some intelligence to the storage device, largely with the goal of masking the details of the physical storage technology from the computer. SCSI devices were more expensive than ST-412 devices, and when the lower-cost Integrated Drive Electronics (IDE) disk drives appeared in 1986, they quickly became the standard in low-cost personal computing. The IDE interface moved nearly all controller intelligence into the drive's on-board electronics, and the external interface board was just that: a way to bridge a computer's expansion bus to the drive's integrated controller. When the IDE interface was standardised by ANSI in 1994, it became known as the AT Attachment (ATA) interface, and later as PATA (for Parallel ATA) to distinguish it from the Serial ATA (SATA) interface, which was introduced in 2003. The ATA interface uses a single cable, which carries 16 data lines and all necessary control lines.

As described earlier, LBA hides the details of internal drive organisation from the computer and its OS. However, the size of the LBA block numbers was limited by the number of bits allocated to them. The earliest IDE block numbers were 22 bits in size, which (with industry standard 512-byte sectors as blocks) could specify only 2GB of storage. The ATA standard increased the block numbers to 28 bits, which allowed 137GB of storage. It was not until the arrival of the ATA version 6 specification in 2001 that block numbers were allocated 48 bits, allowing 144 petabytes of storage. (A petabyte is 1,000 terabytes.)

By the end of the 1990s, ATA throughput was beginning to push the physical limits of the connection between computer and drive. In 2003, a new drive interface standard was published: Serial ATA (SATA). Most of the innovation lay in the physical interface between computer and drive. In SATA, data passes serially over two sets of two shielded conductors, rather than in parallel across 16 unshielded cable conductors, as in PATA.

The most significant difference between PATA and SATA lies all the way at the bottom, in the electrical interface between the controller and the host. PATA uses *single-ended signalling*, which means that each data path travels over a single wire, encoded as a varying voltage referenced against a common ground. Each of PATA's 16 data lines has its own wire on the interconnect cable, as do the various control signals. Single-ended signalling has been used widely in low-speed parallel and serial connections since the days of telegraphy. The RS232 interface uses single-ended signalling, as does VGA video, PS/2 mouse and keyboard connections, and so on.

The problem with single-ended signalling is that crosstalk from other signal lines or external electrical interference can corrupt data passing over the link. A technique called *differential signalling* was developed to address the interference issue. In differential signalling, each data path requires two wires, and a signal is encoded as the difference between the voltage levels on the two wires. Because the two wires are physically adjacent, and often twisted together, interference tends to affect both at once, changing their voltage levels relative to ground but preserving the difference. A circuit called a **differential amplifier** at the receiver detects the difference in voltage between the two signal wires and outputs a clean signal irrespective of random voltage changes common to both wires. Differential signalling allows the use of lower voltage swings, and higher clock speeds, than single-ended signalling, while still providing adequate noise immunity.

PATA uses a 3.3V or 5V swing, and a typical clock speed of 33MHz for a throughput of 133 megabytes per second (MB/s). SATA incorporates differential signalling with a nominal swing of only 250mV and an effective clock rate (for SATA 3.0) of up to 3GHz for a throughput of around 600MB/s.

SATA offers a degree of backward compatibility with PATA drives by using the ATA command set, albeit over a radically different electrical interface. SATA also introduced *hot swapping*, which is the ability to disconnect and replace a drive without powering-down or rebooting the computer. This can be done without fear of damaging the drive; however, the OS must be capable of ensuring that the drive can be removed without corrupting its buffers and configuration data, as well as detecting a new drive inserted in the place of the old.

The Raspberry Pi uses a Secure Digital (SD) format flash card for its primary non-volatile storage, and does not include a drive interface for SATA. Disk drives may be connected to the Raspberry Pi using one of the board's USB ports, which are described in detail in Chapter 12. You can read about flash storage technology and SD cards later in this chapter.

Floppy Disk Drives

Rotating disk drives with removable media far predate microcomputers. IBM, again, spear-headed the technology, introducing the first removable hard disk pack for the Model 1401 mainframe in 1962. The seminal 1973 Xerox Alto workstation foreshadowed the use of removable magnetic disk storage on desktop personal computers by incorporating a 2.5MB single-platter disk cartridge in every unit. IBM developed an 8" (200 millimetre) read-only removable drive unit with flexible media in 1971, originally to store microcode that had to be loaded each time certain System/370 mainframe models were powered up. This flexible "memory disk" remained a mainframe technology until 1972, when Alan Shugart left IBM for Memorex, which created the first inexpensive read/write flexible-medium drive—the Memorex 650. Shugart later formed Shugart Associates to create a small business computer, an effort hampered by the sheer size of the Memorex-style 8" drives to be manufactured for it. Shugart developed the far less bulky 5 ¼" version of the technology to serve the emerging microcomputer market, and while the business computer never left its labs, the firm quickly became the leader in flexible-medium magnetic storage. The term "floppy" was coined in the trade press in about 1970, and was used because the magnetic medium was a coating on thin circular Mylar sheet rather than a rigid platter. The Mylar sheet was informally called a "cookie". The formal term for the cookie mounted inside a protective sleeve was *diskette*.

Early floppy-disk technologies had an interesting way of marking the positions of storage sectors on the flexible medium: equally spaced holes were punched in the cookie near the hub, and each of these sector holes marked the beginning of a new sector. One additional hole was punched in the cookie halfway between two of the sector holes. This was the track index hole, which told the floppy drive the angular position at which the first sector in each track began. A scheme depending on holes for sector positioning was called *hard sectoring* because track and sector positions were dictated by physical holes and could not be changed. Later generations of floppy technology were *soft sectored*, meaning that the sector positions were defined by magnetic markers written to the cookie by the drive heads, as with hard drives. Soft sectoring allowed the density of the diskette to be changed (and thus its capacity) without physical changes to the medium.

Several higher-capacity variations on the floppy disk concept saw broad use from the late 1980s to the early 2000s, including the Iomega Bernoulli Box (10MB) and zip drives (100 and 250MB) and the Compaq SuperDisk drives (120 and 240MB), which would also read conventional 1.44 MB 3 ½" diskettes. Inexpensive CD-ROM drives made the floppy disk less necessary during the late 1990s, and once CD-ROM drives became read/write instead of read-only, the floppy diskette was on its way out. It is no coincidence that floppy disk drives pretty much vanished from consumer-class PCs entirely about the time that USB 2.0 flash-based thumb drives became reliable and inexpensive. The flash storage medium used in thumb drives is smaller, faster, and longer lived, as described in more detail in the "Flash Storage" section later in this chapter.

Partitions and File Systems

The process called *partitioning* divides a physical drive unit into multiple logical units called partitions. Operating systems regard each partition as a separate logical device; a common application of partitioning is to support simultaneous installation of multiple operating systems on a single physical storage device, with each operating system's root file system occupying a separate partition. Much of the technology and terminology around partitioning dates back to the dawn of the PC era, and was introduced in PC DOS 2.0 to support the first consumer-class hard drives for the IBM PC/XT.

At the lowest level, a partition is simply a range of contiguous sectors on a physical drive. How partitions are created and managed is heavily dependent on the overall architecture of the computer (for example, Wintel versus Mac versus Unix) as well as the OS doing the creating and managing. There can be large differences among versions of the same OS: Windows Vista and its successors handle partitioning in a way that is very different from (and incompatible with) Windows 9x, 2000 and XP. What we describe here is a high-level simplification of disk organisation that leaves out many of these details.

Primary Partitions and Extended Partitions

The first sector on a partitioned device contains the master boot record (MBR). The MBR contains a short piece of executable code known as a *bootloader*—which on IBM PC-compatible machines is responsible for loading the OS kernel into random access memory (RAM)—and a table of partition descriptors called the *partition table*. The default number of entries in the table is four. (Certain third-party partitioners/boot managers can increase this to as many as 16, at the cost of rendering the partitioning scheme as a whole incompatible with conventional MBRs.) Each of these four entries describes a *primary partition* and contains the following information:

- A status code indicating whether the partition is active (bootable.) This value is used to select the boot partition in the absence of a boot utility like the one built into Windows, or grub for Linux

- The starting LBA sector number of the partition

- The length of the partition, in sectors

- The location of the first and last sectors of the partition expressed as Cylinder-Head-Sector (CHS) numbers

- The partition ID code, which in most cases specifies which file system the partition was formatted for, and what special attributes the partition may have.

Figure 6-6 illustrates the MBR and partition table.

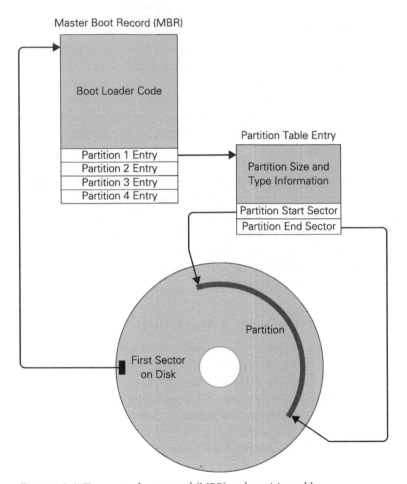

FIGURE 6-6: The master boot record (MBR) and partition table

The limit of four primary partitions is arbitrary and came about in the effort to provide both a minimal bootloader and partition definition data in a single 512-byte sector. Demand for greater flexibility in partitioning led to the development of the extended partition concept in the mid-1980s. An *extended partition* is a primary partition modified to allow it to act as a sort of partition container. Only one of the four primary partitions may be used as an extended partition. Within the sectors allocated to an extended partition, multiple logical partitions may be allocated. Each logical partition has an extended boot record (EBR) that defines its size, type and start/end sector addresses. There is no master table of logical partition descriptors, and thus no arbitrary limit on the number of logical partitions that may be defined. Instead of a table, each individual EBR contains a sector address field that points to the next EBR within the extended partition. The EBRs are thus arranged in a structure called a *linked list*, with each entry in the list pointing to the next. The pointer field is zero-filled to indicate the last EBR in the list.

File Systems and High-Level Formatting

A logical partition on a hard drive is nothing more than a block of sectors offering undifferentiated storage space. Operating systems require components called *file systems* to organise and manage a partition's sectors in a useful way. Provided a logical partition follows the rules laid out in the file system specification, different operating systems with potentially different implementations of the file system software will be able to read and write to the partition interchangeably.

Nearly all file systems organise mass storage volumes as *files* (blocks of storage containing data) and *directories*, which are hierarchical structures acting as indexes for both files and child directories. (Directories are called *folders* in some operating systems.) Internally, file systems are implemented as tables associating file and directory names with blocks of storage space to contain the file contents, and with file metadata. These blocks are contiguous groups of sectors called clusters or allocation units. How file system tables are structured and organised differs by file system, but at some level nearly all file systems consist of tables linked to other tables in data structures called *trees*. (For more on this, see Chapter 8.)

Disk partitions are generally created with a specific file system in mind, and the partitioning tool lays out the foundation of that file system during the partitioning process. This is why you'll see partitions referred to specifically as New Technology File System (NTFS) partitions or ext4 partitions or any of the many different file systems available on desktop computers. ("ext4" is not an acronym and simply means the fourth generation of the Linux extended file system.) During the process of high-level formatting, an empty file system of the appropriate sort is written to the partition. High-level formatting is a fast process that generally replaces a populated directory tree with an empty root directory entry, within which new files and directories may be created. In most cases the underlying data, and large parts of the file system tables, are not overwritten, so utilities exist that can recover most or all of a file system after its volume has been high-level formatted.

High-level formatting may also include options to scan a volume for bad sectors, or for overwriting data with zeros or bit patterns for security reasons. Such operations make the high-level formatting process considerably more time-consuming.

The Future: GUID Partition Tables (GPTs)

The basic mechanism behind FAT has been with us since the DOS era in the early 1980s. It's been enhanced and extended many times, but it still has a number of serious and probably unfixable problems. The three most serious issues are these:

- The MBR exists at only one place on a disk, and if the sole copy of the MBR is damaged or overwritten, the contents of the entire disk may be lost.

- MBR-based systems cannot handle drives with more than 2 terabytes capacity. With 3TB and 4TB drives now common and reasonably inexpensive, this significantly limits the storage that may be installed on one PC.

- MBR is arbitrarily limited to four primary partitions. Getting past this limit requires creating an extended partition with logical partitions inside it, which is an awkward workaround for a problem that shouldn't have existed to begin with.

In the last few years, an entirely new drive organization technology has come on the scene: *GUID partition tables* (GPTs.) GUID means *globally unique identifier*, and it means that literally: a GPT partition is assigned a 122-bit value generated at random that is almost guaranteed to be unique. There are 2^{122} or 3.5×10^{36} possible GUID values, so with good random number generators the likelihood of duplicate GUIDs is almost nil.

The number of partitions GPT supports is basically unlimited, and whatever limits exist are limits of the OS. Windows, for example, only supports 128 GPT partitions because it only allocates 128 partition entries. Also, limits on drive size are for all practical purposes gone. A drive may be up to 8 zebibytes, which is 9.4×10^{21} bytes. Drives of this size will not be arriving any time soon.

GPT finesses the danger of damaging the MBR by creating multiple instances of its partition tables and other crucial data scattered across the drive, and if the primary instance is damaged, GPT can repair it using another instance elsewhere on the drive. GPT stores its data with CRC (cyclic redundancy check) values to assist in reconstructing any damaged data.

Against the possibility that "legacy" tools assuming the presence of an MBR partition may overwrite essential GPT data, GPT provides a feature called a "protective MBR", which is an MBR describing the entire drive as a single partition. The protective MBR is not intended for ordinary use. Legacy tools that access the protective MBR may not work in all details, but at very least the tools will not assume a missing or corrupt MBR and write a new one that corrupts GPT data.

Describing GPT operation in detail is beyond the scope of this book. For more on the topic, see https://en.wikipedia.org/wiki/GUID_Partition_Table.

Partitions on the Raspberry Pi SD Card

While most of the preceding discussion of the history of partitioning has centred on rotating magnetic media, more modern solid-state storage technologies such as SD cards and USB flash drives have inherited the same approach to dividing a bulk physical medium into logical partitions composed of individually addressable sectors. An SD card containing the Raspbian OS is typically divided into two partitions. One, the *boot partition*, is only 60MB. It must be formatted specifically for a virtual file allocation table (FAT) file system (either FAT16 or FAT32) and contains only the code and data necessary to initialise the graphics processing unit (GPU), and bring the OS kernel into memory and run it. The other partition, usually called the *root partition*, contains the rest of the OS and all of your files, and at time of writing is formatted with the ext4 Linux file system. Raspbian does not use a separate swap partition, but instead swaps to a file located in the root file system. Swapping is to be avoided at (nearly) all costs on the Raspberry Pi, as discussed towards the end of Chapter 3.

The Raspberry Pi's boot sequence is a little different from desktop and laptop systems. The BCM2835 boot ROM contains a small piece of code that runs on the VPU (video processing unit) a proprietary reduced instruction set computer (RISC) core that forms part of the GPU. The boot ROM loads a first-stage boot loader with the filename `bootcode.bin` from the FAT boot partition, which in turn loads the main firmware file `start.elf`. Finally, `start.elf` reads an OS kernel from the file `kernel.img` (for armv6 CPUs) or `kernel7.img` (for armv7 and armv8 CPUs) into the start of memory and releases the ARM (Advanced RISC Machine) CPU from reset, which in turn loads the OS proper. Which kernel file the bootloader reads depends on which board you have: the first-generation Raspberry Pi boards have armv6 CPUs and require the `kernel.img` file. The Raspberry Pi 2 and after use `kernel7.img`.

The Raspberry Pi 3 incorporates a 64-bit armv8 Cortex A-53 CPU, but a separate 64-bit OS kernel does not exist at this writing. The Raspberry Pi 3 uses `kernel7.img` and runs in 32-bit mode. The Raspberry Pi foundation chose the Cortex A-53 because it runs very well in 32-bit mode, while having 64-bit features that may be exploited in the future.

NOTE

Since mid-2013, the Raspberry Pi Foundation has provided a utility to make installation of a bootable OS a great deal easier. The system is called the New Out-of-Box Software (NOOBS), and you may downloaded it without charge from the Foundation's download page at `www.raspberrypi.org/downloads`.

A full install of NOOBS requires a minimum of 4GB of SD card space. When you boot the Raspberry Pi for the first time, NOOBS displays a menu of several operating systems and asks which ones you want to install. It then installs your chosen operating system, either from the network or from an image file on the SD card, and allows you to select which of the installed operating systems to boot. NOOBS remains available at boot time, allowing you to repair an existing install or install additional operating systems and edit their configuration files.

For more on Raspberry Pi operating systems and operating systems generally, see Chapter 8.

Optical Discs

Although optical mass-storage technology was first successfully demonstrated around 1960, the goal was video recording rather than data recording. High-end consumer video players using the 30cm analog LaserDisc format appeared in 1978, and while there were some adaptations for computer data storage, none were successful due to high costs and the sheer bulk of the individual discs, which weighed almost 400 grams. It wasn't until the fully digital audio CD format appeared in the early 1980s that inexpensive digital optical storage became possible.

Most read-only optical disc technologies work like this: digital information is imposed as patterns of microscopic pits pressed into a disc of polycarbonate plastic along a spiral track, beginning at the hub of the disc and running towards the outer edge. After pressing, the polycarbonate disc is coated with an extremely thin layer of aluminium metal, and then enclosed in transparent acrylic. A beam from a laser diode follows the spiral track, and a photodiode interprets laser light reflected from the disc. The pits—and the flat regions that separate them, called *lands*—are of variable length. Pits have a depth equal to one quarter of the laser's wavelength, such that light reflected from the bottom of a pit is 180° out of phase with light reflected from the surrounding surface, and destructively interferes with it, resulting in a dimmer reflection from pits than from lands. The spiral track reflects the origins of optical storage as a sound and video technology because those are purely serial in nature. (Further back, it echoes vinyl sound recordings, which encoded sound as analog "waviness" along a spiral track pressed into soft plastic.)

As with hard disk storage, it turns out to be easier to detect transitions between pits and lands than it is to detect the features themselves. Rather than using pits to represent binary 0s and lands to represent binary 1s, the CD standard instead encodes a binary 1 as a change from pit to land or vice versa, and a binary 0 as a continuation of the current pit or land for a short distance. See Figure 6-7 for an example. A further layer of RLL coding, known as *eight-to-fourteen modulation* (EFM) is applied to assist in timing recovery and to maintain a small overall digital sum (the number of binary 1s minus the number of binary 0s).

NOTE   A *photodiode* is a special semiconductor junction diode (a two-element semiconductor device) formulated so that the junction is sensitive to light. When a light photon strikes the junction, an electron/hole pair is created and swept out of an area of the diode to either side of the junction, called the *depletion region*. This causes a small current to flow, proportional to the intensity of the light striking the junction. Photodiodes are used to detect light and changes in light striking the photodiode.

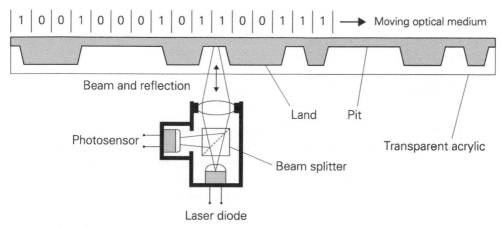

FIGURE 6-7: Optical disk operation

The optical system in nearly all optical drives depends on a device called a *beam splitter*. This is a small prism of glass or plastic with a partially reflective layer imposed within it along a 45-degree angle. (They are typically made by gluing two prisms together along the 45-degree line.) The intense beam from the laser goes through the reflective layer in a straight line towards the disc. When the beam strikes the disc and is reflected back, part of the reflective light is turned aside by the beam splitter and strikes a photosensor, usually a photodiode. A sense amplifier connected to the photosensor detects the difference in intensity of the light reflected from pits compared to lands, and converts those differences into digital pulses. The pulses are "cleaned up" to remove noise, and then they are interpreted as 1s and 0s by the drive electronics.

The bane of optical discs (especially those designed to be handled a lot and not always with sufficient care) is scratching. The CD standard specifies an error correcting code (ECC) scheme based on Reed-Solomon codes, which adds a degree of redundancy to the stored bit stream. This means that multiple copies of data bits are stored in more than one physical area of the disc. The redundant data allows the decoder to reconstruct small amounts of data that had been obscured by scratches. Because scratches tend to destroy many adjacent bits of data at once, data from several nearby regions of the stream are interleaved on the disc, and de-interleaved during playback. This process spreads damage more thinly across a larger stretch of bit stream, reducing the likelihood that it will overwhelm the error-correcting capabilities of the Reed-Solomon code. Reed-Solomon itself involves heavy-duty maths that are beyond the scope of this book, but the Wikipedia entry may be helpful:

```
https://en.wikipedia.org/wiki/Reed%E2%80%93Solomon_error_correction
```

CD-Derived Formats

There are several different kinds of audio-CD-derived optical disc in use today, in the same 12cm format. All have a maximum capacity of roughly 700MB:

- **CD-ROM:** This is the format described earlier. The pits are pressed into the polycarbonate disc at manufacture and cannot be changed.

- **CD-R:** This is a one-time recordable format (in other words, write once). A layer of photosensitive dye is deposited on the plastic disc over the reflective layer. When the disc is being written to, the laser emits strong pulses that permanently change the reflectivity of the dye in spots that are the same size as pits in a non-recordable CD-ROM. When the disc is being read, the laser emits a weaker beam that does not affect the dye layer's properties. The spots on the dye layer are interpreted as pits. The undisturbed dye layer reflects light the same way as the lands do in a CD-ROM.

- **CD-RW:** This format is rewriteable. The dye layer is replaced with a reflective layer of exotic metallic alloy containing indium, tellurium and silver. The alloy is designed to exhibit a phase change when heated by high-intensity laser light. A phase change is a rearrangement of the molecules in a material such that they have different physical properties, such as ice melting into water, or water boiling to produce steam. In this case, the phase change is from a reflective polycrystalline phase to a less-reflective amorphous (glassy) phase. Because the phase affects the reflectivity of the metal, it can be read in the same way as changes in the CD-R dye layer can be read. However, the phase change is not permanent, and can be reversed by using a less intense beam. (The discs are read with an even less intense beam that does not affect the phase of the alloy at all.) The disc may thus be written and rewritten by changing the beam power according to the patterns of 1s and 0s that must be imposed on the disc.

The CD-ROM format is a strong standard and, theoretically, discs written to the CD-R or CD-RW format can be read on any CD-ROM compatible drive. In practice, there are sometimes compatibility issues, especially with older drives that were manufactured before the writeable/rewriteable standards were published.

DVD-Derived Formats

After DVD video became a successful consumer format in about 1995, the format was adapted for computer use as non-volatile storage. In broad terms, the technology works the same way as the earlier CD formats: data is encoded as a pattern of pits or lands on a polycarbonate disc. The dimensions of the spiral track, pits and lands are much smaller than those used in the CD format, and the capacity of DVD-derived formats is much higher. At very minimum, DVD-derived formats can store 4.7GB. Newer formats can store much more. Making the pits and lands smaller is a function of the wavelength of the laser light used to read and write them. At the microscopic scale used to encode data on a disc, shorter wavelengths mean sharper images when the tracks are scanned and the laser light reflected from the pits and lands. Shorter wavelengths mean bluer light. Over the years, the light used in laser imaging has gone from infrared to red to blue. The trademark Blu-ray was coined to reflect the blue light required to encode video at higher resolutions.

Laser colour aside, the biggest technical advance in DVD data storage over CD storage is the ability to create dual-layer discs, which existed in DVD video formats almost from the beginning. This is accomplished by coating the first layer of pits and lands with a transparent lacquer and then bonding on a second transparent plastic layer into which digital data has been pressed before assembly. The second data layer is coated with an extremely thin layer of gold. The gold layer is so thin that it's semi-transparent, and laser light of sufficient intensity passes right through it and is reflected strongly enough from the inner layer to be readable.

When a dual-layer DVD is detected, the DVD reader head changes its optical focus to read either the inner or the outer layer as desired. Whichever layer is not in focus "blurs out" and does not interfere with reading the layer that is in focus.

Dual-layer data discs do not hold twice the amount of data as a single-layer disc. There is a certain amount of overhead required to make the dual-layer technology reliable, and so a dual-layer data disc loses about 10 percent of its capacity over two single-layer discs.

Unlike CD-ROM, there are a number of incompatible refinements on the basic DVD-ROM format. A format war emerged between two competing writeable optical disc standards consortia in the early 2000s. The two groups presented their incompatible standards to the industry as DVD-R and DVD+R. (Both standards were later enhanced to be rewritable.) There are some technical advantages to DVD+R, particularly in terms of reliability and error correction, but today there is still no recognised winner of the war. As with CD-ROM, writeable and rewriteable DVD technology uses photochemical dye and metallic phase change layers to allow changes after manufacture.

Unlike magnetic hard drives, optical discs are not generally partitioned into logical drives. Optical discs have their own, industry-standard file system specification called ISO 9660. The spec lays out how an optical disc is to be read, written and managed in detail. The goal is to allow the optical disc to be a universal interchange medium. If an operating system implements ISO 9660 fully, it is capable of reading from and (where appropriate) writing to any standard optical disc.

Ramdisks

When the IBM PC was first released in 1981, IBM did something a little out of character: it published the full assembly language source code of the machine's Basic Input/Output System (BIOS) in a technical manual. The BIOS in those days controlled just about every interaction between the CPU and peripherals like the keyboard, the text display, printers and disk drives. Having the source code allowed third-party vendors to quickly develop and release add-in products for the machine, which did a great deal to make it the *de facto* standard in desktop computing within a few years of its release.

Not all the add-ins were hardware. By 1982, programmers had written software that allowed the PC to treat a region of system RAM as a PC DOS disk drive. This was called a *ramdisk*, or *RAM drive*. Early ramdisks did not provide a great deal of storage space—typically 64K, out of what might have been 256K or 512K of total memory—but their speed was startling, especially since the standard of performance for the IBM PC at that time was the 360K floppy disk drive. Ramdisks could be three orders of magnitude faster than a floppy drive, and 100 times faster than early 10MB hard drives, for which the "breakthrough price" in 1983 was $1,000.

Device drivers did not exist for DOS PCs. A technology called **terminate and stay resident** (TSR) software allowed ramdisks and many other devices to be accessed by way of standard ROM BIOS calls. A TSR loaded itself alongside DOS in memory, and then "hooked" one or more of the BIOS calls by writing its own address into DOS's table of interrupt vectors at the bottom of memory. When DOS used BIOS to access a disk volume, the ramdisk TSR could choose to intercept the call and then use its own functions to manage the transfer of data to and from the ramdisk's region of memory.

Ramdisks were volatile, of course, and were not used for long-term data storage. They solved the problem of saving out intermediate files during complex builds of software under development. As explained in Chapter 5, native-code compilers operate in several passes, and each pass can generate its own separate temporary files. This took significant time, especially when the only mass storage on the machine was one or two floppy disk drives. Configuring a compiler to write its temporary files to a ramdisk could cut the total build time by 75 percent or more.

As the PC hardware standard matured and RAM grew cheaper, ramdisks were developed using add-in memory beyond the PC's hard limit of 640K. In addition to temporary files, loadable sections of large applications called **overlays** were often copied to ramdisk when the application was run. Instead of grinding the floppy drives every time a new feature set was selected, an overlay stored on a ramdisk was just "there".

The death of floppy drives, along with the arrival of technologies like page caching and virtual memory, which blur the distinction between data held in computer memory and mass storage, greatly reduced the need for explicitly declared ramdisks by the mid-1990s. Ramdisks are still used, especially by live distributions of Unix-derived operating systems. In a live distribution, the OS boots into memory from a CD or DVD optical disc, without being installed on the underlying machine's hard drives. Writeable files are typically stored in ramdisks. Some live distributions can optionally store configuration information on a local hard drive, if the user desires it. This makes a live installation's configuration "persistent" from one run to another. Otherwise, everything associated with the live OS vanishes from memory when the computer is shut down.

In modern Linux systems, including Raspbian, there are two common ramdisk file systems: ramfs and tmpfs. The older ramfs file system does not allow the user to set a maximum amount of memory to be devoted to ramdisk storage: an application writing to a ramfs ramdisk can in theory exhaust the machine's entire supply of physical memory. In contrast, tmpfs partitions can be limited to a set amount of memory and can utilise swap space under memory pressure (albeit at a performance cost). For this reason, tmpfs has largely replaced ramfs.

Flash Storage

Perhaps the single most important advance in non-volatile storage in the last 30 years has been the development of reliable, low-cost flash memory. Flash was invented in the early 1980s by engineers at Toshiba, particularly Dr Fujio Masuoka. After the first detailed presentation of the technology in 1984, it took until 1988 for Intel to field the first commercial chips. In its early days, flash was used as a storage medium for configuration data and BIOS code and firmware in computers; it was also used in consumer electronics like set-top boxes and home broadband routers. Eventually flash became cheap enough to use in mass-storage devices. These fall into four general categories: flash cards (SD, MMC, memory stick, compact flash); USB thumb drives; embedded flash (eMMC, UFS); and flash-based solid-state drives (SSDs) that are designed to replace conventional hard drives.

Flash devices have broad structural similarities to dynamic random access memory (DRAM); the description of DRAM in Chapter 3 will help you during the following discussion of flash technology.

ROMs, PROMs and EPROMs

Flash is a species of non-volatile semiconductor memory, but it is not the first by any means. Mask-programmable *read-only memory* (ROM) chips, which have data permanently recorded in them during manufacture, have existed since the beginning of the semiconductor memory era. Data in a mask-programmable ROM is encoded onto the chip by adjusting one or more photolithographic masks to selectively disconnect or modify the switching behaviour of the chip's individual transistors, which are arranged in a cell matrix similar to that used on SRAM and DRAM chips (see Chapter 3). *Programmable ROM* (PROM) chips allow data to be recorded once (and permanently) onto the chip after manufacture, generally by using a high-current pulse to melt or otherwise open fuses in the cell matrix.

The direct ancestor of flash memory is *erasable PROM* (EPROM), which was invented in 1972. Data stored in an EPROM device may be erased by exposure to ultraviolet (UV) light. Data is stored as charge levels in special floating-gate metal-oxide-semiconductor field-effect transistors (MOSFETs) at each node in the memory cell matrix. The entire EPROM may be erased at once by exposure to intense UV light through a small quartz window in the device package. (Quartz passes UV, whereas ordinary glass does not.) Energetic UV photons create ionisation in the silicon dioxide insulating layer that traps charge in the floating gate MOSFETs, allowing it to leak away to ground. If shielded from light, an EPROM retains its data for at least 20, and as many as 40, years, and it may be erased hundreds of times. Erasing via UV does cause cumulative damage in the insulating layer such that thousands of erase cycles renders a cell unusable, an effect that looms large in flash memory systems.

Flash as EEPROM

Towards the end of the 1970s, various approaches were tried to make EPROM devices erasable without requiring many minutes under a UV light source to do so. As a category, these devices are called *electrically erasable PROM* (EEPROM). As with EPROM, all EEPROM devices store data as levels of electrical charge on a floating MOSFET gate. Bits are erased by removing charge from the gate. Flash is technically an EEPROM technology, one that was designed at the outset to be both fast and scalable. Like most EEPROM technologies, it can be erased selectively; that is, portions of a device's data may be retained while other portions are erased. Today, it is by far the most successful EEPROM technology ever developed.

Like most forms of semiconductor memory, flash is based on individual memory cells in an addressable matrix. The fundamental flash cell is based on the floating-gate MOSFET. Figure 6-8 shows a cross-section of a flash cell and the floating-gate MOSFET symbol.

As mentioned in the digital logic primer in Chapter 4, a MOSFET controls a flow of current by creating a temporary conductive channel between its source and drain terminals under the control of a voltage applied to the its gate terminal. The voltage at which the MOSFET begins to conduct is referred to as the ***threshold voltage***, V_{th}.

In addition to the regular control gate, floating-gate transistors have a second gate electrode, located between the control gate and the channel, which is not connected to the rest of the electronics in the chip; instead, it is enclosed in a layer of insulating material like silicon dioxide. This floating gate may be given a charge by applying a high voltage to the control gate, while placing a voltage across the channel. The voltage across the channel accelerates electrons to the point where they have enough energy (that is, they are "hot" enough) to cross the silicon dioxide insulator separating the floating gate from the channel, imparting a charge to the gate; this process is referred to as ***hot carrier injection*** (HCI). The presence or absence of charge on the floating gate affects the threshold voltage of the transistor; by setting the control gate to a voltage close to V_{th} and measuring the current flowing in the channel it is possible to measure the charge on the floating gate to a high level of accuracy.

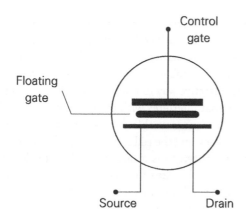

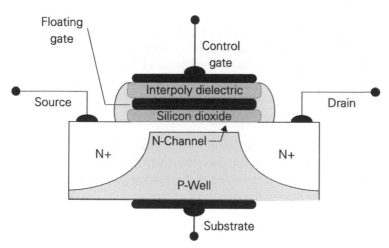

FIGURE 6-8: A flash cell

Charge placed on the floating gate through HCI may be removed by applying a large negative voltage to the control gate. This creates a strong electric field that encourages Fowler-Nordheim tunnelling of "cold" electrons across the barrier between the channel and the floating gate. After a level of charge has been set on the floating gate, the insulating layer surrounding the gate will keep the charge in place on the gate for a remarkably long time. Some research indicates that this retention time could be as much as 100 years under ideal conditions.

When subjected to a sufficiently intense electric field, certain metals will emit low-energy ("cold") electrons. This is called *field emission*. These electrons can tunnel through an insulating layer via quantum effects described by physicists Ralph Fowler and Lothar Nordheim in the late 1920s. This is one type of *quantum tunnelling*, and among the first to be described in detail.

NOTE

Like EPROM and earlier generations of EEPROM cells, flash memory cells have a limitation that is not present in SRAM or DRAM memory cells: flash cells may be written to and/or erased only a certain number of times. HCI causes cumulative damage to the insulating barriers that isolate the floating gate. After a certain number of write/erase cycles, electrons become trapped in the barriers, and there is no effective way to remove them. These trapped electrons give the barriers an unwanted charge that interferes with the measurement of the charge level on the floating gate. At some point the measurable difference between charge and lack of charge (the *threshold window*) disappears, and the cell can no longer be accurately read. The number of times that a cell may be written to is a factor called *endurance*. The endurance of flash cells varies widely depending on the size of the cells, the number of bits stored per cell, and the materials from which the cells are manufactured. Currently, flash endurance ranges from about 1,000 to about 100,000 write/erase cycles.

Single-Level vs. Multi-Level Storage

SRAM encodes data in flip-flops, which have only two possible logic states, and can therefore encode only a single bit. DRAM stores data as charge in microscopic capacitors attached to MOSFET transistors. (See Chapter 3 for a detailed description of DRAM operation.) The charge leaks away quickly, so the actual voltage on the capacitor varies across the time between refresh cycles. The best that we can do is test to see whether a DRAM cell's capacitor is charged or not charged. Again, those two states encode only one bit.

Flash, like DRAM, stores data as charge in a cell. Unlike DRAM, flash can keep a charge in a cell almost unchanged for many years. We can not only detect whether the charge exists in the cell but also, by careful measurement of the effect of the floating gate on the transistor threshold voltage, measure that charge with considerable accuracy.

Being able to measure the charge level in the floating gate allows something very useful: the ability to store multiple bits in a single flash cell. Figure 6-9 shows how this is done. A flash cell that stores only one bit is called a *single-level cell* (SLC). In an SLC, there are only two possible voltage levels. This makes the cell a binary device, which can store either a 0-bit or a 1-bit. If you set up a flash device to store four different voltages in a cell, that cell can encode two bits. If you set up a flash device to store eight different voltages in a cell, the cell can encode three bits.

Strictly speaking, any flash cell that stores more than one bit is called a *multi-level cell* (MLC). At this writing, the most that commercial flash devices can store in a single cell is four bits.

There's a downside to packing more bits into a single cell. In general, the maximum charge level that may be placed on a device's floating gates is limited by other factors and cannot be arbitrarily increased. This means that the difference between charge levels in multi-level devices becomes smaller as the number of bits per cell increases (refer to Figure 6-9). The smaller this difference in voltage is, the more difficult it is to measure, and the more likely it is that there will be both read and write errors. Multi-level cells are more vulnerable to stray charge trapped in the insulating barriers, because stray charge makes the gate charge more difficult to measure. This means that the endurance of MLCs is lower than that of SLCs.

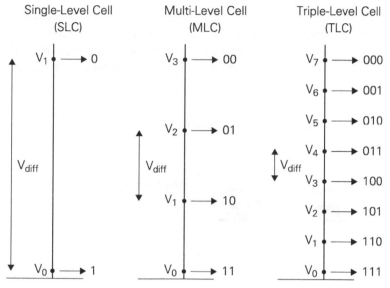

FIGURE 6-9: Single-level and multi-level flash encoding

There are techniques to minimise the effects of cell failures, which we'll return to in the "Wear Levelling and the Flash Translation Layer" section.

NOR vs. NAND Flash

In general, the individual cells in flash devices all work the same way. How the cells are arranged and interconnected on the silicon of a flash storage chip dictates to some extent how that chip is used. There are currently two very different architectures by which flash cells are combined into storage arrays:

- **NOR (Not-OR) flash:** May be written and read down to the resolution of a single machine word, much as DRAM is. NOR is slower to write and erase than NAND flash and is less dense, but is faster to read. It can support in-place execution of code (that is, without first copying it to RAM) and is commonly used for storing firmware in embedded devices.

- **NAND (Not-AND) flash:** Accessed in larger pages of 512 to 4,096 bytes. Pages are combined into blocks of typically 16KB or more. NAND flash is read and written in pages, but erased only in blocks. NAND is faster to write and erase than NOR flash; it's also more dense but is slower to read. In-place execution of code is not generally possible due to the lack of support for rapid random access to the array.

A NOR flash array is shown in Figure 6-10. Note the resemblance to DRAM, as shown in Figure 3-4 from Chapter 3. A single cell is present at the intersection of each bit line and row line. The term NOR is borrowed from digital logic and the basic operation of NOR gates: a single input to a NOR word line produces an inverted (opposite logic level) output on a bit line.

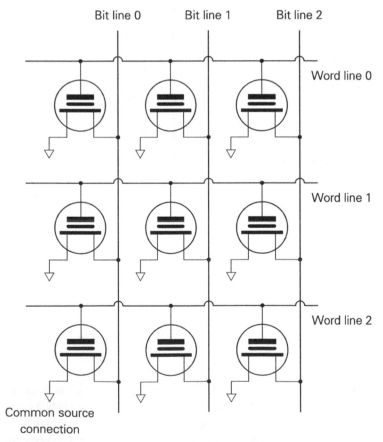

FIGURE 6-10: A NOR flash array

NAND flash was designed to act as mass storage rather than non-volatile RAM. To be cost-effective there must be a great many cells in a storage array. In a NAND array, cells are not addressed singly but in groups of 32 or 64 cells connected in series, as shown in Figure 6-11. Such groups are called *strings*. An entire string is connected to or disconnected from a bit line at once by transistor switches at the beginning and end of the string. This resembles the input circuit of a NAND gate, which has several inputs, all of which must be raised to a logic 1 level to produce a logic 0 level on the output.

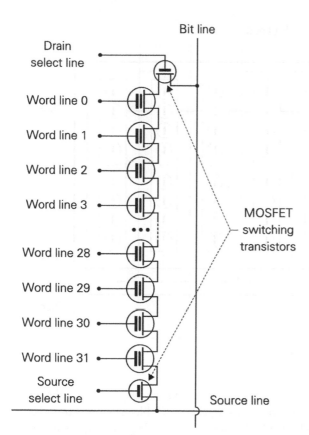

FIGURE 6-11: A NAND cell string

NAND arrays can be denser than NOR arrays because placing multiple cells in series greatly reduces the overhead inherent in connecting individual flash cells to word lines and bit lines. Think of it as less "wiring" on the chip surface, allowing the space saved to be used to fabricate additional cells.

One way to think of the difference between NOR and NAND flash is to see NAND cell strings as occupying the positions that single flash cells occupy in a NOR array. Having multiple cells in a string requires an additional level of addressing, as shown in Figure 6-12. Because they're connected in series, the cells in a NAND string cannot be programmed together. Instead, an array's decoding circuitry treats each corresponding bit in a large number of strings (anywhere from 512 to 4,096) as a unit called a *page*. A NAND page is the smallest unit that may be read from or written to in a single operation.

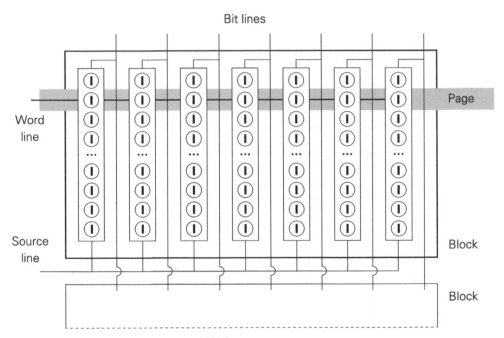

FIGURE 6-12: NAND strings, pages and blocks

Taken together, all the cell strings that span a page are called a *block*. Depending on the number of cells in a string and the number of strings in a page, a NAND block may run from 16KB to 128KB in size. The number of blocks in a NAND array varies widely and is generally from 2,048 and up.

Reading a single cell out of a string of cells in a NAND array requires that the entire series string conduct current; otherwise, there would be no way to test the state of any individual cell. A read operation involves first applying to the control gates of all the MOSFETs, except the one to be read, a voltage that is sufficient to drive the MOSFETs into full conduction, irrespective of the charge state of their floating gates. This essentially takes them out of the circuit as data storage devices and makes them serve temporarily as simple electrical conductors. After the rest of the string has been made to conduct, a near-threshold voltage is applied to the gate of the MOSFET to be read: its conduction, and therefore the conduction of the string as a whole, is then determined by the charge on its floating gate. Depending on the current flowing through the string, the cell is interpreted as a 0-bit or a 1-bit.

Not all of the cells in a flash array are used for storing data. A certain number are used for ECC error detection and correction. Some are also set aside as spare cells, to be used by the flash translation layer in bad block management, as described in the next section.

One other characteristic of flash memory bears on the difference between NOR and NAND: the process for erasing bits is electrically different from the process for writing new bits. Erasing sets all bits in the erased area to 1, and 1-bits are not written to cells except as part of the erase process. When new data is written to flash cells, only the 0-bits in the data are actually written. Whatever bits in the new data are to be 1-bits are simply left alone. This makes flash memory erase-before-write, meaning that every write operation must be preceded by an erase operation, which provides the 1-bits over which 0-bits may be written. A block is the smallest unit of NAND storage that may be erased in one operation. Because NOR must be able to read and write data at the machine word size (anywhere from 8 bits to 64 bits) the machine word is the smallest erasable unit. This allows execute in place (XIP) but also makes writing to NOR arrays slower per byte than NAND.

Wear Levelling and the Flash Translation Layer

The big problem with flash is endurance: cells can only undergo so many erase/rewrite cycles before the floating gate insulation degrades and the cells become unusable. The number of erase/rewrite cycles for TLC NAND can be as low as 1,000 before problems appear. Endurance issues of this sort don't exist with conventional hard drives, and so traditional file systems make no effort to limit the number of writes to a particular sector on a particular hard drive platter.

Clearly, there must be some sort of mechanism for preventing any single block of flash cells from approaching that endurance limit too quickly and for removing unusable blocks from a flash device's active capacity. Such a mechanism is called a *flash translation layer* (FTL) because it interposes itself between a file system and the "raw" flash storage array, accepting hard-disk style commands using LBAs from the file system and translating them to one or more accesses into the flash array. Unlike LBAs in a hard drive, an LBA refers to no fixed location in a flash array. The FTL keeps a mapping table that indicates where an LBA as understood by the file system is currently located in the array. As you'll soon see, this location bounces around inside the flash array quite a bit.

Beyond keeping track of where file system data is stored in an array, an FTL has three significant jobs that may be better categorised as maintenance:

- **Wear levelling:** Keeps track of the number of times that a given flash block has been rewritten and writes new data to blocks that have been used the least

- **Garbage collection:** Blocks marked as available are reclaimed and put back into the pool of available blocks

- **Bad-block management:** Identifies bad blocks, removes them from use and substitutes spare blocks to keep the array at its nominal capacity

Wear levelling is the FTL's most important job. There are a number of ways to handle it. The most common uses a *block aging table* (BAT) to count how many times a given block has undergone an erase/write cycle. New data written to the array is stored in blocks that have seen the least use. This is called *dynamic wear levelling*.

Inherent in the way that computers are used is the fact that some sorts of data change far more often than others. Configuration data changes less often than records in a database, for example. Through a process called *static* or *global wear levelling*, the FTL determines which data changes least often and relocates it to flash blocks that are approaching their endurance limits. Because this data changes rarely, such "old" blocks can remain in use longer than they would if wear levelling were strictly dynamic.

When a flash device is brand new, its write policy is simple: write data to a block that's never been written to before. Remember that flash cells must be erased before they're written, and that erasing a flash block is time-consuming compared to writing new data, by a factor as high as 100. Because all blocks come pre-erased in a new device, this means that performance is very snappy at first. After all blocks have been written to at least once, the FTL must begin erasing blocks to prepare them for writing, and performance may decline.

This effect is worse than it seems at first glance. Writing data to a NAND flash array is done at a page level, but there are many pages in a block, and an entire block must be erased before any one of its pages can be rewritten. For this reason, flash does not allow data to be rewritten "in place". To change one page in a block, the modified page is written to a page that has not been written to since erasure. This may be in the same block, if erased space is still available, or it may be in another block entirely. The original page is then marked as invalid. If no erased space is available, the FTL may first have to erase a block that contains no "fresh" (that is, valid) data. Writing new data to a single page may mean subjecting more pages than one to an erase/write operation. This is called *write amplification*, and it increases wear on the flash array. Keeping write amplification to a minimum is an important priority in any FTL.

To help with wear levelling, when a device is manufactured a certain number of blocks are set aside and are not counted towards the device's marked capacity. This is called *overprovisioning*. Some of these "extra" blocks are later used to replace blocks that fail over time. Most are used as a sort of on-chip cache of free blocks to keep write amplification down. The percentage of overprovisioning varies widely by device and manufacturer but may be as much as 150 percent of the device's marked capacity. Overprovisioning adds to the device's cost but extends its useful life.

Garbage Collection and TRIM

An FTL generally has a background task that gathers "live" pages from blocks that contain one or more invalid pages, and consolidates them on fresh blocks. Blocks that no longer contain live pages may be marked for later erasure. This process is called *garbage collection*, and it is roughly analogous to defragmenting a hard drive. The garbage collection process may also erase blocks with no live data to increase available blocks for new page writes. Erasing is time-intensive, so the FTL performs block erasures during "quiet time" when the device is not busy with read or write requests from the OS.

There is a problem with garbage collection: the FTL only marks a page as invalid after the OS rewrites the LBA that maps to the page. When a file is deleted (and trash emptied) at the OS level, its LBAs are marked as available by the OS. Until fairly recently, the OS had no way to tell the FTL which pages mapped to a deleted file and could therefore be erased and reused at any time. In the late 2000s, the TRIM command was added to the SATA command set. (TRIM is not an acronym, but SATA commands are traditionally given in uppercase.) TRIM is available only to flash devices on a SATA interface, which typically means solid-state drives. (USB thumb drives and SD cards do not support TRIM.) When the OS deletes a file, it issues a TRIM command to the SSD, which includes the LBAs of all sectors belonging to the deleted file. The SSD's FTL can then mark all flash blocks mapping to those LBAs as available for erasure and reuse.

A common misperception is that TRIM is a command telling the flash array, "Erase these LBAs right now". It is not. TRIM simply tells the FTL which file system LBAs have been deleted, and the blocks mapping to those LBAs may be erased whenever the garbage collection code has time. Some very recent flash devices include a separate command called secure TRIM, which suspends other flash array activity until all pages marked for erasure are actually erased.

A significant number of blocks in a flash chip are unusable at the time of manufacture due to minute physical flaws that appear during masking and etching, and these blocks are marked as bad during unit testing. For the same reasons, some usable blocks have higher or lower endurance than others, and a few will fail over time during ordinary use. The FTL notes which blocks generate ECC errors (see Chapter 3 for a brief explanation of ECC) and beyond a threshold number of such errors marks them as unusable. To keep the capacity of the device from gradually shrinking, blocks originally allocated as spares via overprovisioning are added to the available block pool.

The FTL software runs on a special-purpose microcontroller often based on an ARM CPU. Until very recently, the controller chip and the NAND flash storage array chip had each been separate dies in their own IC packages. The two ICs were, integrated with each other at the circuit-board level. NAND arrays and their controllers are now integrated in a single IC package, even though each remains on a separate die. The significant differences between fabrication processes for flash and for microcontroller chips will keep the two from sharing a single die for the foreseeable future. Note that there isn't always a separate CPU for the flash controller software. The cheapest portable music players are essentially USB thumb drives with a two-line LCD display, a headphone jack and a couple of buttons. To reduce cost, the audio codecs and UI manager on such devices often run on the same silicon as the flash controller software, so that the FTL is simply one component of a simple real-time OS, complete with a display and input buttons.

SD Cards

Until fairly recently, flash-based SATA solid-state drives were still a little exotic, but consumer-class flash storage has been on the market since the Compact Flash (CF) card was introduced in 1994. Early CF cards used NOR flash, but changed to the denser NAND flash in response to market demand for higher capacities. The Multimedia Card (MMC) format appeared in 1997, and was less than half the size of CF, at only 24mm × 32mm. In 1999 the SD card added various digital rights management (DRM) features to the basic MMC spec and soon became the dominant card-based removable storage format. SD cards are the same width and height as MMC, but they're 1mm thicker. An MMC will plug into an SD card slot, but not vice versa.

IBM introduced the USB thumb drive in 2000, which allowed removable flash storage to be used in desktop and laptop computers without flash card slots. Even the earliest thumb drives had capacities several times that of 3.5" floppy diskettes, and floppy disk drives began vanishing from desktop computers at about that time.

The Raspberry Pi uses the SD card format for its primary non-volatile storage, including both software and data. The SD format has seen three generations:

- **Secure Digital standard capacity (SDSC):** Stores from 8MB to 2GB

- **Secure Digital high capacity (SDHC):** Stores from 4GB to 32GB

- **Secure Digital extended capacity (SDXC):** Stores from 64GB to 2TB

The generations are backward compatible, meaning that SDHC and SDXC card slots accept and read earlier generations of cards. SDXC cards are usually sold preformatted with the exFAT (extended file allocation table) file system, which allows a higher card capacity than FAT32 without the additional overhead of the NTFS file system. ExFAT is Microsoft proprietary and support under Linux (including Raspbian) is still limited due to patent issues. The Raspberry Pi bootloader cannot boot from an exFAT card, so SDXC cards must be reformatted to FAT32 before use with the Raspberry Pi.

Some SD cards are faster than others. There are several speed classes, where the class number denotes the approximate sustained sequential transfer speed in MB per second. For example, a class 4 card transfers data at 4MB/second, and a class 10 card transfers data at 10 MB/second. A 2009 enhancement to the SD card spec adds ultra-high speed (UHS) formats that change both the card's electrical interface and the controller interface to obtain speeds as high as 100MB/second. UHS cards work in conventional SD interfaces, but are no faster than the older interface allows.

The use of speed class numbers suggests that SD card speed is a simple business, but in truth speed depends heavily on how the card is being used. The vast majority of SD cards are used in devices like digital cameras or music players, in which sequential read and write speed is the primary determinant of performance; for these applications, a speed class value may be enough. In contrast, a general-purpose OS like Raspbian tends to perform frequent smaller reads and writes to non-contiguous areas of the card; in this case, random-access performance becomes the controlling factor, and random access is where SD cards do least well because of the inescapable read-modify-erase-write cycle dictated by the flash technology. If a class 10 card isn't optimised for many relatively small read and write operations, a card with a lower speed class but better random-access performance may perform noticeably better with the Raspberry Pi. This is where the design of the SD card controller comes into play: careful use of buffering minimises the number of reads and writes actually made to the flash array, which in turn improves performance on random access. Unfortunately, there's no standard metric for random performance printed on SD cards. Benchmark roundups published for groups of specific cards may be helpful. You can see a good example at http://thewirecutter.com/reviews/best-sd-card/.

Also note that "fake" SD cards are relatively common; for example, a fake card marked as 32GB might contain only 2 useful GB of storage. Buying from trusted retailers who will honour returns is the best way to avoid this problem.

The current SD card interface bus is 4 bits wide. Early cards used a slower single-bit bus, and so later generations allow the host processor to communicate with the card at startup across the 1-bit bus until the host identifies the card and determines its generation, bus width and feature set. After initialisation, the host uses the full bus width available. The startup protocol also allows the host to determine the card's capacity, speed and features unavailable in the basic SD standard.

The host controls the card using a command set, just as in a hard drive or SSD. The SD command set is adapted from the earlier MMC command set. The differences are primarily associated with the SD standard's DRM security mechanisms.

eMMC

Not all flash storage needs to be removable, or even separate from the circuit board on which the rest of a device like a smartphone or tablet is assembled. There is a class of ICs defined in a standard called *embedded MMC* (eMMC), which is designed to be soldered to a circuit board using a ball-grid array (BGA) package. (Chapter 3 describes BGAs in connection with Raspberry Pi memory chips.) The flash controller and NAND flash arrays are on separate dies but enclosed in the same package, using a technology called *multi-chip packaging* (MCP).

The eMMC interface is an expansion of the original MMC interface. The bus is 8 bits wide, and adds flash-specific SATA commands to the MMC command set. These include TRIM, secure TRIM and secure erase. Secure erase erases the entire NAND array in an unrecoverable fashion, and is said to return the eMMC device to its original out-of-the-box state in terms of data. It does not reverse reduced endurance due to earlier use.

Because eMMC storage is often the only non-volatile storage integral to a device like a smartphone or tablet, the current eMMC standard (v5.1) specifies two different boot partitions plus an additional partition called the *replay-protected memory block* (RPMB) that contains DRM-related code and decryption keys. These partitions are actually imposed on the flash array at manufacture and are roughly equivalent to a factory low-level format on a conventional hard drive. The remaining storage in the eMMC device is considered user space and may contain up to four general-purpose partitions for user data.

Most eMMC devices use either MLC or TLC encoding for enhanced density; MLC is more common in devices targeted at industrial applications (which require long-term reliability but are less cost-sensitive), and TLC in consumer applications (where the reverse applies). The eMMC standard provides for enhanced areas that use single-level cell (SLC) encoding for better reliability, at the cost of lower density. By default, the boot partitions and RPMB are enhanced areas. Sections of user space may optionally be specified as enhanced areas. Establishment of enhanced areas in the flash array may be done only once and may not be undone during the life of the array. The operation is generally performed by the manufacturer of the electronics into which the eMMC is integrated, during assembly and installation of the OS.

A standard released in 2012 called Universal Flash Storage (UFS) may replace eMMC in coming years. UFS incorporates a new standard called M-PHY for the electrical connection with the host processor, and the SCSI architectural model for logical communication with the OS and applications. UFS allows delivery of an SSD in a single IC package that may be soldered to a circuit board. The first UFS devices appeared in early 2015, and at this writing have capacities as high as 256GB.

The Future of Non-Volatile Storage

At this writing, flash has no serious competition in the area of non-volatile semiconductor memory. Flash-based solid-state drives are coming into their own, with 2TB units now widely available. They're still expensive (roughly £500) but if history is any guide, that price will come down quickly in the near future. 512GB SDXC flash cards are on the market, and the SDXC format can embrace cards with as much as 2TB of capacity. Unfortunately, the same physical and economic challenges that face manufacturers of digital logic devices also impose limits on the achievable density of planar (2-D) flash-based storage, and these limits are now in sight. As we approach the 10 nanometre (nm) process node (the next level of ever-smaller semiconductor fabrication technology) it becomes harder to reliably manufacture the well-insulated floating gate structures on which flash depends, and capital investment in new fabrication facilities becomes harder to justify.

To get past such limitations, much research is currently being done on 3-D fabrication, which allows the manufacture of NAND flash cell arrays in which cell strings are arranged vertically rather than in the horizontal dimension of a planar chip. Greater densities thus become possible without reducing the fabrication process size. The first commercial products using 3-D NAND flash are now on the market, and their density will only improve as the techniques are perfected. One caveat is that because 3-D fabrication requires more process steps, it is unlikely to yield the dramatic reductions in cost-per-bit that have historically been provided by moving to new process nodes.

Another promising new technology is resistive RAM (RRAM or ReRAM), an EEPROM mechanism that does away with floating-gate cells entirely. RRAM stores data in cells containing a substance that changes resistance when a sufficiently high voltage is applied across it. Commercial devices are still a few years off, but early indications are that it may permit smaller cell sizes and lower read/write latency than flash.

The overall trend is clear: spinning disks are losing ground, and no-moving-parts solid-state storage is gaining. The trend is being driven to some extent by the parallel increase in the popularity of hand-held computers and the resolution of video. The breathtaking quality of emerging ultra-high definition (UHD) TV content comes at a steep storage cost: a 100-minute movie occupies 15GB of space. A fair number of those will fit on a 1TB hard drive. But once the OS and apps claim their space, not even one will fit on a low-end 16GB tablet. Current SSD and eMMC standards allow for 2TB flash devices. Silicon fabrication is moving relentlessly in that direction, and within a decade spinning disks may seem as archaic as paper tape does today.

Chapter 7
Wired and Wireless Ethernet

FOR A LONG time, there were so few computers in the world that the benefits of connecting them to one another simply didn't occur to anyone. In the mainframe era, "data sharing" consisted of printing out reports on huge piles of paper and sending them to whoever needed the data. Early use of data communications was not for networking but for remote access to user timesharing terminals, card/tape readers and printers. (For more on this, see Chapter 6.) It wasn't about connecting computers to computers but rather about connecting computers to their peripherals. As currently understood, *networking* is the practice of transferring data files and commands between otherwise independent computers.

Only after the cost of computers came down due to the introduction of minicomputers did universities and research organisations have a critical mass of "in-house" computers to interconnect, circa 1965. After that, networking technology advanced quickly. The initial focus was on connecting computers at a distance, in separate buildings or even separate research campuses, in what came to be called a *wide-area network* (WAN). Lawrence Roberts and Thomas Marill did the experimental work on wide-area network hardware at Massachusetts Institute of Technology's Lincoln Labs that led directly to the seminal research network Advanced Research Projects Agency Network (ARPANET) by 1969. Robert Kahn and Vint Cerf created TCP/IP (Transmission Control Protocol/Internet Protocol) that was perfected on ARPANET by 1983 and later became the foundation of the modern Internet.

In 1971, ALOHAnet was successfully deployed by the University of Hawaii, as a means of linking the university's computers spread across several islands via radio signals. It was one of the first packet-based networks, and certainly the first wireless network. ALOHAnet introduced the concept of uncoordinated access to a shared medium (in this case, a block of radio spectrum) with support for collision detection, back-off and retransmission; it was one of the inspirations for Ethernet, which was in development about that time and shares these features, which we'll discuss during the rest of this chapter.

Local-area networks (LANs) came a little later, once multiple computers were deployed in physical proximity within a single building. One of the first operational LANs was the Cambridge Ring, implemented at Cambridge University in 1974 but never commercialised. Xerox Corporation developed what became Ethernet circa 1970 to 1975, published the spec in 1976 and presented Ethernet as a standard in 1980, in cooperation with Digital Equipment Corporation and Intel. In 1983, Ethernet became Institute of Electrical and Electronics Engineers (IEEE) standard 802.3, to tremendous industry enthusiasm. IBM introduced its token ring network architecture in 1985 as a competitor to Ethernet, but the architecture's proprietary nature prevented it from becoming a wide success.

Hundreds of network technologies have appeared and vanished since the 1970s. Some were truly minimal: the XModem and Kermit software packages were widely used for transferring files between two microcomputers in the late 1970s and early 1980s, using serial ports. This mechanism required a special serial crossover cable that was often called a *null modem*. The crossover cable connected the serial transmit line of one computer to the serial receive line of the other, allowing direct communication without passing through other communications gear. Computer bulletin-board systems (CBBS) allowed multiple computers to connect to a remote computer via phone lines and modems, allowing text messaging and file transfers. By the late 1990s, the Internet was the dominant WAN, and Ethernet was the dominant LAN.

The OSI Reference Model for Networking

Networking can be a complicated business, largely because its job is to bridge a great many different technologies spread across computer categories from hand-held devices to desktop computers to servers. Making sense of it requires a roadmap. Fortunately, we've had such a roadmap since the mid-1980s: the *Open System Interconnection* (OSI) reference model, which became an International Organization for Standardization (ISO) standard in 1984.

> **NOTE**   The abbreviation ISO is not an acronym but an adaptation of a classic Greek term *isos,* which is equal.

The OSI model is not a specification in the same sense that the IEEE 802.3 Ethernet document is a specification. It's a way of creating a "big picture" view of the many smaller ideas falling within the larger idea of networking. It's an educational tool, and also a way to help engineers and programmers stay on the same page when discussing networking technologies. The basic idea is to separate computer networking into conceptual layers, from networking applications at the top (think email clients and web browsers) to copper and fibre-optic cables, radio waves, and their associated electronics at the bottom. The journey of data across a network connection begins at the top, moves downward through the model's layers to the physical link at the bottom, across the physical link to another computer, and then up through the layers to the top. Figure 7-1 illustrates the OSI reference model.

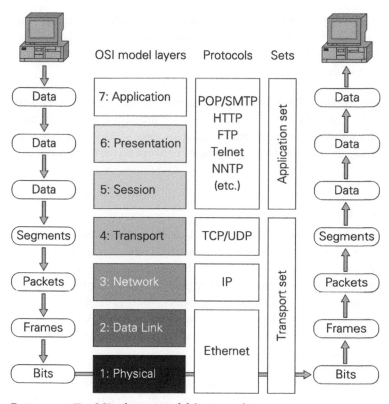

FIGURE 7-1: The OSI reference model for networking

Because the layers of networking machinery are depicted one atop the other in schematic diagrams of the OSI model, they are often referred to as a *network stack*. **NOTE**

We're going to go through the OSI model layer by layer so that you can get a sense for the big picture of networking. This chapter is primarily about wired and wireless Ethernet (both of which are used a great deal with the Raspberry Pi) and so our focus later in the chapter will be on the bottom four layers (called the *transport set*), which encompass Ethernet and two crucial protocols: Transmission Control Protocol (TCP) and Internet Protocol (IP).One way to think of it is that the transport set is about moving data, whereas the top three layers, called the *application set*, are about processing data via networked applications.

Central to the OSI model is the idea of *abstraction*. Each layer conceptually communicates directly with the corresponding layer (its *peer)* on the other layer of the link, without depending on the exact details of the levels below it; these details are said to be *abstracted away*. So a web browser (in the application layer on your computer) can communicate with a web server (in the application layer on another computer) without caring in detail how the underlying TCP/IP stack provides a reliable channel between the two machines, or whether the physical medium supporting the communication is an Ethernet cable, a Wi-Fi link, a fibre-optic backbone or some combination of the three.

The OSI model has its limits. Not all networking systems map neatly onto its layers, and some networking systems (particularly the Internet suite of protocols) have their own layered reference models that predate the OSI model and span some of its several layers. It is, however, an excellent way to confront the complexities of networking the first time you're introduced to them.

The Application Layer

The journey across a network begins when you, the user, launch a network-aware program. That's what the application layer is about: creating or selecting data for transfer. The computer you're using is called a *host*, as is the computer on the other end of the line. The program you're using to communicate across the network is called a *client*. The program at the other end is likely to be a *server*, which is a program that exists purely to send data across a network in response to a request from a client, without human interaction. A server can be thought of as a sort of data robot: your client sends commands or data to the server and the server in turn sends commands and data to your client.

The application layer provides the "human face" of network client programs like email, chat, Usenet, web browsers, FTP, Telnet, and so on. Once the application layer has worked out the commands and data to be sent over the network, and the address of the destination host, these are passed down the stack to the next layer.

The Presentation Layer

The name of the presentation layer is a little misleading. It has nothing to do with displaying data. It's really about data conversion, and about how data will be "presented" to the host on the other end of the connection. As we explained in Chapter 6, there have been numerous character encoding standards, but the three most important are the American Standard for Code Information Interchange (ASCII, used on almost everything today), Unicode (for character sets larger than 256 characters) and Extended Binary Coded Decimal Interchange Code (EBCDIC), which is used only on older "big iron" IBM mainframes. The presentation layer is where encoding differences like that are ironed out. Two other tasks often handled in the presentation layer are encryption and data compression, both of which are optional but these days quite common.

The presentation layer may translate outgoing data into a specified standard network encoding for transmission; the peer will translate incoming data from the standard encoding into that host's preferred encoding before passing it up to the application layer. It may add *headers* to outgoing data before passing it on to the next layer, indicating what encryption or compression has been applied; these are used by the peer to undo the encryption or compression. Headers may be seen as nested envelopes, on each of which is written information relevant to an entity at a particular layer of the stack. Most ISO model layers add one or more headers to the data block passed down from the layer above them. Later on, as the data block passes up the stack on the destination host, the headers are removed in order and interpreted by the peer of the layer that applied them.

This process, called *data encapsulation*, is shown in Figure 7-2. A Protocol Data Unit (PDU) is a chunk of data handled by a particular layer of the OSI model. For the transport layer, this is called a *segment*. For the network layer, this is called a *packet*. For the data link layer, it's called a *frame*. (Note that many people use the terms "packet" and "frame" interchangeably.)

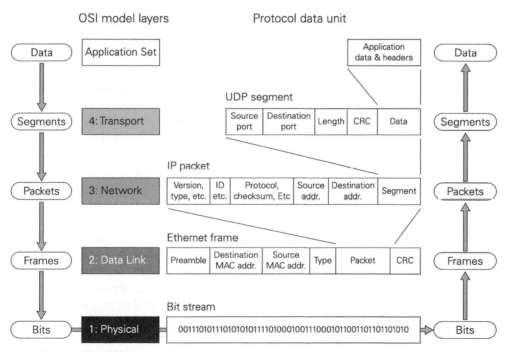

FIGURE 7-2: OSI model data encapsulation

Note that the IP packet and Ethernet frame PDUs are more complex than shown in Figure 7-2 and have been abbreviated to simplify the diagram. The transport layer segment is shown as a User Datagram Protocol (UDP) PDU, also for simplicity's sake. As you will see a little later, the transport layer also supports the much more complex TCP PDU. Either a UDP or TCP segment may be processed at the transport layer.

You'll find it useful to refer to Figures 7-1 and 7-2 during the detailed discussion of the various OSI layers that follow.

The Session Layer

With data in hand from the presentation layer, the session layer opens the actual communication session with the other host. The session layer determines if the other host can in fact be reached. It also determines whether the connection between the two hosts is full duplex or half duplex. *Full duplex* means that data can pass in both directions simultaneously. *Half duplex* means that only one end can transmit at a time, while the other end listens for data and waits for the line to "turn around".

Some network applications can request multiple simultaneous connections to the other host. A web browser, for example, may need an HTML file, a CSS file and perhaps other content files of various sorts in order to render a single web page. The session layer establishes these additional connections and keeps track of what data is moving over which connection. The session layer also provides the highest level of error response, and may attempt to re-establish failed connections automatically.

The session layer is the lowest layer in the application set. Many network applications map to all three layers in the application set, in that a single program (like a web browser or an email client) handles data selection/creation, data presentation and session management. When all requested sessions have been established, the application's work is done. The data is handed down to the transport set, where the focus is less on the data than on getting the data where it needs to go.

The Transport Layer

On the transmit side, the transport layer's primary tasks are to take the data handed down from the session layer by one or more processes, optionally divide it into *segments* that are small enough to handle conveniently (a process called *segmentation*), and queue segments from these processes for transmission over the network (a process called *multiplexing*). At the receive side the transport layer reassembles segments and routes data to the appropriate receiving process.

Transport layer protocols may be categorised as either connection-oriented or connectionless. *Connection-oriented protocols* provide a reliable, ordered stream of data between two processes, and so must generally provide a mechanism on the receive side to reorder segments that arrive out of order (which can occur if the underlying network routes segments via multiple routes with different latencies) and to detect and request retransmission of segments that have been dropped or corrupted by the underlying network. They may also provide flow-control facilities, which prevent the transmitter from sending data faster than it can be processed by the receiver. *Connectionless protocols* are generally much simpler, delegating the handling of errors and out-of-order data upward to the application set; often they provide little more than a multiplexing function.

In the modern Internet, the transport layer is implemented by TCP and UDP. TCP is connection-oriented: it divides the incoming stream of data from a process into segments, and attaches to each segment a header containing a sequence number (which is used to reorder segments at the receive end and detect missing segments) and a checksum (which is used to detect corrupted segments). Flow control is provided by using a sliding window scheme: the segment header contains a window field, which allows each end of the connection to specify how much data it can accept. Multiplexing is provided by means of source and destination port fields in the header, which (along with the source address) are used by the receiver to identify the destination process and stream for each incoming segment.

UDP is a much simpler connectionless protocol. Its header contains only the source and destination port fields required for multiplexing, along with a length field and a checksum; corrupted segments are silently discarded in UDP rather than being retransmitted. UDP is commonly used in applications like Voice over Internet Protocol (VoIP) in which occasional dropped segments can be tolerated but latency must be kept to a minimum.

The Network Layer

The network layer is primarily concerned with *routing*; that is, determining what path the data will take while it travels to the other host. Although the OSI model diagram in Figure 7-1 suggests that the data travels directly from the sending host to the receiving host, in WANs (including the Internet) this is not always the case. A network *path* often includes one or more intermediate "stops" at computers along the way. These *intermediate nodes* don't generally unpack or attempt to interpret the data; they simply look at the destination address on each packet and send the packets on their way. The specialised hardware devices that perform this forwarding are called *routers*. Routers contain tables of network addresses and connections called a *routing table*, and can work out the route to the destination host address using the host address and the routing table. Routers are covered in more detail later in this chapter in the "Routers and the Internet" section.

In the context of the Internet, the network layer is where the IP does most of its work. IP takes segments passed down from the transport layer and builds them into packets with additional information needed for IP processing (refer to Figure 7-2). The IP packet is complex, and its header format is shown in Figure 7-3. Although we can't explain each of the header fields in detail in this book, here's a quick summary:

- **Version:** The IP version number—for example, 4 for IPv4 and 6 for IPv6.
- **IP header length:** The length of the header in 32-bit words, including options and padding.

- **Type of service:** Encodes "quality-of-service" (QoS) values for IP packets. Some packets require special treatment to ensure the quality of the larger data stream. Video, for example, requires that packets be sent in order and with minimum delay (latency) for the highest quality when delivered for display.

- **Total packet length:** Specifies the length of the packet in bytes. This length cannot be longer than 65,535 bytes and includes the segment passed down from the transport layer.

- **Identification:** A 16-bit value given to every packet belonging to a specific message. It allows the destination host to reassemble a message from packets received out of order or mixed with packets belonging to other messages.

- **Flags:** Contains three single-bit control flags that control the splitting of large packets into smaller packets. The first flag is reserved and not used.

- **Fragment offset:** Part of a mechanism to identify the order of packets received out of order.

- **Time to live (TTL):** Specifies the maximum number of "hops" the packet is allowed to take along its route from the source host to the destination host. Time to live is decremented by one at each hop, and when the value goes to zero the packet is assumed to have "got lost" and is discarded. (Note that "TTL" as used here has nothing to do with transistor-transistor logic chips.)

- **Protocol:** Contains an 8-bit code specifying the protocol (generally TCP or UDP) that generated the segment handed down from the transport layer.

- **Header checksum:** Part of a mechanism that detects corrupted packet headers. This checksum does not include payload data.

- **Source IP address:** The 32-bit IP address (that is, its location on the Internet) of the host that generated the packet. We'll explain IP addresses in more detail in the section "Names vs. Addresses" later in this chapter.

- **Destination IP address:** The 32-bit IP address of the host to which the packet was sent.

- **Options:** A variable-length field that may contain one or more optional subfields used for security, testing and debugging.

- **Data:** The payload embedded in the packet. This is generally a segment passed down from the transport layer.

When necessary, the IP can split a segment too large to fit in a single packet into multiple packets. IP doesn't attempt to keep packets in order or detect errors, both of which are handled by layers above the network layer. Its job is to get packets to the next stop along the route.

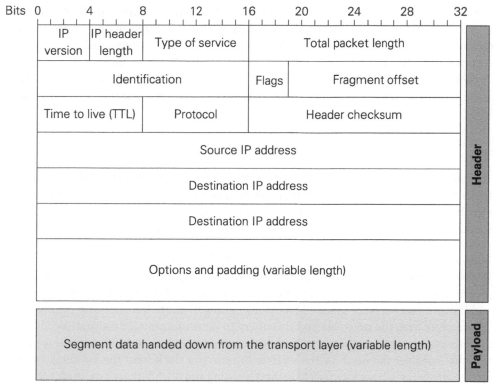

FIGURE 7-3: The Internet Protocol (IP) Version 4 (IPv4) header format

The Data Link Layer

The Internet is not a single network. It's a network of networks with defined, routable connections between them. Networks can be nested within larger networks to any reasonable level, but at some point there is a *local network* in which all computers may connect directly to one another without the involvement of a router. The data link layer manages the flow of data over these direct connections, reorganising data coming from higher layers yet again, this time into *frames* that are of a size and format that the hardware implementing the direct connection can handle. There are many different technologies used in connecting computers on a local network. In the case of technologies that involve communication over a shared medium, a primary function of the data link layer is to arbitrate access to this medium, via a *media access control* (MAC) scheme. This may involve either centralised coordination or decentralised collision detection and avoidance. As discussed later in this chapter in the section "Collision Detection and Avoidance", modern Ethernet technologies (including Wi-Fi) take the latter approach.

The data link layer may also provide local flow control, which ensures that frames are not sent so quickly that the destination host's buffers fill up, and reliable delivery, whereby successfully received frames are acknowledged by the receiver and unacknowledged frames are retained by the transmitter and retransmitted as necessary. Ethernet does not provide either of these services; in the case of protocols that do, it is common to regard the data link layer as comprising an upper *logical link control* sublayer, where these services reside, and a lower MAC sublayer.

The Physical Layer

The physical layer is where the network connection literally "gets physical": the frames handed down from the data link layer are received as strings of bits, which are converted to signals in the physical *medium*. This medium is any physical process onto which data may be encoded: electrical pulses on a cable, modulated microwaves, modulated light, whatever.

Most of the physical layer's operation occurs inside electronic circuitry in a computer's Network Interface Controller (NIC), and varies widely between standards. The transmitter generally adds a *preamble* and delimiter bits that indicate the beginning and end of the data, and transforms each bit or group of bits in turn into a *symbol* to transmit over the medium. The receiver uses the preamble and delimiters to detect incoming data, and decodes the symbols to recover the original bits. In choosing what symbols to transmit over the medium we must consider the need for the receiver to recover a clock from the incoming symbol stream; encoding schemes such as Manchester coding and 4B/5B (there's more on encoding a little later in this chapter in the "Ethernet Encoding Systems" section) guarantee that transitions will occur with a certain minimum frequency, regardless of the input data.

Ethernet spans the data link and physical layers. The Ethernet protocols operate in the data link layer, with a standard interface to any of several Ethernet-specific physical layers, which we'll discuss in more detail shortly. Wi-Fi is analogous to Ethernet with wireless media, in that it too spans the data link and physical layers of the OSI model, with several variations of the medium access (MAC) mechanism and physical layers. Much of the difference between Ethernet and Wi-Fi physical layers are differences of *modulation*; that is, mechanisms for imposing information on radio-frequency energy. For Ethernet, this radio-frequency energy is conducted through cabling of some sort. For Wi-Fi, the radio-frequency energy is transferred over free space using antennas.

Ethernet

Like so many other things, Ethernet came out of the Xerox PARC labs in Palo Alto, California. Robert Metcalfe and David Boggs first circulated the idea within PARC in May 1973, and by November of that year the technology went online. The Ethernet concept was an outgrowth of PARC's research into personal computing, and was intended to link PARC's forward-looking Alto experimental workstations together at a speed of 3 megabits per second (Mbit/s). Metcalfe coined the term "Ethernet" as an allusion to the Victorian idea of the *luminiferous aether*, which was a mysterious (and later shown to be non-existent) medium through which light and radio waves passed. Ethernet was introduced as a commercial product in 1980, and in 1983 was standardised as IEEE 802.3.

Thicknet and Thinnet

The earliest Ethernet implementations used a fairly stiff 10mm diameter coaxial cable. A workstation or other networked device could be connected only at certain points on the cable. The cable, in fact, bore markings every 2.5 metres to indicate where so-called "vampire taps" could be clamped onto it. The interval was calculated to minimise interference from radio-frequency reflections inside the cable. The thickness and stiffness of the cable prompted the nickname "Thicknet", even after the formal IEEE designation 10BASE5 was given to the system. A few years later, a variation using thinner coaxial cable was introduced. The cable was only 6mm in diameter, less expensive, and a great deal more flexible. Taps could be placed at any point on the cable. The system came to be called "Thinnet" and bore the designation 10BASE2.

The IEEE nomenclature is still used, and it's worth a short description here. The "10" indicates the maximum speed of data sent across the cable, in megabits. The 10-megabit value was not the design speed of the interface but the highest speed that the cable-based infrastructure could deliver. Early Ethernet implementations operated at less than half that speed. The "BASE" indicates *baseband* transmission. In baseband transmission, the digital signal on the physical medium is a pattern of actual bits encoded as transitions from 0 volts to some arbitrary line voltage. This is in contrast to *broadband* transmission (think cable TV), which imposes a signal on a radio-frequency carrier wave using various modulation schemes. In both modes of transmission, data travels at frequencies high enough to be considered RF. The number at the end of the designation (here, 5 or 2) indicates the maximum length of a network segment, in hundreds of metres. In 10BASE2 the "2" is an exaggeration; in practice, the segment length maxes out at 185 metres.

The Basic Ethernet Idea

Ethernet has evolved a great deal since its introduction in 1980. To explain its modern form, we have to begin with its original mechanism as implemented in Thicknet and Thinnet. Both forms use coaxial cable to connect some limited number of computers. All computers on the network are *peers*; that is, none have special hardware or software that is not present in all of the others. Any computer on the network can send or receive Ethernet packets to any other computer on the network.

Ethernet originated the idea of a MAC address, and every device attached to the cable (which may include printers and other special-purpose devices like file servers) has a unique 48-bit numeric address, generally expressed as six groups of two hexadecimal digits. Any device with a MAC address, whatever its nature, is called a *node*. The MAC address is in fact more of an ID code than a true address. Unlike IP addresses (which are covered a little later in the "Names vs. Addresses" section) a MAC address says nothing about *where* its device is located on the network and is used only to tell nodes apart. As 48 bits can identify 281 *trillion* different devices, we won't run out of MAC addresses any time soon. That said, a few duplicates are known to have been issued by mistake, and with some equipment, including the Raspberry Pi, it's possible to change the MAC address to mimic another device.

When the network is quiet, all nodes are "listening"; that is, their NICs are ready to receive data from the cable. At any time, a node may place a packet on the cable. On baseband technologies like Ethernet, that simply means that the packet's bits are imposed on the cable as serial changes in voltage levels, one after the other. Each NIC accumulates bits from the cable in a buffer until the complete packet is present. They then strip off the preamble and delimiters and examine the destination MAC address present in the Ethernet frame. If the destination MAC address matches the NIC's MAC address, the frame is retained. Otherwise, the frame is ignored. See Figure 7-4.

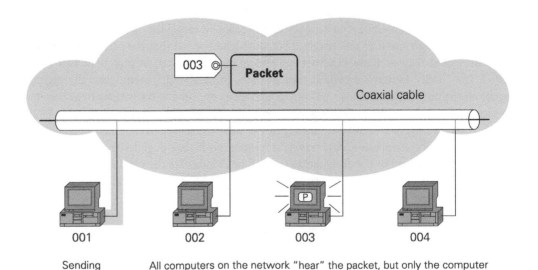

Sending computer

All computers on the network "hear" the packet, but only the computer with the address matching the packet address accepts the packet.

FIGURE 7-4: How Ethernet works

Collision Detection and Avoidance

There's a certain elegance in the original Ethernet idea: *Here's a packet; if it's yours, keep it.* However, there was a downside to the early Ethernet's simplicity: collisions. An Ethernet network has no central controller. Any node may place a packet on the network at any time. The nodes are aware when another node is transmitting, and they wait for the current packet to be sent (plus a short additional time period) before beginning their own transmissions. However, when the network is quiet, nothing prevents two or more nodes from beginning a transmission at the same time. This results in a *packet collision*, which generally means that all packets in the attempt are lost.

Collisions in shared-medium Ethernet are detected in an interesting way: when two pulses from two nodes enter the cable at the same moment, the pulses "add" electrically, and the signal voltage on the cable is higher than during normal network traffic. The NICs monitor the signal voltage while transmitting, and a higher-than-normal voltage indicates a collision.

When any transmitting node detects a collision, it ceases to send the current packet and begins sending out a *jam signal*, which is a bit pattern that disrupts the error-detection bits at the end of the frame. Other nodes on the segment will see the packet as damaged and drop it. When the network becomes quiet, those nodes that had collided wait a random period of time called a *backoff period* (typically only a few microseconds) before attempting to transmit again. The random backoff periods are different for both nodes, making it less likely that the colliding nodes will collide again when they attempt to retransmit their jammed packets.

The backoff period isn't just a random delay value drawn from a fixed distribution. An algorithm called *truncated binary exponential backoff* is used to vary the distribution of the backoff period based on collision frequency. An initial collision triggers a random backoff period of either 0 or 1 slot (where a *slot* is the time normally taken to transmit 512 bits) before attempting retransmission. If packets collide again, a random period of between 0 and 3 slots is used; with each collision the maximum period doubles, until after ten collisions the period is between 0 and 1023 slots in length. The maximum period is then held constant at 1023 slots for a further six collisions, after which the station attempting to transmit stops trying and discards the packet. The overall effect is to slow down network activity during congested periods, "spacing out" retransmitted packets so that the network doesn't simply grind to a halt in a storm of packet collisions.

This protocol is called CSMA/CD, which stands for Carrier Sense Multiple Access with Collision Detection. "Carrier sense" is a bit of a misnomer here. Base band systems like Ethernet have no carrier, which is technically a radio frequency wave on which signals are imposed via modulation. In this case, it only means that nodes on the network have a way to determine when other stations are transmitting.

A network segment containing nodes that may transmit packets that collide is called a *collision domain*. On early Ethernet systems, the entire network was a single collision domain, which meant that throughput degraded as more nodes were added to the network and collisions became more frequent. We'll return to collision domains a little later, in connection with Ethernet bridges and switches.

Ethernet Encoding Systems

Down at the physical level of the OSI model, Ethernet NICs encode the data to be transmitted by imposing a series of voltages on the network medium. The many variations of Ethernet each use a different encoding scheme; here we will briefly describe the schemes used by the 10Mbit standards (10BASE5, 10BASE2 and 10BASE-T), and the dominant 100Mbit (100BASE-TX) and 1Gbit (1000BASE-T) standards.

The electrical design of Ethernet requires us to choose encodings that have a very small DC component (that is, a long-term average voltage of close to zero), regardless of the data being transmitted. Signals from the NIC are inductively coupled onto the shared medium via transformers, which act as high-pass filters; if a DC component were present then this filtering would distort the signal, making it hard for a receiver to accurately recover the transmitted data. An encoding should also be *self-clocking*, possessing sufficiently frequent level transitions to allow the receiver to infer a clock with which to sample the signal. There are obvious parallels here with the encodings used to store data on magnetic media, which is described in Chapter 6.

10BASE5 and 10BASE2 (along with 10BASE-T; see the "10BASE-T and Twisted Pair Cabling" section later in this chapter) encode bits via *Manchester encoding*, shown in Figure 7-5. Each data bit is encoded in one clock cycle, with a transition at the centre of the cycle encoding the bit: a transition from negative to positive is considered a 1-bit, and a transition from positive to negative is considered a 0-bit. If necessary, an extra transition is inserted at the start of a cycle, to put the line into the correct state to encode the bit. The arrows in the figure show you which transitions encode data and which directions the transitions take.

Manchester encoding trivially meets our requirements for being self-clocking (as every bit has at least one transition) and having 0 DC component (as half of each bit period is spent at each voltage level). These properties come at a price, however: the extra transitions introduced by the encoding increase the bandwidth of the signal to around 20MHz. To go beyond 10 Mbps with affordable cabling, it was necessary to devise more efficient encoding schemes.

One such scheme, used by 100BASE-TX Fast Ethernet, is *4B/5B*, so named because it encodes each four data bits into five bits for transmission. The 5-bit encoded group is called a *symbol*. The encoding is performed using a simple static dictionary, shown in Table 7-1, in which each unique 4-bit group translates to a unique 5-bit symbol. The code used in 4B/5B was designed to provide at least a single level transition for every four bits of data. This ensures that the transmitted bitstream is self-clocking, even in the presence of long strings of 0- or 1-bits.

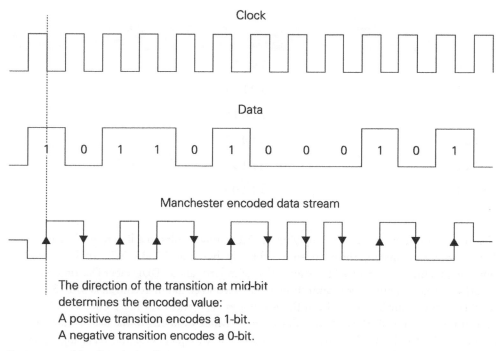

The direction of the transition at mid-bit
determines the encoded value:
A positive transition encodes a 1-bit.
A negative transition encodes a 0-bit.

FIGURE 7-5: Manchester encoding

Table 7-1 **4B/5B Encoding**

Data word	4B/5B code word
0000	11110
0001	01001
0010	10100
0011	10101
0100	01010
0101	01011
0110	01110
0111	01111
1000	10010
1001	10011

continued

Table 7-1   **continued**

Data word	4B/5B code word
1010	10110
1011	10111
1100	11010
1101	11011
1110	11100
1111	11101

Given a data rate of 100Mbit/s, applying 4B/5B coding results in a line rate of 125Mbit/s. Rather than transmitting the encoded bits directly, however, 100BASE-TX applies a second encoding technique, borrowed from an earlier standard called FDDI (Fiber Distributed Data Interface, used in fibre-optics connections). This second encoding technical is MLT-3 (multi-level transmit using 3 levels). Given three voltages -V, 0 and +V, MLT-3 encodes a 0-bit by continuing to transmit the current voltage, and a 1-bit by moving to the next voltage in the sequence (0, +V, 0, -V). The maximum fundamental frequency of the resulting signal is 31.25MHz, as it takes a minimum of four bit periods to cycle through the sequence, allowing us to use cost-effective Category 5 cabling, which is covered in more detail shortly. MLT-3 encoding is shown in Figure 7-6.

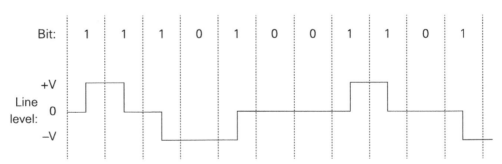

FIGURE 7-6: MLT-3 encoding

While the combination of 4B/5B and MLT-3 coding satisfies the self-clocking requirement, it does not ensure zero DC balance. A partial solution is provided by applying a reversible *scrambling* procedure to the 4B/5B-encoded bitstream. This involves applying the XOR logical operation between the bitstream and a pseudorandom bit sequence and ensures that, in almost all cases, the MLT-3 output spends 25% of its time in the -V state and 25% in the +V state.

Given that the scrambler sequence is known and fixed, it is of course possible to carefully construct a bitstream that cancels out the scrambling, resulting in significant DC bias. Such *killer packets* may be assumed to be rare in practice; nonetheless, most NICs contain circuitry that will detect and compensate for DC offset if it occurs.

100BASE-TX makes use of two pairs of conductors, one carrying data in each direction. Figure 7-7 shows the 100BASE-TX encoding and decoding scheme in its entirety.

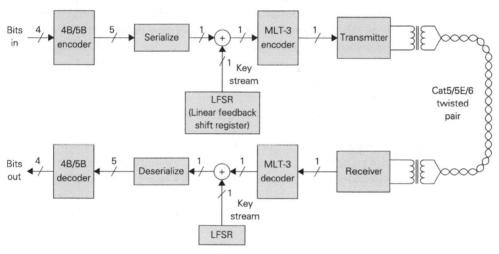

FIGURE 7-7: 100Base TX encoding and decoding

The 1000BASE-T standard provides data rates of 1 gigabit per second while maintaining the same symbol rate as 100BASE-TX (125Msymbols/s). It accomplishes this by using four pairs of conductors (versus one for 100BASE-TX), and by using a denser 5-level amplitude modulation (versus three levels for 100BASE-TX). There are 5^4 = 625 possible symbols, so the theoretical raw bit rate is 125Msymbols/s * log2(625) = 1160 Mbps. The "spare" coding capacity is used to implement a low-density forward error correction scheme known as *trellis coding*, the exact details of which are beyond the scope of this book. This approach effectively compensates for the increase in raw error rate caused by the denser amplitude modulation.

In contrast with 100BASE-TX, which implements full-duplex communication using a dedicated pair of conductors for each direction, 1000BASE-T supports simultaneous bidirectional transmission over the same set of conductors. To accomplish this, each receiver subtracts the (known) output of the local transmitter from the voltage observed on the line, leaving only the incoming signal (if any).

PAM-5 Encoding

After a data stream has been encoded, it must be coupled to the Ethernet medium. This is generally done through small transformers in the NIC. The encoded data stream is a series of digital pulses that exist at one or the other of two voltage levels. When a digital signal is encoded between two voltage levels in this way, it's called *binary signalling*. Typically, a positive voltage level represents a 1-bit and a negative voltage represents a 0-bit.

Higher data rates, like those of Gigabit Ethernet, require denser encoding. The system widely used today is five-level *pulse amplitude modulation*, abbreviated to PAM-5. PAM-5 encodes 2 bits per pulse by varying the signal voltage over five levels rather than only two. Two of the five levels are positive voltages, two are negative voltages and the fifth is 0 voltage. When information is encoded as a varying voltage level in a signal, it's called *amplitude modulation*. PAM-5 varies the amplitude of the pulses that make up the encoded data stream, hence the name pulse amplitude modulation. Schemes like this are called *multi-level signalling*, because more than two voltage levels are used to encode data.

We've drawn a PAM-5 data stream in Figure 7-8, which is a graph of pulse amplitude over time. The grey bars are pulses, and the wide black line is the amplitude for the stream of pulses. Each pulse is considered a symbol, because one pulse encodes two bits. The 0V level does not encode any particular value, and its primary purpose is to allow the receiver to extract a clock signal from the data, and to facilitate error correction using a technology called *forward error correction* (FEC). The details of FEC as used in Gigabit Ethernet are beyond the scope of this book. As a broad overview, though, additional bits are added to a data stream, which allows the receiver to identify and correct a limited number of errors without reversing the line (hence "forward") to request retransmission of data. Forward error correction has much in common with error-correcting code (ECC) memory, which is covered in Chapter 3.

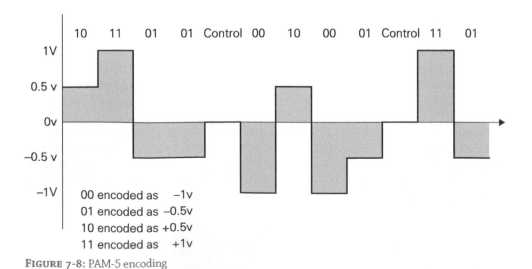

FIGURE 7-8: PAM-5 encoding

The actual graph of a PAM-5 waveform is not as "clean" as the graph in Figure 7-8, especially at gigabit speeds. Noise gets into the waveform, and extracting symbols from the waveform is a serious challenge to the electronics on the receiver side.

10BASE-T and Twisted-Pair Cabling

The early Ethernet implementations based on coaxial cable had a number of problems, collisions being the least of it. 10BASE2, in particular, was vulnerable to mechanical connection issues. Cables had a coaxial connector on each end, and at each node, two cables came together in a coaxial "T" connector; these connectors were inexpensive, and even a comparatively gentle tug on a cable was sometimes enough to interrupt the continuity of the bus. Once the bus had been split in two in this way, radio-frequency signal reflections from the break point would prevent communication even between hosts on the same half. In addition, there were at least twice as many vulnerable connections as there were nodes on the network.

In the late 1980s a new variation of Ethernet appeared: 10BASE-T. The "T" stood for *twisted pair*, which is a way of wrapping two thin (usually 24-gauge) copper wires around one another to reduce interference from external noises sources. To transmit a bit on a coaxial cable, the transmitting NIC applies a voltage to the centre conductor of the cable, with the outer cable shield acting as the ground return path; this is referred to as *single-ended* signalling. To do the same on a twisted-pair cable, the transmitting NIC applies two different voltages to the two conductors: zeros and ones are represented by positive and negative *differences*, rather than by absolute voltages, so this is referred to as *differential* signalling. The receiving NIC can extract the encoded data using a differential amplifier, which converts the voltage difference between its inputs into a single output.

Differential signals travelling over tightly twisted pairs of wires have low electromagnetic emissions (because emissions from one wire will be very nearly cancelled by emissions from the other) and good immunity to interference (because interference will create almost the same voltage change on both wires, without affecting the difference between them). Figure 7-9 illustrates the way differential transmission schemes using balanced lines operate.

A 10BASE-T cable consists of four twisted pairs in one jacket, terminated in 8-conductor modular plugs. A cable of that construction that has been tested to a transmission speed of 100MHz is considered *Category 5* (informally "cat 5"), as defined in the ANSI/EIA-568 cabling standard. Category 5 cables can be used for other sorts of signals, including both audio and video, but Ethernet is now the primary use for Category 5 and its plug-compatible but faster successors, Category 5E and Category 6.

Why four twisted pairs in one jacket? As described earlier, the dominant Gigabit Ethernet technology, 1000BASE-T, achieves its greater throughput in part by splitting a single data stream into four parallel bidirectional streams, each one with its own twisted pair in a Category 5, 5E, or 6 cable. Slower Ethernet technologies may not use all four pairs, and some, like 10BASE-T, use one unidirectional pair for transmit and one for receive.

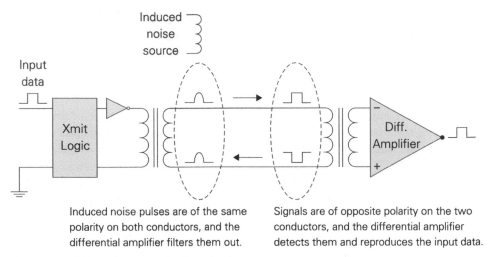

Induced noise pulses are of the same polarity on both conductors, and the differential amplifier filters them out.

Signals are of opposite polarity on the two conductors, and the differential amplifier detects them and reproduces the input data.

FIGURE 7-9: Balanced transmission lines for data

From Bus Topology to Star Topology

Category 5 cabling was not the only change in going from 10BASE2 to 10BASE-T. 10BASE-T networks are a whole different *shape*. The way that nodes are connected in a network is called the network *topology*. 10BASE5 and 10BASE2 networks used *bus topology*, in which all nodes are simply daisy chained along a single stretch of coaxial cable. By contrast, 10BASE-T networks use *star topology*, in which all nodes connect to a central *network hub*. See Figure 7-10 for a comparison of the two topologies.

The central hub was necessary because 10BASE-T networks use separate differential pairs for transmit and receive. This allowed *full duplex* operation, by which a node may send and receive data simultaneously. However, it also required that the transmit wires of each node be connected to the receive wires of every other node. This was done at the hub. Early Ethernet hubs were just passive connectors, in which the appropriate wires from each node were connected to the appropriate wires from all the other nodes. Later hubs reduced *cross-talk* (signal interference between nearby wires due to inductive and capacitive coupling) and *shot noise* (static from motors, relays and similar electrical equipment) by adding digital amplifiers between each leg of the hub and the central connections. This led to fewer damaged packets and improved overall network throughput. Such active hubs were originally called *repeater hubs* or *repeaters* (because the amplifiers took a weak or noisy signal and retransmitted it as a stronger and cleaner signal) but today are known simply as network hubs or Ethernet hubs. Purely passive hubs are no longer used.

In truth, hubs aren't quite as simple as amplifiers that strengthen and "clean up" packets. A hub used as a link between two network segments isolates the segments from one another with respect to cabling disruptions like bad coaxial connectors.

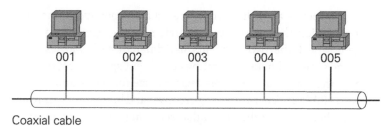

Coaxial cable

A bus topology network

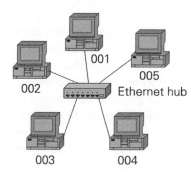

A star topology network

FIGURE 7-10: Bus topology versus star topology

As good as 10BASE-T cabling and hubs were, the system still connected all nodes to all other nodes as a single collision domain. This meant that packet collisions continued to be an issue with hubs, and collision detection schemes had to be present to manage them. Note that hubs are layer 1 devices, and at the physical layer what a hub does is mostly amplify and thus "clean up" the signals passing through the hub. To do more than that, you need more than a hub.

Switched Ethernet

An elegant solution to Ethernet packet collision overhead didn't appear until 1990. The firm Kalpana (later acquired by Cisco) invented a *switching hub* for Ethernet networks. Switching hubs occupy the same position in star topology networks as conventional hubs do, in that all nodes on a star network are connected to one port on the switching hub at the network's centre. However, in contrast to conventional hubs, switching hubs operate at layer 2 on the OSI reference model, having some awareness of the data that is being passed through them. Today, such devices are simply called *network switches*, and Ethernet networks could not be as fast or reliable as they are without them.

Network switch technology grew out of an earlier concept called a *network bridge*. The first network bridges were two-port devices that allowed two separate network segments to communicate. The bridge is necessary if the two segments use different technologies (say, 10BASE2 and 10BASE-T) or the same technology operating at different speeds, or if the size of the entire network exceeds the maximum allowable segment size for the technology in question (185m in the case of 10BASE2). A network bridge receives and buffers packets from one segment, and retransmits them on the other when that segment's medium is quiet; in doing so it prevents the two bridged network segments from becoming a single collision domain. Collisions do not propagate through bridges, allowing each of the two bridged network segments to have more nodes than a single segment could handle.

Very simply put, a network switch creates a momentary dedicated connection between two and only two network nodes. When one node wishes to send a packet to another node connected to a switch, the switch creates the connection for just long enough to allow the packet to pass between them. Because during that brief moment the nodes are on what amounts to an isolated, two-node network, collisions are impossible, and no time or bandwidth is spent on collision detection and retransmission. Other nodes on the network do not see packets passed between the two nodes connected through the switch. Network switches for home use have four, five, or perhaps eight ports. Switches used in corporate environments may have hundreds. Figure 7-11 shows a network switch.

> **NOTE** We need to be very clear that Figure 7-11 is a metaphor: network switches are fully electronic, and there are no mechanical switch contacts inside them. Modern switches are capable of sustaining multiple simultaneous connections between many different pairs of nodes, so that more than a single packet can pass through the switch's *crossbar* (the matrix of electrical switching logic that connects ports to one another) at any given time.

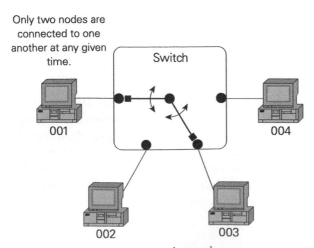

FIGURE 7-11: How network switches work

To do their job, network switches must contain considerably more intelligence than hubs. A switch maintains a table of MAC addresses for all the nodes connected to its ports; using this table, it can instantly associate the MAC address of an incoming packet with an outgoing port and thus make a temporary connection between two hosts. Building and maintaining the table is done in two ways:

- By broadcasting a packet to the reserved MAC address FF:FF:FF:FF:FF:FF, the switch can request that all nodes reachable through the switch's ports respond with their MAC addresses. Some computers also broadcast their own MAC addresses to the network when they are powered up or rebooted.

- By listening to both the sending and receiving addresses in all packets that it handles, a switch can verify the MAC addresses reachable on any of its ports.

The simplest possible switch would buffer incoming packets in memory until it receives an entire packet and verifies that it is complete and not corrupt. Only then does it begin forwarding the packet to the destination host. This is called *store-and-forward* switching. To improve throughput, a technology called *cut-through* switching was developed. In cut-through switching, the switch inspects an incoming packet only until it has the complete destination address, at which time (if no other transmission to the destination is in progress) it immediately begins forwarding the packet to the destination host. Without buffering overhead, this gets the packet to the destination in the shortest possible time. However, cut-through switching does not verify that packets are complete, and will forward incomplete or damaged packets. The destination host will detect the damaged packet and discard it. If this happens often enough, the throughput benefits of cut-through switching will be lost.

Using switches and hubs isn't an either/or situation. They can be freely mixed in Ethernet networks, as shown in Figure 7-12. In the figure, four nodes are connected directly to the Ethernet switch. A hub connecting three additional nodes is also connected to the switch. The key issue in using hubs is that collisions again become possible on the leg of the network connected by a hub. The highlighting in Figure 7-12 shows the four-node collision domain within the network. The switch can create a dedicated connection between node 003 and the hub, but the hub connects nodes 004, 005 and 006 in a way such that the switch cannot reach any of the three individually. If nodes 004 and 006 begin transmitting a packet simultaneously, the packets will collide, and all the usual collision overhead will apply.

The situation illustrated in Figure 7-12 comes up often in wireless networking because wireless access points (APs) are conceptually closer to hubs than to switches.

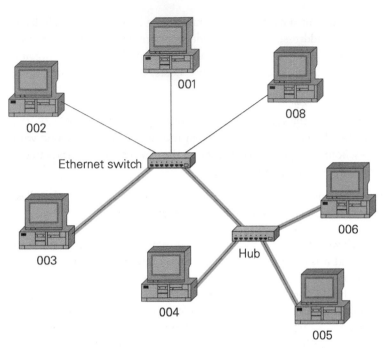

FIGURE 7-12: Mixing switches and hubs

Routers and the Internet

One way to think about LANs versus WANs is that LANs are networks of computers, and WANs are networks of networks. It wasn't that way in the very beginning, when WANs primarily connected large, lonely computers at one company or university with large, lonely computers at other companies and universities. Today, of course, no organisation ever has just one computer, and this is often the case for individuals at home too. No matter how simple or inexpensive, every computer, smartphone or tablet has a network port of some kind, be it wired, wireless or both. With LANs everywhere, the next step is to allow one LAN to network with other LANs. This is what the Internet was designed to do. And although Internet mechanisms go well beyond the stated topic of this chapter (Ethernet) the Internet protocol suite is very much involved in even the smallest local-area network—a network of one device—that connects to the Internet.

Names vs. Addresses

On a LAN, a node is identified by its MAC address. MAC addresses are (ideally) unique, so theoretically a node should be able to contact another node on the other side of the world by placing the MAC address of the faraway node in a packet. This doesn't work for an obvious reason: a MAC address contains no information about where its node actually *is*. As a metaphor, think of people at a meeting around a conference table. Everyone can see everyone else around the table, and when anyone talks, everyone can hear. That's how LANs work. At the same time, other people are sitting around other conference tables in other buildings, talking in the same local way. How can you get two such meetings to talk to one another? If both conference tables have speaker-phones, one table's phone can call the other, and the two conference tables will be in communication.

A phone number isn't just an ID code. A phone number consists of several parts in most nations. In the U.S., this is a country code, an area code, an exchange and a subscriber number. Each level contains information about the physical location of the phone and each level narrows the location down further. For example, a phone might be in the U.S. (North America code +1), in the Colorado Springs metro area (area code 719), in an exchange (674) and at some four-digit subscriber number within that exchange.

The Internet uses a system very much like this. As we've mentioned briefly earlier in the chapter, the collection of rules and techniques that enable packet-based communication over the Internet is called the *Internet Protocol* (IP). Within the Internet protocol is an addressing scheme based on a type of numeric address called the *IP address*. The IP is intimately connected with a higher-level protocol called *Transmission Control Protocol* (TCP). If you refer to Figure 7-1, you see that TCP is immediately above IP on the OSI reference model.

The IP is focused on addressing and routing *packets*; the TCP is focused on establishing and maintaining *connections* between computers so that packets may be transferred. TCP is the Internet's delivery mechanism: it makes sure that packets actually get where they're going, and that the order of a stream of packets is preserved as it travels from computer to computer. IP and TCP work together and are rarely used separately. This is why most of the time you'll see them referred to as TCP/IP.

IP Addresses and TCP Ports

An IP address has two parts. One is the address of a network, and the other is the address of a particular node (in Internet jargon, a *host*) present on that network. Unlike a MAC address, which is more of a name or an ID code, an IP address really is an address, and allows a network appliance called a *router* to locate a network and a host based on that address.

By convention, IP addresses are usually written out this way, as a so-called *dotted quad*:

```
264.136.8.101
```

Each group of numbers separated by periods is called an *octet*, which in computer science means an 8-bit quantity. If you're sharp you may have noticed that 264 is not expressible in 8 bits. That was deliberate. In writing this chapter, we don't want to use someone's actual IP address, and the custom in books and papers is to create imaginary addresses for examples by using a value greater than 255 for the first octet.

In an IP address, one or more of the higher-order octets contains the network address, and one or more of the lower-order octets contains the host address. In Figure 7-13, on the right is a LAN with four hosts. Between the LAN and the outside world is a router. In this case, the three higher-order octets contain the address of the network. The lowest octet contains the address of a particular host. Given an address like 264.136.8.101, a host anywhere in the world can create a TCP connection with the top computer in Figure 7-13.

Larger networks with more than 255 hosts divide the IP address differently, with more octets devoted to the host portion of the address, and fewer to the network portion of the address. The split between the network portion and the host portion of an IP address is specified by a four-octet bit pattern called a *subnetwork mask*. ("Subnetwork" is often shortened to "subnet".) The mask is used to separate the two portions of the address for further processing. Where networks are nested one inside another, a separate subnetwork mask (informally called a "subnet mask") is used for each of the separate networks.

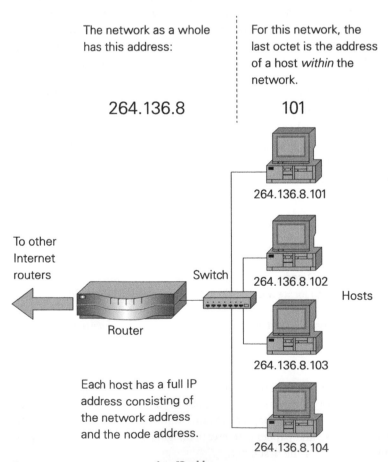

FIGURE 7-13: The two parts of an IP address

Internet routing is complex, and the details of how routers work internally is beyond the scope of this book. As mentioned earlier in this chapter, they use an internal routing table to look up network addresses to discover how to reach them. An entry in the routing table provides information allowing the router to choose a route by which the destination network may be reached. A given router cannot necessarily access any arbitrary network with one single connection. It may take several sequential connections (called *hops*) to reach a given destination. At the end of each hop there's another router, and that router forwards the packet to the next router along the route. Eventually the packet arrives at the destination network, and that network's router forwards the packet to the individual host to which the packet was addressed.

Routers come in many sizes, from a home network router that can fit in the palm of your hand to a cabinet the size of a refrigerator that weighs hundreds of pounds. The routing table in a large router may have hundreds of thousands of entries. The routing table on a home router typically has only one, which contains the address of the home's ISP's router. Any packet originating on a home router has only one possible path—through its ISP—to the rest of the Internet. So the home router forwards all packets to the ISP's much larger and more powerful router, which then selects the next hop on the route.

The TCP protocol creates connections between two hosts (one or both of which may be servers) using IP addresses. These connections, however, are not simply between computers or other network devices. Connections are actually between two software applications running on those computers. (Refer to Figure 7-1, and the application set of the OSI reference model.) A web browser on your tablet or computer connects to a web server on a remote host. An email client on your tablet or computer connects to an email server on the remote host. This final piece of routing is accomplished using *port numbers*, which are 16-bit values that (as we saw earlier) are present in every IP packet and allow the network stack on a host to identify which application should receive each packet. We refer to the act of splitting a single stream of incoming packets from the network into multiple streams of packets on the basis of destination port numbers as *demultiplexing*.

When a client application wants to establish a TCP connection to a server application, it begins by assigning an arbitrary unused local port number to uniquely identify its end of the connection. It then sends a connection request, specifying a destination port number; this is not an arbitrary number but instead is generally one of several *well-known port numbers*, which are associated with a higher-level protocol. HTTP is associated with port 80, email with ports 25 (sending via SMTP) and 110 (receiving via POP), SSL (Secure Sockets Layer) with port 443, FTP (File Transfer Protocol) with port 21, and so on. A server application must "listen" to a port for TCP to make a connection to that port; if there is nobody listening on port 80, for example, there is no web server in operation at the remote host. When a connection is accepted, an arbitrary unused port number is assigned to the server end of the connection; further communication happens via this port number, freeing up the well-known port to accept further incoming connections.

Routers can block connections that use specific port numbers as a security measure, to prevent remote connections to unauthorised servers. For example, a common way to combat email spam is for hosting services to configure their routers to block port 25, which is assigned to the Simple Mail Transfer Protocol (SMTP). Certain software is difficult to block by port number because the protocols allow the use of any open port via "port discovery", which basically means that the two hosts attempt a connection on a range of ports until they find one that works. (BitTorrent is a good example of such an adaptable protocol.)

Ports are also important in a router-based function called Network Address Translation (NAT), which is covered a little later in the "Network Address Translation" section.

Local IP Addresses and DHCP

When the architects of the original Internet defined the suite of Internet protocols that include the IP addressing system, they never imagined that the general public would one day be connecting to the Internet by the billions. They also didn't envision that devices as mundane as telephones, TV sets and even refrigerators would someday want their own IP addresses as well. This has led to a serious problem: there only 4.3 billion possible 32-bit IP addresses, which isn't nearly enough to give one to every person (or refrigerator) on Earth.

Several things are being done to deal with this shortage of IP addresses. The high road is to create a whole new addressing scheme with larger addresses, which is being done in the IPv6 project. (The current 32-bit IP addressing system is called IPv4.) The IPv6 address space is 128 bits wide. This allows it to support up to 2^{128} different addresses. That number works out at 3.4×10^{38}, which dwarfs the total number of stars, planets, moons and asteroids in the observable universe.

At this writing, only about 10% of Internet traffic uses IPv6 addresses. The expectation is that IPv6 will eventually dominate the Internet. In the meantime, the shortage has been ameliorated to some extent by the use of *local IP addresses*. The Internet Assigned Numbers Authority (IANA) has set aside four blocks of IP addresses as local, meaning that they cannot be routed and are basically invisible except within their own local networks. This makes them sound useless, but in fact local IP addresses make it possible to use the TCP/IP-based Internet services within a LAN, where there is no router between any two hosts. Because local IP addresses cannot be seen outside of their local network, there's no danger in reusing them. Hundreds of millions of people can use the address 192.168.1.100 at the same time. The following are the four blocks of local IP addresses:

```
10.0.0.0- 10.255.255.255

169.254.0.1 - 169.254.255.254

172.16.0.0 - 172.31.255.255

192.168.0.0 - 192.268.255.255
```

Local IP addresses can't be seen past a router, but in nearly all home networks, the router performs an important service: it distributes local IP addresses to the nodes in its own network. A piece of software called a *Dynamic Host Configuration Protocol* (DHCP) server runs in the router, and when a node comes online and asks for network configuration, the DHCP server scans the addresses in its local IP address table and sends down a local address that isn't already being used. A number of other configuration options (including the subnet mask) are sent down at the same time with the local IP address, but they're beyond the scope of this chapter.

The node making the request gets a *lease* on the IP address for a limited period of time, often 24 hours. When the lease expires, the address goes back into the free address pool. If a node is still on the network when its IP address lease expires, it simply requests that the lease be renewed. A reasonable expiration period on DHCP leases (24 hours or more) allows nodes to be powered down overnight without losing their leases. The next time a node is powered up, it will still have the same IP address.

DHCP isn't used only for distributing local IP addresses to LANs. Internet service providers (ISPs) run DHCP servers as well, and when a home router connects to its ISP, the ISP's DHCP server sends down configuration information to the home router, including a *global* IP address. This address is how your LAN is known to other networks across the Internet.

An IP address distributed by a DHCP server, whether local or global, is called a *dynamic IP address*. Dynamic IP addresses are used in situations where the address may change without disrupting network operation. Server software that can be accessed from the Internet requires an IP address that doesn't change. Such an address is a *static IP address*. Internet hosting services that allow you to run your own servers on the Internet are allocated blocks of static IP addresses. When you establish an account with a hosting service, you are provided with a static IP address for your server. That one static IP address is how people and other servers on the Internet can find your server.

It's possible to manually assign static local IP addresses to nodes on a LAN. Such addresses are not leased and don't expire. They are useful for nodes like network printers that are accessed by other network nodes via their IP address. If a network printer's IP address changes, some nodes on the network may not be able to access it. Most network printers include instructions and sometimes software allowing a static local IP address to be assigned to the printer.

The local IP addresses that begin with 169.254 have a special use: all Windows versions from Windows 2000 onwards implement a service called *Automatic Private IP Addressing* (APIPA), which provides a local IP address from the 169.254 block any time a DHCP server is not available to provide a local address. A Windows node with an APIPA address can communicate with any other node on its local network segment that has an APIPA address. This allows small numbers of computers to connect through a switch without requiring a router. The more general term for a system that automatically provides local network addresses and other configuration parameters is *zero-configuration networking*. A similar system called Avahi exists for Linux, but Raspbian does not include it by default and it must be installed manually if it is desired. Zero-configuration networking is primarily useful for small networks that have no connection to the Internet and thus no router or DHCP server to handle local segment configuration.

Network Address Translation

Local IP addresses are invisible to other networks beyond the local router. How, then, can TCP/IP allow nodes with local IP addresses to connect to the Internet? The answer is another software service running on the router: *Network Address Translation* (NAT). Simply put, NAT translates a non-routable local IP address into a global, routable IP address. In addition, it provides, almost as a by-product, fairly strong protection against unwanted connections from outside the local network. Figure 7-14 is a sketch of a possible home network setup: four computers, a router, and a switch. In many, or even most, cases these days, the router and the switch are combined into a single physical appliance. (They're broken out here for conceptual clarity.) Each of the network's four computers has a local, non-routable IP address. NAT is running inside the router. NAT keeps these local IP addresses in a table that it maintains for its own use.

As we explained earlier, the network as a whole has a single public, routable IP address that is the only address for any network node that can be seen by the outside world. This address resides in the network's router, and for home networks it is generally provided by the ISP's DHCP server. Local IP addresses are not routable, and to create connections between individual computers on a local network segment and hosts on the other side of the router, the router creates "extended" IP addresses by combining the local IP address assigned to a device on the local network with a TCP port number. Which port number is used isn't important, as long as it isn't already used by anything else on that particular network. (There are more than 65,000 different port numbers, so finding a free one on even a modest-sized network is rarely a problem.) NAT stores extended IP addresses for its local nodes in an internal table that acts as a sort of "internal phone book" for devices on the local network segment. This table is not accessible from the Internet. Only NAT can read it or change it. On Linux systems, this process is called *IP masquerading*. In a sense, the router is assigning port numbers as ID codes to the computers on its local network.

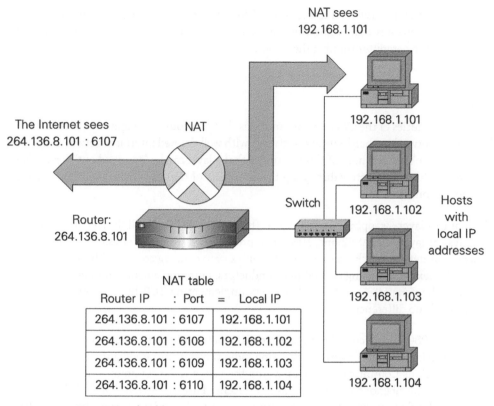

FIGURE 7-14: How Network Address Translation (NAT) works

When one of the computers inside the network wants to connect (for example) to a web server, NAT takes the web page request and places an extended IP address consisting of the router's IP address plus the requesting computer's port number into the request. When the web server establishes a connection, it uses this extended IP address, and not the internal, local IP address of the computer to which it connects. The connection is thus established with the router, *not* the computer—and the router decides what material delivered from the web server can reach the computer. The web server has no knowledge of the requesting computer beyond its port number, and the port number alone does not allow a connection to a local IP address. Because the address that servers outside the local network must use is created by NAT, the connection must be initiated by NAT, in cooperation with one of the local network nodes. This prevents unsolicited connections from outside the local network.

NAT complicates matters when a user of a computer on a local network wants to run a publicly available server on the computer. Because outside users must be allowed to make a connection to the server, a way for connections initiated outside the network must be provided by the router. This is done through *port forwarding*, in which an outside request for a server connection is forwarded to a local IP address for the computer on which the server is running. NAT ensures that connections are made only to the server, and not to any other software on the computer running the server.

Wi-Fi

One of the beauties of the OSI reference model is that it encourages engineers to "layer" their designs for networking hardware and software, with well-defined interfaces between adjacent layers. A non-obvious benefit of this layering is that a layer can be "swapped out" for a different layer without completely disrupting the operation of the stack from the perspective of the application layer.

Much of this layer-swapping has occurred at the bottom, at the data link layer and especially the physical layer. 10BASE2 and 10BASE-T provide two different physical media for the transport of network packets: one is a half-duplex system using coaxial cable, and the other is a full-duplex system using twisted-pair conductors. Both implement Ethernet networking, and from the perspective of the higher layers implementing TCP/IP and network applications, there's no difference.

In the mid-1980s, researchers began to explore the notion of creating Ethernet-like data link and physical layers without wires at all, using radio waves or infrared light. The U.S. Federal Communications Commission, which governs the use of radio communication in the U.S., had opened a number of frequency bands to unlicensed use in 1985. In 1987, NCR created a wireless technology to link its cashier station products. It worked very well, and the firm developed the technology into a commercial product line called WaveLAN, which was placed on the market in 1988. A similar but incompatible system was developed by Canadian firm Telesystems SLW at about the same time, and was eventually spun off as Aironet. Hoping to see its technology incorporated into the IEEE 802 LAN standard, NCR contributed the design to the 802 standards committee in 1990. The IEEE proposed a new standard for wireless Ethernet and called it 802.11. The standard was published in 1997. This original 802.11 spec embraced a number of existing modulation technologies, bit rates and MAC schemes, making it more of a menu than a standard. (For example, it included a physical layer spec for modulated infrared light that never saw broad adoption.) There were so many choices that even products completely compliant with the standard could be incompatible with other compliant products.

Most wireless networking products that adhere to the 802.11 standard are referred to using the name *Wi-Fi*, from an early play on the term "hi-fi" for audio technology. "Wi-Fi" is a trademark owned by a trade group called the Wi-Fi Alliance, and rights to use the term on products are not granted until the products are tested for compliance with the pertinent sections of the IEEE 802.11 standard.

Standards within Standards

Quite apart from compatibility issues, early 802.11 products billed as "wireless Ethernet" offered bit rates of only 1 Mbps or 2 Mbps. This was far slower than 10 Mbps technologies like 10BASE2 and 10BASE-T, and the 100 Mbps and 1000 Mbps technologies that followed them. In the years after 1997, the IEEE 802.11 committee began work on several addenda to the 802.11 standard, defining new wireless technologies focused on improving throughput:

- **802.11a:** Operates on the 5GHz band, with a nominal bit rate of 54 Mbps, and a practical throughput of about half that, using TCP. The spec was finalised in 2000.

- **802.11b:** Operates on the 2.4GHz band, with a nominal bit rate of 11 Mbps, and a practical TCP throughput of about 6 Mbps. The spec was finalised in 1999.

- **802.11g:** Operates on the 2.4GHz band, but uses several technologies originally developed for the 802.11a standard to allow bit rates of up to 54 Mbps. As with 802.11a, practical TCP throughput is less than half that, at about 22 Mbps. The spec was finalised in late 2003.

- **802.11n:** Operates on either the 2.4GHz band or the 5GHz band. It achieves much higher throughput than earlier technologies by using twice the channel bandwidth (40MHz) when possible, and multiple antennas with a technology called multiple-input, multiple-output (MIMO). Maximum bit rate can theoretically be as high as 600 Mbps, but the practical bit rate and TCP throughput depend heavily on local channel congestion and rarely top 100 Mbps. The spec was finalised in 2009.

- **802.11ac:** Operates only on the 5GHz band. Its technology is an evolutionary extension of 802.11n, and achieves throughput close to 1000BASE-T (gigabit Ethernet) by using additional antennas and "bonding" adjacent 40MHz channels into 80 or 160MHz channels, where local spectrum use allows. The spec was approved at the beginning of 2014, and commercial products began appearing in large numbers later that year.

Although the IEEE formally withdraws addenda like these once they have been folded into the larger 802.11 spec and ratified, terms like *Wireless-B* and *Wireless-G* continue to be used to differentiate products that do not support all available technologies. In practice, nearly all commercial products at this writing support standards b, g, and n on 2.4GHz, with some lines supporting 802.11a on 5GHz as well.

Many other addenda to 802.11 have been published and ratified since 1997, generally providing refinements to the primary spec in areas like mobile device roaming, quality of service, bridging networks and security.

Facing the Real World

Going wireless complicates networking in a number of ways. Wired Ethernet keeps its signal inside a cable of some sort and, beyond certain physical limitations (especially the radius at which an Ethernet cable may be bent), where the cable can go, the signal goes. Wi-Fi uses microwaves travelling freely through the air, in and among buildings and other structures. The problems related to the microwave physical medium fall into several categories:

- Attenuation (reduction of signal strength) due to distance through free space, and the presence of walls and water-rich exterior factors like broadleaf trees, rain or snow

- Microwave shadows cast by large metallic objects such as aluminium sides, filing cabinets, refrigerators and industrial equipment

- Multipath interference caused by signals taking paths of different lengths from the transmit antenna to the receive antenna, and interfering with one another constructively or destructively at the receive antenna

- Channel congestion, which is interference from Wi-Fi signals on the same or adjacent channels

- Interference from other technologies using the same frequencies as Wi-Fi, including Bluetooth gear, cordless phones, medical devices, sensor networks and, on some frequencies, amateur radio transceivers

- The hidden node problem, in which not all terminals participating in a network can see each other, causing difficulties for MAC

Even along unobstructed paths, microwaves transmitted from an omnidirectional antenna are attenuated by distance according to the inverse square law. When Wi-Fi hardware is used in fixed *point-to-point service*, as in links between buildings, directional antennas may be used to focus microwave energy along the path between a link's two endpoints. This allows communication across gaps that would be impossible with omnidirectional antennas at the same power level.

Microwaves are electromagnetic radiation, and may be reflected as they travel from transmitter to receiver. Wi-Fi signals bounce off walls, floors, ceilings and large objects, especially objects made of metal. This causes multiple wavefronts to arrive at the receiver along paths of different lengths, and thus at (very) slightly different times. If two or more wavefronts arrive precisely "in phase" they can theoretically boost signal strength at the receive antenna. However, in virtually all cases, the many wavefronts interfere with one another in unpredictable ways, causing *fading*. Even worse, multipath fading effects can be strongly frequency-dependent, causing not just fading but distortion of wideband signals. Figure 7-15 illustrates multipath interference.

In most Wi-Fi gear going back to the original Wireless-B, access points and wireless routers incorporate two antennas to deal with multipath interference. The ideal distance between them is one wavelength, which at 2.4GHz is 12.5cm, or just under five inches. The Wi-Fi receiver continuously samples signals on both antennas, and chooses the stronger of the two. This is called *diversity reception*. Having the antennas one wavelength apart optimises the chances that a usable signal is present on one antenna when the other antenna is subject to multipath interference.

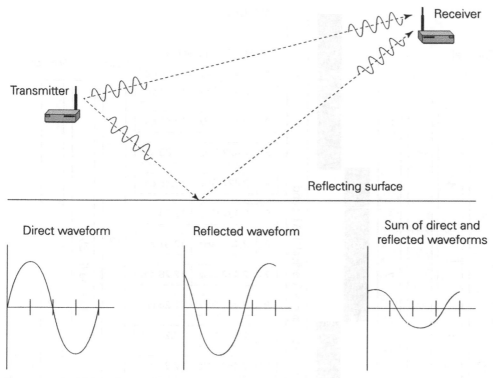

Receiver

Transmitter

Reflecting surface

Direct waveform

Reflected waveform

Sum of direct and
reflected waveforms

FIGURE 7-15: Multipath interference

Channel congestion is a consequence of a small number of distinct channels and of the way microwave spectrum space is allocated to those channels. Wi-Fi channels on 2.4GHz are not laid out nose-to-tail across the band, but overlap, as shown in Figure 7-16. Only three non-overlapping channels exist: channels 1, 6 and 11.

Channels 1, 6 and 11 do not overlap with one another, but *do* overlap with the channels to either side of them. A strong signal of some sort on channel 5 may make channel 6 unusable, for example.

NOTE

In crowded urban areas, interference from Wi-Fi gear on adjacent channels makes selecting a channel for use difficult. There are Wi-Fi survey apps available for mobile devices like tablets and smartphones that sample Wi-Fi signals and plot out their distribution across the 2.4GHz band on graphs. Once a survey app determines where neighbouring Wi-Fi gear is operating on the band, it becomes possible to choose the quietest channel currently available.

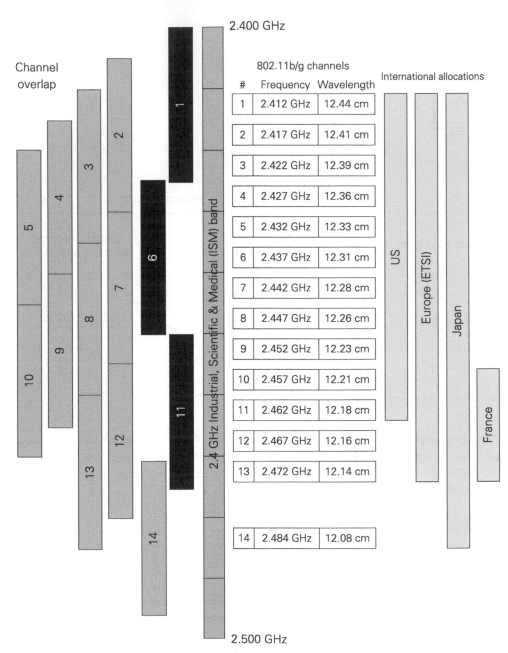

FIGURE 7-16: Wi-Fi frequency allocation on the 2.4GHz ISM band

Exactly which channels are available is dependent on national radio frequency regulations. In the U.S., only the first 11 channels may be used. Additional channels 12 and 13 are available in many other countries, including the UK. Channel 14 is available only in Japan. France allows only channels 10-13, and Spain only channels 10-11. Channel allocation on the 5GHz band is complex and difficult to summarise. The band is larger and the individual channels wider, so high bit-rate technologies like Wireless-N work best at 5GHz.

The 2.4GHz band does not belong to Wi-Fi alone. Its formal name is the industrial, scientific, and medical (ISM) band, and many different classes of devices use it. Interference from such devices is not only possible but likely. The most familiar is the short-range Bluetooth wireless technology. Inexpensive cordless phones use 2.4GHz and are a common source of interference, as are microwave ovens, which may emit enough stray microwave energy to cause frequent frame retransmissions and a visibly slower link. If interference from industrial or medical equipment occurs, Wi-Fi users have no recourse but to relocate their gear to a different channel.

Wi-Fi Equipment in Use

The simplest way to think of a wireless network is to replace a conventional wired Ethernet hub with a Wi-Fi appliance called a *wireless access point* (AP.) The network shown in Figure 7-12 then becomes something very much like Figure 7-17. A Wi-Fi AP *is* an Ethernet hub, using the Wi-Fi data link and physical layers rather than the data link and physical layer for twisted pair network technologies like 10BASE-T, 100BASE-TX or 1000BASE-T. Nodes (often called *stations* in technical literature) that connect wirelessly use a type of NIC called a *wireless client adapter*. The term "client" here alludes to a sort of client/server relationship with the access point, which "serves" an Ethernet connection to one or more wireless clients. A wireless client adapter can be an add-on device (as it generally is in desktop computers) or an integral part of a mobile device like a laptop, tablet or smartphone.

All nodes connecting through the access point become part of a single collision domain, because there is no physical mechanism to support Ethernet switching through a wireless access point. Furthermore, like an early 10BASE5 or 10BASE2 network, Wi-Fi networks are half-duplex, with data travelling in only one direction at a time.

Access points have a number of jobs in a typical Wi-Fi network:

- **Broadcasting its presence:** There is a type of 802.11 management frame called a *beacon frame*, which is broadcast periodically to let stations know that the network is there under a particular name and is available for connection.

- **Station authentication and encryption:** This happens through Wi-Fi security protocols like EAP, WEP, WPA and WPA-2. Although it is possible to authenticate a station without encrypting subsequent traffic, authentication and encryption are generally handled together. The exceptions are some public hotspots in restaurants and coffee shops, which simply leave the AP open for everyone. This is a security risk, as others in the location can monitor network traffic using "sniffing" utilities.

- **Forwarding frames between stations:** All frames travelling between stations associated to an access point travel via the access point, even if the two stations are within range of each other. The access point receives the frame from the sender, and repeats it to the receiver.

- **Bridging to the wired portions of the network:** Because an AP connects a hubbed subnetwork to a switched network, it must perform the function of a network bridge.

- **Media access control (MAC):** The access point may provide centralised control of media access, explicitly notifying stations when they are free to transmit. Few products implement this *point coordination function* (PCF), relying instead on a distributed approach, described in the section "Wi-Fi Distributed Media Access."

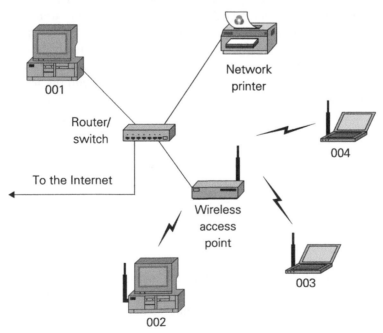

FIGURE 7-17: A simple wireless network

Early in the Wi-Fi era, wireless access points were separate units, intended to be added onto an existing wired network with its own router/switch appliance. Since the mid-2000s, the router/switch and wireless access point have generally been combined into a single appliance that incorporates a network router governing an Internet connection, a wired Ethernet switch with several Category 5 connectors and a wireless access point. This combination appliance is called a *wireless router*. In early days wireless access points and wireless routers had external, "steerable" antennas. Today most wireless devices (whether wireless routers or mobile clients) have antennas hidden inside the device case.

Infrastructure Networks vs. Ad Hoc Networks

The technical term for the sort of network shown in Figure 7-14 is *infrastructure network*. The term "infrastructure" is used because such a network is planned and constructed in a particular way, like a highway system. The access point and the stations associated with it form a *Basic Service Set* (BSS); this is given a distinctive human-readable name, called the *Service Set Identifier* (SSID), which wireless stations use to locate and connect to the infrastructure network when they come online. Stations may connect to or disconnect from the AP, but the overall shape of the network does not change. In modern infrastructure networks, there is almost always a router associated with one or more access points, providing a connection to larger wired networks or the global Internet.

From its inception, the 802.11 standard defined another, very different sort of network: the *ad hoc wireless network*. In an ad hoc network, wireless stations connect to one another, without the intermediation of an access point, forming an *Independent Basic Service Set* (IBSS). This requires that the stations place their Wi-Fi client adapters in ad hoc mode instead of infrastructure mode. "Ad hoc" here indicates that the network is unplanned and assembled when necessary, but it vanishes when the stations disconnect. (Think of a network of laptops convened on a conference table to share documents pertinent to a meeting.) Any station in an ad hoc network may communicate with any other station in the network, just as would be possible in an infrastructure network, but in this case frames travel directly from the sender to the receiver rather than via an access point. See Figure 7-18.

Ad hoc networks have some advantages over infrastructure networks. For short-lived networks, they avoid the cost and effort of providing an access point. Also, peak throughput between two stations in a quiet network is doubled, as each frame is transmitted once (from sender to receiver) rather than twice (from sender to access point and from access point to receiver). However, they also suffer from some significant disadvantages:

- All 802.11 wireless networks require that each station maintains an accurate current time, which is used for power management (allowing a station to "go to sleep" for a period when idle) and MAC. In an infrastructure network, each beacon frame transmitted by the access point contains a time, which the other stations in its BSS use to synchronise their clocks. In an ad hoc network this timing synchronisation function (TSF) must instead be implemented in a distributed fashion. Each station periodically attempts to transmit a beacon frame containing its current time; on receiving a beacon frame, a station updates its current time if the time indicated in the beacon frame is later than the current time. This scheme has been shown to scale poorly with the number of stations in the network; beyond a certain limit, contention causes beacons to be lost, and some stations (generally those with the fastest clocks) may become desynchronised from the rest of the network.

- As stations in an ad hoc network must be within radio range of one another to communicate, the maximum separation between stations is roughly half that of an infrastructure network, where a well-placed access point can relay frames between stations on opposite sides of its coverage area. Furthermore, it is often possible to site an access point in an elevated position with good sight lines, extending its footprint.

Not all operating systems support ad hoc mode adequately, or at all, even though the client adapter hardware may be fully Wi-Fi compliant.

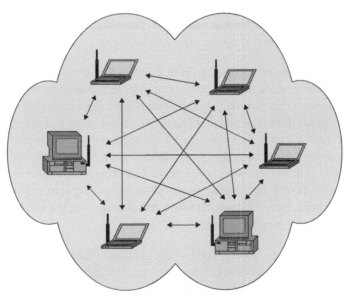

FIGURE 7-18: An ad hoc wireless network

Wi-Fi Distributed Media Access

As noted earlier, very few products implement the centralised PCF scheme for MAC. In the absence of PCF, stations are still able to regulate their access to the medium using the *distributed coordination function* (DCF). While the DCF has some similarities to the CSMA/CD approach used in wired Ethernet, a key difference is that it is not generally feasible for a station to sense the wireless medium while transmitting, as the relatively strong local transmitted signal will tend to drown out the relatively weak signals from other stations. This precludes conventional collision detection.

In the absence of reliable collision detection, Wi-Fi networks instead employ *Carrier Sense Multiple Access/Collision Avoidance* (CSMA/CA), which aims to *avoid* packet collisions rather than detect them, which works this way: as in CSMA/CD, a station first listens to the channel to detect the signal of another station transmitting. This is called *physical carrier sensing*, because it involves the station actually detecting a signal on the medium. If such a signal is heard, the station wishing to transmit waits for a calculated period of time before listening again. It listens until the channel is clear, and then transmits the packet in its entirety. There is no "after the fact" collision detection, and no jam signal. (A jam signal is impossible because the Wi-Fi radio medium is half-duplex, and stations cannot listen for a jam signal while they are transmitting.)

There are a number of subtleties to the implementation of DCF:

- Rather than transmitting immediately when the medium becomes idle, a station must first wait for a fixed period known as the *distributed inter-frame space* (DIFS); if the medium remains idle during the DIFS, the station then waits for a further random backoff period before transmitting. The DIFS allows higher-priority traffic, such as PCF frames or acknowledgment frames, preferential access to the medium. As in the case of wired Ethernet, the backoff period reduces the likelihood of two stations that are waiting for the medium to begin transmitting simultaneously, resulting in a collision.

- The backoff period is chosen randomly to lie within a contention window. Too small a window increases the likelihood that two stations will choose the same backoff value; too large a window degrades efficiency as the medium tends to spend more time idle. The solution is to use a dynamic window, which varies based on how much contention is encountered. Initially a station's window is set to a fixed minimum value; each unsuccessful transmission doubles the size of the window, up to a fixed maximum value, whereas a successful transmission resets it to the minimum value.

- Because dropped frames are far more frequent in wireless networks than wired ones, 802.11 implements a MAC-level acknowledgement and retransmission protocol. When a station successfully receives a frame, it waits for the *short inter-frame space* (SIFS, where SIFS is less than DIFS, ensuring priority) and then sends an acknowledgement (ACK) frame. If a transmitting station fails to receive an ACK, it can conclude that a collision, or other interfering event, has occurred, and should then retransmit the frame.

  Physically sensing the medium consumes power. To mitigate this, 802.11 implements a virtual carrier sensing mechanism: each frame contains a duration field, which allows the transmitter to indicate how long it (and any associated ACK frame) will occupy the medium. When a station receives a packet, even a packet intended for another station, it copies the duration field into a local timer known as the *network allocation vector* (NAV), and postpones any transmissions until the timer has expired. Stations generally put their radio hardware into a low-power state while waiting.

Carrier Sense and the Hidden Node Problem

Both infrastructure and ad hoc Wi-Fi networks have a similar problem: unless every station participating in the network can "hear" every other station, problems arise. The most important of these is the breakdown of the physical and virtual carrier sensing mechanisms described earlier in the section "Wi-Fi Distributed Media Access." Such a breakdown leads to an increase in the packet collision rate. See Figure 7-19.

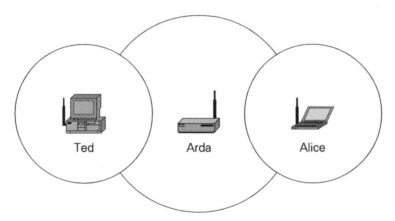

FIGURE 7-19: The hidden node problem

In Figure 7-19, wireless stations Ted and Alice are both connected to Arda, an AP physically about halfway between them. Ted and Alice are far enough apart so that their radios do not have the range to detect one another's signals. Physical distance has "hidden" Ted from Alice and vice versa. This is called the *hidden node problem*. When two Wi-Fi nodes are hidden from one another, they cannot avoid transmitting colliding packets because they cannot monitor the channel for one another's transmissions.

To address the hidden node problem, the 802.11 standard defines a virtual carrier sensing mechanism called *request to send/clear to send* (RTS/CTS). Instead of simply listening for a clear channel, a transmitting station first performs a *handshake* with the intended receiving station by sending it an RTS frame and waiting for a CTS frame in response. Only after this handshake is complete is data transmitted. This greatly mitigates the hidden node problem: in the example, although Alice cannot receive Ted's RTS frame, she does receive Arda's CTS response and is able to update her NAV value, which in turn causes her to postpone any future transmissions until Ted has finished.

Here's how it works, broken out into steps (see Figure 7-20):

1. When a station wants to send a packet, it first checks to see that the channel is quiet and waits for the DIFS before sending out an RTS frame. The duration field of the RTS frame is set to the total time required to complete the CTS, data transmission and ACK.

2. All stations that hear the RTS frame copy its duration field to their NAV timers.

3. Assuming that the destination station hears the RTS, it waits for the SIFS and replies with a CTS frame. The duration field of the CTS frame is set to the total time required to complete the data transmission and ACK (a slightly smaller value than in the RTS frame).

4. Some stations may not have heard the original RTS frame due to the hidden-node problem. If those stations hear the CTS frame, they copy its duration field into their NAV timers.

5. After the transmitting station receives CTS, it waits for a SIFS interval and begins sending the data frame proper.

6. When the receiving station has successfully received the data packet, it waits for another SIFS interval and sends an ACK frame back to the sending station.

7. By the time the ACK frame has been sent, all the NAV timers associated with the transaction will have timed out. All stations then wait for a DIFS interval before checking the channel for idleness and beginning the process again.

Of course, it's still possible for two stations that are hidden from each other to send overlapping RTS frames, which will then collide and be dropped. The key benefit of the RTS/CTS protocol is that it reduces the period of vulnerability during which a hidden-node collision can occur from the comparatively long data transmission time to the comparatively short time required to transmit the RTS frame. Because the RTS/CTS handshake introduces a substantial overhead, and because its benefits are most pronounced for longer frames, it is common to apply a size threshold below which frames are transmitted without handshaking. Handshaking is often disabled completely for small networks, especially those with stations at fixed positions.

Fragmentation

Because longer frames have a proportionally higher chance of encountering interference and collisions than shorter frames, Wi-Fi networks provide a configurable option called a *fragmentation threshold*, which specifies the maximum size of frame that may be transmitted in one piece. A frame that is larger than the fragmentation threshold is broken into a numbered series of fragments, which are individually acknowledged and may be individually retransmitted if the acknowledgment does not arrive.

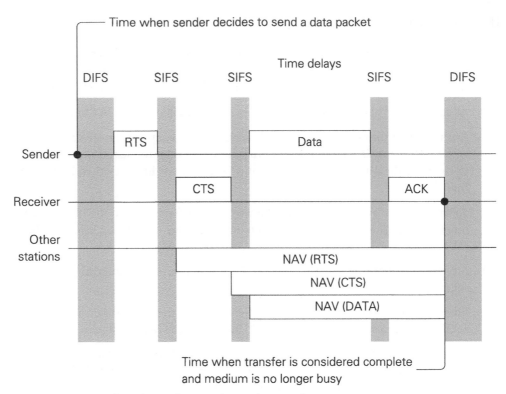

FIGURE 7-20: How the DCF coordinates a data packet transfer

Fragments are transmitted on the medium separated by the SIFS, and so will not be interrupted by other DCF-coordinated traffic. The duration field of each transmitted fragment specifies the time required to transmit all the remaining fragments, rather than just the current one. When used with RTS/CTS handshaking, the duration field of the RTS frame specifies the total time required to transmit the CTS and all the fragments, so the medium is reserved for the entire duration of the fragmented transmission.

Amplitude Modulation, Phase Modulation and QAM

Before we discuss the operation of the various 802.11 physical layers, it is helpful to review a few basic radio concepts.

All radio technologies transmit information over the air by changing or *modulating* one or more properties of a carrier wave in response to that information. Figure 7-21 illustrates two analogue modulation schemes that you have doubtless encountered in everyday life: amplitude modulation (AM) and frequency modulation (FM). The former holds the frequency of the carrier constant and varies its amplitude; the latter holds the amplitude constant and varies the carrier's frequency about a central value.

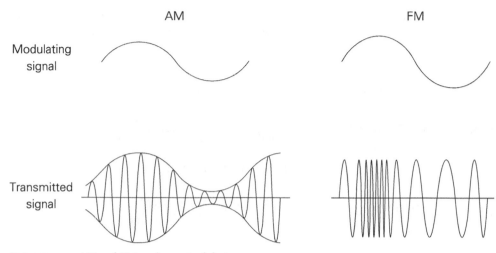

FIGURE 7-21: AM and FM analogue modulation

In contrast with analogue modulation, whose goal is to encode a continuous and continually varying signal, digital modulation schemes transmit a discrete series of symbols (such as, in the simplest case, bits). In the rest of this discussion we are concerned with digital rather than analogue modulation.

Figure 7-22 illustrates four digital modulation schemes for transmitting binary data. The first two are digital equivalents of our familiar analogue schemes: *binary amplitude-shift keying* (BASK)—sometimes also referred to as on-off keying (OOK)—transmits a binary 0 by emitting nothing and a binary 1 by emitting the carrier wave; *binary frequency-shift keying* (BFSK) transmits 0s and 1s by changing the carrier frequency between two defined values. *Binary phase-shift keying* (BPSK) transmits a binary 0 by emitting the carrier wave and a binary 1 by emitting the carrier wave phase-shifted by 180° (that is, inverted). In practice, *differential BPSK* (DBPSK) is often used in place of BPSK; this eliminates the requirement for a fixed phase reference, encoding a binary 0 by continuing to transmit the carrier with its current phase and a binary 1 by shifting the current phase by 180°.

The extension from binary to m-ary symbols (symbols that can take m values) is straightforward. For mASK we permit m possible amplitudes for the carrier, rather than simply on and off; for mFSK we permit m possible frequencies; and for mPSK we allow phase shifts that are finer than just 180". If we double m from two to four we can transmit twice as much data over the same channel, as each symbol can represent two bits; doubling m again gives a further 50% increase in capacity, as each symbol can now represent three bits. Ultimately our ability to keep increasing m is limited by noise, which makes it hard for the receiver to accurately discriminate between increasingly finely spaced amplitude levels or frequency or phase shifts. This is in accordance with the Shannon-Hartley theorem, which informally states that the information-carrying capacity of a channel decreases with the signal-to-noise ratio of the channel.

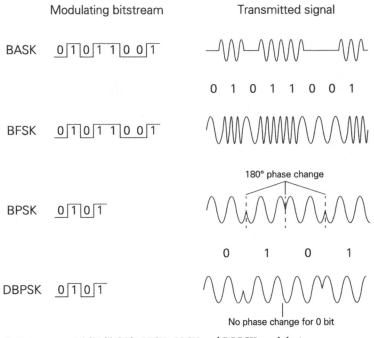

FIGURE 7-22: BASK (OOK), BFSK, BPSK and DBPSK modulation

We can, of course, choose to combine amplitude and phase modulation or keying. The resulting modulation scheme is referred to as *quadrature amplitude modulation* (QAM), because modulating amplitude and phase together is equivalent to modulating the amplitude of two carriers that are 90° degrees out of phase (in quadrature) with each other, and summing the result. A digital QAM scheme is characterised by the set of discrete (phase, amplitude) values used. These are often represented as a *constellation* (that is, a specific arrangement of values) in the complex plane, as shown in Figure 7-23. In the figure, distance from the origin corresponds to the amplitude, and angular position corresponds to the phase shift. In 16QAM, there are 16 different possible combinations of amplitude and angular position, allowing 16 bits to be encoded by a single pair of phase and amplitude values. QAM systems have to be carefully designed to keep noise immunity high. An engineer will generally attempt to maximise the Euclidean (straight line) distance between any two points in the constellation, maximising the chance that a receiver will be able to identify the intended point in the presence of noise.

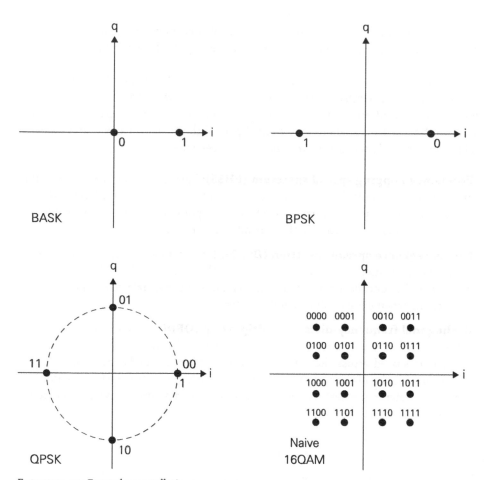

FIGURE 7-23: Example constellations

Spread-Spectrum Techniques

The 2.4GHz and 5GHz ISM frequency bands used by Wi-Fi represent a particularly challenging environment in which to transmit data. Standards intended for use in these bands must offer some degree of resilience in the face of interference from a variety of sources:

- Other communication technologies that use the band (such as Bluetooth and ZigBee)

- Non-communication devices such as microwave ovens

- Clients attached to other Wi-Fi networks with overlapping channel assignments, which do not participate in this network's collision-avoidance regime

- Time-delayed reflections of signals (multipath interference; refer to Figure 7-15)

Transmitters in the ISM bands are also subject to regulatory limits on the total amount of power that they may radiate in a given frequency window (spectral power density).

The Wi-Fi family of standards use a variety of *spread-spectrum* techniques to address these challenges. As the name suggests, these spread a signal across a wider bandwidth than would otherwise be the case, offering improved resilience to interference (and in particular to narrowband interference that occupies only a small part of the frequency band) and reduced spectral power density. Three distinct techniques have been used:

- **Frequency-hopping spread spectrum (FHSS):** This approach is used only by the original 802.11 standard, at data rates of 1 to 2 Mbps. It uses 2- or 4-level FSK, and "hops" the frequency of the carrier wave to another point in the channel every 400ms, in a sequence that is known to both transmitter and receiver.

- **Direct-sequence spread spectrum (DSSS):** This combines the stream of data bits with a faster stream of *chips*. In the case of 802.11b operating at 1 or 2 Mbps, a repeating 11-chip Barker code is combined with each bit. The closely related complementary-code keying scheme is used at higher data rates.

- **Orthogonal frequency-division multiplexing (OFDM):** Data is split into many streams, each of which is modulated at a comparatively low rate onto one of many subcarriers spaced across the band. Since 802.11g, all standards have used OFDM, relying on wider bands, denser modulations and spatial diversity (which is described in more detail later in the next section) to deliver higher data rates in low-noise environments.

Wi-Fi Modulation and Coding in Detail

It's time to take a look at the DSSS and OFDM modulation schemes used by 802.11b and 802.11g in more detail. Understanding the modulation schemes thoroughly is not necessary to use Wi-Fi, but it is necessary to comprehend the challenges of wireless networking, as compared to conventional wired Ethernet.

At a data rate of 1 Mbps, the incoming bits are multiplied by a spreading sequence (in this case the 11-digit Barker code) running at a chipping rate of 11 Mbps; each bit in the source stream now corresponds to 11 bits in the spread stream. The spread stream is used to DBPSK-modulate a carrier wave. To achieve a doubling of throughput to 2 Mbps, DQPSK modulation replaces DBPSK. Figure 7-24 shows these two configurations. The 11-digit Barker code:

+1 -1 +1 +1 -1 +1 +1 +1 -1 -1 -1

is used as the spreading sequence. It has extremely low autocorrelation: if you multiply the sequence by a shifted version of itself and sum the products, then for any shift that is not a multiple of 11 you get a maximum sum of between -1 and +1, whereas for a shift that is a multiple of 11, the products clearly sum to +11. For a shift of two, the products would be the following, which yields a sum of -1:

+1	-1	+1	+1	-1	+1	+1	+1	-1	-1	-1
×	×	×	×	×	×	×	×	×	×	×
+1	+1	-1	+1	+1	+1	-1	-1	-1	+1	-1
=	=	=	=	=	=	=	=	=	=	=
+1	-1	-1	+1	-1	+1	-1	-1	+1	-1	+1

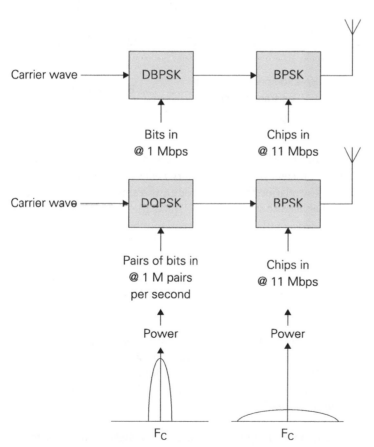

FIGURE 7-24: Spread-spectrum transmission at 1 Mbps and 2 Mbps using 11-digit Barker code

The receiver demodulates the incoming signal, and multiplies the resulting spread stream by the spreading sequence to recover the original data, as shown in Figure 7-25; before doing so, it must synchronise its spreading sequence with that of the transmitter, a task that is simplified by the Barker code's low autocorrelation. Multiplying by the spreading sequence in the receiver suppresses both inter-symbol interference due to multipath effects (because of the Barker code's low autocorrelation) and other noise (because it broadens the noise spectrum, allowing it to be rejected by the integrating action of the receiver).

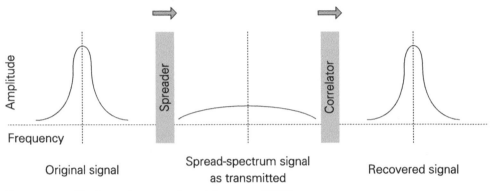

FIGURE 7-25: The Direct-Sequence Spread-Spectrum (DSSS) process

To achieve data rates of 5.5 Mbps and 11 Mbps with the same channel bandwidth, we require an approach with greater spectral efficiency. Complementary codes are sets of codes that, like the Barker code, have low autocorrelation (between a code and a shifted version of itself, as before) and cross-correlation (between codes in the set). Unlike the Barker code, however, the codes used here are polyphase codes: rather than being real numbers drawn from the set {-1, 1}, code values are complex numbers drawn from the set {-1, 1, -j, j}. When used as spreading sequences, they have the same advantages as the Barker code in terms of synchronisation and interference rejection, but as there is more than one code in the set, we are now able to convey additional information through our choice of the code used to spread a given symbol.

To transmit at 11 Mbps, we group the incoming bits into 8-bit bytes. Six bits are used to select one of 64 8-bit complementary codes, and the remaining two bits are used to phase-modulate the entire code. The chipping rate remains 11 Mbps, and as eight bits are transmitted for every eight chips, the data throughput is also 11 Mbps. When transmitting at 5.5 Mbps, the number of codes is reduced to four.

The 802.11g standard supports data rates of up to 54 Mbps on the 2.4GHz band. To achieve this, it adopts an OFDM modulation scheme first used (on the 5GHz band) by 802.11a. Each 20MHz channel is divided into 52 subchannels; four channels are reserved for pilot signals, and data is modulated onto the remaining 48 subcarriers using 64-QAM (for 52 Mbps and 48 Mbps modes), 16-QAM (for 36 Mbps and 24 Mbps), QPSK (for 18 Mbps and 12 Mbps) or BPSK (for 9 Mbps and 6 Mbps). A symbol is transmitted every 4μs, so the raw throughput in 64QAM mode is given by

48 channels × 250,000 symbols/s × 6 bits/symbol = 72 Mbps

The difference between the raw throughput of 72 Mbps and the actual throughput of 54 Mbps is accounted for by the use of a FEC code with a code rate of 3/4 (that is, four bits are transmitted for every three bits of data). Each 802.11g data rate uses forward error correction, with code rates of 1/2 (for 24 Mbps, 12 Mbps and 6 Mbps), 2/3 (for 48 Mbps) or 3/4 (for 54 Mbps, 36 Mbps, 18 Mbps and 9 Mbps).

The OFDM scheme provides resilience both to narrowband interference and to frequency-selective fading; the FEC code allows the receiver to reconstruct a certain amount of missing data from one or more corrupted subcarriers. The relatively slow modulation rate permits the insertion of a guard interval between each symbol, reducing inter-symbol interference.

How Wi-Fi Connections Happen

Connecting a Wi-Fi device to a wireless access point is not as simple as it might seem at first. There may be multiple APs and multiple client adapters visible in the same physical location. APs and clients may be scattered across several channels. Not all clients may be authorised to connect to certain APs. At the highest level, resolving such issues is a three-step process:

1. Client adapters need to determine which APs are available on what channels. This process is called *scanning*.

2. The APs need to be able to determine which clients are theirs, and vice versa. This process is called *authentication*.

3. After authentication, the authenticated client may connect to the AP that authenticated it. This process is called *association*.

Scanning may be active or passive. In *passive scanning*, an AP is configured to periodically broadcast a frame containing its SSID. Client adapters listen for these broadcast frames across all channels and build a list. If they have connected to an AP before, they will choose that AP. If they don't see an SSID that they've connected to before, they will attempt to connect to the AP with the strongest signal. How the connection happens and how the user gets involved are implementation dependent. Most modern Wi-Fi software has a *Connect Automatically?* dialog that appears on first connection and requires user confirmation before automatic connections can happen in the future. The user of the client adapter's computer may also be given a chance to choose an AP from the list that the client gathers from broadcast SSID frames.

In *active scanning*, a client adapter sends out a *probe request frame* to all APs within range. The probe request frame may contain the SSID of a preferred AP, in essence asking, "Are you there, `blackwave`?" If the `blackwave` AP is out there, it issues a probe response to the client. The probe request frame may alternatively contain a null (empty) SSID field, which amounts to asking, "Who's out there?" In that case, any AP within range may send a probe response back to the client, which in most cases will choose the AP with the strongest signal.

Active scanning with a null SSID is done because in some wireless networks, the APs are configured *not* to broadcast their SSIDs. An active scan is thus the only way for a client to determine what APs are within range. In most home networks and "coffee shop" Wi-Fi providers, the APs broadcast their SSIDs, and passive scanning is sufficient.

After a client adapter identifies the AP that it wants to connect to, the authentication process determines whether the connection is authorised. There are two types of authentication: open and shared-key. *Open authentication* does not depend on passwords. The client sends an authentication request frame to the AP. This frame includes the client's MAC address. An AP may be configured to exclude certain client MAC addresses, or only permit certain client MAC addresses. Depending on how the AP is configured, it either grants or refuses the client's authentication request. If it refuses, the conversation is over, and the connection does not happen. If the AP grants the request, the process moves on to association.

Authentication by MAC address is done less and less often, because clients transmit their MAC addresses as *cleartext* (that is, without encryption) and an attacker can compile a list of valid MAC addresses with software that simply monitors the channel. Because many client adapters allow users to change their MAC addresses to arbitrary values, the attacker could then "spoof" a legitimate MAC address and connect to the network.

Shared-key authentication uses one of several protocols that involve encryption. The most common protocol for small networks today is called WPA-2, which has been mandatory on new-build Wi-Fi gear since 2006. (WPA-2 is covered in more detail in the next section.) Large corporate networks and those with strong security requirements use a separate authentication server (often one called RADIUS) that implements an IEEE authentication standard called 802.1X. Small networks handle shared-key authentication directly between AP and client. A conversation occurs between AP and client, in which the AP and client require one another to complete a cryptographic challenge. If both AP and client possess the same shared key, the challenge can be completed successfully and authentication is granted. Thereafter, all communication between AP and client is encrypted.

The final connection step is association. After the AP and client adapter have authenticated one another, the client sends the AP an *association request frame*. If granted, the association process goes to completion, after which the client may obtain network configuration parameters and an IP address through the network's DHCP server. The AP may still refuse association for other reasons; for example, if the number of clients associated with it has already reached a pre-set maximum value. In most cases, however, the association request is granted, and the client connects.

Wi-Fi Security

There is some inherent security in wired networks: without physical access to a network jack or network equipment, connecting to the network is impossible. Wi-Fi signals can pass through walls and do not limit connections to physical jacks, so security becomes a matter of great importance. The original 802.11 standard specified a simple encryption mechanism called *wired equivalent privacy* (WEP). A WEP key is a string of hexadecimal digits and not a conventional password. Some Wi-Fi hardware incorporated key generators to convert a human-readable password or passphrase to a hexadecimal WEP key.

In 2001, security researchers found a flaw in WEP's encryption algorithm that allowed a wireless access point protected by WEP to be cracked after as little as 10 minutes of examining encrypted packets passing over the network. Once the nature of the flaw became generally known, WEP became useless. In 2004, the 802.11 committee ratified addendum 802.11i, which became known as *Wi-Fi Protected Access version 2*, or WPA-2. WPA-2 replaced a short-lived interim solution called WPA, which was not as strong; like WEP, it's no longer used. WPA-2 uses a 256-bit encryption protocol called the *Advanced Encryption Standard* (AES). AES is a *block cipher* that encrypts and decrypts data a block at a time. Older Wi-Fi protocols such as WEP and WPA used *stream ciphers*, which deal with single characters at a time and are much more vulnerable to attack.

WPA-2 allows for ASCII keyphrases up to 63 characters in length, and if the keyphrase consists of random characters, 20 to 30 characters is generally sufficient for home networks. Note that attackers do not simply transmit passwords to a wireless router one after the other until they find one that works. Instead, a utility called a *packet sniffer* captures encrypted packets off the air and saves them to disk as files. Then, an *offline brute-force attack* can be attempted. In this type of attack, dictionaries of ordinary words and commonly used passwords are tried against the encrypted packets stored on an attacker's computer, using a fast application that can attempt tens of thousands of passwords per second. If the attacker is willing to let the software keep trying for weeks or months, a weak password or a concatenation of common dictionary words could be vulnerable. There is some comfort in the "low-hanging fruit" effect: because some people use short or otherwise weak passwords, attackers are less likely to spend months of time on a brute-force attack against a strong password. That assumes that you are not a corporate or military site storing important information. Few attackers will waste that much time breaking your password just to steal your MP3s.

Not all parts of WPA-2 are as secure as the main encryption algorithm. In 2011, a critical flaw was discovered in a WPA-2 accessory technology called Wi-Fi Protected Setup (WPS) that runs in the firmware of wireless routers and allows easy password distribution for small networks. It was found that the WPS protocol "leaks" portions of a PIN code, and allows a brute-force attack to succeed in as little as two hours. WPS is now considered compromised and security professionals recommend that it be disabled in devices that include it.

On the client side, WPA-2 is implemented as a piece of software called a *supplicant*, which runs on the computer that wants to connect to the network and not in the client adapter itself. For Linux distributions (including Raspbian) the supplicant software is called `wpa_supplicant`, and its configuration file `wpa_supplicant.conf` is located in the folder `/etc/wpa_supplicant`. The supplicant "asks" its chosen AP for authentication, and then engages in the WPA-2 protocol with the AP. Some supplicant implementations include a graphical user interface (GUI) for management, whereas others are command-line based and read keyphrases and other information from an editable configuration file.

Wi-Fi on the Raspberry Pi

Most models of the Raspberry Pi have a wired Ethernet port that is standard and will work without any tweaking on Linux distributions like Raspbian. (The older Model A boards and the Raspberry Pi Zero do not have Ethernet ports.) If you connect your Raspberry Pi board via cable to your router's Ethernet port with a running DHCP server, Raspbian requests DHCP configuration, which includes a local IP address. After DHCP has configured Raspbian's networking parameters, the board should be able to communicate with other nodes on your local network as well as the Internet at large, using its IP address.

Raspbian (and most Unix-derived operating systems) includes a command-line utility called `ifconfig`, which allows you to display the configuration of your wired Ethernet port. (There is a better configuration utility for Wi-Fi, which we'll get to shortly.) Simply open a terminal window and execute this command:

```
ifconfig eth0
```

Here, `eth0` is the default name of the Raspberry Pi's wired Ethernet port. The utility displays the current status of the port, including its MAC address and IP address. If you're not using the wired Ethernet port on your Raspberry Pi, it's a good idea to disable it, especially if you intend to use a Wi-Fi adapter. You disable `eth0` with `ifconfig`:

```
sudo ifconfig eth0 down
```

Note that changing parameters (as distinct from merely displaying them) requires the use of admin privileges, via `sudo`. To enable the port again, enter this command:

```
sudo ifconfig eth0 up
```

Unless you have a Raspberry Pi 3 (which has both Wi-Fi and Bluetooth right on the circuit board), you'll have to obtain a USB Wi-Fi client adapter. Make sure that your board is running the latest image of Raspbian, which includes most available Wi-Fi drivers and tools. There are extremely compact Wi-Fi client adapters that can be plugged into one of the two on-board USB ports or into a powered USB hub. You can find a list of other tested and known-compatible Wi-Fi client units at http://elinux.org/RPi_USB_Wi-Fi_Adapters.

Make sure that your board is running from a robust power source like a powered hub. No matter how compact, a Wi-Fi adapter includes a microwave radio transmitter, and it needs a certain amount of current to do its job. Adding such an adapter to a board that's close to overloading its power supply is almost guaranteed to make it fail. When choosing a power supply for a Raspberry Pi installation, always err on the side of more current rather than less. Most of the common problems getting a Raspberry Pi system to work stem from inadequate current from the power supply.

The WPA-2 supplicant that comes preinstalled with Raspbian has a GUI, and if Raspbian has a driver for your client adapter, connecting to your access point can be done entirely using the GUI. Follow these steps:

1. Run the supplicant software by launching Wi-Fi Config from the Raspbian desktop. The wpa_gui main window is shown in Figure 7-26.

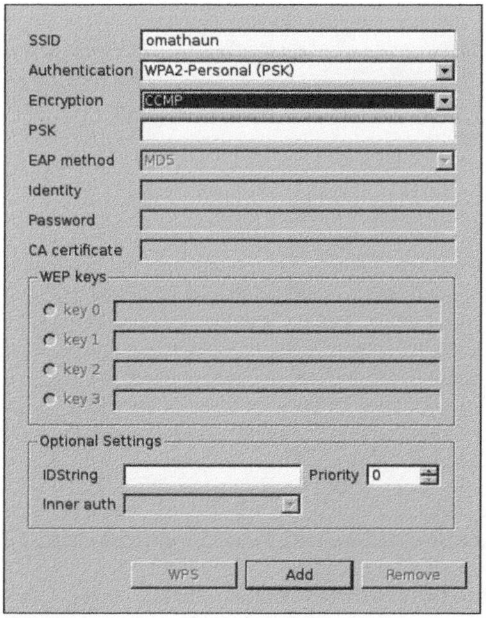

FIGURE 7-26: The wpa_gui main window

2. Click the Scan button. The supplicant scans for available APs and displays a list in a new window. See Figure 7-27.

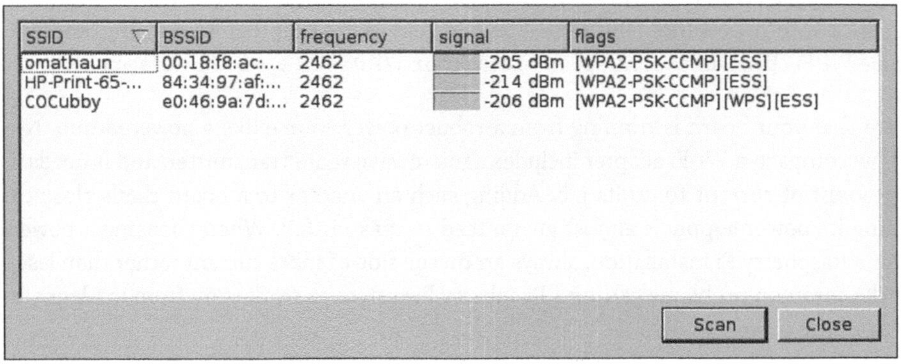

SSID ▽	BSSID	frequency	signal	flags
omathaun	00:18:f8:ac:...	2462	-205 dBm	[WPA2-PSK-CCMP][ESS]
HP-Print-65-...	84:34:97:af:...	2462	-214 dBm	[WPA2-PSK-CCMP][ESS]
COCubby	e0:46:9a:7d:...	2462	-206 dBm	[WPA2-PSK-CCMP][WPS][ESS]

Scan   Close

FIGURE 7-27: The Scan window

3. Assuming that one of the listed APs is your own, double-click its line in the Scan window. The NetworkConfig window opens (see Figure 7-28). If you don't see your AP listed, your Raspberry Pi may be too far away, or there may be some configuration conflict.

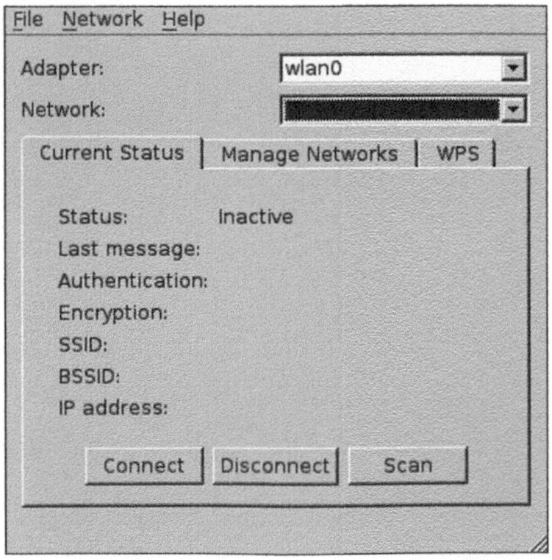

File Network Help

Adapter: wlan0

Network:

Current Status | Manage Networks | WPS

Status: Inactive
Last message:
Authentication:
Encryption:
SSID:
BSSID:
IP address:

Connect   Disconnect   Scan

FIGURE 7-28: The Network Config window

4. Enter your AP's shared key in the PSK field.

5. Click Add. Assuming you entered the shared key correctly, the supplicant connects to your AP. At that point, the Status tab of the wpa_gui main window shows Completed (Station) in the Status field.

6. Test your new connection by launching Midori and accessing any web page. You can use the `wpa_gui` application for ongoing configuration as well, say if you install a new wireless access point or change your SSID or shared key. For simple status display, another Linux command-line utility provides more information. After you have your Wi-Fi connection established and configured, open a terminal window and enter the following command:

iwconfig

The utility displays an eight-line text summary including the AP's SSID, the wireless technology (a/b/g/n), the AP's MAC address, the current bit rate, indicators for signal level, link quality and cumulative counts for various errors.

Even More Networking

Networking is a field that is both broad and deep, and there's a great deal to learn beyond what we can show in one chapter. Here are some useful topics for independent research:

- **Samba:** A software package that allows Linux operating systems like Raspbian to transfer files with Windows or other non-Linux operating systems. Samba is free and may be installed without charge from the Raspberry Pi repositories.

- **Ethernet bridges:** Special Ethernet appliances that forward Ethernet frames from one physical medium to another. This is often from Category 5 cabling to Wi-Fi or vice versa, but there are bridges that can implement Ethernet over residential power wiring, and allow a Category 5 connection on both ends. (As a category, this is called *Powerline Networking*, and it's often used for bringing a network connection to locations in a building where Wi-Fi cannot reach.) With special software, a Raspberry Pi board can be configured to bridge between wired Ethernet and Wi-Fi.

- **Power over Ethernet (PoE):** A technology that uses special adapters to send a modest amount of current through unused twisted pairs in a Category 5 Ethernet cable, or over the signalling conductors if there are no unused pairs available. Because the POE voltage is the same on both pairs of the twisted pair carrying data, the NICs ignore the voltage, which does not interfere with data. Implemented correctly, PoE can allow an Ethernet bridge or even an entire Raspberry Pi computer to be located on a mast or some other location where conventional power isn't available.

There are also a great many devices like cameras and sensors that can be attached to a computer network through a Category 5 Ethernet cable. More and more everyday household devices are joining the "Internet of Things" and may be controlled via Wi-Fi from computers of all sorts. Learning Ethernet and TCP/IP thoroughly will allow you to extend your reach anywhere that Ethernet cables—or Wi-Fi microwaves—can reach.

Chapter 8

Operating Systems

BEFORE EXPLORING THE world of operating systems, we should be clear about what they are. Here's a basic definition from the online version of the *Merriam-Webster* dictionary, of all places, that hits it better than many computer books: it says an operating system is "the main program in a computer that controls the way the computer works and makes it possible for other programs to function".

We can expand on this definition by saying that the operating system (OS) consists of software that controls the use of computer hardware and software resources, enables user interaction via applications (programs), or gives direct access to various functions outside of applications, such as copying or deleting files, updating the OS itself, and so forth. We understand the OS hides way out of sight but it makes everything the computer does possible. Figure 8-1 shows a basic computer system.

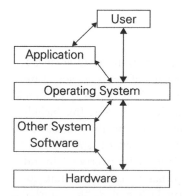

FIGURE 8-1: A basic computer system

This chapter first looks at operating systems in general, including their fascinating history. We explore concepts like time-sharing, in which the OS controls slices of processor time, memory usage, mass storage reads and writes, and all the system's other facilities and resources to enable multitasking (running more than one application at essentially the same time). Time-sharing also allows multiuser modes in which several users—or even millions (think Google and Facebook as examples)—each run one or more applications simultaneously.

We also explore kernels in this chapter. The kernel is software that oversees and exerts basic control for a computer's hardware, memory access, central processing unit (CPU), storage devices and file systems, and all the rest of its resources. The OS's kernel provides the necessary interface for applications to use the computer's hardware. Word processing software, web browsers, email clients, media players and so on would be useless if they could not access and save data and perform operations on that data when it became available to the software. The kernel serves as both the heart and the brains of an OS. Through discussions of how the OS manages file systems, working memory and similar resources, you will see how the kernel manages operations in detail.

The "Enablers and Assistants to the Operating System" section covers ways in which the OS accesses and/or administers the sharing of CPU time, memory, media access, and all other facets of multitasking/time sharing. It encompasses what is required in the way of interfacing for complete control of the computer's hardware and software. We examine firmware (small programs usually kept in flash memory or some other permanent storage media) used to boot and enable the kernel for operation, and we also look at device drivers, which give the system access to various hardware peripherals such as keyboards, displays, mice and other pointing devices, and disk drives, USB peripherals of all sorts, printers, scanners and so on.

> **NOTE** It's worth noting here that not all device drivers are firmware; many device drivers reside on the hard drive—or, in the case of the Raspberry Pi, the SD card—and become available as the operating system establishes access to that type of storage.

Finally, getting back to the Raspberry Pi specifically, the last section in this chapter gives an overview of various OSs for the Raspberry Pi (the different flavours of Linux are sometimes called distros, or distributions). It provides sources for OS downloads as well as applications and other software such as utility programs, source code and device drivers. This includes specific considerations of the Raspberry Pi's computer architecture and its available OSs from various versions of GNU/Linux, such as Debian, to the most popular Raspberry Pi distro, Raspbian Linux (a version of Debian that's been optimised for the Raspberry Pi). In addition, we look at the new wealth of OSs that has opened up thanks to the new four-core Advanced RISC Machine (ARM) processor in the Raspberry Pi 2 and 3. These include Raspberry Pi–enhanced versions of Ubuntu, Fedora and Gentoo, as well as Windows 10.

Introduction to Operating Systems

A full understanding of modern-day OSs requires a look at how and why they came about. Significant OSs include Unix and Linux, which have had a profound influence on Windows, the Mac OS, and smartphone OSs of more recent vintage. Like humanity itself, any operating system contains the physical heredity if those that existing before.

History of Operating Systems

Early computers ran one program at a time. Without an OS to parcel out simultaneous tasks, they proceeded from the beginning of a problem to the end. Their utility lay in fast number crunching, far faster than human operators could match even if they were using mechanical calculation machines. In short, although these first computers had rudimentary memory and program control, their design was influenced greatly by what calculators did well—arithmetic. Early computers were basically super calculators. This changed, as we will soon see, with the advent of true operating systems supervising much more powerful uses of computers.

Although some experts consider the Atanasoff–Berry computer built in 1937 at Iowa State University or the Colossus Mark 1 used at Bletchley Park during World War II to be the first digital electronic computers, ENIAC (which stands for Electronic Numerical Integrator And Computer) is the one that caught the public's attention. It was secretly built during World War II and announced publicly in 1946.

Newspapers called ENIAC the "Giant Brain". It could solve a wide range of numerical problems around 1,000 times faster than previous electromechanical computers. Inside the large racks that made up ENIAC were 17,468 vacuum tubes, 7,200 crystal diodes, 1,500 relays, 70,000 resistors, 10,000 capacitors and something like five million hand-solder connections. It weighed about 30 tons and took up 1,800 square feet while consuming 150 kilowatts of power. As shown in Figure 8-2, it was big, and what you see in the figure is only part of the entire thing.

Mainframes

Huge computers called mainframes proliferated in large companies, universities and government agencies, computerising a variety of applications that had once required rooms full of people doing manual calculating. However, although big computers solved problems, they presented a huge problem.

That difficulty was the linear nature of the early mainframes. The need to manage resources and speed up the process was obvious. Manufacturers started adding libraries of code controlling operations such as input and output functions, which meant programmers no longer had to write often-used routines for every program. Instead, they put a link in the code to call the required library of instructions. Because the code did not execute until the program was actually running the computer, these prepackaged routines were termed runtime libraries.

FIGURE 8-2: ENIAC, 1940s
Figure courtesy of the United States Army

Early Operating Systems

As with many things in computer science history, there is some dispute over what was the first real OS. Some historians say LEO 1 (which stands for Lyons Electronic Office), which was developed in 1950 for the electronic delay storage automatic calculator (EDSAC) computing platform, was the first. However, other sources say the first OS came from General Motors in 1956 and was written for the company's IBM 704 mainframe. Essentially, all of the early OSs came about from mainframe customers who were trying to answer specific needs in their industry. When new machines were purchased, these systems required rewriting and recompiling for the new machine.

By the 1960s, computer manufacturers began attempting to provide OSs for their machines. An example of an early manufacturer OS was OS/360, which consisted of several different versions developed by IBM for their 360 series. Because of differences in hardware and thus performance, OS/360 was more a family of OSs than one unified OS.

Operating systems, driven by competition to sell mainframes, were becoming more complex and, most importantly, they were becoming more useful. Earlier computers were limited in the tasks they could accomplish, or gave computers flexibility and scope. UNIVAC, Burroughs, GE and others presented their own OSs.

Smaller Computers, Better Operating Systems

The 1970s brought true change to computing. The first indication was the minicomputer, which truly earned its designation as "mini" because it was many times physically smaller than mainframes. No longer were large computer rooms with raised floors (for cables to run underneath) and special cooling systems required. And operators stopped wearing white coats like doctors or research scientists.

Smaller companies could purchase a minicomputer and put it in their offices. The cooling fans on these babies were so loud that a vacant office was often converted into "the computer room".

Personal Computers

The personal or microcomputer came about in the late 1970s. Computer usage exploded, and with it came a demand for ease of use. Now just about anyone could have a home computer, a hobby computer or a computer on the desk at work. On this smaller computer architecture (remember the word *micro*), tight control of resources was paramount in avoiding slowdowns and actually getting work done or games played.

Selling computers to consumers and small businesses called for *features,* which were both useful and simply imagination-catching things the computer could do (graphics, sound, and so forth). The features required fast advances in operating systems.

Companies like Commodore, Radio Shack and Apple appeared and, yes, IBM was back with the personal computer (PC) starting in 1982. Soon thereafter, a ton of manufacturers were building IBM clones, PCs that ran the disk operating system (DOS). Figure 8-3 shows IBM's first PC from 1981.

PCs proliferated and all sorts of peripherals—displays, keyboards, printers, game controllers, etc., etc.—were soon hung off them. Operating systems to support all this demand went into massive and continuous development and improvement.

Xerox's famous Palo Alto research centre came up with the computer mouse and a workable graphical user interface (GUI), making WYSIWYG (what you see is what you get) possible. With WYSIWYG, whatever you see on the screen looks the same way when printed or otherwise output. Before the first GUI, as an example, word processing depended upon some sort of mark-up for formatting. You had no idea what the final product would look like until you sent it to the printer. GUI, thus, presented a seminal advance in ease of computing.

FIGURE 8-3: The first IBM PC, model 5150 with model number 5151 monitor and IBM PC keyboard
Photo courtesy of Ruben de Rijcke via Wikimedia Commons

The OSs on Apple's Macintosh and Microsoft's Windows built on Xerox's start, making the personal computer a great deal more user friendly than the big machines preceding it. This new *ease of use* resulted in wider acceptance by consumers and rapidly growing small computer sales. Underlying this explosive success were the new microcomputer operating systems enabling anyone who could push a mouse to use computers.

Today, computers continue decreasing in size, speeding up, getting multicore CPUs and demanding a similar expansion in the power of the OSs running them. This allows OSs to do more things, faster.

The Basics of Operating Systems

The major benefits of an operating system include

- It gives applications easy but safe access to hardware, "safe" meaning in a manner that performs the desired actions without danger of crashing the system.

- It manages sharing of data and security to prevent unauthorised access or any sort of corruption of the data from occurring, all making for more efficient and accurate operation.

- It enables use of resources, such as memory, storage, sockets for networking and the Internet.

The first point in this list brings up one of the original problems from the mainframe days. This problem contributed a lot of the impetus for developing some sort of resource management.

Programmers punched their programs on stacks of paper cards and presented them to a computer operator. The operator fed the cards into a punch reader, and the program—in direct control of the computer hardware, since there was no OS layer—ran until it ended or, horrors, crashed that huge hunk of iron.

Scores, or even hundreds, of programmers might be submitting program decks for that mainframe. In effect, during the time his or her program ran, every single programmer totally controlled the machine. If one programmer had an error in a routine requesting a write to the output cardpunch or tape drive, the whole computer could crash, causing damage costing a million dollars or more.

At the very least, loss of time occurred as operators rushed to correct the crash or were even forced to reboot the whole machine. Meanwhile cards piled up on the submission table and other programmers became agitated as they waited in line for the running of their urgent jobs.

Isolating user programs—applications—from directly commanding hardware or at least controlling their use is the norm today. GUIs incorporated into OSs such as Xerox's original GUI computers, Apple's Mac OS (and its newer incarnation OS X), Microsoft Windows, and the many variants of UNIX and Linux (via X Windows) force application compliance. For an application to print, save to disk, read a file and so on requires going through the OS.

Operating systems today multitask, whether they are managing desktop computers, laptops, smartphones or even huge machines that utilise hundreds or thousands of parallel processors. Multitasking allows the OS to share system resources by slicing CPU time into little chunks allocated to simultaneous users and/or background processes. Multitasking is achieved with interrupts, and most computers today are described as interrupt-driven.

Interrupts

A computer executes one instruction at a time, one after the other. It will continue running a set of instructions (a program) until it finishes or receives an interrupt signal. Interrupts order the computer's CPU and other hardware to stop the current operation, run another set of instructions—or two or three—and then return to the program in progress. This allows time slicing to work and is the basis for multitasking.

Interrupts are completed at computer speed, so the user or users normally notice no slowdown in applications as the computer runs other programs, background processes, and the like. The OS accomplishes its "housekeeping" tasks in this manner.

Background processes include such mundane tasks as time and date keeping, checking for software upgrades, monitoring for keyboard or other input and so forth. They also enable applications to periodically request service and receive their data. A good example of the latter is an email client looking for and receiving incoming messages.

The OS contains a scheduling program, the interrupt handler, that runs to track and prioritise interrupts to be executed in the proper sequence. The scheduler lets the OS determine which program gets a slice of runtime next.

The OS also makes scheduling even more effective by looking for chunks of downtime in which to cram interrupts and to speed multitasking even more. As the words in this paragraph are punched into the word processor, the OS notes and uses any pauses in typing or times when the writer stops to think about what comes next, and it runs slices for scores of other jobs in the queue. Users may dawdle, but the OS always works.

There are three types of interrupts to the OS:

1. **Hardware interrupts:** Come from devices connected to the computer, such as disk drives, keyboards, network cards, etc. These interrupts alert the OS to some event, such as a key pressed on a keyboard or the movement of a mouse, or incoming data from a network. They are asking, "What do I do now?"

2. **Software interrupts:** Come from applications requesting an operation they want the OS to do, such as saving a file.

3. **Traps:** Come from the CPU and occur when it detects an error. The CPU essentially informs the OS of the error and asks for a solution.

Interrupts also prove useful to users in giving an application a higher priority. That means the OS runs it immediately, slowing the background processes by giving them fewer slices of time. It permits greater efficiency and flexibility.

Layers

Distilling an OS to its simplest form, we find four "operating" layers (refer to Figure 8-1). For example:

1. Users—mostly human but also robots, machines, programmed switches and more—input data, require steps to be executed, and save data or generate output.

2. The application responds to requests, such as saving a file, by passing it along to the OS.

3. In the layer below the application, the OS instructs the hardware to write the file and relays the result back to the application, which, for example, informs the user of a successful save. Users also may bypass the application level for direct instructions to the OS. There is a sublayer (labelled as Other System Software in Figure 8-1) that has software such as drivers, which assist the OS.

4. At the lowest level is the hardware, the physical computer. It follows instructions from the OS and does the tasks requested—copying files, writing to disks, acknowledging interrupts, performing multitasking, etc. To be precise, the kernel performs actions. The OS, as described here, consists of more than just the kernel. You can read more about the kernel later in this chapter in the section, "The Kernel: The Basic Facilitator of Operating Systems".

The most important of these levels, the kernel and relevant device drivers, make the hardware useful. The OS converts expensive but totally stupid collections of electronic components into a powerful computing system that does the tasks requested of it and accomplishes useful jobs. This all due to the operating system telling these components what to do and when to do it—millions of times each second if needed.

In short, the user inputs something, such as typing words into word processing software or clicking a menu choice in a spreadsheet. The application decides what to do and requests help from the OS for hardware-required operations.

The OS allocates resources for the application's runtime while using interrupts to cause the hardware to accomplish the desired task, accepting the result and passing it back up to the application—for example, the words typed into a new Facebook post in your browser or the flick of your wrist moving the mouse to make a game character show up on the screen.

Deep down in the kernel, interrupts make these and other actions happen. Pressing a key or moving a mouse triggers hardware interrupts. These interrupts instruct the CPU to read the keystroke or mouse position. For example, when you press A on the keyboard, a hardware interrupt causes the CPU to convert that keystroke and pass it to the current cursor position in the application. Consequently, the letter appears on the screen in the application you're using and the cursor position moves one character space, ready to make the next input.

Meanwhile, in the spaces of time in between requests from the user and application, the OS does a hundred other things. Remember, OSs are always doing tasks, running processes, verifying that attached peripherals are online and much, much more.

Computer Architecture

The hardware of a computer—its physical structure, which includes the CPU, related circuitry and attached devices—controls the design of the OS, or the system management software. A computer, in its most basic form, consists of:

- CPU (one or more and/or multicores)

- Working memory, such as random access memory (RAM)

- Devices as needed for storage, input and output, etc.

As shown in Figure 8-4, the CPU sends and receives instructions and data to and from the working memory. Devices provide to and accept from the CPU input/output requests, data and interrupts. Some devices also have direct memory access (DMA), which is a feature allowing designated hardware subsystems to access the working memory independently of the CPU.

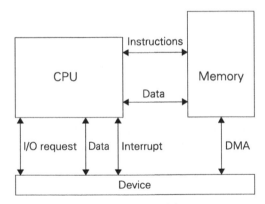

FIGURE 8-4: Basic computer architecture

The typical PC motherboard from years past included a CPU, of course, but also usually associated two additional integrated chips to the CPU, referred to as the core logic chipset. These two chips were the northbridge (a memory controller hub) and the southbridge (an I/O controller hub). The northbridge assisted the CPU in memory-related operations (reading, writing, etc.), whereas the southbridge handled input and output to and from the various hardware devices and ports in the computer. In short, they managed communications for the CPU.

As CPU speeds became faster, having these operations in separate chips often caused bottlenecks. The trend in computer architecture moved to including such logic chips with the CPU in a single chip, called a system-on-a-chip (SoC). You can read more about these later in this chapter. The core logic for all Raspberry Pi models reside in their SoCs.

The CPU has no free will. Its marching orders come from the OS. It accepts instructions and executes them, depending on the step received, in four basic ways:

- **Arithmetic:** Adds, subtracts, multiplies, etc. and sends a result

- **Logic:** Processes true, false, and, or, nor operations and sends a result

- **IO:** Takes data in from "here" and puts it out to "there" or vice versa

- **Control:** Tells devices what to do or enables a function depending on what devices are doing, etc.

While CPU design has changed and evolved over the past decades, basics of operation remain the same but the physical package is different from those huge old mainframes. CPUs blaze along much, much faster today and physically are a great deal smaller. These take of small, encapsulted packages are typically are called integrated circuits (ICs), usually not a lot different in size from our thumbs.

Additionally, the IC package probably contains other CPUs (called cores and which enable parallel processing), working memory, read only memory, device interfaces and other components of a computer system. These ICs are sometimes called SoCs, and allow sophisticated computers to be built in compact configurations, such as that smartphone in your pocket or purse, or on your belt.

The major components of a CPU are the arithmetic logic unit (ALU), the process registers (small amounts of working memory that supply input and accept output from the ALU) and the control unit, which accepts instructions from the OS. The control unit accomplishes these program steps by directing and coordinating the ALU, process registers and other components.

Getting into the structure and function of CPUs is beyond the scope of this chapter, so let's get back on track with our discussion of OSs.

The Purpose of Operating Systems

Operating systems in general accomplish four major functions:

- **Process management:** A process is a set of instructions, which you might call a program. When it is running, the process needs certain resources allocated to it and the OS rations out those resources and controls execution of the process.

- **Memory management:** The operating system shares memory between processes, applications and various system needs, allocating memory space as needed for the current jobs. The OS also helps itself constantly to varying amounts of memory needed for performing its job. Being the boss has its benefits.

- **File system management:** Hundreds or thousands of files exist on the storage devices (hard drives mostly) of a computer with much coming and going, especially the many temporary files applications and other processes created in their normal run-times. The OS keeps track of all the files and does its best to keep the storage medium from being corrupted by all the read and write and list calls whizzing through it.

- **Device management:** This function occurs when the OS uses system calls (a method provided for applications and other processes to interface with the OS to request hardware or other services). This might be providing access to a hard drive or giving run-time to software starting and executing a new process.

To accomplish the four general tasks, any OS needs a host of components. We have met some of them already but now's the time to consider the many parts under the bonnet of any good OS.

Operating Systems' Building Blocks

The building blocks of the OS are the programs, processes, subroutines, libraries and other components that allow the OS to manage the computer.

We can break this down into four main areas that, taken together, create a powerful OS:

- **Kernel:** This program is the heart of any OS. It forms a bridge between applications and other processes, enabling and controlling the CPU and other hardware doing the actual data processing while managing and allocating the resources of memory, CPU time and everything else required for the desired result. In the next section of this chapter, we look at the kernel in detail.

- **Networking:** Under control of the kernel is this often complex subsystem with kernel and userspace components, which provides and supports various network protocols and devices, such as Ethernet cards, and makes client/server networking possible. A client is a program that connects with another computer called a server. Most OSs' networking facilities can run both client and server processes.

- **Security:** Keeping a computer secure in today's environment of constant probes by those eager to take over the computer's resources for nefarious purposes, looms large on the must-do list for any OS. The OS needs to be on constant guard and recognise bogus requests, both from outside and internal to the system. The security subsystem provides such services as authentication (usernames and passwords are one), audits, logging, permissions schemes and more.

- **User interface:** The user interface—which is most often visual but is sometime audible or in Braille for the sight impaired—lets the OS communicate results from applications to the user. In addition, the user can request services, such as file directory listings, directly from the OS. The command line—a text interface utilising typed commands—was the rule in early computing. Since Xerox's development of the GUI and the release of the Mac OS in the early 1980s, most computer OSs today provide GUI capacities.

Now that we know about the history and basic parts of the OS, let's move on to the centre of the OS: the kernel.

The Kernel: The Basic Facilitator of Operating Systems

Laypersons, encouraged by decades of bad science fiction, often think the CPU is a computer's "brain". This is far from the truth. The real boss is the OS kernel, which is software that controls the input/output requests from other software and converts them into data processing instructions that are spoon-fed to the CPU. Figure 8-5 shows how the kernel controls access to the computer's resources.

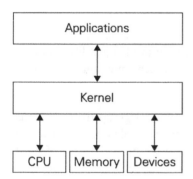

FIGURE 8-5: The kernel controls access to and from the computer's resources.

The kernel also performs the magic of multitasking. Multitasking occurs when the OS employs interrupts to "slice" CPU time into bits for each running process, which essentially allows scores—or even hundreds—of processes, applications and requests from multiple users to run at the same time. This is aided by the kernel drivers, which are small programs sitting somewhere between the kernel and applications. The kernel drivers sort of act as both a glue that holds together the system operation-wise and a communication enabler that makes sure processes talk with the OS and get controlled by it.

Today's multicore CPUs up the ante, so to speak. Instead of time slicing one CPU, a multicore CPU has several CPUs (the Raspberry Pi 2 has four). Thus tasks can be divided, with parts of the task processing in parallel for greater speed (the big advantage of a multicore CPU). Doing this requires a property in the programming of processes that in modern data processing is termed *concurrency*.

Concurrency and parallel processing uses various methods beyond the scope of this book to explain—such as Petri nets, process calculi, the Parallel Random Access Machine model, the Actor model and the Reo Coordination language—in giving the operating system additional scope and power. The result of these methods in processes generated by programs, algorithms and so on, is to break tasks into parts (decomposability), which are acted on simultaneously by the cores (parallelism) and then the results are reconstituted.

Here's a simple analogy: you have a stack of four white cards, which you want respectively coloured red, green, blue, and yellow. You could hand the stack of cards to a guy sitting at a table with four markers, and get him to colour each card, one at a time, and stack each one as he finishes it on the other side of the table. It would take a while.

Alternatively, you could have three guys and a gal at the table. You hand one card to each person. They each colour a card and place it in the stack. Your processing now takes a quarter of the time. That's a good congruency of parallelism.

The OS does tasks like parallel processing while also managing file systems, memory allocation and so on. The Raspberry Pi's OS kernel provides this multitasking just like on much larger computers. In this section, we also look at the ways in which computer architecture influences kernel design.

An OS kernel consists of a collection of programs (components) grouped into various subsystems, which run processes as needed to fill the various managerial tasks of the OS. The next sections explore the components of modern OSs designed for the architecture of small computers. Or, in the case of the Raspberry Pi, a tiny powerhouse fitting in the palm of your hand.

Operating System Control

We have discussed multitasking several times already, where the OS allocates slices of time to applications and other processes. The result, at computer speed, achieves what appears to be simultaneous execution of many programs. That's part of program execution.

The OS is made up of many small programs, so it also takes a share of CPU cycles for its own use. These small programs, when running, comprise processes needed by the OS in its ongoing business of managing the computer.

Figure 8-6 shows a screen capture of some of the processes running on a Raspberry Pi 2 Model B after boot-up. The figure shows the command-line interfaces via Secure Shell (SSH) from a Windows computer. The Raspberry Pi's Raspbian OS, just after booting up, already runs 117 processes.

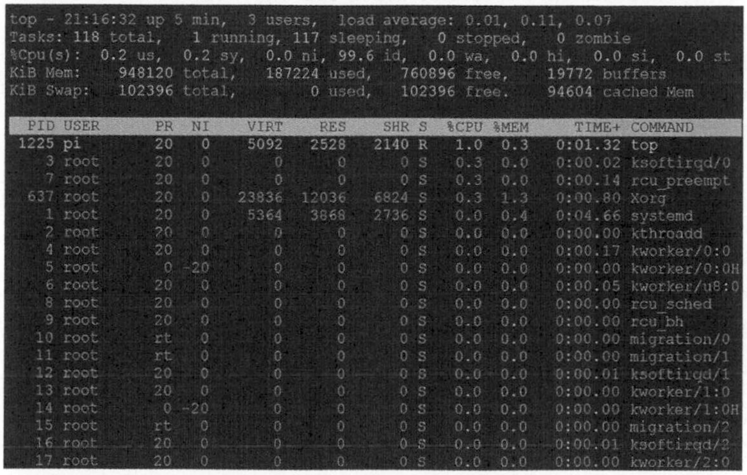

```
top - 21:16:32 up 5 min,  3 users,  load average: 0.01, 0.11, 0.07
Tasks: 118 total,   1 running, 117 sleeping,   0 stopped,   0 zombie
%Cpu(s):  0.2 us,  0.2 sy,  0.0 ni, 99.6 id,  0.0 wa,  0.0 hi,  0.0 si,  0.0 st
KiB Mem:   948120 total,   187224 used,   760896 free,    19772 buffers
KiB Swap:  102396 total,        0 used,   102396 free.    94604 cached Mem

  PID USER      PR  NI    VIRT    RES    SHR S  %CPU %MEM     TIME+ COMMAND
 1225 pi        20   0    5092   2528   2140 R   1.0  0.3   0:01.32 top
    3 root      20   0       0      0      0 S   0.3  0.0   0:00.02 ksoftirqd/0
    7 root      20   0       0      0      0 S   0.3  0.0   0:00.14 rcu_preempt
  637 root      20   0   23836  12036   6824 S   0.3  1.3   0:00.80 Xorg
    1 root      20   0    5364   3868   2736 S   0.0  0.4   0:04.66 systemd
    2 root      20   0       0      0      0 S   0.0  0.0   0:00.00 kthreadd
    4 root      20   0       0      0      0 S   0.0  0.0   0:00.17 kworker/0:0
    5 root       0 -20       0      0      0 S   0.0  0.0   0:00.00 kworker/0:0H
    6 root      20   0       0      0      0 S   0.0  0.0   0:00.05 kworker/u8:0
    8 root      20   0       0      0      0 S   0.0  0.0   0:00.00 rcu_sched
    9 root      20   0       0      0      0 S   0.0  0.0   0:00.00 rcu_bh
   10 root      rt   0       0      0      0 S   0.0  0.0   0:00.00 migration/0
   11 root      rt   0       0      0      0 S   0.0  0.0   0:00.00 migration/1
   12 root      20   0       0      0      0 S   0.0  0.0   0:00.01 ksoftirqd/1
   13 root      20   0       0      0      0 S   0.0  0.0   0:00.00 kworker/1:0
   14 root       0 -20       0      0      0 S   0.0  0.0   0:00.00 kworker/1:0H
   15 root      rt   0       0      0      0 S   0.0  0.0   0:00.00 migration/2
   16 root      20   0       0      0      0 S   0.0  0.0   0:00.01 ksoftirqd/2
   17 root      20   0       0      0      0 S   0.0  0.0   0:00.00 kworker/2:0
```

FIGURE 8-6: Multitasking allows the running of many tasks.

A lot of behind-the-scenes activity goes on deep down in the OS of any computer. Some of these processes run permanently after the computer boots. One such process, used in most Linux-based OSs including several available for the Raspberry Pi, is cron. Cron got its name from the word chronological, meaning "in order of time". When you need a backup of your files every Friday at 3am, cron makes it happen.

Other processes come and go as needed. Computers may look idle when they are not in use but in actuality, scores of little programs are whizzing data around as the OS goes about its duties.

Modes

Walk into any large office building and you will find many places you cannot enter or where entry requires special permission. Such places have locked or guarded doors and sensitive areas protected by carefully controlled access. On a computer, this analogy correlates to file and program permissions. The OS controls which users can access which files and run which programs.

Modes carry security a step further and at a much lower level. They are more like secret vaults in a basement sublevel that's so secret that no one knows it exists. CPUs today give us several modes of operation. Two of these, supervisor mode and protected mode, facilitate immense power for the OS.

Operating systems use the all-powerful supervisor mode sparingly. However, one time when the supervisor mode runs without governance from the OS occurs during the boot process. Because it's not awake yet, the OS has no control. In fact, the initial programs when a computer powers up, like the bootloader routine, must have unfettered access to hardware. The capability of a CPU running in protected mode can be set up only with supervisor mode.

After the OS comes alive, it places the CPU into protected mode. The protected mode is restricted to a limited set of possible CPU instructions, preventing all programs from mucking about with the hardware. At almost all times, the OS enforces protected mode on applications and even its own processes.

When the OS allows the CPU to run in kernel mode, the steps executed have unlimited direct access to all the hardware. The OS opens this gate wide when certain tasks that need unrestricted access run. Handling how processes write to memory or erase (clean up after itself) are a good example. Both of these types of operation require care. Mess up the working memory, and processes can crash all over the place, which can bring down the computer entirely. Glitch the display even slightly and it blanks or locks, leaving users locked out, unable to use their application.

Of course, applications do often need access to hardware for memory manipulations and updating the screen via its graphic card. The program calls for this by triggering an interrupt, which was discussed earlier in this chapter. The OS kernel takes the CPU out of protected mode for the application while maintaining control over its access.

Ah, but what if the application commits an error while in either supervisor mode or protected mode? There are usually CPU "protected mode resource" registers with data the program does not have authority to change. If it tries, the OS uses supervisor mode to prevent a crash, usually by killing the application or other process.

Memory Management

One of the kernel's main functions lies in allocating memory resources. Every one of the processes and programs running in the computer reside in the working memory and use even more of it for manipulating data. The OS performs a complex dance for keeping all these processes from overwriting each other.

Remember those protected mode registers in the CPU that we described in the previous section about modes? This provides one of the several methods by which the kernel limits a memory-hungry process from taking up too many memory locations and possibly causing a crash. Others include memory segmentation and paging—hardware-dependent techniques aiding in memory control and allocation.

Virtual Memory

On older submarines with limited space, such as those during World War II, sailors used the "hot bunk" or "hot rack" system. A bed was assigned to more than one sailor, all on different shifts, with one sleeping while the others were on duty — thus allowing the vessel carrying two or three times the crew limited sleeping facilities would otherwise dictate.

Virtual memory techniques control which memory locations process access at any given time. Therefore, the kernel uses the same memory address for several processes, just not at exactly the same time. So, under OS control, computers effectively have several times their actual physical memory available to run programs.

Often even efficiently employing the same memory addresses for different programs does not meet demand. The kernel then adds more memory space by moving lesser-used memory into a file (called a swap file) on a disk drive. If a process calls for data in memory in the swap file, the kernel brings it back into working memory, moving something else out, if need be.

Again, virtual memory techniques cause the working memory to look a lot larger than it really is, to both programs and users.

Another, arguably even more important, use takes care of fragmentation, which means that the OS stores parts of processes and data wherever empty memory locations exist. When a computer is running lots of concurrent processes with data coming and going, expanding and contracting, stuff is soon broken up and stuffed into memory locations all over the place (or fragmented). Virtual memory keeps this reality transparent to programs, and they continue to operate as if all parts were in adjacent memory slots.

Speaking of the kernel doing all these time-slicing and virtual-memory tricks, it's time we looked at multitasking again.

Multitasking

In sleight-of-hand tricks with playing cards, one of the basic secrets is a move called the "back palm". A magician holds a card up to the audience. He makes a motion and it disappears. He shows you the back of his hand, sliding the card into a "front palm" so it remains hidden. Turning his hand around, he produces the card seemingly out of thin air. Or he might start with several cards in his back palm, producing them one at a time in a rain of cards from apparently nowhere. Numerous YouTube videos give tutorials on how this sleight of hand works.

If you practice the simple moves and do it fast, it truly looks like magic. That's how multitasking works. The OS kernel moves program steps and memory allocations in and out of sight so fast it looks like magic. Hundreds of things seem to be happening simultaneously—which, of course, they are.

Again, time slicing is the trick. The kernel has a scheduling program that decides the amount of CPU time a program gets as well as its priority. If the CPU has multiple cores, the use of concurrency, as we saw earlier, to achieve parallel processing comes into play as well. With this scheduling program, the kernel controls every process's ration of CPU time and amount of memory access.

Disk Access and File Systems

Just as the kernel controls the amount of memory "real estate", a process can occupy in working memory, the same holds true for storage. The main method of storage in modern computers is hard disks, either the old spinning disk or solid-state flash memory drives.

Data is stored on media such as hard drives in files. A computer file holds some similarity (which inspired the name) to paper file folders and their contents. Instead of paper, the information in a computer file consists of binary ones and zeros written magnetically on media such as hard drives or electrically like on SSDs.

The OS organises the binary information into an array of a manageable format (called a "file"), allowing the OS to write, retrieve and manage the available space for other files. The scheme used for file manipulation is a file system (an organized collection of many hundreds or thousands of files). The OS then controls finding, reading and writing of these files as required by applications.

The old, often-used analogy comparing file systems to a physical office file cabinet has some validity. The file system equals the cabinet. Drawers are directories and file folders are the files. However, to make this analogy hold up for modern file systems, you need a file cabinet that has drawers within drawers. In addition, the filing cabinet would know where each and every file was, what was in it, who had permission to read it, and how much space was left in the cabinet, and the cabinet would do all this while spinning at 7,200 rpm.

Numerous types of file system exist. Many of the current OSs can read and manage several types at the same time. For example, when you mount an external drive formatted under

Windows to a Linux machine, the OS manages the Windows file system in parallel with the Linux file system.

Device Drivers

The usefulness of a computer depends on input of data and output of answers. Fulfilling this need for millions of applications on millions of computers results in millions of peripherals developed and sold. A peripheral can be any hardware device installed in or attached to a computer for the purpose of input and/or output. Printers, speakers, keyboards, various mouse-like pointer devices, external disc drives, keyboards, USB gadgets, and so forth, all fall into the peripheral category.

If an OS contained routines for every possible peripheral that currently exists or will come into existence in the next ten years—even narrowing it down to only those from this country or that—the OS would require a hard drive the size of Wales just to store itself. Drivers are a simple but quite elegant solution to this issue.

Most peripherals have small programs specifically written for an OS; these small programs are called drivers. When installed, a driver shows the OS what the device can do and translates OS instructions for the peripheral, enabling the printer to be a printer, the speaker to play audio files, and so on.

Now you've had a brief introduction to what an OS kernel does and how it does it. Next, we see how the OS enables applications in using hardware resources.

Enablers and Assistants to the Operating System

The OS uses device drivers to assist with input and output, but other programs assist the OS as well. This section delves into the booting procedure (booting or boot-up occurs when the computer powers up), firmware (hardware-specific programs to assist the OS), and finally more detail about how the OS manages memory and storage.

Waking Up the OS

Push a computer's power switch to the On position and it begins waking up (booting). The term booting derives from the old cliché of pulling yourself up by your bootstraps. Bootstrapping, in its original usage, meant someone trying to achieve an impossible task. In the case of a computer, an OS readying a computer for practical use seems impossible because the OS is not even there yet—it's just on a file on a hard drive or other memory storage device. Something has to wake the boss.

Booting in General

In modern computers, the something that wakes the OS consists of a "bootloader" (or "bootstrap loader"), a small program stored on read-only memory (ROM). The loader runs automatically on power-up, setting up access and providing some bits of necessary data so the OS's programs get loaded into working memory and executed.

The ROM containing the loader and other information about the computer is often Basic Input/Output System (BIOS). BIOS performs hardware initialisation whenever the computer boots. Newer computers have a replacement for BIOS called Unified Extensible Firmware interface (UEFI). Both BIOS and UEFI are firmware—small programs specific to the hardware and embedded via permanent memory, such as ROM, erasable, reprogrammable read-only memory (EPROM), or flash memory. You can read more about firmware later in this section.

The sequence of booting usually goes something like this:

1. When power is applied to the BIOS or UEFI chip, diagnostics run (to make sure the hardware is okay), components get initialised (for example, disk drives spin up) and the bootstrap program is started.

2. The loader loads the OS into working memory from storage and starts it.

3. The OS creates data structures in working memory, sets needed registers in the CPU and starts a user-level program. From then on, the OS accepts interrupts and the computer is open for business.

These steps outline booting in general terms. Two additional methods of booting, the first more often used, also need mentioning.

Second-Stage Boot Loaders

Bootstrap programs have limitations, one of which derives from the relatively small amount of storage space on ROMs. Therefore, when requirements call for a more sophisticated booting process, a two-stage loader provides the solution. It is a simple concept with the following payoffs:

- The limited bootstrap program loads a more advanced "second-stage" loader from disk into working memory. The new loader has additional features and power, resulting in more options. One such is the ability to configure the loader for things like choosing which of two or more OSs to load.

  For example, a dual-boot PC that uses this method gives the user the choice of running Windows or a Linux distro. Other choices might be booting into a safe or rescue mode, or even booting into a basic shell provided by the second-stage loader.

A widely used second-stage loader is GRand Unified Bootloader (GNU GRUB), from the GNU Project and the Free Software Foundation. GRUB assists the boot process in most Linux OSs. GRUB includes shell capacity, allowing low-level operations before the OS gets loaded; sometimes this is exceptionally useful in rescuing a system that no longer brings up the OS. To expand on all this, as we'll see shortly in the Raspberry Pi's boot sequence, sometimes a third-stage loader gives booting even more power.

- The second-stage loader also facilitates network booting, which is explained in the next section.

Network Booting

A second-stage loader, with its larger and more complex program, can include the capacity of booting from a network. This eliminates the need for a hard drive on the local computer, which is handy for small, embedded computers in machinery, appliances and other uses.

In addition, network booting simplifies the job of IT managers responsible for hundreds or thousands of computers in a company. If every computer on the network boots from the same copy of the OS, keeping that one OS updated with all the latest security and other upgrades is a breeze.

In network booting, the second-stage boot loader accesses the OS copy stored on a network drive with simple protocols provided from ROM. It then transfers the necessary parts to the local computer's working memory for the OS to finish loading itself and start.

Now, let us get specific with the Raspberry Pi.

Booting the Raspberry Pi

The computer architecture of a single-board computer like the Raspberry Pi certainly affects its design. However, the boot process still follows the general precepts we have already seen, with some compromises.

One compromise—for cost and space reduction—involves not including separate non-volatile memory (ROMs, flash memory, etc.). The Raspberry Pi still needs some sort of boot-strap program, however. The design accomplishes this by using the SoC described earlier in this chapter. The SoC is an integrated circuit, which contains the CPU and other components. One of those "other components" entails a small amount of ROM.

Many things happen during booting. Figure 8-7 shows a Raspberry Pi 2 booting, and you can see all the processes being set up, configured and tested.

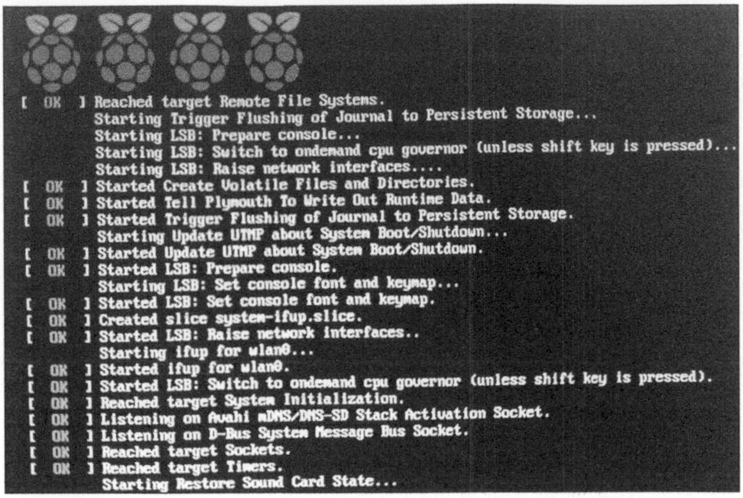

FIGURE 8-7: Detail of Raspberry Pi 2 screen messages during booting

On the Raspberry Pi 3, we get four cores in the CPUs running at 1.2 Ghz. During normal operation—that is, after the OS has taken charge—the GPU drives the display, if present. However, during booting, it plays another role.

The CPUs used on all Raspberry Pi boards are ARM-designed. When powered up, the boot process then begins, and proceeds like this:

1. The Raspberry Pi's design has the GPU on when the board powers up—the ARM core(s) remain off.

2. The GPU executes the first stage boot loader from ROM on the SoC.

3. The first stage reads the SD or (on newer models) the microSD card, and loads bootcode.bin, the second-stage boot loader, for whatever OS is on the card, into the L2 cache (caches being areas of very fast memory available to CPUs or, here, the GPU) and executes it.

4. Next, bootcode.bin turns on SDRAM (the separate memory chip physically stacked on top of the SoC), loads the third-stage program—loader.bin—and starts it.

5. loader.bin reads start.elf, the GPU's firmware (which is covered in the next section).

6. start.elf reads config.txt, cmdline.txt and kernel.img, and starts the OS (this refers to a Linux-based OS such as Raspbian, and is not necessarily valid for any other type of OS).

Which OS gets started by this booting procedure runs on your Raspberry Pi when power is applied. There are a growing number of choices. We look at these in the final section of this chapter. Before that, a brief look at firmware will be beneficial.

ARM (ARM Holding plc) is a British multinational semiconductor and software company. Its main business consists of researching and designing power-efficient CPUs often used in smartphones, tablets and single-board computers such as the Raspberry Pi. The company licenses its designs to other manufacturers.

NOTE

Firmware

Software design for control, monitoring and various types of data manipulation embedded in a device on non-volatile memory (ROM, flash, and so on) is called firmware. Firmware controls or assists in a wide range of devices today. These include phones, cameras, watches, thermostats, refrigerators, stoves and, of course, computers. Almost all digital things have some sort of firmware installed.

The firmware in some devices has no provision for updates and is truly permanent for the life of the device. It's hard, for example, to envision upgrading the firmware in a cheap digital watch from the local discount store. It is what it is. Keeping firmware current in other devices, especially computers, is possible and even desirable.

Upgrading the BIOS or UEFI in a computer sometimes requires a bit of effort. To update it manually, you must find the manufacturer of the software, which resides on an EPROM in your device. Then you secure a utility program that allows you to flash (erase and rewrite) the replacement code onto the EPROM. This process is a pain and creates some danger of erasing the BIOS or UEFI instead of rewriting it. In modern computers and other devices featuring firmware updates, the manufacturers often supply automated procedures for downloading and upgrading.

Many operating systems, including Raspbian, handle the details of application, OS and firmware updates for us. However, you often must manually enter a command for this to occur, instructing the OS to check online software depositories, download the updates available and install those updates. This is something you should do often to maintain the security of you system, apply bug fixes and add new features. If running Raspbian, the most popular Linux OS on the Raspberry Pi, enter the following command on the command line to update:

```
sudo apt-get update && sudo apt-get upgrade
```

The first half of the preceding command tells the OS to search the appropriate repositories and download updates. The second orders it to install those updates (that is, upgrade the OS).

Now, it's time to examine OS choices for the Raspberry Pi.

Operating Systems for Raspberry Pi

This section gives an overview of the various OSs for the Raspberry Pi, and includes a look at the wealth of new OSs that have become available thanks to the new four-core ARM processor in the Raspberry Pi 2; these include Raspberry Pi–enhanced versions of Ubuntu, Fedora and Gentoo as well as Windows 10. In other words, any OS that has ARM support works on the Raspberry Pi's computer architecture.

The OSs in this section aren't meant to be a complete list. Instead we're touching on some of the more interesting OSs. Included are the ones optimised for the Raspberry Pi's architecture to deliver powerful solutions on this credit-card-sized monster of a minicomputer.

In choosing an OS for the Raspberry Pi, you should consider the solutions you want the board to accomplish. The truly neat thing about the Raspberry Pi is that changing the OS entails simply replacing the SD or microSD card with another one. (Try that with a PC, Mac, or Linux box!) This ease of switching opens up all sorts of possibilities.

NOOBS

The New Out-Of-Box Software (NOOBS) software package presents a selection of OSs optimised for the Raspberry Pi. You can download them free from the official Raspberry Pi website at www.raspberrypi.org/downloads/ (see Figure 8-8). They also feature third-party OS images—*images* being a complete file system in the proper format to boot up and run. You may also purchase NOOBS on SD or microSD cards (the newer Model B+ and 2.0, and 3.0 Raspberry Pis use the latter) on the site or from many other vendors.

Running the NOOBS card walks you through setting up an OS. You have six choices:

- **Raspbian:** A port (converted and optimised to run on the Raspberry Pi) of the popular Debian Linux distribution and recommended by the Raspberry Pi Foundation and many thousands of experimenters as the best OS for the Raspberry Pi. The latest version of this Linux distro is Debian 8, "Jessie".

- **Arch Linux:** A Raspberry Pi version for Arch Linux designed to run on ARM central processor chips.

- **Pidora:** A version of Red Hat's Fedora Linux distribution. Fedora has always been on the cutting edge of Linux (although just remember—sometimes you bleed on the cutting edge).

- **OpenELEC:** A dedicated media centre distribution designed for playing video and music by the use of a small, dedicated OS that doesn't hog resources and leaves more memory for showing movies, blasting the latest tunes and so forth.

- **RaspBMC:** A media centre distribution based on Raspbian that saves resources for serving media files.

- **Reduced instruction set computing (RISC) OS:** Created by the team that designed the ARM CPU. It offers fast execution on small hardware and is worth experimenting with.

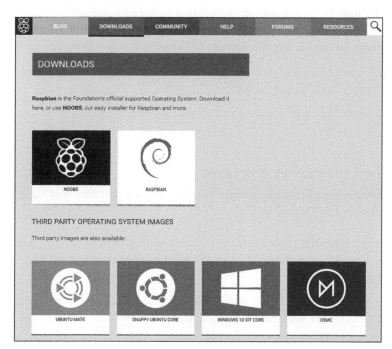

FIGURE 8-8: The Downloads page on the Raspberry Pi site presents a good starting selection of operating systems.

Of the six OSs listed here, Raspbian is the most popular. If you're used to Debian-type Linux distros (Debian itself, Ubuntu and so on), you'll be right at home running Raspbian on a Raspberry Pi.

Third-Party Operating Systems

The official Raspberry Pi site includes several third-party images, which are free for download. Images allow you to write an SD or microSD card that installs the OS on your Raspberry Pi. Two of these OSs were discussed in the preceding section—OpenELEC and RISC OS—so we'll skip those. Of the ones remaining, one may shock you (Windows) and, yes, it's free:

- **Ubuntu MATE:** A Raspberry Pi-optimised version of the popular Ubuntu distro that features the MATE desktop (a desktop environment forked from the now-unmaintained code base of GNOME 2).

- **Snappy Ubuntu Core:** A distro that came about as a project for Ubuntu users on smartphones. It supports Docker, which means it is a good platform for cloud applications.

- **Windows 10 IoT Core:** The latest version of the often maligned but often indispensible Microsoft OS comes to the Raspberry Pi (requires Raspberry 2.0). IoT refers to the Internet of Things, so this OS lets you develop IoT apps on the Raspberry Pi.

- **OSMC:** A free open source media centre "built for the people, by the people". It's similar to the proprietary OpenELEC, but it's free.

- **PiNet:** Provides a centralised user accounts and file storage system for a Raspberry Pi classroom.

Other Available Operating Systems

Other versions of OS distributions for the Raspberry Pi exist. Here's a smattering of some interesting ones. Most require the Raspberry Pi 2:

- **Gentoo:** A fast and popular (because of its near-unlimited adaptability) Linux. Look for the Raspberry Pi version on the Gentoo site at `https://wiki.gentoo.org/wiki/Raspberry_Pi`.

- **FreeBSD:** Before Linux there was UNIX, and FreeBSD is still very actively supported (see `www.FreeBSD.org`). It's been ported to the Raspberry Pi; visit `https://www.raspberrypi.org/blog/freebsd-is-here/`.

- **Firefox OS:** Mozilla's Firefox OS is now on Raspberry Pi. Find additional information at `https://wiki.mozilla.org/Fxos_on_RaspberryPi`.

- **IPFire:** This OS provides a system featuring an exceptionally strong firewall, which gives protection against intrusion but retains ease of use and has the functionality required for corporate and institutional usage. Visit `www.ipfire.org/` to download the ARM version.

- **OpenSUSE:** A popular Linux distro, especially in Europe, that now has an ARM version that runs on the Pi. See `https://en.opensuse.org/HCL:Raspberry_Pi`.

- **Plan 9:** An OS from Bell Labs that's named after everyone's favourite so-bad-it's-good movie, *Plan 9 from Outer Space*. You can find more info and instructions for installing Plan 9 on the Raspberry Pi at `https://www.raspberrypi.org/forums/viewtopic.php?f=80&t=24480`.

- **SliTaz:** An OS touted as a simple and fast Linux OS system that has low resource requirements for servers and desktops. Find the link for the Raspberry Pi version at `www.slitaz.org/en/`.

- **Tiny Core:** A simple (limited subset) Linux OS that takes up less memory space and fewer other resources but still provides reasonable computer power. Find downloads and info at `http://distro.ibiblio.org/tinycorelinux/ports.html`.

An increasing number of other OSs are out there. Googling "operating systems for Raspberry Pi" returns quite a lot of possibilities for you to explore. Again, one of the great advantages of the Raspberry Pi lies in its capacity to change OSs in seconds. Unplug the current SD or microSD card and plug into another card with an entirely different OS. Boot it up and go.

The only limit to the number of OSs you can have lies in how many SD cards you can afford. Prices on SDs and microSDs continue to drop. It's pretty darn wonderful.

Chapter 9
Video Codecs and Video Compression

A VIDEO IS a sequence of images that are shown one after the other. In principle, you could store them as a digital flip-book, with a picture for each frame. Without compression, roughly 3 bytes per pixel (one to store each of the red, green and blue colour components) are required to avoid introducing perceptible *quantisation artefacts* (visible steps in brightness or colour). If you wanted to store video even at a relatively low resolution (640 × 480 pixels) at 25 frames a second, each second would then take up 3 * 640 * 480 * 25 bytes, which works out to just more than 23 megabytes (MB) per second. A two-hour film would take up more than 165 gigabytes (GB), which is equivalent to 10 double-sided, double-layer DVDs. Applying a generic lossless compression algorithm such as ZIP might make it a little smaller, but you'd still need several of these disks.

Storing footage as just described would basically make almost any form of digital video distribution completely impractical. Changing the side of a DVD every six minutes would be annoying, and downloading a TV show would take days. YouTube would only work for clips a few seconds long. Video chat would require either an image too small to be useful or the fastest Internet connection available.

In order to make digital video distribution possible, it's essential to find ways to make the videos much smaller. This shrinking of files is known as compression. There are two basic types of compression: lossless and lossy. In *lossless* compression, the file is shrunk in such a way that it's possible to recreate the original file perfectly from the compressed file, down to the level of individual bits. This is how file formats such as `.zip` or `tar.gz` work. However, there's a limit to how small you can make a file with lossless compression, and lossless compression on its own generally isn't sufficient for most video applications.

In contrast with lossless compression, *lossy* compression makes a file smaller by removing some of the information. After lossy compression, it is no longer possible to recreate the original file perfectly from the compressed file. As a trivial example of lossy video compression, imagine simply halving the horizontal and vertical resolution of each image in the video stream. The resulting video file would shrink by a factor of four, at the cost of a significant reduction in visual fidelity. The art of designing lossy video compression algorithms and encoder implementations lies in keeping the perceived quality of the decoded stream as high as possible while making the file as small as possible.

Most video encoders use both lossless and lossy compression techniques to get the files as small as possible.

The First Video Codecs

The International Telecommunication Union (ITU) developed the first widely used video compression standard (known as H.261) to enable video calls over Integrated Services Digital Network (ISDN) lines in 1988. In comparison to more modern standards, H.261 delivered relatively poor image quality for a given bit rate, but it is notable for having laid the technical foundations for future video compression standards. Compression standards are often known informally as codecs, a mash-up of *coder-deco*der. More formally, the term codec refers to an implementation of a standard in software, hardware or a combination of the two.

The Moving Picture Experts Group (MPEG) was formed in 1988 by the International Organization for Standardization (ISO) and International Electrotechnical Commission (IEC) to take this foundation and build it up to support higher video quality than was possible over ISDN lines. Both the ITU and MPEG continue to develop codecs, often in collaboration with one another. Since 2001 much of this work has been done under the auspices of the Joint Video Team (JVT), which was responsible for the successful H.264/MPEG-4 AVC codec. The MPEG series of standards includes more than just video. It includes the file structure, audio and other parts needed to make a fully functional video file.

The first standard developed by MPEG (known as MPEG-1) was released in 1993. There are two ways the designers of MPEG-1 sought to minimise file size while maximising image quality:

- Preferentially removing information that humans find hard to perceive (exploiting the eye)
- Exploiting the sort of information that videos hold (exploiting the data)

Exploiting the Eye

Our eyes possess two types of receptors that detect light: rods that detect brightness and cones that detect colour. Rods are more sensitive than cones, which is why we lose the ability to see colours when it gets dark, although we can still make out shapes. We also have about 20 times as many rods as cones. This means that we're far better at making out fine variations in brightness than in colour. It's a little quirk of human physiology that can be exploited when compressing video since there's no point in storing information that the eye can't see.

To treat brightness and colour differently in a codec, it is helpful first to transform the image from the RGB colorspace, where each pixel is represented by a red, a green and a blue value, to the so-called $Y'C_bC_r$ colorspace, where each pixel is represented by a *luma* (brightness) value Y' and two *chroma* (colour) values C_b and C_r. Luma corresponds to perceived brightness and is computed as a weighted sum of the original red, green and blue values. There are several slightly different YC_bC_r colorspaces, which are used for different applications. The weights and sums for the commonly used ITU-R BT.601standard are:

$Y' = 0.257R + 0.504G + 0.098B + 16$

$Cr = 0.439R - 0.368G - 0.071B + 128$

$Cb = -0.148R - 0.219G + 0.439B + 128$

If we visualise the 24-bit RGB colorspace as a cube, increasing luma moves us roughly along a leading diagonal from black (0,0,0) to white (255,255,255), through 254 shades of grey. The chroma values represent movement away from the diagonal: roughly speaking, C_b and C_r represent how much of a blue or red tint the colour has, respectively.

Changing the colorspace like this doesn't make the image any smaller (each pixel is still represented by three numbers, and each number requires roughly the same number of bits of precision as before), but it splits up the brightness from the colour. In effect, there are three independent images, or *channels*: one of brightness, one of "redness" and one of "blueness". The individual pixel values that make up a channel are referred to as *samples*. These are displayed together, but they can be stored in different ways. Because we have so many more rods, which are for seeing detail, it doesn't matter if the colour values are at a lower resolution. The first, and simplest, stage of MPEG-1 compression is chroma subsampling. This leaves the luma channel at full resolution, but halves the horizontal and vertical resolution of both chroma channels, shrinking the space they occupy by a factor of four (see Figures 9-1, 9-2 and 9-3). The overall space occupied by the image is thus halved (because $1 + ¼ + ¼ = ½ \times 3$) at no cost in visual quality. Not bad for a first step!

FIGURE 9-1: The luma channel of the image

FIGURE 9-2: The chroma red channel of the image

FIGURE 9-3: The chroma blue channel of the image

Exploiting the Data

The second technique that video compression can use is to make assumptions about the properties of the content being transmitted. Typically, each image in a video isn't completely different to those before and after it. If it was, the screen would just display different unrelated images in quick succession, and you wouldn't be able to make much sense of what is happening. Instead, most frames are very similar to the ones before and after it. Perhaps most of the background is the same with just a few static or slowly changing objects moving around, or perhaps the whole frame moves as the camera pans. Either way, this means that most of the information is already available in a preceding frame. Sometimes the whole image changes as the video cuts to a new scene, but this is infrequent considering there may be between 24 and 60 frames per second.

To take advantage of this feature of video data, an MPEG-1 encoder splits the sequence of frames into I frames, P frames and B frames.

I Frames

Intra-frames, or I frames, are stored in a way that allows them to be decoded by themselves, without reference to any other frame in the video. From a technical perspective, I frames are encoded in a very similar way to the JPEG format for storing still images; the compression techniques you'll see used on I frames work in much the same way to keep photographs small.

The first stage is to split each channel (Y', C_b and C_r) of the I-frame image into 8×8 sample blocks. Because the chroma channels have already been subsampled, a single 8×8 block in the chroma channel corresponds to four adjacent 8×8 blocks in the luma channel. This collection of six blocks (one C_b, one C_r and four Y') is known as a macroblock. We'll look at how these macroblocks are used later on, but first let's take a look at the other types of frame.

P Frames

Predicted frames, or P frames, depend on image data from the preceding I or P frame. They don't describe the whole image, just the bits that have changed. As such, they can't be decoded without the preceding I or P frame being decoded first. The P frames are divided into macroblocks in exactly the same way as I frames.

As previously mentioned, a large portion of each image will probably be the same as in the previous image, just moved slightly. When encoding a P frame, the encoder looks at each macroblock in the image in turn and tries to find similar macroblock-sized areas in the preceding frame; this procedure is known as *motion search*. If the encoder finds a similar area, it doesn't encode the new macroblock from scratch; instead it encodes a motion vector indicating where in the previous frame the match has been found. A macroblock encoded in this way is known as a P macroblock; when the decoder comes to decode a P macroblock it decodes the motion vector and copies the appropriate area of the preceding frame. If the encoder fails to find a sufficiently similar macroblock in the previous frame, it stores the macroblock in exactly the same way that macroblocks are stored in I frames. A macroblock encoded in this way is known as an I macroblock.

Even if motion search has identified a good candidate for prediction, it's likely that there will still be some small differences between the current frame and the corresponding section of the preceding frame. For example, a macroblock may contain a bird flying across the screen. As it flies, it also changes shape as its wings flap. This difference is known as the *prediction error* or *residual*. The encoder may choose to encode the residual using the same techniques that it would use for I macroblock image data and store the encoded residual along with the motion vector; when the decoder comes to decode the macroblock, it decodes the residual and combines it with the image data copied from the preceding frame.

The smaller the residual, the less information there is to store, and therefore the smaller the file size. In order to capture movement as accurately as possible, MPEG-1 motion vectors can be specified down to the half-pixel (also called half-pel) level in both x and y directions. If it decodes a half-pel motion vector for a macroblock, the decoder must do more than just copy pixels from the previous frame: it must also have a scheme for generating the "missing" pixel values that lie halfway between the real pixel values. This process is called interpolation. If you visualize a single line of pixels, in a single channel, you'll have a single sample for each pixel. These could be plotted on a graph to show how the sample value changes along the line of pixels. The easiest interpolation scheme, used by MPEG-1, is to draw a straight line between the two points and plot the middle point on this line (mathematically, we take the average of the two adjacent samples); this is known as linear interpolation.

Of course, in a 2D picture, we need to do this vertically as well as horizontally. Motion vectors that have integer x or y components (for example (1, ½) or (3½, 2)) are straightforward, as they require linear interpolation in one direction only. Motion vectors that have half-pel *x* and *y* components (for example (2½, ½)) require us to average four adjacent samples in the source image. This is known as bilinear interpolation. See Figure 9-4 for details.

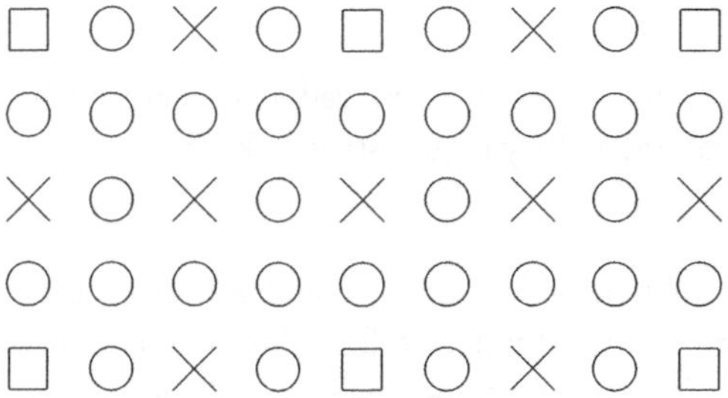

FIGURE 9-4: The location of the full pixels (squares) and the half-pixel values (crosses) on a 2×1 grid. Later video standards also use quarter-pixel values (circles).

This encoding of movement is obvious if you've ever seen a corrupted MPEG video. Parts of the frame still move around, but because the preceding frame is wrong, the images that are moving are incorrect.

B Frames

Bi-directional frames, or B frames, are much like P frames except that they can contain elements from the preceding I or P frame and the subsequent I or P frame; note that no frame is ever predicted off a B frame.

Each macroblock in a B frame can be predicted off areas in one or both of these frames. If it's predicted off both, then the encoder must store two motion vectors, and the decoder computes a weighted average of the two areas before combining it with the residual (if any).

If the video stream has a large number of B frames in a row, one of the reference frames could be quite a way ahead. This could create a problem for the decoder because it would have to read forward all the way to the reference frame and decode that before coming back to decode the B frame. In order to simplify this problem, the encoder doesn't write frames to the file in the order they appear on the screen, but so that the reference frames are always before the frames that are predicted off them. Table 9-1 shows an example video stream.

This would be stored in the order 1,4,2,3,7,5,6. First the decoder gets to frame 1. This is an I frame so it can be decoded independently. Then the decoder gets to frame 4. This is a P frame, so it's predicted off an earlier frame. Because frames 2 and 3 are B frames, it's predicted off frame 1, which has already been decoded. Then the decoder gets to frame 2, which is a B frame. The two reference frames (1 and 4) have already been decoded, and likewise for frame 3, which has the same reference frames. The same method is used to reorder the second half of the frames.

Table 9-1   Example Group of Pictures with Frame Types

Frame number	1	2	3	4	5	6	7
Frame type	I	B	B	P	B	B	I

This reordering doesn't change the order in which the frames are displayed on the screen (the *presentation order*). That is still done in numerical order. They're just stored like this to make life easier for the decoder.

There isn't a set way for MPEG-1 encoders to split the video into I, P and B frames. Each piece of encoding software does it a little differently. Most videos follow the pattern shown in Table 9-1, with I frames at regular intervals, P frames evenly spaced between I frames, and B frames for the rest. An I frame and its successive P and B frames are known as a *group of pictures* (GOP); the pattern of P and B frames is known as the *GOP structure*; and the size of the gap between I frames is known as the *GOP size*.

The GOP size and structure can be set by the encoder depending on the required bit rate, and how easily we wish to be able to seek through a video. Because only I frames can be decoded independently, we can only seek to a GOP boundary; a small GOP size makes it easier to seek to an arbitrary location in the video, generally at the cost of requiring a higher bit rate for a given quality due to the increased number of expensive I frames.

Available bandwidth is particularly important because videos are usually intended to be played without buffering. We typically think of bandwidth today in terms of an Internet connection, but when the MPEG-1 codec was designed, other factors were more important because streaming video over the web wasn't yet possible. MPEG-1 was designed to work at a range of bit rates, but the key one for the designers was the speed at which a CD-ROM drive could read data (1.5 megabits per second (Mbits/s)). MPEG-1 provides roughly the same quality as a VHS video cassette at this bit rate. The Video CD format, a precursor to DVDs, stores 74 minutes of MPEG-1 video on a standard CD.

Video CD is a good example of a "constant bit rate" format: it isn't possible to run the CD faster to get more bit rate to encode a rapidly changing scene, or to run it more slowly to conserve space when the scene isn't changing. Modern streaming video codecs often vary their bit rate (within limits) according to scene complexity. There are a variety of techniques an encoder can use to keep the video stream at the required bit rate. First you need to understand how MPEG-1 encodes image data and residuals.

Understanding Frequency Transform

As previously described, MPEG-1 exploits the eye's inability to distinguish fine changes in colour through chroma subsampling. Another helpful (for codec designers) attribute of the human visual system is that we find it harder to detect fine (high-frequency) changes in either brightness or colour than to detect coarser-grained (low-frequency) changes. In principle, we can represent high-frequency details in the scene less accurately, or even discard them altogether, without compromising perceptual quality.

Just as we transformed the image into the $Y'C_bC_r$ colorspace to allow us to separate and subsample chroma, we must transform our data again to allow us to discard high-frequency details. This time, the four 8×8 luma blocks and two 8×8 chroma blocks that make up a macroblock are each passed through a discrete cosine transformation (DCT). The mathematical details are beyond the scope of this book, but the key is that after applying the DCT we no longer store a grid of 8×8 sample values, one for each point (a *spatial representation*), but instead store details of how the samples change as we move across the block in the x and y directions (a *frequency representation*).

It's easiest to understand the DCT by first thinking of the one-dimensional case: a single line of an 8×8 sample block. This one line has eight sample values that could be displayed as a line graph. The DCT decomposes this line into a weighted sum of several cosine waves (*basis functions*) of different frequencies. When added together, these functions have the same value as the line (at least at the sample points). The cosine waves are described by coefficients that give the amplitude of each cosine wave. It turns out that eight coefficients (and eight waves of different frequencies) are enough to accurately capture the original signal—we've traded eight spatial-domain samples for eight frequency-domain coefficients. In the two-dimensional case, it turns out that we need 64 two-dimensional cosine waves (surfaces that vary at different rates in the x and y directions) and 64 coefficients.

It is helpful to write the 64 coefficients in an 8×8 block, with the ones in the top left representing the lower frequencies, and the ones in the bottom right representing the higher frequencies (see Figure 9-5). The top-left value is known as the DC coefficient and is always equal to the average value of all the samples in the block. In other words, it's the value of the block without taking into account any of the spatial changes.

The name DC comes from direct current and is a relic from when similar methods were used to analyse electricity.   **NOTE**

All the other values are called AC (alternating current) coefficients. In Figure 9-5, the top line represents changes in purely the horizontal direction, with the leftmost AC coefficient (next to the DC) holding the lowest frequency data, while the rightmost one holds the highest frequency data. Similarly, the leftmost column holds information about changes in purely the vertical direction. The other values hold information about changes in both directions. For example, the rightmost value on the second row corresponds to high-frequency change in the horizontal direction and low-frequency change in the vertical direction.

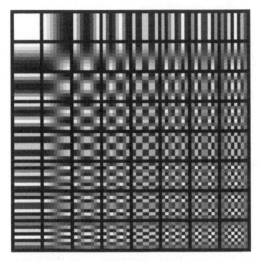

FIGURE 9-5: The spatial frequencies that each coefficient represents

Just as when we transformed from RGB to Y'CbCr, the DCT hasn't compressed the image itself: the cosine coefficients take up roughly the same amount of space as the original data. However, once again it has set us up to be able to apply a subsequent lossy compression step in a way that minimises the perceived impact on visual quality. The lossy step in this case is *quantisation*— dividing each coefficient by a number and rounding down during encoding, and then multiplying by the same number during decoding to get back a similar (but generally not quite identical) number. As human eyes are more able to detect errors in low-frequency data than high-frequency data, the encoder generally quantises the high-frequency coefficients more coarsely.

Take a look at Figures 9-6, 9-7 and 9-8, which contain a frame with increasingly large amounts of compression. As the file size gets smaller, more and more errors start to creep into the higher-frequency portions of the image.

Per-coefficient quantisation is performed by applying a *quantisation matrix*, which can be varied on a frame-by-frame basis to hit the target bit rate. This matrix has the same dimensions as the matrix holding the output from the DCT, and each entry in the quantisation matrix is the level of quantisation for the corresponding coefficient in the DCT output. The DCT value is divided by the quantisation value, and this result is rounded down. This reduces the numbers to a smaller range, and smaller ranges take less space to store.

FIGURE 9-6: At maximum quality, there's little quantisation, so both the high- and low-frequency portions of the image are displayed well. This image has about 6 bits per pixel.

FIGURE 9-7: As the quantisation starts to come in, the high-frequency portions of the image (like edges) start to lose definition. This image has 0.9 bits per pixel.

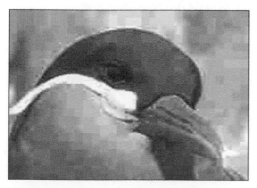

FIGURE 9-8: With a high level of quantisation, only the low-frequency image is really visible, and you can see the boundaries between macroblocks. This image has 0.3 bits per pixel.

In general, quantisation usually reduces many of the higher-frequency portions of the DCT to 0. Having a large proportion of the numbers the same makes the next step (entropy coding) efficient.

Figures 9-9, 9-10 and 9-11 show the quantisation matrices that were used in Figures 9-6, 9-7 and 9-8, respectively. You can extract these from JPEG images (which are very similar to MPEG-1 I frames) on your Raspberry Pi using djpeg. First you need to install it with

```
sudo apt-get install libjpeg-progs
```

Then you can run the following where image.jpeg is the name of the JPEG file:

```
djpeg -verbose -verbose image.jpeg > /dev/null
```

Normally this gives two matrices—one for the luma values and one for the chroma values—but these images are black and white so only have luma values. If you're testing the output of the Raspberry Pi camera module, you may find that the quantisation matrix is set to not quantise at all (that is, it's all 1s) unless you specify a quality option in the raspistill command (for example, -q 50).

```
1   1   1   1   1   1   1   1
1   1   1   1   1   1   1   1
1   1   1   1   1   1   1   1
1   1   1   1   1   1   1   1
1   1   1   1   1   1   1   1
1   1   1   1   1   1   1   1
1   1   1   1   1   1   1   1
1   1   1   1   1   1   1   1
```

FIGURE 9-9: There's no quantisation, which means that all of the frequency data is kept.

```
16   11   10   16    24    40    51    61
12   12   14   19    26    58    60    55
14   13   16   24    40    57    69    56
14   17   22   29    51    87    80    62
18   22   37   56    68   109   103    77
24   35   55   64    81   104   113    92
49   64   78   87   103   121   120   101
72   92   95   98   112   100   103    99
```

FIGURE 9-10: Quite a lot of quantisation, and heavily focused on the higher-frequency portions

80	55	50	80	120	200	255	255
60	60	70	95	130	255	255	255
70	65	80	120	200	255	255	255
70	85	110	145	255	255	255	255
90	110	185	255	255	255	255	255
120	175	255	255	255	255	255	255
245	255	255	255	255	255	255	255
255	255	255	255	255	255	255	255

FIGURE 9-11: Much of the high-frequency data is removed entirely.

As you can see in Figures 9-10 and 9-11, the quantisation values tend to be roughly equal along trailing diagonals. This is because these lines contain coefficients to which our eyes have roughly the same sensitivity. For example, in Figure 9-11, the fourth value across the top line corresponds to the same frequency horizontally as the fourth one down on the leftmost line does vertically. One has a quantised coefficient of 80, whereas the other has one of 70; they're not exactly the same because empirical studies have found that slightly asymmetric matrices yield slightly better perceptual quality at a given bit rate. The two coefficients between them (65 and 70) correspond to DCT basis functions with slightly lower horizontal frequency and slightly higher vertical frequency, and are similar in magnitude.

The matrix of quantised DCT coefficients has to be serialised into a single stream of numbers in order to be stored in a file or transmitted over a network. Usually when serialising a matrix like this, each row is sent one after the other; in this case, however, the final step (entropy coding) is more efficient if the matrix is serialised in a zig-zag pattern.

This zig-zag pattern starts with the coefficient that our eyes are most sensitive to and moves through them in the order of decreasing sensitivity. This should roughly equate to quantisation levels getting higher and higher. As the quantisation level gets higher, more and more of the quantised values will be zero, and this string of zeros is very effectively compressed in the next stage. See Figure 9-12 for an example.

Using Lossless Encoding Techniques

The final part of the MPEG-1 encoding process applies lossless compression techniques to the quantised coefficients and other data including mode choice flags and motion vectors. There are three methods that MPEG-1 uses to get the file size as small as possible:

- Differential pulse-code modulation (DPCM)

- Run-length encoding (RLE)

- Huffman coding

DCT Coefficents

34	27	101	129	42	9	30	19
21	92	47	23	107	134	21	10
119	15	137	191	105	104	110	168
45	49	52	29	40	28	21	46
4	41	73	203	37	73	33	84
17	111	67	55	69	73	20	1
121	22	172	89	81	80	56	50
38	72	71	94	99	95	99	92

Quantisation Matrix

16	11	10	16	24	40	51	61
12	12	14	19	26	58	60	55
14	13	16	24	40	57	69	56
14	17	22	29	51	87	80	62
18	22	37	56	68	109	103	77
24	35	55	64	81	104	113	92
49	64	78	87	103	121	120	101
72	92	95	98	112	100	103	99

Step 1

Quantised Coefficents

2	2	10	8	1	0	0	0
1	7	3	1	4	2	0	0
8	1	8	7	2	1	1	2
3	2	2	1	0	0	0	0
0	1	1	3	0	0	0	0
0	3	1	0	0	0	0	0
2	0	2	1	0	0	0	0
0	0	0	0	0	0	0	0

Step 2

Step 3   Serialised and Quantised Coefficents

2 2 1 8 7 10 8 3 1 3 0 2 8 1 1 0 4 7 2 1 0 2 3 1 1 2 2 0 0 0 1 0 3 1 0 0 0 2 0 0 0 1 0 2 0 0 0 0 0 0 0 0 0 0 0 0 0 0

FIGURE 9-12: The process of quantising and serialising the output from MPEG-1 I frame DCT

Certain parameters, notably DC coefficients and motion vectors, are strongly correlated between successive macroblocks. DPCM exploits this correlation by storing only the difference between the last value and the current value. The differences have a tighter frequency distribution than the values themselves, and so respond better to Huffman coding.

RLE is simply the process of shortening strings of the same value. For example, if a quantised DCT matrix ends with a series of 40 zeros, this could be represented by 40 repetitions of the number zero. However, in RLE, it's represented by the zero once, and a count of 40 times. This is particularly effective in MPEG encoding because the zigzag ordering of coefficients ensures that this situation happens very frequently, especially at higher quantisation levels.

Huffman coding also removes duplicated data, but it works on sequences of symbols that are repeated at different locations in the data, not simply blocks of repeated identical symbols. Sequences that occur frequently are assigned short binary representations, while those that occur rarely are assigned longer representations. For example, if the text of this chapter were Huffman coded, the encoder might see that the word "encoded" is repeated many times and so replace this with a representation that's only 1 byte long, saving space. The statistics of the MPEG-1 symbol stream are such that Huffman encoding typically performs very well.

Changing with the Times

These basic techniques in MPEG-1 still form the basis of modern video compression today, more than 20 years after they were first introduced, that is:

- Colorspace transformation, where incoming data in the RGB colorspace is transformed into the $Y'C_bC_r$ colorspace and subsampled to exploit the eye's differential sensitivity to luma and chroma

- Splitting into GOPs comprising I, P and B frames and applying motion compensation to exploit the fact than many frames are similar

- A frequency domain transform (DCT or other) to transform the spatial representation into a frequency representation

- Quantisation that reduces the amount of data in the DCT coefficient matrix, exploiting the eye's differential sensitivity to high- and low-frequency data

- Entropy coding

However, modern video codecs have developed more efficient ways of performing each of these tasks.

MPEG-1 started the digital video revolution, but some limitations quickly became apparent. It supported only two audio channels (stereo) but not surround sound. Also, it didn't properly support interlaced video .

Interlaced video is a video technique to increase the apparent frame rate of a video. It's commonly used in broadcast TV. **NOTE**

With these weaknesses corrected, MPEG-2 was the first digital video format to really become popular. Although nearly 20 years old at the time of writing, it still forms the basis of much commercial video compression, such as broadcast digital TV and DVDs. These applications place a premium on quality at reasonable file sizes. The MPEG-2 video compression standard is the same as the ITU's H.262 standard.

Initially, an MPEG-3 video encoding standard was designed as an extension to MPEG-2. However, many of the proposed techniques were incorporated into MPEG-2 and the formal MPEG-3 designation was retired. The audio standard commonly known as MPEG-3 is, in fact, MPEG-1 layer 3, the most sophisticated of three possible audio encoding schemes specified alongside the MPEG-1 standard.

In parallel with the development of new standards, numerous encoder techniques have been developed that can be used to improve compression or perceptual quality in older standards as well as in newer ones.

Just as our eyes are more sensitive to lower spatial frequencies, they're also more sensitive to changes in brightness at some levels, particularly in the middle of the brightness range. *Lumi masking* is the process where the encoder preferentially removes detail from areas of the image that are either very bright or very dark. This can assign more bitstream space to encoding medium-brightness blocks, which means that the frame looks better for a particular bit rate.

Encoders have considerable latitude in how they choose to quantise individual transform coefficients. The straightforward division-with-rounding approach described in the earlier "Understanding Frequency Transform" section minimises error, but does not fully take into account the bit rate benefits of choosing small coefficients, which have shorter entropy codes, and of discarding isolated non-zero coefficients that break up long runs of zeros, which are cheap to encode using RLE. Techniques such as uniform or adaptive deadzone and trellis quantisation attempt to capture these benefits by biasing coefficients toward zero. Trellis quantisation, as implemented by the popular x264 encoder, uses a comparatively detailed model of a codec's RLE and entropy coding schemes to identify quantisation choices that yield significant bit rate savings.

Both lumi-masking and trellis quantisation can be used in older and newer MPEG standards.

The Latest Standards from MPEG

Just as digital video using MPEG-2 was starting to become popular, the landscape changed when home Internet connections started to become fast enough to download video.

If you're putting a film on DVD, it really doesn't matter what size the file is as long as it's smaller than the capacity of the disc (4.7–9.4GB per side depending on the type of disk). However, when streaming video over the Internet, every megabyte counts. Smaller file sizes mean cheaper storage costs, less buffering for the viewer and lower bandwidth. What's more, the playback devices for Internet viewing tend to be more powerful than digital TV set-top boxes. This extra processing power can be used to perform more complex decoding.

There are two video compression sections to MPEG-4: parts 2 and 10. Part 2 was the first to become popular, and it introduced many new features such as quarter-pel motion vectors and global motion compensation. The term MPEG-4 is generally used informally to refer to the part 2 standard. Two implementations, Xvid and DivX, were particularly popular in the early days of illegal file sharing because they had small file sizes compared to the MPEG-2 DVDs from which the files were usually ripped. The implementations differed slightly in their implementation of the standard, so the implementations wouldn't always play the same files.

MPEG didn't release the entire MPEG-4 suite of standard in one go. MPEG-4 part 2 was released in 1999, whereas part 10 (more commonly known by its equivalent ITU designation,

H.264) didn't emerge for another four years. This meant that hardware had again improved, and part 10 is more complex (with a corresponding increase in compression performance) than any of the preceding standards.

One of the main ways in which H.264 improves on its predecessors is by increasing the flexibility and precision of the motion compensation scheme.

In previous standards, B frames could be predicted off two adjacent reference frames; H.264 increases this to a (probably excessive) maximum of 16 nearby frames, depending on resolution. As with MPEG-4, motion vectors are specified to quarter-pel precision. Earlier we said that MPEG-1 uses bilinear interpolation to calculate values halfway between integer sample positions. With quarter-pel motion vectors, there are three possible locations between any two pixels. It is possible to use the same bilinear interpolation to generate estimated sample values at these locations, but better results are possible with a more advanced interpolation method. Think again of the graph showing the sample values for a single channel along one line of pixels. Using linear interpolation, we said, was the same as drawing a straight line between adjacent samples and reading the value off that. A more effective way would be to try to fit a smooth curve against the line of samples using more than just the two immediately adjacent values, and using this to calculate the intermediate values.

The sub-pel values are calculated in two stages in H.264. Firstly, the half-pel values are calculated using a six-tap filter. It has six taps because it takes into account the value of six nearby samples when calculating the value; in contrast, a bilinear filter has two taps. Although this enables it to calculate the half-pel values more accurately, it can take more time and energy to perform. So once the half-pel values have been calculated, we use linear interpolation to derive quarter-pel values as the average of two adjacent half- or whole-pel values.

Where MPEG-1 performs motion compensation on a whole macroblock at a time, H.264 macroblocks can be split into smaller partitions for motion compensation. These can be as small as 4×4 luma pixels (which corresponds to 2×2 chroma pixels because these have been subsampled). These smaller areas can capture some motion better, though, of course, there is a decreased return because more motion vectors need to be stored should the small partitions be used.

H.264 also allows more efficient entropy coding methods including Context Adaptive Binary Arithmetic Coding (CABAC) and Context Adaptive Variable Length Coding (CAVLC). Both these coding methods exploit the fact that some things are more likely to appear when surrounded by other pieces of data. For example, look at this sentence:

Europe and America are separated by the ********* ocean.

You can probably guess that the missing word is Atlantic. Moreover, whenever you see the word ocean, it's probably preceded by Atlantic, Pacific, Arctic, Indian or Southern. In these cases, you're getting some information about what the word is, based on its context. Both CABAC and CAVLC use this sense of context to perform the final, lossless, stage of encoding more efficiently than the Huffman coding used in earlier video compression formats. As always, the trade-off is that these schemes require significantly more processing power to encode and decode.

At high levels of quantisation, DCT-based video compression methods have a tendency to introduce *blocking artefacts*. These appear at the borders of transform blocks (8×8 pixel DCT blocks in the MPEG-1 case) and manifest as sudden step changes in brightness or colour. Prior to the introduction of H.264, some decoders implemented *deblocking filters,* which are context-aware, low-pass filters that act to reduce blocking artefacts by tweaking the sample values on each side of transform block edges that are deemed to be "blocky". These filters were not standardised and were generally out-of-loop, which is to say that they were applied immediately prior to displaying a frame and dependent P or B frames would fetch them from the non-deblocked image.

H.264 introduced a sophisticated, standardised, in-loop deblocking filter. This is applied as the last stage of the frame decoding process, generally before the frame is written to memory, so dependent P or B frames now fetch their motion-compensation data from the (hopefully higher quality) deblocked image.

Take a look at Figures 9-13 and 9-14 to see the improvements in I frame compression between MPEG-1 and MPEG-4 part 10. Both of these are compressed at the same bit rate (0.9 bits per pixel). Because these are I frames, the image quality isn't helped by the improved motion compensation.

FIGURE 9-13: MPEG-4 part 10 compressed I frame. Notice how there are few artefacts (the slight blurriness is because it's zoomed in to show detail).

FIGURE 9-14: MPEG-1 compressed I frame. At this level of compression, the quantisation errors are significant.

None of these improvements fundamentally changes the overall shape of the video codec pipeline. In fact, it hasn't really changed since MPEG-1. However, the improvements do result in a significant increase in compression at the cost of requiring significantly more processing power for both encoding and decoding.

On the Raspberry Pi, VideoCore is capable of doing more or less all the work of video decoding. This is controlled through Open Media Acceleration (OpenMAX), an API that allows programmers to utilise the hardware acceleration in a standard way. Not all video software for the Raspberry Pi makes full use of VideoCore capability, but Raspbian does come with the source code for a simple H.264 player to demonstrate how to use VideoCore.

To test video encoding on your Raspberry Pi, the first thing you need to do is compile the example code. Launch LXTerminal and type the following command:

```
cd /opt/vc/src/hello_pi
./rebuild.sh
```

Then you can run the example video by entering this:

```
cd hello_video
./hello_video.bin test.h264
```

An H.264 video plays in full-screen mode. The first thing you should notice when the video is finished is that it didn't use much CPU power (the green graph at the bottom right stayed quite low).

Similarly, you can use OpenMAX to help encode video. You can test this out using the hello_encode example program with the following:

```
cd ../hello_encode
./hello_encode.bin
```

You may notice that this process hogs the CPU for a few seconds because not all of the encoding functions can be run on the GPU. However, it's still far faster than CPU-only encoding.

This creates a file called test.h264. You can play this file with the hello_video player with:

```
../hello_video/hello_video.bin test.h264
```

H.265

H.264 is the most advanced video codec in wide use at the time of writing. However, it doesn't represent the end of the road for video compression. Work has recently finished on the High Efficiency Video Codec (HEVC) standard, generally known by its ITU name, H.265.

The goal of H.265 is to reduce bit rate at constant quality by 50 percent compared to H.264 without significantly increasing the computational complexity of the decoding process.

To achieve this goal, H.265 uses a new structure for storing the information. Instead of macroblocks, it uses coding tree units (CTUs). These fulfil roughly the same role as macroblocks in motion compensation, but they can be much larger (up to 64×64 luma pixels), and are recursively subdivided as needed. Larger CTUs allow graphically simple regions, such as clear blue sky or plain-coloured walls, to be encoded simply, whereas smaller CTUs allow regions with finer detail to be properly captured.

The final ITU H.265 standard was released in April 2013, but is only beginning to see widespread use. One reason for this is the lack of available decoding hardware. Although high-power CPUs like the ones found in modern desktop computers can decode HEVC, lower power devices, such as smartphones or the Raspberry Pi, need the assistance of the GPU; older GPUs aren't able to decode H.265.

Motion Search

As we have seen, one of the key ways that encoders compress videos is by finding motion vectors that accurately describe the movement of one block compared to the previous frame, thereby minimising the residual and its associated bitstream requirement.

This begs the question, how do you calculate these motion vectors? In principle—for P frames at least—the process is easy. You take each block and compare it to all the potential locations on the preceding I or P frame (or other eligible frames depending on the compression standard). For each location, you compute the residual and work out the length of bitstream required to encode it, remembering to add the bits required to encode the motion vector: the DPCM and Huffman coding (in the case of MPEG-1) applied to the vector components means that it is generally cheapest to encode a vector very similar to that of the previous macroblock. The location that results in the smallest overall number of bits emitted "wins" and is used to construct the final stream (unless its cost exceeds that of simply encoding an I macroblock).

The problem with this is that it would take far too long to calculate all the differences, so instead encoders use algorithms that cut down the search area in some way, often using a hill-climbing hierarchical approach.

One such option is the diamond search. In this search, nine points in the reference frame are chosen in a diamond pattern around the place the block is located in the frame to be encoded. Then the search step takes place, which is:

- If the centre point has the lowest errors, move on to the final step. Otherwise, centre a new diamond around the point that has the lowest error rate.

- Once you have located a diamond where the lowest error rate is in the middle, the final step is to switch to a smaller diamond. This subdivides the centre of the diamond into five sections, and the one with the smallest difference is chosen.

Figure 9-15 shows this algorithm in action. Step 1 shows the starting grid around the point (the circle). In Step 2, the grid moves again. In Step 3, the point with the smallest difference is the centre point, so it moves on to the final step with a smaller grid. This is only performed once in Step 4, and the point with the smallest difference is used.

You may think that there's a good chance that this algorithm misses the actual motion, particularly in the case of fast motion, corresponding to many pixels per frame. This is correct, but the point here is not to create a perfect algorithm; the algorithm only needs to be good enough and run quickly enough to be useful. The described diamond search runs quite fast, but it doesn't always find the optimum motion vectors. Remember that the residual (the difference between the motion compensation result and the actual source frame) is encoded, so even if the motion estimation isn't perfect, the frame can still have a high image quality; it just needs to include more data in each frame.

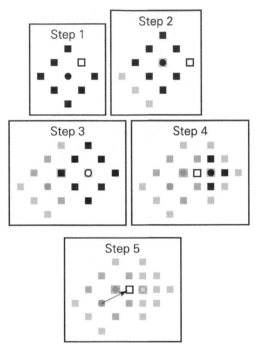

FIGURE 9-15: The diamond motion search algorithm. The circle represents the starting point for that step and the hollow shape is the point with the smallest difference.

When encoding a video, you have to make a choice between the quality of the motion estimation and the amount of time you want the encoding to take. Lower quality motion estimation results in either lower quality videos or larger file sizes (depending on how you set up the encoder), but lower quality motion estimation also results in a correspondingly shorter execution time.

Take a look at Table 9-2 for the difference between encoding time and file size for a video using the avconv command on the Raspberry Pi.

Table 9-2   A Comparison of Motion Search Algorithms

Motion search algorithm	Filesize (bytes)	Time taken to encode (seconds)
Exhaustive search algorithm (esa)	89961	39
Diamond (dia)	90713	23
Hadamard exhaustive search (tesa)	90004	44

The times in Table 9-2 are based on a 2-second, 200×200 pixel video recorded on the Raspberry Pi camera module. You may have noticed that this takes far longer than `hello_encode.bin` despite this video being shorter. This shows just how much of a speed-up the GPU gives the encoder.

You can experiment with this yourself using the `avconv` command:

```
sudo apt-get install libav-tools
```

The basic usage is

```
avconv -i inputfile -vcodec libx264 -me_method method-name -crf 15
  -g GOPsize outputfilename.mp4
```

where `method-name` is replaced with `dia`, `esa` or `tesa`, and `GOPsize` is replaced with the group of pictures size you want.

At the end of the encoding, the output is various pieces of information, including details of the different frame types. Here's the section from one of the preceding runs:

```
[libx264 @ 0x8b6360] frame I:3     Avg QP:12.69  size:  3229
[libx264 @ 0x8b6360] frame P:32    Avg QP:15.66  size:  2050
[libx264 @ 0x8b6360] frame B:13    Avg QP:18.11  size:   973
```

This shows you the breakdown in the number of frame types as well as their average size. QP is the quantisation parameter and is used to select a quantisation matrix on a per-frame or even per-macroblock basis; higher QPs mean higher quantisation. Remember that P frames and B frames can use I macroblocks as well as P macroblocks, so this also accounts for some of the size of the P frames in the preceding example.

Try this for yourself to see how different quality settings (the number after `-crf`)—between 0 (very little compression) and 51 (very high compression)—change these numbers.

If you remove `-g GOPsize` the encoder calculates which size it thinks is best. You can use this with different CRF values to see how this changes things.

Video Quality

We've talked about how the encoder can get rid of some of the information to make the file smaller. As more and more information is removed to make the file size smaller, the video quality gets worse—but how much worse?

This is actually a difficult question to answer because the important fact is how good we humans perceive the quality to be. Something like the chroma subsampling would be very obvious to a computer checking for distortion, but it's difficult for the eye to see. Other things are very obvious to the eye, but have less difference to synthetic quality metrics.

The best way to assess video quality is to get real people to watch video samples and rate the comparative quality. This is the method MPEG uses when comparing different proposals for inclusion in a standard. However, it's not really practical for most video encoding. Instead, you need a way of estimating the quality computationally. The most common method is the peak signal to noise ratio (PSNR).

PSNR is calculated by comparing what the image should be (the signal) to the difference between the image as it should be and the image as it is displayed after compression (the noise). The error rate is squared, so the PSNR can be calculated with the following equation:

$$PSNR = 20 * \log_{10}(Max/squareroot(MSE))$$

MSE (which stands for mean squared error) is calculated by taking the difference between the correct and actual values for each pixel, squaring this value and then taking the average across all the pixels. Max is the maximum value that a pixel can take. In most cases, video has 8 bits per colour channel, so this will be 255.

It's important to realise, though, that PSNR doesn't correlate exactly to image quality as it's perceived by the eye.

PSNR looks at the image like a computer does: as a grid of data. The Structural Similarity (SSIM) index is an alternative that attempts to look at the image like a person does. Therefore, it doesn't look at an image on a pixel-by-pixel basis; instead it compares the image in three different ways: the luminance, the contrast and the structure. Each thing is calculated across the image as a whole and then compared with the results from the frame before compression.

Processing Power

Playing video is often thought of as a basic function of a computer. After all, even cheap DVD players can do it without a problem. However, it actually entails a huge amount of processing power to perform, and this increases as demand for higher and higher resolution video increases. Many computers use the extra power in their GPUs to help them perform quickly. That's not the only use of the GPU, as we'll explore further in the next chapter.

Chapter 10
3D Graphics

HISTORICALLY, THE UNDERSTANDING of classical computer systems architectures has focused squarely on the interaction between the central processing unit (CPU) and the memory infrastructure. However, a new breed of system is upon us, in which the graphics processing unit (GPU) plays an integral role and is as important as both these key components.

As software developers and consumers have demanded increased photorealism from games and more complexity and fluidity from their user interfaces, the requirements of computer graphics have increased. The humble GPU has been catapulted from a simple line-drawing accelerator to a highly parallel, multithreaded subsystem in its own right, with such computing power that it has become integral to modern computer architectures.

However, to understand the potential of graphics technology we must focus on its primary purpose and make sense of it in the context of modern 3D graphics.

A Brief History of 3D Graphics

Although William Fetter is credited with coining the term "computer graphics" to describe his work on human body animation with Boeing in the early 1960s, the origin of 3D graphics can be traced back to the 1950s and military flight simulators (see Figure 10-1). As early as 1951, the Whirlwind computer at the Massachusetts Institute of Technology (MIT) was being used as a visualisation tool. The Whirlwind computer allowed oscilloscope-style graphics with user input via a device resembling a *light pen*. The Whirlwind was developed as part of the U.S. Navy's Airplane Stability and Control Analyzer (ASCA) project, and the digital computer provided a programmable flight simulation environment where radar information was used to superimpose an aircraft symbol on top of a set of pre-programmed geographical data points. The result was viewed on a cathode-ray tube (CRT) display. By pointing the light pen at the CRT, the user could query the state of the aircraft, such as its location and speed.

> **NOTE** A light pen is a photo-sensitive device, like a wand, which can be used to point to or highlight objects on a CRT screen in the same way a finger can be used on a touchscreen device.

Throughout the 1950s and 1960s various parallel streams of research developed the ideas of computer-aided design (CAD) and visualisation. By the mid-1950s, IBM was able to demonstrate the first system capable of displaying vector graphics; the IBM 740 (CRT recorder) was attached to the IBM 701 (data processing system) to record a series of points onto 35-millimetre (mm) photographic film. With variations in exposure, these points could be captured as lines and curves, and with the use of special programming techniques, the 740 could be used to display alphanumeric symbols, graphs and simple shapes. This was fundamental to the advent of computer-aided graphical design, but for a rental price of $2,850 per month it was prohibitively expensive even for commercial use. General Motors had also begun research into CAD with IBM, and this collaboration resulted in the world's first computer-aided drawing system, the DAC-1, in the early 1960s, which was also capable of scanning in drawings provided by the user.

> **NOTE** Vector graphics involve using *geometrical primitives* (simple graphical building blocks) based on mathematical expressions to represent graphical images.

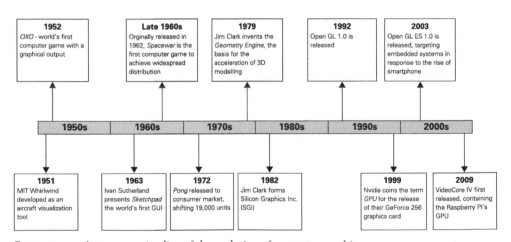

FIGURE 10-1: A summary timeline of the evolution of computer graphics

The Graphical User Interface (GUI)

In 1963, Ivan Sutherland, a PhD student at MIT, presented a thesis entitled "Sketchpad: A Man-Machine Graphical Communication System", which consolidated much of the research of the late 1950s and introduced the first graphical user interface (GUI). Using MIT's TX-2 computer equipped with the man-machine graphic communication system, a user could draw lines and curves directly onto a point plotter display using a light pen. In addition to this being the first complete GUI for a computer, it also allowed the user to constrain the geometric properties of the shapes on the screen, such as line lengths and the angles between them. Sutherland is widely regarded as a founding father of object-oriented programming (OOP) and modern day GUIs. In the mid-1960s he began research into "remote reality" in the quest to replace camera images with computer-generated scenes; these were nothing more than wireframe models, but Sutherland's work was pioneering in the field of virtual reality and, together with Dr David Evans, he created a company to market these vector systems using custom hardware and software.

Raster vs. Vector Graphics

All modern displays are a matrix of luminescent pixels with each pixel being a coloured dot or point at a particular screen location. Two different methods are used to describe how the dots are arranged on the screen to form an image. Images formed by these two methods are referred to as either raster graphics or vector graphics.

Raster graphics are images with these characteristics:

- They are stored as an array of pixels, each of which is assigned a red-green-blue (RGB) colour value and (optionally) a transparency value.

- They are generally simpler to conceptualise than vector graphics because the pixels are arranged in a dot matrix (a grid), sort of like colouring in squares on graph paper. However, large images require storage of much more data because instructions are required to specify the position and colour of each individual pixel.

- They have *resolution* typically determined by the number of dots per inch (dpi). Making the image larger decreases its quality and may result in the image looking blurry, as shown in Figure 10-2.

- They are generally used for photographs and other images that require *continuous tone*: smoothly merging colours and shades as opposed to sharply outlined shapes.

Vector graphics are images with these characteristics:

- They are stored as a collection of mathematically defined points, lines, curves, and fills.

- They generally result in smaller files, because the mathematical formulas describe points, paths and fills instead of having to define the location and colour of each and every pixel.

- They can be made larger without any loss of quality, as shown in Figure 10-2.

- They are the preferred format for fonts, logos and illustrations that require smooth, well-defined edges and flat colours.

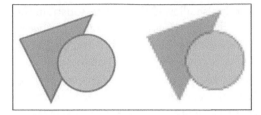

FIGURE 10-2: Magnified vector (left) and raster (right) graphics images

During the late 1960s and 1970s, computer graphics technology was being applied in various fields. For example, in medical imaging, X-ray images were captured digitally and processed on computers before being displayed. NASA also commissioned General Electric to develop a real-time colour raster graphics system as part of a monitor to train astronauts. (See the nearby sidebar for an explanation of raster graphics.) However, the cost of these systems, though falling, meant that computer graphics were limited to military and well-funded commercial applications. It wasn't until the advent of personal computing that this technology became of interest to everyone, and the result was the inevitable flurry of activity in the industry as companies sought to take control of a potentially lucrative market.

3D Graphics in Video Games

Alongside the research into computer graphics in the early 1950s, academics also began experimenting with games as part of their computer science and artificial intelligence research. The first computer game credited with a graphical output was *OXO* in 1952. This was a noughts and crosses puzzle where the players used a rotary telephone controller to determine in which square to place their next move. In this game, which was developed by Alexander Douglas in Cambridge, the user played against the computer, and the noughts and crosses board was displayed on a simple CRT display.

Another early computer game with graphical output was *Tennis for Two*. Developed by William Higinbotham to alleviate the boredom of visitors to Brookhaven National Laboratory, the game allowed two people to play against each other. A side view of a tennis court was displayed on an oscilloscope and each user could deflect a moving ball to each other using their own controller, with a knob for navigation and a button-press to hit the ball. The circuit would correctly model the trajectory of the ball on hitting the edge of the screen or net, and simulate drag as the ball moved through the air. The game was popular with the public, but after two seasons was dismantled to allow the hardware to be reused for other projects. As with many of these early examples, interest and resources focused very much on research rather than the opportunity to commercialise these games.

Perhaps the first game to achieve widespread distribution was *Spacewar!* Developed as a hack by Steve Russell and a group of friends at MIT, and inspired by the visual potential of the high-quality vector display of Digital Equipment Corporation's (DEC's) PDP-1, this two-player game involved user-controlled spaceships that could fire missiles at each other whilst manoeuvring around the gravitational well of a central sun. By the end of the 1960s, most U.S. university computer labs possessed a copy of the game, as DEC decided to distribute it as test software with every PDP-1. However, the huge $120,000 price tag meant that only 50 PDP-1s were ever made, thus limiting the game's commercial viability despite its huge popularity.

As computer hardware became cheaper, the coin-operated game market could seriously consider introducing video gaming to the general public. In the early 1970s, arcade-game developers pioneered rich visual displays and electronic sound effects in an attempt to capture the imagination of the masses. Two engineers, Nolan Bushnell and Ted Dabney, introduced *Computer Space,* a derivative of *Spacewar!,* to the coin-operated arcades of California, but this ended up being too costly and too complex to succeed. However, after forming Atari Inc. together in 1972, Bushnell and Dabney created *Pong.* Similar to table tennis, *Pong* was a two-player bat and ball game where each player attempted to direct a moving ball past their opponent on the other side of a net. Derived from a simple game provided with the Magnavox Odyssey, the world's first home console, they decided to manufacture this for public distribution, and with 19,000 units sold it became the first arcade game to achieve commercial success. Arcades flourished throughout the 1970s and early 1980s, helping to fuel the growing popularity of video gaming and with it the promise of a bright future for computer graphics.

Personal Computing and the Graphics Card

During the early 1970s, distributed video games were manufactured as single-purpose devices, designed and manufactured solely to play a single game. The problem with this approach was that consumers had to purchase a new device each time they wanted to play a new game. (*Pong* was such a game.) By the mid-1970s manufacturers had a solution for this problem—the microprocessor. Games could be run on general-purpose computing hardware; each game was essentially a new set of instructions to be run by the microprocessor in the system and could be sold separately from the gaming unit. The first console of this kind was the Video Entertainment System (VES) released by Fairchild in 1976. Games were released as cartridges containing read-only-memory (ROM) and could be swapped and plugged into the VES console to form an equivalent electrical circuit to that previously built from discrete components. Although game design and translation to ROM code were very much specialist skills, the microprocessor, and therefore the computer, became the next gaming platform.

Parallel Developments in the Film Industry

The need for computer generated images (CGI) drove the film industry to pioneer techniques that underpin modern 3D graphics hardware, from the GRAphics Symbiosis System (GRASS)-based transformations used to model the Death Star for the 1977 release of *Star Wars*, to the 15 minutes of computer-generated animation employing depth-cueing for 1984's *Tron*, to the 1993 full photorealism of the dinosaurs in *Jurassic Park*. Similar developments for industrial applications were equally groundbreaking; Alan Sutcliffe's demonstrations of wireframe terrain models using hidden line removal occurred as early as 1979, and Evans and Sutherland's Picture System series and flight simulators, which employed depth cueing, were capable of manipulating large wireframe models in real time. These technological developments predated their use in gaming and in the personal computer by nearly 15 years, and as such their contribution to 3D graphics standards was hugely significant.

Following are brief descriptions of graphics technologies either attributed to or made famous by the film industry:

- *GRASS* is a programming language designed to create 2D vector graphics animations, allowing scaling, rotation, translation and colour changes over time. It was first developed by Tom DeFanti in 1974 and was most famously used to rotate and scale the Death Star in the attack sequences of *Star Wars*.

- *Hidden line removal* is an optimisation of wireframe modelling where edges and lines that lie behind other visible surfaces are not drawn. The general principle is to avoid drawing what the eye cannot see, as this is wasteful in terms of performance and power. (A *wireframe* is a skeletal shape containing none of the detail of the object it represents.)

- *Depth-cueing* is the process by which the eye is given the perception of depth in a scene. The eye makes use of many "cues" or "hints" to place objects within a three-dimensional world. These include *perspective* (distant objects are smaller than near ones), *occlusion* (distant objects are blocked from view by near ones) and *distance fog* (distant objects are duller and more blurred due to light scattering by the atmosphere). *Tron* employed the most primitive form of distance fog, whereby distant objects were gradually mixed with black to fade them out as they moved away from the scene—so the phrase was coined "if in doubt, black it out!"

From the late 1970s onward, 3D graphics developed at a rapid pace, fuelled by users' desire for more immersive experiences and more complex geometries to be modelled and animated in life-like ways. Many industries contributed to this dramatic and rapid advancement. For the purposes of this brief history, we're focusing on the development of hardware for the personal computer.

Apart from custom-built and hugely expensive hardware that was largely tied to research—graphics and computer animation had been confined to complex algorithms written for general-purpose processors, with, at best, simple video address generators that performed some form of translation between the CPU and the display. It was inevitable that hardware acceleration would follow in order to support the growing processing demands of increasingly complex graphics.

In 1979, Jim Clark, an associate professor of electrical engineering at Stanford University, California, developed what he called a geometry engine, which was the foundation of modern hardware to accelerate 3D modelling. This engine transformed objects from representations in standalone models to a position and orientation on a computer screen. The lighting and shading steps were still handled by the main processor. Clark anticipated commercial success for the engine and formed Silicon Graphics Inc. (SGI) in 1982. The company was instrumental in bringing 3D computer graphics to the mass market.

Around the same time, the home PC market began in earnest with the hugely successful IBM PC and the Apple II, both of which came with graphics cards that supported colour displays. This captured the minds of families and businesses alike, and the first computer with a graphical user interface followed with the Apple Macintosh in 1984. The many competing platforms thrust computing and gaming into the limelight via aggressive advertising campaigns, and this pushed the graphics industry forward still further. Popular cross-platform games such as *Elite* started to make use of wireframe models and techniques such as hidden line removal; another game, *Alpha Waves*, provided the first fully immersive 3D experience for gamers, with interaction of 3D objects in a simple 3D world. High-performing 3D graphics would soon become a requirement of personal computers.

Meanwhile, SGI began the development of products for high-performance graphics terminals, beginning with their customised Integrated Raster Imaging System (IRIS) hardware, which could be attached to a general-purpose computer. Developers were exposed to this hardware via SGI's proprietary application programming interface (API) called the IRIS graphics language (IRIS GL), which was mainly geared toward the provision of efficient floating point mathematics (used to represent an object's shape by specifying its vertices in three-dimensional space; see the "Geometry Specification and Attributes" section later in this chapter) via Clark's geometry engine. The follow-up IRIS 2000 series formed part of fully functional UNIX workstations, but as systems evolved to accelerate 3D rendering, as well as geometry processing, it became clear that across the host of PCs and consumer devices a standard API was required for cross-platform support. In addition, companies such as IBM and Sun Microsystems were planning releases of 3D hardware that competed directly with IRIS, and so SGI sought to consolidate its market share by releasing a derivation of IRIS GL called OpenGL, which was the first API for 2D and 3D graphics that was not manufacturer-specific. OpenGL allowed developers access to all hardware platforms that supported it, and, critically, any unsupported hardware feature could be offloaded to software running on the main processor.

UNIX is a widely used multitasking, multiuser operating system. For additional information about operating systems, see Chapter 8.

Two Competing Standards

It is here that we move away from graphics hardware to discuss the development of features through graphics standards. With the release of OpenGL 1.0 in 1992, SGI gained the support of various companies, including Apple, ATI, Sun Microsystems and, initially, Microsoft. To ensure the promotion and development of the open standard, SGI led the formation of the Architecture Review Board (ARB) later that year, and so numerous revisions of OpenGL followed. OpenGL 1.0 introduced the concept of model-space geometry, transformation to screen space, colour and depth information, textures, lighting and materials. Its aim was to provide an abstraction layer above the underlying hardware so that developers could port (transfer) their applications to various platforms without having to rewrite their code. Although well supported, this approach came at a performance cost, and early hardware platforms struggled as a result.

An *abstraction layer* is used in programming to hide implementation details such that the same code can be used multiple times or on multiple platforms. For example, suppose you made a list of jobs for somebody to do in a day, one of which was washing your clothes. The output from this task would be a clean set of clothes. Sure, you might set some quality guarantees such that nothing is shrunk or the colours don't run, but at this level you don't care *how* the washing is done. Moreover, you could pass the same list to somebody else (subject to the same guarantees) and they could achieve the same result. The mechanics of which machine is used, which cleaning agents, how the clothes are dried and which garments are mixed with others are unimportant details. This is a level of abstraction.

Early in 1993, Microsoft exited the OpenGL working group; in a bid to be competitive in the market, Microsoft bought a company called RenderMorphics to work on 3D graphics for Windows 95. RenderMorphics had developed an API in the field of CAD and medical imaging, and in 1995 Microsoft released the first versions of its own Direct3D API based on the RenderMorphics software: Direct X 2.0 and Direct X 3.0. Whilst developers appreciated the direct control of hardware that the immediate mode provided, it was hard to program, which led to calls for OpenGL to be adopted as the one true standard. In addition, a company called 3Dfx was developing a proprietary API (called Glide) for its Voodoo hardware, and the huge performance advantages of this approach brought the company some success. However, even 3Dfx was forced to adopt a subset of OpenGL features (Mini GL) in 1996 when a company called id Software released *Quake* and included a Windows port targeting OpenGL.

Immediate mode is a rendering style for graphic library APIs that allows for the direct display of graphics objects to the screen.

As processing capabilities improved, proprietary APIs declined in favour of the flexibility provided by Direct 3D and cross-platform support provided by OpenGL. An intense battle ensued. Although OpenGL was the favoured API of many hardware vendors, Direct3D 4 was to prove revolutionary because it allowed rendering to arbitrary surfaces that could be used in subsequent rendering passes. OpenGL had to be extended to provide such a mechanism. Similar advances followed, most notably with the move to programmable processing steps from the old fixed-function pipeline. This led to the first major revision of OpenGL, and although both APIs have since remained independent, feature sets have remained broadly similar between the two standards. However, OpenGL remains the only cross-platform graphics API supported by various operating systems such as Linux, Android and iOS. By contrast, Direct3D is purely targeted at Microsoft Windows. In 2003 OpenGL ES 1.0—a derivative of OpenGL 1.3—was released to target embedded devices (the ES suffix stands for embedded systems). This release was in direct response to the proliferation of smartphones, tablets and mobile platforms. OpenGL ES 1.0 has since undergone several major revisions.

A *fixed-function hardware pipeline* is a collection of processing stages, each of which is tightly mapped to a dedicated set of logic gates (building blocks of a digital circuit). A *programmable hardware pipeline* is a more loosely defined general-purpose platform on which the same functionality can be achieved with much more flexibility and, unfortunately, a potential degradation of performance. The programming interface is conceptually more complex (as a program needs to be written to perform each task rather than directly calling a specific hardware function), but the scope to achieve more sophisticated techniques means that programmable pipelines now underpin all modern graphics processors.

NOTE

Before you move on to looking at OpenGL in more detail, we should mention NVIDIA, the company that first coined the phrase "graphics processing unit" (GPU). This term is widely used to describe the single-chip processor dedicated to geometry processing, transform and lighting, texture mapping and shading. NVIDIA first used the term in 1999 for the release of its GeForce 256 core and the first Direct3D 7-compliant hardware accelerator. The Raspberry Pi contains Broadcom's VideoCoreIV GPU.

The OpenGL Graphics Pipeline

This section delves deeper into the OpenGL graphics pipeline. All modern computer hardware—from desktop PCs to smartphones—contains some form of GPU specifically designed to accelerate all but the simplest of 3D graphics tasks. We will take a look at the principal stages of the classical graphics pipeline and understand the key concepts before moving on to how modern GPUs accelerate these steps.

OpenGL neither requires that any features be accelerated by special hardware nor specifies any minimum performance targets; it merely sets out requirements that any implementation must meet to comply with the specification. It would therefore be perfectly acceptable, though perhaps undesirable, for the API to be implemented entirely in software running on a general purpose CPU. It is also important to recognise that OpenGL dictates only 3D rendering and not how input data is passed to the pipeline or how these images are to be displayed on screen.

OpenGL is a huge topic in its own right, worthy of several textbooks. As we touch on the basics of the graphics pipeline we will refer to OpenGL ES versions to demonstrate how the standard has evolved to improve flexibility for developers, and in turn has placed greater demands on the hardware itself. For reference, the Raspberry Pi GPU supports both OpenGL ES 1.1 and OpenGL ES 2.0 standards.

Figure 10-3 illustrates a high-level view of a graphics pipeline broken down into the following four stages:

1. **Vertex processing:** Vertices are placed to define the position and shape of an object.

2. **Rasterization:** Primitives (connected vertices) are converted into fragments with each fragment containing the data necessary to generate one pixel of a primitive.

3. **Fragment processing:** Fragments undergo a series of operations, including texturing and blending in preparation of converting them into coloured pixels.

4. **Output merging:** Fragments of primitives in three-dimensional space are combined to render a three-dimensional objects on a two-dimensional screen. For example, if a portion of one object is behind another in three-dimensional space, the pixels of that portion of the object in back will be hidden behind the pixels of the object in front.

FIGURE 10-3: A simple graphics pipeline diagram

Because the process is linear it is described as a pipeline: data passes through successive stages, where each stage can start only after the previous one has completed. However, many stages may be simultaneously active as the pipeline queues up processing steps in preparation for when the next stage can accept its data. Consider Figure 10-4 in which we represent three stages of cleaning: washing, drying and ironing. We could perform washing and then drying and then ironing for each load, but this only achieves a throughput (one complete cleaning cycle) of one load for every three processes. Given that washing, drying and ironing can be performed in parallel, we can start the next wash load as soon as the previous load is being dried. The same is true of the subsequent drying and ironing steps. Apart from the initial time taken to fill the pipeline (that is, to get to the point in time when washing, drying and ironing are all active), throughput is now one load for every process.

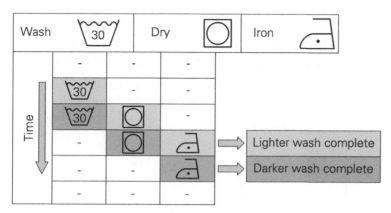

FIGURE 10-4: Visual metaphor of a pipeline, where several steps can be performed in parallel to improve computational efficiency.

Geometry Specification and Attributes

Objects in OpenGL ES are composed of points, lines and triangles. Complex shapes are created from these basic building blocks, or *primitives*. The inputs to OpenGL ES are the (three-dimensional) coordinates of the vertices of these building blocks; a point has one vertex, a line has two vertices, and a triangle has three vertices. As described later in this section, vertices may also have other data attached to them apart from their position in the modelview-space. The data associated with each vertex are known as *attributes*.

Three coordinates are required to describe the position of a vertex in a three-dimensional world: x, y and z (see Figure 10-5). These coordinates are grouped as three-component vectors. In the absence of any transformation the default orientation of the coordinate axes are such that x and y represent the horizontal and vertical screen axes, and z the axis perpendicular to the screen. The default range of these axes is from -1 to +1. Any shape that lies inside the cube defined by these axes is projected onto the two-dimensional viewing surface (that is, the screen). If a shape has coordinates that lie outside of this range, it is clipped and may be removed from the scene entirely, as it will not be visible.

OpenGL ES supports seven primitives that may be used to construct more complex shapes. These primitives are shown in Figure 10-6:

- A point is a single vertex with a default size of one pixel. The user may change the size of a point primitive.

- A line is defined by two connected vertices.

- A line strip is formed by connecting three or more vertices without connecting the first and last vertices, thus forming an open shape.

- A line loop is a line strip with the first and last vertices connected to form a closed shape.

- A triangle is formed by connecting three vertices.

- A triangle strip is formed where three vertices are used to describe an initial triangle, and each successive vertex forms a new triangle using two previous vertices and the new vertex.

- A triangle fan is similar to a triangle strip except that each triangle has the initial vertex in common.

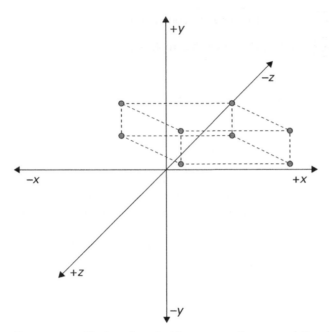

FIGURE 10-5: Vertices plotted with x, y, z coordinates can define three-dimensional shapes.

All shapes in OpenGL ES are constructed from these primitive types, with the type specified as an input by the developer. The default format for these coordinates is 32-bit floating point (a format that provides a wide dynamic range of values to support precise positioning) but again, the user may specify different a data type.

In addition to position, other per-input-vertex data may be specified by the user. This is data that will be used in subsequent 3D rendering steps and may include colour, normal vectors (used in lighting calculations) and coordinates of textures (used in texturing). Colour is assigned to each vertex in OpenGL ES. When different colours are set for different vertices, the pipeline automatically blends them for screen pixels that lie inside the shape. Colours are specified with up to four components: red, green, blue and, optionally, alpha, which is used to represent the transparency of the colour. When multiple objects overlay one pixel in a scene, the relative depth of these objects and the alpha colour components determine how colours must be blended to give the illusion of transparency.

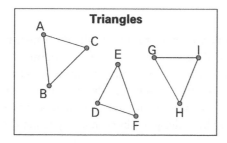

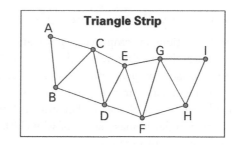

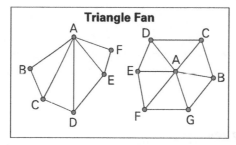

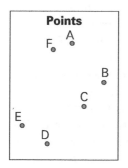

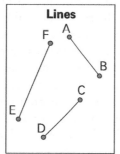

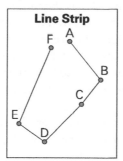

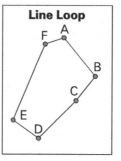

FIGURE 10-6: Open GL primitive types

A *normal vector* (or *normal*) represents a direction that is perpendicular to the surface of an object. **NOTE**

The definition of additional attributes is well-defined in OpenGL ES 1.1 as it only exposes a fixed function rendering pipeline. Because the OpenGL ES 2.0 pipeline is flexible, these other attributes are essentially any data that may or may not be used by any processing step later in the pipeline. You can read more about how this data may be used in later sections of this chapter.

Geometry Transformation

Transformations in computer graphics are essentially changes to the coordinate system in which each object exists. Whilst the inputs to OpenGL ES are the abstract object coordinates specific to each component of the scene, each object undergoes several transformations that may change its appearance or remove it entirely from the "screen". Hardware implementations handle most of the mathematics behind the scenes, but it pays to understand this concept in order to make sense of why GPUs have been designed in such a way to aid the transformation process.

> **NOTE** We talk about the "screen" here, but the output of rendering need not necessarily end up on the display. Many applications process a scene multiple times before outputting an image to the screen; each intermediate processing step (or render) will not necessarily be visible to the user.

Transformation Types

The first vertex processing step is the modelling transformation, which positions and sizes the object in the context of the overall scene. The system of world coordinates is used to define the relative positions of these objects in the 3D world that is being created. Following this, a second transformation occurs to account for what the observer of the scene can actually see. Only the view of the world from the perspective of the observer is what is rendered to the screen. This is the system of *eye coordinates*, having undergone what is termed as the viewing transformation. In practice, OpenGL ES does not separate these two transforms, as it is impossible to distinguish between the two from the output of these two stages. For example, imagine a scene of a woman walking her dog, where the dog is directly in front of the woman. In the next frame, the dog is to the left of the woman. Has this resulted from the dog moving to the (stationary) woman's left (a modelling transformation of the dog), or from the woman moving to the right of the dog (a viewing transformation from the woman)? The difference is purely conceptual, and so OpenGL ES makes no attempt to distinguish between the two; there is only one modelview transformation (see Figure 10-7).

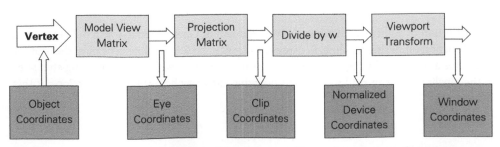

FIGURE 10-7: OpenGL ES uses a single modelview for modelling and viewing transformations.

OpenGL ES supports three basic modelview transformations: translation, scaling and rotation:

- Translation simply adds an offset to each component of the position vector, thereby moving it within the new coordinate system. For example, for an offset of (-off_x, +off_y, +off_z), a vector (x, y, z) would become (x-off_x, y+off_y, z+off_z). On its own, it does not change the size of the overall object.

- Scaling multiplies each component of the position vector by a scale factor, thereby resizing the overall object. For example, for a scale factor of (sf_x, sf_y, sf_z), a vector (x, y, z) would become (sf_x*x, sf_y*y, sf_z*z).

- Rotation requires a bit more understanding of three-dimensional coordinate systems. Whereas rotation in two dimensions occurs around a point, in three dimensions this must happen around an axis. Once this axis is defined, a convention must then be used to define whether clockwise or anticlockwise rotation occurs for positive values of rotation around this axis. OpenGL ES uses a right-handed coordinate system so the right-hand rule applies: curling the fingers of your right hand as you point your thumb in the air shows you the direction of positive rotation around an axis pointing in the direction of your thumb. For example, an axis defined by the vector (dx, dy, dz) with respect to the origin (where at least one of dx, dy or dz are non-zero) defines an axis about which each vertex can be rotated by a user-defined angle (which we call θ). (See Figure 10-8.)

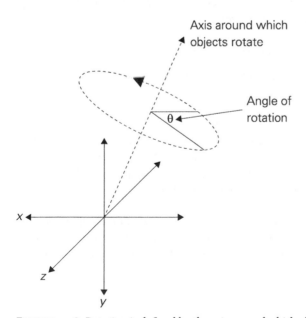

FIGURE 10-8: Rotation is defined by the axis around which objects rotate and the angle of rotation.

OpenGL ES 1.1 provides a fixed set of functions to describe these various transformations, namely `glTranslate`, `glScale` and `glRotate`, whereas OpenGL ES 2.0 hands much more control to the developer by providing programmable stages in which to process geometry.

After positioning objects within this imaginary 3D world, the view of this world needs to be projected onto a two-dimensional viewing surface, for which there are two more stages of transformation. The projection transformation first converts from eye coordinates to clip coordinates, and this is necessary for two reasons:

- The observer cannot see the entire three-dimensional world, so the limits within which this 2D scene is viewed (the viewport) must be bound to the set of objects rendered to the display.

- The observer can see objects only within a certain range of distances, so limits must be placed on the depths of transformed components.

Objects that lie outside of these ranges are said to be "clipped," hence the term *clip coordinates*. Rather than a 2D rectangle within which a scene must be displayed, a viewing volume defines the observable region, accounting for the relative depths of objects in the scene.

In theory, this viewing volume might resemble an infinitely "deep" rectangle, with a cross-section equal to the 2D window through which the scene is viewed; in practice the viewing volume does not resemble such a window, for two reasons:

- Perspective: objects further from the observer appear smaller.
- The field-of-view extends as distance from the observer increases.

All lifelike images are processed using perspective projection to account for distance from the viewer. Perspective projection would imply an infinitely deep pyramidal viewing volume extending from the observer. However, because it would be impossible to store an infinite range of depth values, the regions of this pyramid within which objects can be observed are limited. In effect, the viewing volume is a truncated pyramid, as shown in Figure 10-9. This is also known as the frustrum, and is discussed later in this chapter.

The final transformation is to convert the 2D clip coordinates to a set of coordinates scaled to the device on which the scene is being displayed (such as a rectangle of pixels on a screen). The viewport transformation performs this step and is the final stage of vertex processing.

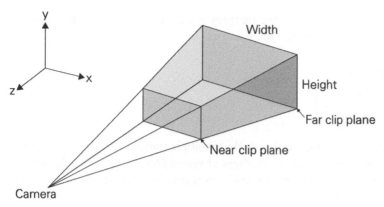

FIGURE 10-9: OpenGL ES viewing volume, or frustrum. In addition to the viewport boundaries, near and far clip planes must be supplied to fully define the set of valid clip coordinates as a result of the projection transformation. (Clip planes pass through the frustrum; anything closer to the viewport than the near clip plane or farther than the far clip plane are cut out of the scene.)

The Maths behind Transformations: Transformation Matrices

Now that you have a general understanding of the geometry transformations in the coordinate plane, you are ready to look more closely at the mathematics involved in performing transformations. As stated earlier, the position of vertices in a 3D coordinate space are represented in Cartesian form by a three-component vector, where the magnitude of each component represents the distance of the point from the origin in the x, y and z dimensions respectively. For now we represent each vertex by a triple of numbers in the form (x,y,z).

A transformation results in some change in a graphical object, such as its position (translation), its size (scaling) or its angle relative to a rotational axis. (rotation). To perform such transformations, the object's vertices must be moved in the coordinate plane in a certain direction and magnitude. To determine the new location of a vertex, mathematical operations are performed on the vertex's x, y and z values. Matrices facilitate these mathematical operations.

Matrices are rectangular arrays of numbers and are used to represent the modelview transformations described earlier. They are used to pre-multiply each vector by per-component factors to compute an output vector of the same dimension. To be able to multiply two matrices, the number of columns in the first matrix must equal the number of rows in the second matrix. To multiply two matrices, you multiply each value in the first row of the first matrix by its corresponding value in the first column of the second matrix and then sum the results. This is repeated for all rows and columns as shown:

$$\begin{pmatrix} a & b & c \\ d & e & f \\ g & h & i \end{pmatrix} \begin{pmatrix} x \\ y \\ z \end{pmatrix} = \begin{pmatrix} ax+by+cz \\ dx+ey+fz \\ gx+hy+iz \end{pmatrix}$$

Following is an example of how multiplying matrices is used to scale a three-dimensional vector by each of the scale factors `sf_x, sf_y` and `sf_z`:

$$S = \begin{pmatrix} sf_x & 0 & 0 \\ 0 & sf_y & 0 \\ 0 & 0 & sf_z \end{pmatrix} \begin{pmatrix} x \\ y \\ z \end{pmatrix} = \begin{pmatrix} sf_x * x \\ sf_y * y \\ sf_z * z \end{pmatrix}$$

The most powerful feature of using matrices is that multiple transformations can be combined by multiplying matrices. This allows all stages of vertex processing to be reduced to a single matrix multiplication, thus making the whole process more efficient and amenable to dedicated hardware processing.

> **NOTE**   Although the matrix examples show a 3×3 matrix that corresponds to the three axes, x, y and z, you will commonly see a 4×4 matrix. The fourth column accounts for the origin (the point at which the three axes intersect). This fourth column enables you to change the position of the coordinate origin, which is required to perform a translation.

Lighting and Materials

Lighting and materials contribute directly to the realism of objects displayed in the scene, and this is one area that has undergone significant changes through major revisions of OpenGL ES. This section touches on basic lighting concepts as seen in OpenGL ES 1.1. Note that for OpenGL ES 2.0 onwards, the lighting system (together with the geometric transformation stage discussed in the last section) was replaced by an entirely programmable pipeline allowing for more customization. Previously, only a limited set of fixed-function calls were made available to the application developer.

The interaction of light with objects and their materials is key to the way an observer perceives the world. A mirror looks shiny because it reflects a lot of light; a wool sweater looks fluffy because it absorbs more light and produces diffuse reflections according to the surface contours of the material. For our constructed 3D world to appear lifelike, these effects must be modelled in ways that fit with the properties expected of objects we see every day. Note that lighting is computed per vertex for an object, the properties of which are then interpolated over the entire primitive like other vertex attributes.

OpenGL ES defines a series of properties that must be defined for the light sources and the objects placed in the scene. Two types of reflection are defined: specular reflection and diffuse reflection (see Figure 10-10).

- **Specular reflection:** The rays of light are reflected almost entirely in one direction by a surface, such that the observer views regions that are highly coloured according to the observer's precise position. A real-world example would be the glare of sunlight from a mirror. This is easily avoided by moving slightly to one side. Areas of an object that are intensely lit in this way are called specular highlights.

- **Diffuse reflection:** The propensity of a material to scatter light in all directions, such that it appears fuzzy and dull. The observer views contributions of colour from the whole surface.

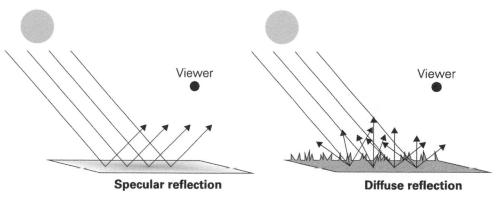

Specular reflection   **Diffuse reflection**

FIGURE 10-10: Specular versus diffuse reflection

These properties together govern how shiny a material appears. OpenGL ES defines a specular colour and a diffuse colour for an object, together with two additional colours. The ambient colour is the colour an object reflects when illuminated by indirect light, and the emission colour is the "glow" emitted from the object without any external illumination.

In addition to the properties of a surface, the colour of an object depends on the angle at which light is emitted or reflected. A flat-shaded curved surface appears to vary in colour, according to the angle at which light is reflected from it. OpenGL ES captures this information by way of a normal vector, which represents a direction perpendicular to an object's surface. In fact, normal vectors are defined for each vertex, much like colour and texture coordinates, and are transformed and interpolated for a primitive like any other vertex attribute. This is because although a triangle is planar, this may be shaped around a curved surface and so the normal vector gradually changes over the length and breadth of the primitive. As the normal vector varies, the resultant calculations that use this vary, which affects the computed colour we would naturally expect to see. One further detail about normal vectors is the direction in which they point: the direction of a normal vector is governed by whether the primitive is front-facing or back-facing. A front-facing primitive forms the side of an object that faces the viewer so that the normal vector points towards the viewer. A back-facing primitive has a normal vector that points away from the viewer, as its surface points away from them. The way a primitive faces is captured in the geometry specification stage by way of a winding order of vertices. By default, vertices defined in an anticlockwise order form a front-facing primitive, and those defined in a clockwise order form a back-facing primitive. Figure 10-11 shows an example of the winding order for front-facing and back-facing primitives.

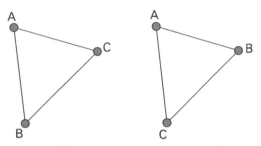

FIGURE 10-11: The triangle on the left shows an anticlockwise winding order. Under the standard convention, this would be a forward-facing primitive. The triangle on the right shows a clockwise winding order, which would be a back-facing primitive.

> **NOTE** The actual surfaces, especially of CAD models coming from a non-uniform rational basis spline (NURBS) translation, are only approximated by the vertices and triangles in OpenGL. It is the interpolation of the reflections between vertices that gives the model the smooth continuous appearance rather than the tell-tale tessellation (tiling of a surface with geometric shapes) that gives away images as computer generated rather than natural. (NURBS is a mathematical model for generating curves and surfaces.)

With the material and light source properties defined, a set of lighting calculations are performed to derive each vertex colour. Essentially vertex colour is formed from the ambient and emission colours of the material, plus a set of contributions per light source in the scene. These contributions are scaled in intensity according to the direction of the surface with respect to the light source (using the normal vector), the position of the viewer with respect to the surface (for specular contributions) and the distance of the light source and viewer from the surface. For the latter, imagine that the influence of a light is essentially a cone of energy spreading out from the source, such that the relative intensity of light follows the familiar inverse square law, becoming less intense at the edges of the cone's base. Vertex colour is modified still further by the spectacular colour of the material and the light source, the angle between the reflected ray and the viewer, and the shininess of the material, with shinier materials decreasing the amount of visible light as this angle increases. Diffuse contributions are derived from the diffuse colour components in a similar way, except that the angle between the source ray and surface normal is used; as a result surfaces that are parallel to the source ray do not appear lit.

Because the colour of a vertex is the sum of contributions from all light sources, their combined intensity can easily result in the loss of all colour detail in the scene. This is similar to the concept of a photograph being overexposed. Lighting levels must be carefully tuned to achieve the desired output.

As we explained earlier, for versions of OpenGL ES 2.0 and later, the process of transformation and lighting were made much more flexible. They are now known as *vertex shading*, and they're entirely programmable by the user. Programs specified in an OpenGL ES–specific shader language called GL Shader Language (GLSL) are submitted to the implementation to perform these transformations, and where hardware is provided this may take the form of a GLSL-specific processor where GLSL programs are compiled as needed to perform all the computation required.

Primitive Assembly and Rasterisation

Up to this point an application-supplied list of vertex attributes has been transformed into a new list of attributes, converted to the coordinate system of the intended display device. However, these vertices must be used to construct the shapes as we see them on screen. Preparing shapes for display is a two-step process:

1. **Primitive assembly:** Vertices for each shape are grouped allowing the pipeline to compute how all shapes are to appear in the final output image.

2. **Rasterisation:** Shapes are converted to collections of pixels to be displayed on screen or processed in further rendering steps (see Figure 10-12).

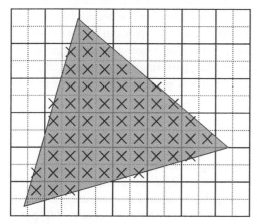

FIGURE 10-12: Rasterisation. The crosses indicate primitive samples that will be shaded during fragment processing.

During rasterization, all pixels lying inside the boundaries of the shape must be shaded using the data associated with its vertices; those outside should be left unchanged. After these pixels are determined, the attributes associated with each vertex must be interpolated so that each included pixel inherits a weighted average of those belonging to the primitive, depending on its distance from the corners. Attributes such as colour, normal vectors (used in lighting) and texture coordinates may all be interpolated in this way in preparation for per-pixel processing (known as fragment shading in OpenGL ES 2.0). Because these values vary across the shape, at the input to the fragment shading step these are known as *varyings*.

Although the rasterisation process is largely hidden from and invisible to an OpenGL ES user, it is helpful to know how this step works. Imagine that the *output frame-buffer*, a part of random access memory (RAM) containing a bitmap with a complete frame of data, is divided into a grid of squares representing each of the pixels to be displayed on screen. Coverage of a pixel by a primitive is determined by one or more sample points within the "square" that the pixel represents. When more than one sample point is used per pixel, it's called multi-sampling and this may be used to improve the output image quality. When multi-sampling is not enabled, a single sample point at the centre of the pixel is used to represent its exact position. If two primitives share an edge through a particular pixel, this must only result in a single output fragment. A set of rules—called *tie break rules*—determine which primitive is chosen in various cases. These rules ensure consistency in the rasterisation process. Also note that an included pixel at this stage is called a *fragment* because it contains more than just colour information; texture coordinates, depth and stencil information are also associated with each frame-buffer location.

If multi-sampling is enabled each pixel may have many sample points, allowing for partial coverage to be represented in the frame-buffer. The single coverage value per pixel contains 1 bit per sample point. The colour and texture coordinates for all samples can be the same, but depth and stencil information are stored per sample. In this way, edge anti-aliasing (smoothing jagged edges) may be achieved without compromising performance, as colour computation (including texture sampling) need only be performed per-pixel. The output pixel is simply an average of the number of included sample points.

Having decided which pixels are covered by a particular primitive, it is necessary to compute all the attributes associated with these pixels (known as fragments) from the vertex attributes for the entire primitive. This is done using interpolation and the barycentric coordinates (see Figure 10-13) of each of the primitive's vertices. By determining the distance of each fragment from the vertices, simple linear interpolation is used to compute colour and texture coordinates, together with any other per-vertex attributes necessary for pixel processing. There is one problem, however. Linear interpolation in device coordinates, post perspective-projection, does not compute consistent results because perspective projection in itself is not a linear transformation. This is where w comes in. By dividing each vertex attribute by its respective w term, interpolating the 1/w term and then dividing each interpolated attribute by this interpolated 1/w perspective-correct interpolation is achieved.

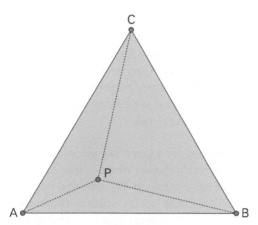

FIGURE 10-13: Barycentric coordinates represent the sizes of mass placed at an object's corners such that the point lies at the centre of mass for the overall object.

Barycentric coordinates represent the position of a point inside an object relative to the influence of the object's vertices. This is usually thought of in terms of the size of mass placed at each vertex such that the point lies at the centre of mass for the overall object. For triangles, this can be visualized more easily using areas rather than masses. In Figure 10-13, the barycentric coordinates of a general point P, inside a triangle ABC, represent the relative ratios of the areas of PBC, PCA and PAB, respectively. By definition, the coordinates of point P add up to one. This makes varyings interpolation easy as the computed output is simply the sum of each vertex attribute multiplied by its barycentric coordinate component. Perspective-correct computation must include 1/w interpolation, which must be divided through once each sample varying has been determined.

Pixel Processing (Fragment Shading)

Fragments that are determined to be inside the primitive and have all their interpolated varyings computed are ready for per-pixel processing. However, fragments may still be invisible as they may lie behind other shapes that also overlap the same fragment location; they are said to be *occluded*. Transparency may also mean that the colour value associated with the fragment is not the final colour written to the frame-buffer; it must be blended with the object behind it as this colour is, in part, also visible to the viewer. Such decisions are handled by a series of tests to influence the resultant operation to the frame-buffer. In OpenGL ES 1.1, sample data computation is limited to a series of fixed-function operations, whereas in OpenGL ES 2.0 general purpose fragment shading gives the application writer much more freedom to compute the colour, depth and stencil values associated with each fragment. We focus first on OpenGL ES 1.1 functionality.

Fragments that exit the rasterisation pipeline first make use of any textures that are bound to them. This will be described in more detail in the next section, but essentially a map of a texture stored in memory may be applied directly or used to modify the colour of a fragment sample. Texturing may be used in various ways to achieve lifelike visualisations at low computational cost. OpenGL ES 1.1's fixed function pipeline then applies a colour sum stage, where a secondary colour may be added to the fragment colour or used to modify the texture colour further (for specular highlights, for example). The final stage in fragment processing is to apply fog, which is used to reduce the visibility of objects that are further away from the viewer so that as objects approach the far clip plane, they tend to fade.

Before we deal with how these colour values are updated for a given sample location, we should mention that it is the depth and stencil data that influence whether this colour is even updated at all. The scene depicts objects in three dimensions, so it follows that parts of objects, or even whole objects, may lie behind others and may not be visible in the frame-buffer. One technique for handling this, called the *painter's algorithm*, might be to change the order of primitives to be drawn from back to front, allowing those in the foreground to be rendered later and thus appear first. However, not only does the painter's algorithm fail when different parts of objects intersect and overlap in different portions of the image, but every time the viewing position changes this order would need to be recomputed.

Instead, OpenGL ES uses a depth buffer to store the position of each visible frame-buffer sample in the scene. For each primitive, the depth of a sample to be updated is compared with that in the frame-buffer; if it is occluded, the colour value is not updated; otherwise, the colour is written to the frame-buffer and the depth value is also updated. There is one further wrinkle with this technique. Following transformation and rasterisation it is possible that two primitives lie in the same plane, but the interpolation of depth is not consistently computed. This can lead to depth fighting, where pixels of one object can "bleed" into those of another co-planar object, which is particularly obvious during animation where the transformations are likely to change subtly from frame to frame. OpenGL ES provides a mechanism called *polygon offset* to set displacements of primitives based on their slope and/or bias. However, care from the application writer together with consistent varyings interpolation can ensure that these effects are minimised.

The depth test is one example of a fragment test—an operation that may be used to control the update of a sample in the final frame-buffer. There are other tests, but the general principle is to perform a comparison of a computed value against the existing value in the frame-buffer; based on the outcome the value may be updated or not.

Other fragment tests include the alpha test and the stencil test. The alpha test performs the fragment test on the alpha channel of a given sample, and depending on the test result may be used to discard portions of a primitive pixel by pixel. The stencil test may also be used to eliminate fragments based on a comparison of a reference value and a stored frame-buffer value. However, it may also modify the contents of the stencil buffer for a sample, depending on the outcome of the depth and stencil tests.

Following the fragment tests, the final colour in the frame-buffer may be replaced directly or modified further according to the configuration specified by the user. Blending is one of these stages, which derives an output pixel colour as a linear combination of the sample and existing frame-buffer colours. Blend factors are individually applied to the source (sample) and destination (frame-buffer) colours before addition or subtraction to form the new colour to be written to the frame-buffer.

In addition to blending, a set of logical operations is available to the user. These provide a set of bitwise operations that can be used to modify the frame-buffer contents using source and destination colours. Each operation is separately applied to each colour component and can be disabled to allow the sample colour to be written straight to the frame-buffer.

Again, OpenGL ES 2.0 completely transformed the fragment processing pipeline by providing a general-purpose platform on which processing could be performed on each sample. An additional set of GLSL functions completely replace the fixed-function texture environment, colour sum and fog components of the pipeline. For hardware implementations these GLSL functions are again compiled as needed to run on custom shader processor cores, part of the process now called *fragment shading*.

Texturing

Texture mapping is a fundamental resource used extensively to compute the colours of rendered surfaces, either directly from an image in memory or via additional processing that may depend on image or geometry data. With texture mapping, coordinates of vertices are matched up with coordinates of a texture. The functionality available to the OpenGL ES programmer has improved dramatically over the years, but the fundamental concepts remain the same.

A *texture* is a digital image stored in memory. It can be sampled as part of fragment processing in order to derive a colour for each sample or each pixel to be written to the frame-buffer. In its simplest form, texturing is a computationally cheap way of adding detail to the surface of an object. Consider rendering a three-dimensional model of a brick-built house. The walls could be constructed brick by brick, each brick transformed and lit individually, together with its surrounding mortar. The quality of the resulting scene would be high, but this would be at the expense of complex geometry and a high number of calculations to be computed as the scene is animated. The wall itself is a complete entity; each brick does not move in relation to the others. All that is required is a repeatable pattern of bricks and mortar to be pasted onto a model of a complete wall. This is where texturing comes in. An image of bricks and mortar is stored in memory, and as pixels are rendered across a primitive spanning the whole wall they simply sample the next colour stored in memory. In effect, the image stored in memory is copied to the surface of the object in the frame-buffer. As the wall is transformed in the scene, this image may need to be scaled and filtered, but this is all possible via texture mapping. Textures may be used to colour objects, to apply effects to existing object surfaces or purely as a general source of data to the more recent OpenGL ES 2.0 fragment shaders.

Textures are stored in memory as rectangular arrays of image data in much the same way as image data is stored in the frame-buffer. Each element is known as a *texel*. Originally, the dimensions of textures were restricted to power-of-two sizes (for example, 32, 64 or 2^n texels in width/height) to simplify the sampling calculations, but in OpenGL ES 2.0 these restrictions have been lifted. Texture images are referenced via texture coordinates—per-vertex attributes that detail where in each dimension to sample the texture. The whole texture can be referenced by a coordinate in the range [0,1]; individual texels may be accessed by multiplying the coordinates by the appropriate dimensions of the image. If the coordinates lie outside the range [0,1] one of several things may happen. If wrapping is enabled, the texture may repeat (by ignoring the whole part of the coordinate and sampling using the fractional part), or it may be clamped so that the outermost texel is sampled (clamp-to-edge) or a border texel is sampled (clamp-to-border). This is configurable by the application writer, depending on the desired output.

The sampling of textures may also vary depending on the specified filtering mode. Texture coordinates specify an exact location at which to sample the image stored in memory, but this is highly unlikely to fall in the centre of a specific texel. If nearest filtering is selected, the nearest texel to the sampling point is chosen, which is cheap and simple to implement. A more precise result may be obtained (in two dimensions) by choosing the four texels that are nearest to the sampling point and taking a weighted average of these according to the distance of the sampling point from each of them. This is known as *bilinear filtering* because a simple 2×2 box filter is used to derive the appropriate texel colour, as shown in Figure 10-14.

Texture images may be applied to objects that are large and close to the viewer or small objects that are much further away. The texel sampling rate for distant objects can cause noticeable visual artefacts (distortions): two adjacent screen pixels of an object far in the distance may correspond to texels spaced a long way apart in the same texture. Simply applying bilinear filtering for successive pixels can result in a huge loss of detail and undesirable moiré patterns. The correct process would be to compute the average of all the texels surrounding each sample point such that successive samples capture all the image data. At full resolution this could result in averaging hundreds of texels at huge computational cost. The solution is called *mipmapping*. Mipmaps are a sequence of precomputed down-filtered textures stored with the original image. Each mipmap is half the width and half the height of the previous image. (See Figure 10-15.) A complete set of mipmaps is computed, right down to an image of just 1×1 texel. The cost of storing a full set of quarter-size images is 33%, but the improved quality in texturing and reduction in filtering computation more than makes up for this.

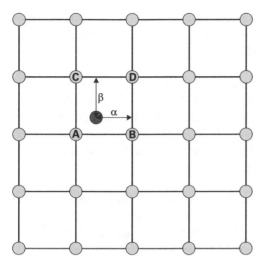

FIGURE 10-14: The dark grey dot indicates the sample position against the texture in memory. If nearest filtering is selected, texel A will be chosen. If bilinear filtering is selected, the colour data from texels A, B, C and D will be blended together linearly, using the fractional distances α and β.

FIGURE 10-15: A collection of mipmaps, each half the width and half the height of the previous level.

To take advantage of mipmaps, it is necessary to compute a suitable size at which to sample the texture. This is known as the correct *level-of-detail* (*LOD*). The most detailed image is level 0; as the level increases the image size shrinks and less detail is visible. To work out a suitable LOD, we pick adjacent screen space pixels of a primitive and compute the spacing of their texture coordinates in each dimension. Note that these texture coordinates have been interpolated from the original texture coordinates of the constituent vertices. The LOD is then increased until the spacing of texels most closely matches the spacing of adjacent pixels.

As each level increases, adjacent texels contain information from all of the pixels of the original image through successive averaging, thereby reducing the likelihood of visual artefacts. Bilinear filtering can now be performed at the chosen LOD.

However, bilinear filtering also has its limitations. Transitions in LOD as an object moves away from the viewer can lead to obvious changes in the sharpness of the sampled image. This is alleviated by a method called *trilinear filtering*. Instead of choosing the LOD that most closely matches the pixel spacing, we choose the levels directly below and directly above the optimal spacing, perform a bilinear filter at each level and then blend these two results. This ensures smooth transitions between chosen mipmaps.

So far we have described the texturing process for simple two-dimensional lookups. Using the texture coordinates for a pixel and its neighbours, we choose an appropriate LOD, from which sample points are derived for texels that must be fetched from the image stored in memory. Once fetched, they may be blended according to the filtering mode specified by the user.

OpenGL ES 2.0 also adds support for cube-map textures. A cube map is six-sided block with a different image of the same scene on each side (face). The cube structure is especially useful for creating light and reflection maps that are applied to surfaces to control their brightness. Three texture coordinates (s, t and r) are used to describe a normalised vector pointing from the cube's centre towards a particular face. The magnitude of the largest component is used to select a face, with the remaining two coordinates used to reference a sample point in the desired 2D image. Although the edges (or seams) of the cube faces can result in undesirable visual effects, the computational efficiency of building reflection and complex light maps have cemented cube-mapping as a valuable tool for developers.

In OpenGL ES 1.1, when the fetch and filtering of texels is complete, this data is supplied to the fragment processing pipeline by way of a texture environment. In this final step the (untextured) fragment colour is combined with the filtered texel value and an optional environment colour according to one of a set of fixed-function combination functions. These range from modulation of the existing fragment colour to an alpha blended value or complete replacement with the textured colour. Note that OpenGL ES 1.1 also permits multi-texturing, where more than one texture can be independently sampled and used to compute the output colour for a given fragment. Although these texture pipelines are conceptually separate, the combination of textured colours is performed in ascending order of texture units under one texture environment. However, the limited number of units, together with the inability to move data between texture stages, forces a multi-pass approach to achieve complex texturing effects.

In OpenGL ES 2.0 there is full flexibility in the combination of textured colours through the generic fragment shading pipeline. Texture units are accessed via fragment shaders and texture results are combined as part of the user-defined program supplied by the developer.

Modern Graphics Hardware

Now that you have an understanding of the OpenGL ES graphics pipeline, you're in a position to see how various stages are candidates for specialised hardware acceleration. In order for hardware acceleration to be possible, a layer of software must exist between the standard OpenGL ES API and the GPU; this is called the *driver*, and it runs on the main CPU. In addition to implementing features on the CPU, which aren't accelerated by graphics hardware, the driver interprets API calls and translates them into a set of controls that are used to configure and initiate the GPU to perform rendering. Vertex-attribute buffers, textures and programs must be derived and positioned in memory, where they are accessible to the graphics core before any instruction is given to begin processing.

As with features at the API level there are competing requirements in terms of performance and cost that drive the decision to offload functionality to specialised hardware, but OpenGL ES is specified loosely enough to allow implementers some freedom to choose different approaches.

At the end of this section we review in more detail Raspberry Pi's graphics hardware: the VideoCore IV GPU.

Tiled Rendering

One of the key questions facing graphics hardware architects is how to deal with the immense amount of data transferred to and from memory. Considering the frame-buffer traffic alone, rendering to a 1080p resolution, 4× multi-sampled buffer with 32 bits of colour and 32 bits of depth-stencil data constitutes approximately 64 megabytes (MB) of data. Updating this buffer at 60 frames per second (smooth user-interface transitions demand such a frame rate) requires a bandwidth to main memory of more than 3.6 gigabytes per second (GB/s). However, this assumes that each and every fragment sample is rendered only once. Transparent objects or occluded objects that can't be discarded earlier in the pipeline mean that even for 2× overdraw (that is, each sample is rendered twice per frame), it would be necessary to read each sample from memory once and write to each sample twice. The required bandwidth would exceed 10GB/s without accounting for reading of the vertex attributes and textures necessary to compute the desired fragment data.

Immediate mode renderers store frame-buffer data in off-chip memory (memory that's not built into the processor), such that as each draw call (request to the GPU to render an image) is processed, the colour, depth and stencil data is immediately updated. In order for this to be efficient, a huge *bandwidth* between graphics hardware (GPU) and graphics memory must be provided, which is expensive in terms of cost and power. In the PC and console domain, graphics cards contain large configurations of dedicated dynamic random access memory (DRAM), with up to 8GB of addressable memory accessible at up to 32GB/s. Such configurations are impractical for mobile devices, however. To cope with reduced bandwidth and a smaller power envelope, *tile-based rendering* was devised.

NOTE   Bandwidth is the capacity of a link through which information is provided.

Tiled renderers divide the output frame-buffer into an array of squares or rectangles (called tiles), each containing a subset of the pixels to be rendered for the scene. Tiles are typically small (approximately 16×16 or 32×32 pixels) and need not be square. Each tile is then rendered separately but only once for all primitives that contribute to that particular portion of the image. To do this the GPU must first work out which primitives contribute to each tile in the image. This process is known as *tile binning* (see Figure 10-16). The hardware calculates the position of each primitive in device coordinates, and if any part lies within a tile boundary it is appended to the list of primitives to be rendered for that tile. Rendering then proceeds tile-by-tile, focusing only on the geometry that contributes to the output image for that tile. The immediate bandwidth can be provided by local on-chip memory and the main frame-buffer need only be written to once, reducing the power associated with accessing off-chip DRAM.

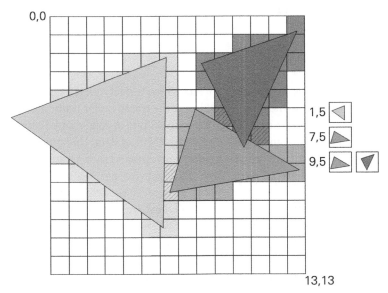

FIGURE 10-16: Tile binning. The set of primitives that overlap each tile is recorded in memory. Rendering is processed on a tile-by-tile basis for each overlapping primitive.

The amount of processing performed during the binning step may also vary between architectures. By sorting incoming primitives from front to back it is also possible to remove occluded objects entirely from the rendering step, thus saving further processing power and memory bandwidth later in the pipeline. This technique is known as *tile-based deferred rendering*. Other similar techniques are described in the next section.

Geometry Rejection

In additional to the large amount of data associated with 3D rendering, the increased complexity of geometry meshes, lighting and fragment processing means that the computation required for each output pixel can limit the achievable frame-rates for modern applications. It is therefore highly advantageous to discard objects that are invisible to the viewer as early as possible in the pipeline. Rejection of objects is achieved through a selection process commonly referred to as culling.

One of the key requirements of a modern hardware GPU is to accelerate the lighting and transformation parts of the pipeline efficiently, which is done using a process known as *vertex shading* in OpenGL ES 2.0. To achieve this, primitive data in the form of vertex references must be supplied to the hardware, together with the addresses in memory of the attributes associated with these vertices. These must be processed to determine the position of an object in the scene; for tiled renderers this is essential for tile binning. A dedicated memory fetch engine accumulates these attributes, which may be spread across more than one array structure in memory depending on how these have been set up via the OpenGL ES API. Note that some form of caching is probably sensible at this stage; depending on the order of vertex references and primitive type, some reuse of vertex attributes is expected as they are likely to be referenced more than once in the primitive stream. The references themselves follow a convention to specify whether the surface is facing towards or away from the viewer. If an anticlockwise winding order is used to define front facing polygons then any primitive that has been specified with clockwise-ordered vertices in screen space may not be visible. This information is particularly useful for opaque objects where the back-facing primitives are occluded by the front-facing ones. The hardware can spot this by computing the surface normal vector of the primitive and working out its direction with respect to the position of the viewer. If the shape faces away from the viewer it may be discarded from the pipeline; this is known as back-face culling. By doing this, the rasterisation and fragment processing steps are avoided, which improves performance without having any effect on the output image.

There are also other ways in which invisible geometry may be discarded. Recall the viewing volume mentioned earlier; this is the three-dimensional region that is visible to the observer and is approximated by a truncated pyramid known as the frustrum, which determines which objects are included and which are cut out of a scene. Objects that undergo geometric transformations may end up completely outside of the frustrum and can be discarded entirely prior to rasterisation. Note that objects may also lie so far into the distance that they do not influence the colour of any pixels, despite lying inside the far clip plane.

Of course, objects may lie only partially outside of the viewing volume. In this case only the visible portions of the primitive should be rendered and the rest discarded. This process is known as *clipping*. When a primitive is clipped it cannot be represented as a triangle by the original vertices. One or two new triangles may be required (see Figure 10-17), with two new vertices containing attributes interpolated from the original unclipped primitive. These are fed into the pipeline in place of the original primitive so that the rasteriser need only fill visible samples in preparation for fragment processing. Care must be taken to ensure that the varyings are consistent along the newly created edge.

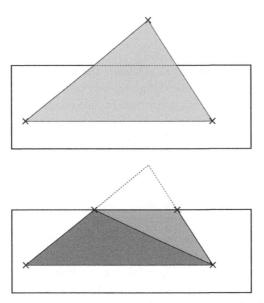

FIGURE 10-17: The top image shows a triangle that lies partially outside of the viewing volume. Clipping creates two new vertices on the frustrum boundary, and one triangle now becomes two.

Rasterisation is largely a fixed-function task, which lends itself to dedicated hardware acceleration of vector arithmetic to compute the included pixels for primitives being passed through the pipeline. Following transformation, the depth value associated with each vertex is interpolated as the polygon is rasterised, thus providing a per-sample value for the position of the primitive in the scene. Samples that lie behind other opaque objects can be discarded as they will not be visible, but it's desirable to reject these prior to fragment processing to reduce memory traffic and improve performance. As long as fragment processing does not update the depth of the sample, and the existing object in the scene is opaque, samples may be discarded early if their depth value is smaller than that of the sample currently occupying the frame-buffer; this is known as *early depth rejection* or *early-z*. There is an obvious latency (delay) issue here; the depth buffer may yet be updated by fragments already being processed in the hardware pipeline, but these are known to lie closer to the viewer than the existing sample. Anything that lies behind the existing sample is safely rejected, but reducing the time between the early depth test and the depth update improves the efficacy of early-z. Note that implementations may choose to perform the early-z test using bounded objects to improve rejection throughput at the expense of accuracy. Some hardware architectures make use of a multi-pass approach where the depth component of all samples for all primitives is computed before any fragment processing takes place. The second pass then only processes fragments for the nearest pixels, reducing the workload significantly. This technique is known as *deferred rendering*.

Shading

As we've already discussed, OpenGL ES 2.0 introduced much more flexible transform, lighting and pixel processing pipelines with the introduction of programmable vertex and fragment shaders. These programs are designed to run on general purpose processors, derived from the native GL shading language (GLSL). Hardware implementations of the OpenGL ES 2.0 pipeline typically contain custom digital signal processors (DSPs), which are closely coupled to the pipeline functions that give or receive (source or sink) data from these stages. Vertex shaders receive vertex positions and properties, known as attributes, and a set of matrix multiplication coefficients and lighting model constants, known as *uniforms*. They output interpolants used later in fragment shading, known as *varyings*. Fragment shaders receive varyings and via built-in texture lookup functions can access textures in memory, outputting colour, depth and stencil data to the frame-buffer. Since both shader types are derived from the same underlying language, they can be targeted at the same DSP allowing for dynamic partitioning of shading resources across different workloads. This is known as *unified shader architecture* and is common to many GPU shader processors. The lack of required integer support also means that these DSPs, at least initially, are hardened single precision floating-point processors, highly optimised for vector and matrix operations whilst remaining small and low power.

Perhaps the most distinctive property of graphics processing, and specifically shading, is the way in which many operations can be performed in parallel. Vertex shaders run independently for each vertex, and fragment shaders run independently for each sample, which has led to highly parallelised architectures where the same operation is applied to many different inputs at the same time. These are known as single-instruction, multiple data (SIMD) architectures. For every element (that is, a vertex or a fragment sample), these SIMD DSPs possess a huge amount of compute capability for relatively modest instruction bandwidths because the same instruction can be executed many times across different data. It is for this reason that GPUs have become highly desirable platforms for non-graphics related computation, as you will see later in this chapter.

Given the highly parallel nature of shading, the performance bottlenecks are frequently the result of accesses to shared resources, such as special functions or textures in memory. Multithreading is used to hide the latency associated with such accesses, so when a program stalls on an access, a task switch ensures that another program can make progress, thus hiding the latency. Take a look at the example in Figure 10-18. Note how thread 0 issues a texture request midway through the program. Once the request is issued, we switch to thread 1 to make use of the processor while thread 0 is stalled, only to return either when thread 1 stalls or ends. When we return to thread 0 the texture access has completed and the latency has been "hidden". It is common for shader processors to have many more than two threads, trading off complexity with enough parallelism to keep the processor cores busy. Similarly, given the very high number of samples involved in fragment shading there are typically many instances of these SIMD processor cores, all operating simultaneously. The Raspberry Pi GPU has 12 shader processor cores in total; typical PC graphics cards have many hundreds of cores.

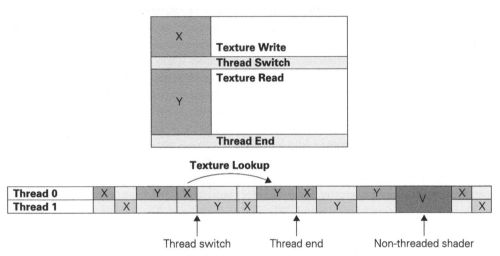

FIGURE 10-18: A threaded shader is divided into two sections (X and Y), which can take turns processing data in order to reduce or hide latency issues related to the need to access the same data for different processes.

Caching

Graphics processing is a memory-intensive task that involves frequently moving large amounts of data into and out of memory. Memory resources are further strained by fluctuating demand and limited bandwidth (restrictions inherent in the pipeline through which data travels in and out of memory). Modern GPUs make extensive use of a hierarchy of caches to meet the immediate bandwidth requirements at the lowest level, whilst providing enough local memory so that the stress on the main system memory is reduced. Due to multi-threaded shaders and highly parallel architectures, GPUs are fairly tolerant to high system-memory latencies.

A fully hardware-accelerated OpenGL ES pipeline must read from and write to various data streams during each frame. Many of these streams are backed by a cache in hardware. Vertex positions and properties must be fetched from main memory into the core, and depending on the order in which primitives have been specified these may be reused as the primitive stream is processed. For OpenGL ES 2.0 cores, transformation and lighting are performed through vertex shading, requiring program instructions and uniforms to be fetched from main memory. The SIMD nature of these programs makes caching of this data extremely worthwhile.

The extensive use of textures during fragment processing and its inherent nature as a shading bottleneck mean that sizing and tuning texture caching is also critical to the performance of the system. Textures (and even regions of textures) are likely to have only a finite context, which is very much dependent on the locality of specific objects in the scene. For example, when rendering the wall of a house it is highly likely that, given the correct LOD selection, adjacent frame-buffer samples will correspond to adjacent texture samples. For this reason hardware designers commonly optimise the efficiency of 2D access patterns or create 2D blocks of data to map to consecutive addresses in memory. This improves texture cache efficiency and thus reduces the impact on system memory bandwidth, and therefore power.

Immediate mode renderers may also implement a cache between the frame-buffer and main memory, again to reduce the load on the main memory system. However, due to the increasing resolution of images and colour depths this caching has become less effective; it is more common to dedicate many megabytes of local frame-buffer memory to facilitate these architectures. Various seventh-generation consoles, such as the Xbox 360 and Playstation 3, use embedded DRAM for this purpose.

Raspberry Pi GPU

The Raspberry Pi is built on Broadcom's BCM2835 application processor (BCM2836 for Raspberry Pi 2), which both contain the VideoCore IV GPU—a highly optimised hardware graphics engine for embedded systems. This GPU supports hardware acceleration of OpenGL ES 1.1 and OpenGL ES 2.0, and makes use of various techniques and optimisations discussed earlier in this section.

The VideoCore IV GPU (also known as V3D) is split into a single *core* module (single processing entity), comprised of the main vertex and primitive pipeline, rasteriser and tile memory, together with a number of compute units called slices, which contain up to four custom 32-bit floating point processors, caches, a special functions unit and up to two dedicated texture fetch and filtering engines. BCM2835 and BCM2836 contain a V3D with three of these slices, each containing four floating point shader processors and two texture units.

Also note that VideoCore IV is a tile-based renderer with deferred vertex shading, which means that full vertex shading only takes place per-tile after binning has occurred. In fact, in order to work out which primitives lie in each tile, a streamlined vertex shader is used to compute just the position of the transformed vertices. This information, along with the other vertex attributes, is then recomputed during rendering in the subsequent pass, minimising the amount of data stored to (and loaded from) memory. This position-only computation during binning is called *coordinate shading*. The front end of the hardware is divided into two distinct pipelines (perhaps confusingly called *threads*): one for binning and one for rendering. To keep things simple we will describe the binning pipeline followed by the rendering pipeline, but these are capable of running simultaneously and dynamically sharing the resources available to them throughout the graphics core.

The Control List Executor (CLE) is the entry point to the hardware, and it fetches the list of control items from memory that is required to configure the core. It dispatches this configuration information to other hardware blocks within the GPU, ensuring that every state set up via the OpenGL ES API is reflected in the hardware processes that follow. Note the distinction between control items and instructions; for clarity, the information used to configure the GPU pipeline as a whole is communicated through control items, whereas information compiled from GLSL shaders and used in vertex and fragment shading is composed of instructions.

The first few hardware modules in the binning pipeline are concerned with loading vertex attributes from memory in preparation for coordinate shading. References to vertex attributes are fed to the hardware via the CLE in the form of a list of indices—essentially pointers to attributes within the set of arrays set up via the OpenGL ES driver. These indices are fed to the Vertex Cache Manager (VCM), which, in conjunction with the Vertex Cache Direct Memory Access engine (VCD), fetches the vertex attributes from GPU memory and stores them in the Vertex Pipeline Memory (VPM). The VCM caches these pointers to vertex attributes because vertices are often reused in triangle strips and fans, and this caching reduces the number of accesses to the same vertex information in GPU memory, which therefore reduces power and memory bandwidth requirements. The VCM also gathers the vertex attributes into SIMD batches for shading on the custom shader processor (known as the Quad Processing Unit or QPU). Note that the same coordinate shader may be run many times for different vertices, hence the ability to group the vertex data into batches that share a single instruction stream. We will cover the QPU in more detail later. The VPM is a 12 kilobyte (KB) block of on-chip SRAM, which can be accessed in two dimensions. All the information associated with a *vertex* is stored *vertically* in a single column, such that a batch is stored as a series of VPM columns. Individual attributes, such as an individual colour component or texture coordinate, can be accessed via a specific *row* of the memory. This is particularly helpful during coordinate and vertex shading, which computes per-attribute data across the whole SIMD batch of vertices.

After all vertex attributes are present in the VPM, coordinate shading can commence. Coordinate shading is performed on one of the QPUs and is initiated via the QPU Scheduler (QPS), which assumes control of all shading tasks, ensuring a fair distribution of coordinate, vertex and fragment shaders across all available processors (remember that binning and rendering can occur in parallel). The driver is responsible for compiling and linking shader programs to be run on the QPU; locations of the specific instructions and data for the coordinate shader associated with this batch are provided via the CLE. Coordinate shading computes the transformed position of the batch of vertices, which are then used to work out which tiles each primitive intersects. This vertex information is stored in another area (or segment) of the VPM, which can be accessed directly by the Primitive Tile Binner (PTB). The PTB is responsible for tile binning, essentially generating a list of configuration data and primitives that must be processed when rendering each tile. Because it has access to the position data it also performs the first stage of clipping, removing primitives that are completely outside the viewing volume and generating new vertices for primitives that intersect the clip boundaries. The PTB stores tile lists to GPU memory, which contain per-tile control items and primitives that can be read directly by the rendering thread of the CLE. Once this data has been written to memory, rendering can begin for each tile in turn; the core may also begin binning for the next frame simultaneously.

The first stages of the rendering pipeline operate very much like binning. The CLE has a separate hardware thread to process the per-tile control list and fetch the indices for the set of primitives that lie in each tile. Vertex attribute data is refetched from memory via a separate VCM and the single, shared VCD. When all vertex attributes (now including all the vertex data and not just the position components) have been fetched into the VPM, the QPS schedules vertex shading on one of the 12 available QPUs. Vertex shading computes the transformed vertex positions and other attributes, including texture coordinates and lighting, storing this data in a separate VPM segment. However, instead of the PTB, the Primitive Setup Engine (PSE) reads this shaded vertex data from the VPM and begins primitive assembly. Using the indices fetched by the CLE and the associated vertex data in the VPM, the PSE computes the equations for the edges of each input primitive, as well as the plane equations necessary for later interpolation steps. If necessary the PSE also performs the second stage of clipping by fetching the PTB-generated vertices that have been clamped to the viewing volume and preparing associated attributes for subsequent interpolation. The Front-End Pipe (FEP) performs rasterisation, generating a series of 2×2 fragments (or quads) that relate to pixels within the frame-buffer that are covered by the primitive. Quads are chosen to simplify the LOD calculations that may be necessary for texturing during the subsequent fragment shading step. The FEP also stores the depth of each fragment in a buffer so that any later rasterised primitive whose fragments lie behind another visible object may be discarded early in the pipeline. This saves needless computation during fragment shading, and therefore improves performance and saves power.

Quads are gathered into SIMD-sized batches for fragment shading, whilst their positions with respect to the original primitive vertices are used to compute the interpolated attributes or varyings, ready for use by the fragment shader. This is done by the Varyings Interpolator (VRI), one of which exists for each slice, shared between four QPUs. Once a batch is ready to be shaded, the QPS allocates a QPU on which to process the samples. The fragment shader itself is a collection of instructions and data compiled and linked by the driver and placed in GPU memory; the locations of these are again made available to the QPU via the CLE. Note also that the fragment shader may be threaded; that is to say it may be run in parallel (but not simultaneously with) another fragment shader on the same QPU. As we discussed earlier, this allows the latency of accesses to memory to be hidden and improves utilisation of the processors.

Fragment shading essentially computes the colour (and optionally depth and stencil) components for each sample in the frame-buffer. Each shader may access a shared special functions unit (SFU) for complex mathematical expressions such as logarithms, exponents and reciprocals, together with a specialised texture and memory fetch unit (TMU) for retrieving and filtering texture data.

Once complete, the fragment information is written to the tile buffer (TLB), which tests each fragment and performs additional operations prior to updating the sample data. Here, the sample data may be discarded or used to modify the existing frame-buffer contents according to the depth and stencil tests. After all the primitives for the tile are processed and fragment shading is complete, the full tile is flushed to GPU memory. Multisampled outputs simply average the four samples together per output-pixel, which is done seamlessly as the tile data is written to main memory. Tiles are 64×64 pixels in size on the Raspberry Pi (32×32 pixels in multisample mode). After the tile has been flushed, the next tile is processed. Note that when transparent objects are rendered on top of one another the order in which fragments are shaded affects the blended output colour; a hardware scoreboard (SCB) is used to ensure fragments that are being shaded in parallel update the TLB in their specified order.

At the heart of both vertex and fragment processing on VideoCore IV's GPU is the Quad Processing Unit or QPU. This is a multithreaded, 16-way SIMD, 32-bit floating point processor with a customised instruction set for graphics programs. The QPU is physically a four-way SIMD (hence the term quad), designed so that it operates on 2×2 fragments simultaneously and performs the same instruction over four successive clock cycles, thus appearing to the programmer as a 16-way SIMD engine. This allows floating point arithmetic to be performed over multiple cycles, thereby reducing power consumption. Each QPU possesses 32 general purpose registers, which may be split between two threads for fragment shading where latency tolerance is specifically desired. The QPU also has access to a number of closely coupled hardware peripherals, such as the single, shared SFU and VRI units, together with a TMU for every two QPUs. Specific instructions are used to access these units, and results from these peripherals are mapped into two of five temporary working registers (accumulators), which are also shared between threads. There are two ALU pipelines (one for addition and one for multiplication), so that in total, the VideoCore IV GPU can process 24 billion floating point operations per second (24 GFLOPs). It is this immense compute power that software developers want to unlock by way of APIs dedicated to general-purpose computing, such as OpenCL.

The general philosophy behind the VideoCore IV architecture is to offload as much as possible from software and minimise the interaction between the driver and the hardware itself. As a result, interfaces to the rest of the chip infrastructure are limited to a simple programming interface to communicate with the core, a memory access interface to read from and write to GPU memory, and an interrupt for notifying the CPU when binning and rendering jobs are complete. The extensive use of parallelism and low-power techniques mean that the V3D is a highly efficient GPU for mobile devices, proving very effective in accelerating the OpenGL ES pipeline and bringing high-quality GUIs and immersive gaming to embedded systems.

Open VG

Until now we have focused on OpenGL and the dawn of specialised hardware to accelerate 3D graphics rendering. However, efficient implementation of 2D graphics is also highly desirable. The advent of web browsing has increased the importance of scalable font rendering such that a user can pan and zoom page content at little or no performance cost. Similarly, being able to cheaply compute smooth curves and edges is necessary in a wide array of applications, such as the display of maps and navigation aids in modern smartphones or more directly in graphic design software. A separate open standard was devised for vector graphics, principally aimed at achieving cross-vendor support for exactly these cases: Open Vector Graphics (Open VG). The Raspberry Pi GPU supports OpenVG 1.1.

Vector graphics is built upon several key concepts: paths, stroking and filling. A path is comprised of one or more line segments, connected by two or more anchor points. These line segments need not be straight. Curved segments may join two points, described by mathematical equations and the path's associated control points (see Figure 10-19). These curved segments are known as Bézier curves and are named after the French mathematician Pierre Bézier. The areas between curves may be filled with flat-shaded or gradient colour. Open paths consist of start and end points that don't meet; closed paths join start and end points together. Path definitions include jumps between points, quadratic and cubic equations to join points and methods to obtain the interpolated position along a path, a path bounding box or a tangent to the path at a particular location.

Stroking is the process by which outlines are defined around the path, such as the line width, joining style at the corner of two edges (such as a bevel, round or mitre) and the end caps of all lines. These outlines, coupled with the path definitions form objects that are ready to be transformed and rasterised in a similar way to OpenGL ES. However, the purpose of rasterisation is to compute a filtered alpha value for each pixel depending on the coverage of the surrounding geometry. This effectively provides a weighting factor for the subsequent paint stages. The geometry may be windowed using clip rectangles prior to painting, to limit the regions over which colour is applied. This may be further modified by a per-pixel mask, much like the stencil buffer in OpenGL ES, via a series of fixed-function operations such as explicit clearing or adding to or subtracting from application-supplied values.

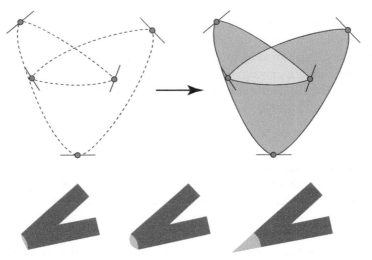

FIGURE 10-19: In OpenVG shapes are constructed from points linked by paths described by Bézier curves.

Painting is the process by which colour is applied to the geometry, either via flat shading, linear gradients or radial gradients, or by sampling and tiling an image from memory. Blending the painted colour values with the output of rasterisation results in a per-pixel colour to be output to the frame-buffer. Filling is the application of paint to any area within a path. Note that stroking and filling may both incur painting; these are done via separate objects in separate processing steps.

OpenVG was defined with hardware acceleration in mind, together with an API that resembled OpenGL ES. Although completely separate, the similarities mean that the same hardware (with a few simple additions) can be repurposed to support OpenVG. The OpenVG driver must first assemble a list of OpenVG-specific control items to configure the GPU via the existing CLE. The Bézier curve for each path segment is split into a series of straight-line sections using a QPU program generated by the driver. In doing this, the geometry regions that are required to be painted are then covered by a series of triangles in a fan with one common, central vertex. The vertices of these triangles are stored in the VPM. Note that tile binning is still applicable—having computed the position of each triangle, the set of these primitives covering each tile is stored so that rendering can proceed on per-tile basis.

Rendering is performed as a second step, with the set of transformed vertices processed as a triangle fan by the rasteriser. However, depending on the path, multiple triangles may overlay each other indicating whether the pixel lies inside or outside the fill region. A compressed coverage buffer accumulates the count at each pixel location, thereby providing a mask of which fragments must be shaded during painting. This coverage accumulation pipe (CAP) is only present for OpenVG use. Painting and frame-buffer modifications are mapped to the fragment shading process of OpenGL ES 2.0, which provides sufficient flexibility to achieve all required colour effects. One aspect of this, the tiling of image data within a fill region, is supported via an additional child image mode in the TMU. This allows the user to supply an arbitrary window within a texture from which to sample in memory.

OpenVG is able to be supported with little additional hardware cost due to the flexibility of the hardware architecture required to support OpenGL ES 2.0. Although OpenVG is not as popular as it once was, it remains a good example of how thoughtful architecture can provide a valuable platform for functionality beyond the primary requirements, something that we also find with the advent of general purpose computing on GPUs, discussed next.

General Purpose GPUs

As the demands of graphics APIs have increased, GPU hardware architectures have evolved to provide large numbers of general purpose processors on which to perform vertex and fragment shading in parallel. This has resulted in huge floating-point computation potential, which application developers and researchers want to utilise for non-graphics functionality. The Raspberry Pi GPU, with 12 QPUs and 3 SFUs, provides a compute platform of up to 27 billion floating point operations per second. PC graphics cards contain GPUs with hundreds of shader processors and more than 1 teraflop (1 trillion floating point operations per second) of 32-bit floating point performance. Such computation is already used for complex physics simulations and to implement high-quality image processing algorithms on platforms that don't already contain specialised hardware for this purpose.

Heterogeneous Architectures

To leverage the available compute power, system architectures must be designed to make offloading tasks to the GPU simple. Architectures that aim to make use of compute elements beyond just the CPU (most commonly the CPU and GPU together) are known as *heterogeneous architectures*. The aim of these systems is to ensure the passing of data between the CPU and GPU is efficient, usually via shared memory.

Traditional computer architectures require an algorithm designer to set up data structures in CPU memory (accessible only by the CPU) and copy them to a region of memory accessible only by the GPU. The GPU operates on the data and writes the results back to GPU memory.

These results are then copied from GPU memory back to CPU memory for the program to continue. The problem with this is that complex algorithms with large data sets require a lot of data to be moved around, which is prohibitively slow and expensive in terms of memory bandwidth and power.

A far better solution is to allow the CPU and GPU access to a shared region of memory so that copying of data is no longer required. A couple of features are required to make this realisable. The first is virtual memory. Virtual memory is a technique whereby the locations of data structures referenced by processing units are translated before being used to access the physical locations in the memory itself. As a result, the address space in which the CPU or GPU operates does not directly correspond to the address space of the data structures in memory. This address translation is performed by a memory management unit (MMU). The CPU and GPU address virtual memory and each MMU maps virtual memory addresses to physical addresses in main memory. Conceptually, blocks of memory may be shared by providing the same MMU mappings to the CPU and GPU. Pointers to memory are effectively passed between units rather than the data itself. The second feature is memory coherence. Although the CPU and GPU may be given the same view of main memory, each contains a hierarchy of caches to take advantage of data reuse. If both have a copy of the same data in their local caches and one of them updates the data, how does the other unit know to update their copy? Either a hardware broadcast must be sent to all users to inform them that the data must be refetched from main memory (thus guaranteeing coherence in the system), or the developer must track buffer usage and explicitly flush caches that contain stale copies of the data. Both issues are non-trivial to solve.

Now that the CPU and GPU share access to the same memory, we must decide what tasks to offload and how these should be managed. Shader processors are designed with parallelism in mind, so it is common for software to split computation into independent groups, allowing them to run simultaneously. Groups of work are usually sized to match the SIMD width of each shader core to make full use of the parallelism on offer. Image processing naturally lends itself to GPU acceleration as filter kernels must operate on many pixels simultaneously; these kernels benefit greatly from the texture caching hardware used in graphics, as each image sample may be used by multiple kernels at the same time. However, it is not always possible to dispatch groups of work where each element is independent. It may be necessary to ensure that all elements of a group have completed before beginning the next stage of a program. Synchronisation primitives are provided to handle this very case. A barrier is a point in a program that all elements must reach before execution is allowed to continue. This may be achieved in many ways, but dedicated hardware to handle these cases is becoming increasingly common to reduce overhead of the driver software.

> Allowing the CPU and GPU to share access to memory is only one solution for addressing issues related to limited bandwidth and processing power. Other solutions focus on bypassing bottlenecks. For example, direct memory access (DMA) is a method that allows input/output (I/O) devices to exchange data directly with the main memory, bypassing the CPU, which frees up the CPU for other tasks while streamlining communications between the I/O devices and memory. Another solution enables the GPU to communicate directly a field programmable gate array (FPGA, an integrated circuit that developers can configure) through a PCI Express (PCIe) bus to bypass system memory.
>
> **NOTE**

OpenCL

The Open Computing Language (OpenCL) was first released by Apple in 2009 as a vendor-independent framework through which programs could be executed across heterogeneous systems, including CPUs, GPUs, FPGAs, and DSPs. In short, it provides a standard interface for parallel computing. It also defines a four-level memory hierarchy: global memory, read-only memory (writeable by the CPU only), local memory (shared by processing elements) and private memory (per processing element). However, it is not required that each level in the memory hierarchy is implemented in hardware, and shared memory between the CPU and GPU is not explicitly mandated. These relaxations have allowed OpenCL portability between platforms, at the expense of performance guarantees due to the range of permissible implementations. However, such is the popularity of exposing general compute capability that OpenGL ES has introduced the concept of compute shaders in version 3.1 of the API; these now coexist with vertex and fragment shaders in the standard graphics pipeline.

Although the Raspberry Pi GPU does not natively support OpenCL, it does provide a mechanism for executing general-purpose shaders, known in VideoCore IV as *user shaders*. These are programs written for execution on the QPU, which can be directly issued to the hardware by programming start addresses for the data and instructions to be fetched from memory. User shaders have been used to write a fast-fourier transform (FFT) library for the VideoCore IV V3D, available through the Raspberry Pi website at `https://www.raspberrypi.org/blog/accelerating-fourier-transforms-using-the-gpu/`.

Chapter 11
Audio

SOUND CAPABILITY ON computers is certainly a significant matter. An old adage in the film and video industry states, "Sound is 70 percent of your production". Sound accentuates the visual, sets moods, increases excitement, inspires the user and more. Computer games are one great example that demonstrates the importance of sound.

In short, this chapter is an exploration of sound on computers in general and specifically how the architecture of the Raspberry Pi supports music and all sorts of other sound manipulations. We discuss analog versus digital audio, sound over High Definition Multimedia Interface (HDMI), 1-bit digital analog conversion (DAC), both signal and sound processing, and Inter-IC Sound (I^2S, a communications protocol for carrying digital audio signals).

We also cover the Raspberry Pi's onboard sound, both the input and output features. We begin with the basics of sound on computers and a little history.

Can You Hear Me Now?

Right after World War II ended, the first computers were silent—except, of course, for the grinding and clacking of gears in the mechanical computers, the buzzing of power supplies and the *plink* of vacuum tubes burning out in electronic mainframes. Then there was also the often-colourful language of operators when these monsters crashed due to faulty programs and the lack of operating systems to prevent or recover from the software mishap, necessitating a lengthy reboot.

The "language" we're referring to is not COBOL or FORTRAN—or, to be more modern, Python or JavaScript. We're talking about those nifty words learned by the soldiers, sailors, and airmen in combat during the war and generously passed to their fellow operators after they came into the growing data processing field.

Notice that when you read the preceding two paragraphs you hear sounds, even if they're only in your head. Sound sets the stage and creates atmosphere. Sound is important. Think of this classic movie moment, the computer HAL 9000 singing "Daisy Bell" in the film *2001: A Space Odyssey*. Inspired by the IBM 7094 (from 1961), Hal provided an iconic moment in cinema and computer-generated sound/voice history. Although special effects were used at the time, computer sound capabilities quickly have become reality.

MIDI

The true dawn of sound on computers, at least so far as widespread user interest is concerned, came with the advent of the personal computer. For the purposes of this discussion we consider that to have happened in 1980, when the Commodore 64, Radio Shack's TRS-80 and the Apple II were popular. Then in 1981, IBM's first IBM PC came on the market and more people started using personal computers for pleasure, such as playing games, as well as doing real work. Consequently, the sounds made by personal computers started to matter more and more, especially as people interested in music were figuring out ways for computers to assist them.

In 1981, the Musical Instrument Digital Interface (MIDI) hit the music industry. It caused a lot of excitement among both professional and amateur musicians. Now you could turn music into *data* right on your personal computer. You could load it into a device called a sequencer, edit it, save it and play it back later. Cool!

Of course, it occurred to many people that *their* personal computers would be ideal for this purpose. Soon MIDI add-on cards and sequencing software hit the market. People could add a MIDI player to their computers and download all sorts of MIDI music from bulletin boards (which were precursors to the Internet).

Sound Cards

Of course, it is rather hard to enjoy music if you cannot hear it. Yes, many of the early computers, such as the IBM PC, came with tiny built-in speakers. These were good for little more than the occasional diagnostic beep or other system sound. In fact, that was their design purpose. They provided a limited audio frequency range and very low power. It was useless to hope for decent music reproduction from them.

For quite some time, the best way to achieve good sound in a personal computer was with an add-on card. It took about six years for sound cards to become common built-in features in computers.

Beginning around 1988, sound cards became common and several good choices existed, which meant digital audio moved from being a possibility to a necessity for many computer owners. These cards included capability for sound amplification and they supported external speakers, which remains the norm for personal computers today.

Most modern personal computers come boxed with decent sound cards, speakers, network adapters and other accessories for which you once had to buy additional cards. However, for the very best in sound, great alternatives exist, from speakers to a separate subwoofer bass box that can shake your whole house.

Computers with add-on sound cards had the capability to digitally record output from the speakers to the microphone input. A number of truly professional sound cards are available for turning your computer into a studio-level sound editor and mixer.

Today, computer sound rocks. Now you need to know how it works.

Analog vs. Digital

People began using and recording sound in the nineteenth century—think of Alexander Graham Bell's telephone (see Figure 11-1), Thomas Edison's phonograph, and so on. This type of producing sound and the recording of it used a *transducer* (a microphone is one of those) to convert variations in air pressure to an electrical waveform that changed in frequency and amplitude to match the actual sounds. When played back on a speaker (which is like a reverse transducer), people heard a close approximation of the recorded sounds. This type of recording is known as *analog*.

Over the next hundred years, analog sound recording techniques got very good indeed. Tapes and records played through high-end stereo equipment certainly approached the quality of "being there". So, you might now ask, "If analog is so good, why change?"

FIGURE 11-1: An 1876 photo of Alexander Graham Bell's famous first call on the first telephone, "Come here, Mr. Watson, I want to see you," was all analog sound.

The answer is simple: only the first generation (the original) recording is good. If you copy, say, the master tape from a recording studio onto another tape, it creates a little noise, and all those squiggly audio waves become slightly distorted. Copying the copy introduces more noise, and so on. Static, hisses, whistles. Besides, because computers are digital, they can't manipulate recorded sound.

Digital audio solves the noise problem and makes for easy editing in many ways. When sound comes into a digital recorder—via a microphone or from a recorded analog tape or some other medium—the recorder changes the waveforms into binary 1s and 0s that the computer can understand. In other words, the sounds become *data* and can be formatted and saved as an audio file such as .wav or .mp3.

A digital audio file can be copied hundreds, thousands, millions of times and remain exactly the same quality as the first-generation file. No noise is introduced. In addition, the file is now in digital format and thus available for editing, cutting, enhancing and mixing in all sorts of ways.

It was once true that analog techniques provided all electronic sound, the sound itself being a recording of what humans could actually hear. That's not the case anymore. Software can create music and other sounds from scratch, all digitally. Hundreds of music creation programs, which are available on the Internet, aid in this creation of virtual music, sound effects and even synthesis of artificial "human" speech.

To sum up, in a comparison of analog and digital audio, digital wins for three major reasons:

- Sounds and/or music become computer data, which is easy to manipulate.

- No noise is introduced, regardless of how many generations of copies you make.

- Software can create digital music and sound with any analog input.

Sound and Signal Processing

Processing audio refers to several things, most of which concern deliberately modifying a recorded or created digital audio file. This section gives a general overview of audio processing. An explanation of the hardware specifics and computer architecture that make sound, input and output possible follow later in this chapter. The chapter concludes with information about how to actually edit sound using the Raspberry Pi and its onboard sound hardware.

With the advent of digital audio, manipulating audio with computers rapidly replaced the old methods, and digital audio now dominates in the music industry, broadcasting, home recording and so forth. Podcasts (recorded segments like radio programs but intended to be played online) proliferate on the Internet, and music lovers download millions upon millions of music files daily.

Computerised audio manipulation can take several forms:

- Editing the file to delete or add sounds, adjust the volume, and so on
- Recording the audio with special effects (reverb, for example) or adding effects during editing.
- Compressing the file to make high and low amplitudes even out and improve sound
- Encoding or decoding information from audio for the purpose of computer operation, data collection or various modes of digital communication

Editing

In the days of analog-only sound, editing was a pain. To remove a small bit of annoying noise in a recording, one had to cue the tape, guess where the offending sound lay, use a razor blade or scissors to cut out the section and then glue the tape back together. (Film editing used the same process.) Precise? Definitely not.

To edit digital audio today, you look at the waveform or waveforms, use a mouse pointer to highlight the part that needs to go and press the Delete button. When you play the file, you cannot tell where the edits took place.

Editing enables you to adjust volume, reduce noise—including wind pops in microphones that happen while recording outdoors, or someone's cough during a concert—and do many other things such as adding various enhancing effects, which is covered in the next section.

Editing includes *mixing* (combining audio waves) of many *tracks*. During recording of an orchestra, for example, there might be 20 or more microphones spread around to record different tracks. By combining or emphasising various tracks, the person editing the final release of this recording can work all sorts of magic to get a more pleasing and inspiring result.

Compression

Compression of an audio waveform allows better quality audio on transmission media than other degrade reproduction. Recordings of old time AM broadcast and movies from the 1930s and 1940s provide a prime example. Voices especially sound tinny, less full and rich than they do in modern broadcast and movie audio. In radio audio, this tininess was emphasized by audio-limiting circuits designed to protect transmitters from over-modulation damage as well as preventing distortion. In other words, an announcer shouting on air could blow an expensive transmitter and shut down the station.

Pioneering effects, such as the CBS radio network's Audimax system in the 1960s, changed that by making earlier attempts at compression practical. Compression techniques allow reproduction of voice and music more accurately and distortion free.

Two types of compression are popular and available in software (such as Audacity) for the Raspberry Pi:

- **Audio compression:** Reduces the amount of data in an audio waveform to effect accurate reproduction via CD, MP3, Internet radio and so forth with little or no loss of quality
- **Dynamic range compression:** Reduces the difference between loud and quiet, again resulting in accurate reproduction

Recording with Effects

Features that enable you to modify all or parts of sound files are called *effects*. Effects add ambience, excitement, fullness and other changes to sounds that do not exist in the original recording. Effects can turn drab reality into a magical virtual soundscape. You can even use more than one effect on a sound. Some standard examples of effects include:

- **Echo:** Gives the effect of sound echoing off the walls of a large hall or cavern
- **Chorus:** Adds a very slight delay to make one recorded voice sound like more than one person or make a group of recorded voices sound like many more
- **Pitch shift:** Moves the pitch of music or other sounds up or down; for example, you could copy a track, move the pitch of the copy up or down an octave and mix it with the original track for an interesting effect. You can also change the pitch of an actor's voice to use for a cartoon character. Pitch shift can also be used to change the pitch of an out-of-tune singer so that their voice is in tune.

NOTE   Some karaoke machines use pitch shift in real time to assist singers, making them sound better than they actually are. Called *autotune*, this technique is common in pop culture these days and is even used by professional singers.

- **Robotic voice effects:** Turns the human voice into a mechanical synthesised version. Add a pitch shift effect for a scary result
- **Time stretching:** Increases or decreases speed of an audio signal without affecting its pitch

Hundreds more effects exist, either in audio editing software or available to be downloaded and added as needed. Figure 11-2 shows an example of Adobe Audition, which is part of the Creative Cloud suite and offers extensive sound editing capabilities.

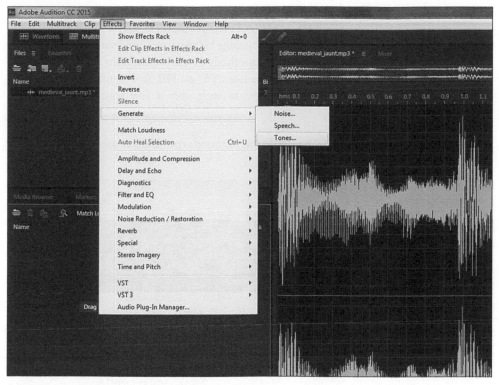

FIGURE 11-2: Adobe Audition professional sound editing program showing some of the many effects available

Encoding and Decoding Information for Communication

Voice recognition is an example of encoding information for controlling software and computers. For example, when you say "Stop" and a program on a computer ends, it's because your word is compared against an encoded version of the word *stop* and recognized, and the command is initiated. (Naturally the computer must have a microphone attached and software for identifying and comparing words to their encoded versions.)

Sensors, industrial instruments, satellites and thousands of other devices on the Internet of Things use variously modulated audio signals to accept and return information. These audio signals are not necessarily words but various commands and other data encoded into audio waveforms. *Decoding* is the process by which the information is extracted and acted on.

Broadcast radio and TV stations add modulated sound waves to their radio frequency carriers to send out voice and music. The radio waveform is encoded with the program material. Your receiver decodes it and converts the voice and music to sound for your enjoyment.

Here's another example: if you've ever seen an amateur radio operator sending Morse code, that's sound manipulation, resulting in *dits* and *dahs* reproduced after being sent through the air to another radio ham's receiver and a message being passed hundreds or thousands of miles. The same is true of more sophisticated methods of communications like radioteletype (RTTY) and technically cutting-edge advances like JT65 or JT9 (low signal modes allowing consistent communications between continents with only a few watts), as shown in Figure 11-3.

The multitude of sound and signal processing applications continues to grow rapidly.

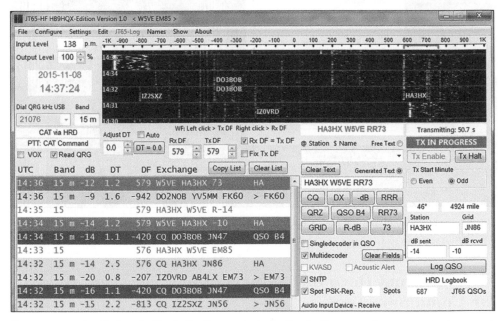

FIGURE 11-3: A radio ham in North Carolina contacts another in Hungary using a computer to convert typed messages into digital waveforms which modulate a radio signal received and decoded by the computer of the ham in Europe.

1-Bit DAC

DAC stands for digital-to-analog converter and ADC stands for analog-to-digital converter. DAC is also known as a bitstream converter.

Earlier in the chapter we discussed the advantages of digital audio over analog, but this does not mean digital audio has totally replaced analog audio. Why? After all, you can plug headphones into the 3.5mm audio jack on the Raspberry Pi board and hear music. Headphones are transducers that convert recorded analog waveforms to sound waves (which are vibrations in the air) and flings them against your eardrums. To make this happen, some kind of digital-to-analog conversion has to happen on the Raspberry Pi board. If you want to use both video and audio via the audio jack on a Raspberry Pi 2 or B+, you need a connector like the one shown in Figure 11-4.

> The type of connector shown in Figure 11-4 includes provision for video as well as audio, whereas the audio jack on the older Model B is a standard stereo configuration with the composite video jack separate. **NOTE**
>
> Prior to Raspberry Pi 2, the stereo jack was not the "3 pole" variety, and it was used only for audio. But there's good news: the plug in Figure 11-4 is 4-pole (TRRS or Tip, Ring, Ring, Sleeve), but the conventional 3-pole stereo plug (such as the one on headphones) still works! Only when you're using video does this plug require a 4-pole connector.

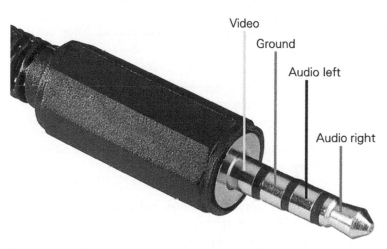

FIGURE 11-4: Connections on a 3.5mm plug to match the Raspberry Pi

Bear in mind that a computer costing around £30 retail might not have the highest possible quality of audio. The quality isn't terrible, though, and the HDMI connector supplies very acceptable sound. The audio from the 3.5mm stereo audio jack, however, does not have as much quality. What is the difference between the two? The 3.5mm jack outputs analog audio and the HDMI jack outputs digital audio.

The Raspberry Pi's onboard DAC conversion is generated by the Pulse Width Modulation (PWM) module and is 1-bit. This is not bad. Many CD players, boom boxes, and other sound-producing consumer electronic devices use 1-bit DACs (or the equivalent) with great results. The 1-bit DAC samples audio at several times its actual rate, converting with quality similar to 16 to 20 bits; in the Raspberry P, however, it's stated as being equivalent to only 11 bit. 1-bit DAC is also cheap, which is something important to manufacturers of low-cost units.

An ADC measures analog audio amplitudes many times each second, storing those as numbers in a file. The most common format used for this in computers is pulse code modulation (PCM). The digital-to-analog conversion DAC, such as the PWM emulation of 1-bit DAC on the Raspberry Pi board, samples a PCM audio file and reconstructs the analog waveform according to the numeric data in the PCM file.

To simplify, a soundwave varies continuously in amplitude over time. The ADC rapidly measures the wave many times a second, recording the amplitude of the wave each time. These points then are encoded into a digital pulse width waveform. When that PWM waveform is decoded, the original analog waveform is reconstruction and can drive a speaker or headphone thus playing the original content.

The problem here is that you may have beautiful music produced in a studio and turned into a 24-bit audio file. Although the 1-bit DAC reads the file okay, it's reconstructing the analog waveform of the music based on its overrate sampling technique which is 11-bit (in the Raspberry Pi's case) to 20-bit, instead of the file's native 24-bit quality. Small distortions due to this faster sampling might also creep in.

> **NOTE** The term *overrate* in the preceding paragraph is significant for bandwidth-limited waveforms such as those produced by the type of DAC described earlier. There is a term in signal processing called the *Nyquist rate*, which is twice the highest frequency in a waveform. Theoretically, at least, such a waveform can be more accurately decoded if sampled above the Nyquist rate, thus reducing noise and distortion. This over-rate technique is how the equivalent 11-bit rate is achieved from a 1-bit DAC encoded file.

When using the Raspberry Pi as a media centre driving high-end amplifiers and speaker systems, you want the best sound possible. The Raspberry Pi can do it, but you need to hang a higher quality DAC from it, which is a cheap and easy solution. With a 24-bit DAC, you will get more clarity and depth of sound. The difference is subtle, but it is definitely there.

So, how does the Raspberry Pi communicate with this better DAC? It happens via a sound transport protocol referred to as I²S.

I²S

I²S—which is short for Inter-IC Sound, Interchip Sound or IIS—is a type of serial bus interface standard that connects digital audio devices to one another. As an example, I²S connects the Raspberry Pi to an external DAC.

But wait. You may have noticed we have nothing labelled "I²S Connector" on the Raspberry Pi board. We could use one of the USB ports for outputting PCM audio to a DAC, but that can introduce distortion. The best solution is to use the general purpose input output (GPIO) pins on the Raspberry Pi board. Also, it's best to use the shortest path possible. Consequently, external DAC boards for the Raspberry Pi plug directly into the GPIO pins.

You might want to check out the following list of DAC boards, all of which cost less than £25:

- **SainSmart HIFI DAC Audio Sound Card Module for Raspberry Pi 2** (`www.sainsmart.com/sainsmart-hifi-dac-audio-sound-card-module-i2s-interface-for-raspberry-pi-2-b.html`): Plugs directly to the Raspberry Pi board.

- **HiFiBerry DAC+** (`www.hifiberry.com/dac/`): Plugs into A, B, B+, and 2, but it may not work with some older As and Bs.

- **Eleduino HIFI DAC Audio Sound Card Module** (`http://www.eleduino.com/HIFI-DAC-Audio-Sound-Card-Module-I2S-interface-for-Raspberry-pi-B-Raspberry-Pi-2-Model-B-p10546.html`)

- **Arducam HIFI DAC Audio Sound Card Module** (`http://www.amazon.com/Arducam-Audio-Module-Interface-Raspberry/dp/B013JZI3DS`)

You can find other options for DAC boards by searching for "Raspberry Pi DAC".   **NOTE**

Raspberry Pi Sound Input/Output

The Raspberry Pi supplies two types of connector for getting sound into and out of it: the audio output jack and the HDMI jack.

Audio Output Jack

The Raspberry Pi board provides a standard 3.5mm audio stereo jack. Here you can plug in headphones, powered speakers or anything else that takes and plays audio input and matches the connections of the jack.

A limitation of this output is the quality of sound. The audio out from this connector, as specs state, is 11-bit. (For truly good sounding music you want 16-bit or 24-bit.)

No worries, though: like other Raspberry Pi limitations, solutions abound. For example, you can add a generic USB/audio adapter. One of these adapters puts out better sound and allows for microphone *input* as well. This lets you use the Raspberry Pi as a voice or music recorder, or teach it to work via voice commands, and so forth. Alternatively, as mentioned earlier in the chapter, an external DAC board is the yellow brick road to high-end quality sound.

HDMI

HDMI was developed in the early 2000s as a method of transferring high-quality video and audio to playback devices. A number of versions exist, but they all use the same cable and connectors. The Raspberry Pi includes an HDMI connector on its board.

> **NOTE** HDMI is a proprietary interface owned by a consortium of large flat-screen TV manufacturers. The development of HDMI technology paralleled and contributed to the rise of these big entertainment devices. Big screens require better picture quality, and home theatre sound systems require better audio.

There's nothing as fine as a nice big display that shows the colourful graphic user interface (GUI) of the Raspberry Pi and enables you to watch videos, play games and do all the stuff you expect a computer to do. The best solution involves HDMI, and here are two of the advantages of using HDMI output:

- HDMI allows the transfer of video and audio from an HDMI-compliant display controller (think Raspberry Pi here) to compatible computer monitors, projectors, digital TVs or digital audio devices.

- HDMI's higher quality provides a marked advantage over composite video (such as what comes out of the yellow or sometimes black connector on the Raspberry Pi board). This also provides a display that's much easier on the eyes and provides higher resolution instead of composite video's noisy and sometimes distorted video and/or audio.

> **WARNING** It is important to know that HDMI-to-HDMI connections include *both* video and audio. For connections that convert HDMI to DVI (Digital Video Interface) or VGA (Video Graphics Array), only video goes through the connection. Your options for audio include a separate audio cable from the audio out port of the Raspberry Pi. Alternatively, some adapters recommended earlier in this chapter have audio ports. You still need to run an audio cable from the converter's connector to the audio input on the monitor or to separate speakers.

Remember, audio coming from the HDMI output of the Raspberry Pi is better quality than from the 3.5mm audio output jack. Although it might seem like a good idea to plug in nice computer speakers that include a built-in amplifier, or any other powered speaker, the best method employs the Raspberry Pi's onboard I^{2}S to a separate DAC.

Sound on the Raspberry Pi

Do not mistake our suggestion of using an external DAC for a complaint that the Raspberry Pi has bad sound. It does not. It has *great* sound features. In this section, we look at the

Raspberry Pi's onboard sound hardware and then see how this fantastic little computer enables us to manipulate sound in all sorts of good ways.

Raspberry Pi Sound on Board

As of the Raspberry Pi 2, all of the Raspberry Pi 2's magic occurs in the Broadcom BM2535 system-on-a-chip (SoC). Among other things, this chip provides the following three things that provide the Raspberry Pi 2's audio features:

- DAC conversion providing left and right stereo analog audio for the 3.5mm jack

- HDMI digital audio

- Support of I^{2}S audio transport

Now that you know where the magic happens, it's time to do something practical, such as editing audio.

Manipulating Sound on the Raspberry Pi

As mentioned in Chapter 8, Raspbian (a version of Debian Linux optimised for the Raspberry Pi) is a good starting point for installing as an operating system. The audio editing techniques in this section work in most Linux distros on the Raspberry Pi, but we have used Raspbian for our examples.

Selecting Audio Devices

Like many devices with powerful modern operating systems, the Raspberry Pi recognises several methods of achieving most goals. For example, there's more than one way to select the audio device.

The Raspberry Pi comes with two methods of audio playback. The first is analog stereo with digital files converted to work with headphones or speakers. The second is HDMI, which features higher-quality digital sound. A 4-pole connector is supplied for analog audio output and there's also an HDMI connector for cabling to TVs, stereo systems and other HDMI-enabled devices.

The default output method is to use the 4-pole 3.5mm socket on the Raspberry Pi board (video output possible in addition to sound). As explained earlier in this chapter, using a standard 3-pole mini stereo plug, such as those on the end of headphones or computer speakers, works by design also, so you can use any powered computer speakers and your Raspberry Pi will sound good.

Making a Permanent Change

Let's say you're using the Raspberry Pi as an entertainment centre controller hooked to a TV and/or stereo system. In that case, manually selecting HDMI after booting the Raspberry Pi would become a pain. Here's the solution for that:

1. Open the command-line terminal (usually the little TV-like icon with a black screen).

2. Type the command `sudo raspi-config`. (The `sudo` means super user do, giving you permission to change configuration—in this case the way the board boots up.)

3. After the Raspberry Pi Software Configuration Tool screen appears (see Figure 11-5), use the down arrow key and select 9 Advanced Options. Press Enter.

4. Select A9 Audio.

5. On the Choose the Audio Output screen, select 2 Force HDMI.

6. Click OK and then click Finish.

7. Reboot the Raspberry Pi.

From now on, the Raspberry Pi boots up with the HDMI as the default audio output device.

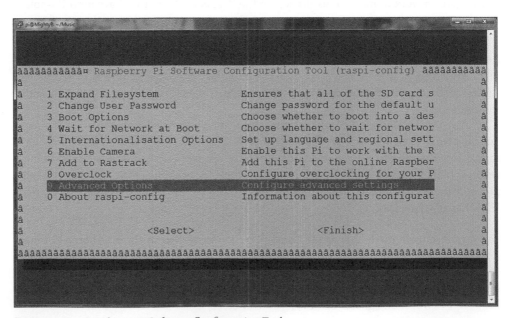

FIGURE 11-5: Raspberry Pi Software Configuration Tool

Selecting Output Manually

Manual selection of how you want sound output from a Raspberry Pi is easy. To begin simply, we can use the omxplayer utility, which is included in Raspbian. This player not only plays standard audio digital file formats such as `.wav` and `.mp3` but it also plays video formats including `.mp4` and `.avi`.

`.mp3` is a very popular format for music, but it's a proprietary format. To play it, you'll need to install an encoder/decoder, such as lame. It's free. Install it using the command **NOTE**

```
sudo apt-get install lame
```

Then omxplayer plays MP3s without further effort on your part.

The omxplayer utility has no GUI capability, so you use it in the terminal with command-line instructions. For example, you invoke omxplayer with only the name of a digital file. The command

```
omxplayer Beethoven_Ode_To_Joy.wav
```

plays the file on the default device, depending on what you've set in the procedure described in the preceding section.

The command

```
omxplayer -local Beethoven_Ode_To_Joy.wav
```

produces output to the 3.5mm audio connector and the command

```
omxplayer -hdmi Beethoven_Ode_To_Joy.wav
```

produces output to the HDMI connector.

The omxplayer utility contains many other options. Type its name in the terminal without parameters to get a list of these.

Playing Audio

A number of media players—software that plays both audio and video files—exist for the Raspberry Pi. These allow operation from the desktop in your operating system. On Raspbian, a good starting point is XiX. You can download the Linux ARM version and installation instructions at www.xixmusicplayer.org.

| NOTE | Media players should not be confused with media centre software. The latter does much more in setting up libraries and all the other functions expected of a media centre in selecting and serving entertainment. Some of the major software packages for PC and Mac also have versions that run on the Raspberry Pi, such as XBMC and Kodi. |

As previously mentioned, the Raspberry Pi is certainly capable of better sound than it outputs through the 3.5mm audio connector or even the HDMI output. An inexpensive (and we mean *really inexpensive*) method involves adding a USB sound card (which is less than £7 from major online retailers). Many of these have microphone input in addition to speaker/ headphone output. They are similar to the sound cards in PCs and have many of the same features, albeit in a smaller package.

These inexpensive USB sound card dongles do not require drivers. To install one, power down your Raspberry Pi, plug the dongle into a USB receptacle, and then boot up the Raspberry Pi.

You also need to switch the audio output device to the USB sound card. You can't use the omxplayer utility for that because it currently doesn't support USB sound. Instead, use a player called aplay. Like omxplayer, aplay is controlled through the command line using a terminal utility.

Use these steps to get aplay on Raspbian:

1. Type the following in the command line:

   ```
   sudo apt-get install aplay
   ```

2. Get the device number for your USB sound card by typing the following on the command line:

   ```
   aplay -l
   ```

| NOTE | The parameter in that command is not the digit one (1) but a lowercase L (l). |

Look for the device number of the USB sound card and make a note of it. The listing on our test Raspberry Pi 2 shows several lines, but the following two show the sound devices:

```
card 0: ALSA [bcm2835 ALSA], device 1: bcm2835 ALSA [bcm2835
  IEC958/HDMI]

card 1: Device [C-Media USB Audio Device], device 0: USB Audio
  [USB Audio]
```

The first, `card 0`, has 2835 in it; that's the number of the Broadcom SoC, so we can deduce it's the default sound output that came as part of our Raspberry Pi. The second, `card 1`, tells us it's a C-Media USB Audio Device.

3. Get the device number, which is a little confusing because `card 1` is considered *device 0* (because it's the second card going to the first device—computer cards, devices, disks and so on often start numbering at 0 instead of 1). With that information, you're ready to play music with your headphones or powered speakers plugged into the USB dongle itself.

4. Find the PCM method for your USB sound card by typing the following command (this time using an uppercase "L"):

```
aplay -L
```

> **NOTE**
> PCM is the format generated by the Raspberry Pi when converting a digital file into an analog sound output. You are going to use the `-D` option to specify a PCM method.

You see several lines of output. Look at the two listings showing the name of your USB device. In our test here using C-Media, the first line sends the digital signal without conversion. This is useful if you have a device plugged in, such as one of the DACs discussed earlier in the chapter. However, headphones, speakers and audio inputs to TVs and stereo sets are generally still analog, so you want PCM audio coming out of the USB dongle.

```
hw:CARD=Device,DEV=0

    C-Media USB Audio Device, USB Audio

    Direct hardware device without any conversions

plughw:CARD=Device,DEV=0

    C-Media USB Audio Device, USB Audio

    Hardware device with all software conversions
```

For this example, `plughw:CARD=Device,DEV=0` is the information you need for the `-D` parameter required to the desired digital file (`Beethoven Ode to Joy.wav`, in this example).

5. Use the following command to play an audio file through the USB sound card:

```
aplay -D plughw:CARD=Device,DEV=0 Beethoven_Ode_To_Joy.wav
```

Wait, we need one more item of information. It lies in the *-D* stuff above. As in omxplayer and many other utilities you'll encounter, entering its name without parameters generates a list of its available commands. Doing that and looking at the -D line, we find:

```
-D  --device=NAME       select PCM by name
```

You'll probably want to install a player with a nice GUI and run it from the desktop. Many players have a desktop icon you can click to switch the audio output.

Installing a Powerful Free Sound Editor

A good choice for an all-around useful editor that runs as it is on Raspbian (and can be installed from Raspbian) is Audacity, which you can download from `www.audacityteam.org`.

Audacity is a useful tool for all sorts of purposes, such as producing blogs, creating multi-layered sound effects, grabbing cuts of audio for presentations, and so forth.

To install Audacity on your Raspberry Pi, make sure the board is connected to the Internet and type:

```
sudo apt-get install audacity
```

Click the Menu button (which is next to the raspberry on the Raspbian GUI) and then type the command `audacity` in the Run box. The program starts and displays a screen like the example shown in Figure 11-6. An audio file of Beethoven's stirring "Ode to Joy" (a `.wav` digital audio file) is already loaded in and ready to edit.

Editing an audio file is very similar to using a word processor to edit a text document. You insert the cursor where you want to make a change, hold down the left mouse button and drag to select an area of the wave form. Click the Delete button to erase the selected section, and the waveform is shortened seamlessly. The copy, paste and undo functions all work very much the same as they do in the word processor.

Audacity includes lots of effects, and you can download and install more. Figure 11-7 shows a few of the included effects. Click Help on the menu bar for information on how and why to use them.

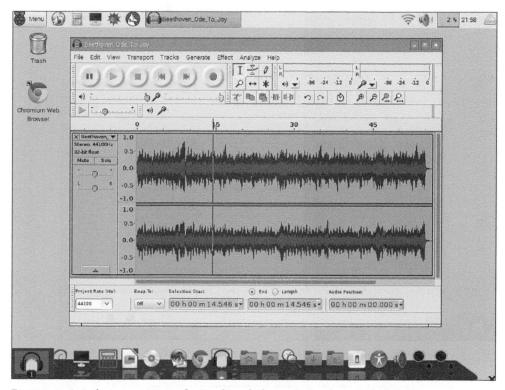

FIGURE 11-6: Audacity running on the Raspbian desktop of a Raspberry Pi 2 Model B

Figure 11-6 shows a stereo waveform with left and right channels, or two tracks. However, nothing limits you to only two tracks. Record yourself playing a guitar. Add in another track playing the same music on a banjo, on a trumpet, some drums, and so on. Sync it up, add a few effects, and you have a major musical production. Mix all the tracks down into left and right for stereo and you've got a hit on your hands.

Figure 11-8 shows four tracks in Audacity. The two original "Ode to Joy" tracks have been copied and pasted slightly offset into an additional two tracks. Playing the result gives an interesting sound—not good, kind of weird, but interesting.

Some Specifics of Encoding and Decoding

Audio and video files use standards called codecs. A *codec* is a device or software for encoding and/or decoding a digital stream or signal. Reasons for doing this include compressing a file to save space, encrypting for copy protection and improving playback. The Raspberry Pi hardware knows how to decode the most common formats. You can also add other formats as needed.

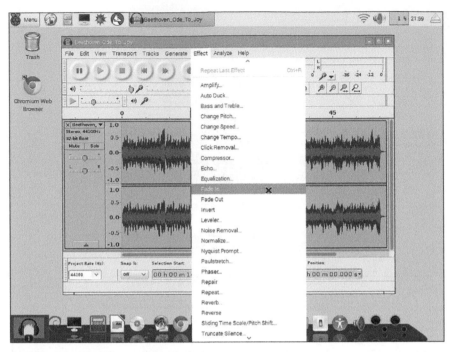

FIGURE 11-7: The Effect menu in Audacity

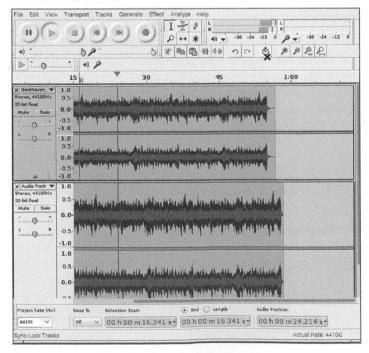

FIGURE 11-8: Additional tracks in Audacity

Chapter 12
Input/Output

WHEN WE DISTIL computerised data processing down to its very essence, we require only two things of our computers—*input* and *output*, or *I/O*. You put data and commands in, and you receive processed data out. It's a simple enough concept, but more than 70 years of electronic computers and the allied development of a veritable galaxy of peripheral devices make it more complicated.

This chapter attempts to demystify this complexity via an overview of I/O and the computer architecture behind it. Of course, there's special emphasis on the Raspberry Pi, with an eye to some practical uses.

We begin with a short history of interfaces and their related protocols. Next, we examine various I/O schemes involving UARTs, USB, SCSI, IDE/PATA, SATA, I²S, I²C, SPI, GPIO and others. Yes, that is a double handful of acronyms, but most of them provide rather elegant solutions to specific I/O needs that we define and explain in this chapter.

The chapter concludes with a Raspberry Pi-specific section on using general purpose input output (GPIO). The two rows of GPIO pins on all the Raspberry Pi models differentiate them from most computers. Using these programmable inputs and outputs allow this credit-card-sized board (even smaller in the case of the Raspberry Pi Zero) to control everything from a tiny blinking LED light to massive electric motors drawing thousands of watts of power.

So, let us meet those cybernetic brothers: input and output.

Introducing Input/Output

Computing devices have been around for a lot longer than many people realise. The abacus—that simple adding and subtracting instrument that uses beads strung on wires—most likely originated in Babylon in the mists of history, several centuries BC. The famous Antikythera device discovered in an ancient shipwreck appears to be a mechanism for predicting the movement of stars and planets, dating from about the first century BC. Tools like these work differently from modern computers, but they both take input and produce output.

The advent of modern I/O took place much more recently, and began with a mouse.

Early computing focused on things the computer was good at, essentially arithmetic calculations and data processing. However, for computers to become the universal helpmates they are today, better methods of input and output were needed. Punched cards and magnetic tape were slow. The advent of terminals where the operator typed text on a keyboard and the computer returned words on a screen was an improvement but it was still cumbersome, even after the keyboard became attached to the computer.

Computers and people needed a better interface. In addition, computers needed to talk with other computers (network) and exchange various forms of data at great speeds *accurately*. Therefore, a proliferation of I/O hardware methods and communications protocols was developed. Those things are the basic subject matter of this chapter, but first we must consider the computer/human interface.

Two inventions changed the face (literally) of the computer: the graphical user interface (GUI) and the now ubiquitous mouse. Which came first? Somewhat surprisingly, it was the mouse, and it was a military secret!

The Mouse

A *mouse* is a computer peripheral that detects two-dimensional motion on a flat surface and converts it into the movement of a cursor (an arrow or other graphic on a computer's screen). Clicking the mouse's button or buttons results in various commands transmitted to the computer.

Early mice used a small rubberised ball to sense motion. Most mice today employ use LED light sources and an array of photo sensors. Many now are also wireless, eliminating the cord coming out of the back like a real mouse's tail (the source of the device's name).

Douglas Engelbart and his team at the Stanford Research Institute developed and named the original mouse in the 1960s (see Figure 12-1). Engelbart did much more than just make today's many varieties of mice possible, but he's a hero to all of us who make our daily bread by moving a mouse around on our desk.

If the mouse is such a great idea, why wasn't it invented sooner? Well, like many great concepts, precursors to the mouse did exist. In 1941, Ralph Benjamin developed a trackball to control a fire-control radar plotting system for the Royal Navy. The fire-control system originally used a joystick device and analog computers in calculating the future position of aircraft for targeting. Benjamin decided a better input method was required and invented a trackball, which he called a "roller ball". In the 1950s, the Royal Canadian Navy controlled digital computer systems with trackballs. Both of these uses fell under the cloak of military secrecy and didn't spread to the larger computing world.

So, Doug Engelbart independently invented the mouse. Sadly, he never received a cent in royalties, but we all owe him our thanks for his immense contribution to computer I/O. With Engelbart's invention, we now had a means of pointing, and computers needed something to make pointing useful. Enter the GUI.

The Graphical User Interface

A graphical user interface (GUI, pronounced "gooey") lets us interact with computers and other devices by the use of text, icons and other visual indicators. The older text-only displays often required the typing of long, counter-intuitive commands as opposed to the faster and easier GUI solution of pointing and clicking.

Doug Engelbart made another contribution. This time, it was his turn to provide us with the precursor to something, in this case text-based hyperlinks/hypertext (*a la* the Internet) that could be clicked on using a mouse (which, thanks to him, already existed) making the link do something, like take you to another screen or perform a command.

From there, Palo Alto Research Center (PARC, owned by Xerox) and Alan Kay, one of the key researchers at PARC, moved computers past text-based hyperlinks and into the world of GUIs. In 1973, the Xerox Alto computer was released. It was the first computer to use a GUI as its main interface, and it accepted input from both the keyboard and a pointing device. This GUI, called the PARC user interface, had elements that are familiar to us today—windows, menus, buttons and check boxes.

The first GUI didn't include icons. Icons came along later thanks to one of Alan Kay's team, David Smith. **NOTE**

It took several years for GUIs to become available on the market. The first commercial release of a computer with a GUI was the Xerox Star 8010 in 1981 (see Figure 12-1). In 1983, Apple got into the game and produced the first Apple with a GUI, the Lisa. Lisa was not an outright success, but it did introduce a menu bar and windows controls, which are things we take for granted in today's GUIs.

FIGURE 12-1: Xerox Star 8010, commercial GUI

Then, in 1984, Apple released the Macintosh computer, which was *truly* the game changer for GUIs. Given the success of the Mac, several other computer manufacturers and software companies were looking at GUI. Atari and Commodore joined their ranks in 1985, and Microsoft pushed out Windows 1.0 later that same year. No one's looked back since.

Today, most operating systems—Windows, Linux, Mac, Android, iOS, you name it—sport GUIs as their primary interface with humans. Advantages of GUIs include:

- They're easy to use, especially for newcomers to computing.
- What you see is what you get (WYSIWYG, pronounced "wizzywig"), meaning that what you see on the screen is exactly how the printed product will look.
- They usually provide Help facilities.
- They can be used without long strings of commands. You just point to a menu and click to see a list of possible commands.

Server installations worldwide still use commands typed at the command line, and those commands are exceptionally useful and worth learning. **NOTE**

- They offer simple ways of moving data between applications, such as drag and drop or copy and paste.

- They allow photos and other graphics to be easily manipulated.

Of course, like anything, GUIs also have disadvantages:

- They require more RAM (working memory).

- They take up more space on hard drives or other permanent storage, such as the Raspberry Pi's microSD.

- They require more overheads for software developers to create them.

GUIs dominate computer operating systems and have made it easier for humans to interact with computers. Yet computers talk not only to us but also to all sorts of devices, both locally and over networks. So let's look at some very important types of I/O and the computer architecture supporting them.

I/O Enablers

The concept of computer I/O devices, also called computer *peripherals*, consists of devices that accept data input, output processed data, or perform both in and out functions.

Here's a simplification of how I/O devices work. They include *sensors*, which are often some sort of device that detects and responds to input from the physical environment. Sensors detect motion, temperature, changes in air or gas pressure and so on, and the sensors feed data or instructions to a computer for processing, storing or initiating a command. The computer may then (if required) present the results to a human or to a machine it controls. Basically, one or both of the following functions occur:

- **Input:** The device converts analog or digital data and instructions, sending an electrical signal in binary format (1s and 0s, digital format) to the computer.

- **Output:** The computer sends digital signals back to the device, which converts those signals into whatever format the device understands.

Table 12-1 lists some examples of I/O devices.

The next sections examine some specific ways I/O happens.

Table 12-1   **I/O Devices**

Input	Output	Input/Output
A mouse inputs signals from its movement on a two-dimensional surface.	Printers print pages sent from the computer.	A network card makes possible continuous communication with other computers on the network as well as on the Internet.
Keyboards report keys pressed.	Displays show a GUI with windows, menus, buttons, the mouse's moving cursor and so on.	Disk drives store and retrieve data via a Serial AT Attachment (SATA) or other type of interface.
Motion sensors report true or false that a motion has occurred.	On the detection of motion in a secure area, the computer causes a siren to sound and/or alerts a designated human guard.	USB peripherals send status and receive commands from the operating system assisted by the driver program for that device.

Universal Serial Bus

Universal Serial Bus (USB) is a method of both input and output. Where the Raspberry Pi is concerned, it is not by accident that the newer models boast four USB plugs (see Figure 12-2) because USB has become indispensable. You'll find four ports a bare minimum for many projects.

FIGURE 12-2: The four USB receptacles on the Raspberry Pi 2

USB allows easy and convenient connection of all sorts of devices, including keyboards, mice and other pointing devices, portable hard drives and thumb drives, network adapters, microphones, CD and DVD drives and much, much more. Even smartphones and game consoles include USB plugs these days.

We begin with some history of USB and its evolution through the various versions (1.0, 1.1, 2.0, 3.0 and 3.1) and then we then offer some detail on the versatility of USB for the Raspberry Pi.

History of USB

Beginning in the early 1980s, the explosive popularisation of personal computing meant a vast proliferation of peripherals was developed for this lucrative market. This often created a rat's nest of cables and power supplies behind computers and spilling off the desk and onto the floor.

USB came about to standardise and eliminate much of this clutter. USB replaced and/or consolidated many earlier types of interface. Parallel ports, serial ports and many separate power supplies landed in the dustbin of computer history, thanks to USB plugs, power and other standards.

USB, as an industry standard, was first released in the mid-1990s. The standard specifies the necessary cables, connectors, communications protocols and the power supply between computers and peripheral devices. All of the preceding specifications enable USB to be implemented by many manufacturers and work interchangeably.

Originally, a consortium of seven companies—Compaq, DEC, IBM, Intel, Microsoft, NEC and Nortel—pushed the development of USB. Today, the developers and maintainers of the USB standard (the current version is version 3.1) form the USB Implementers Forum, which is a non-profit organisation.

Versions of USB

There have been three releases of USB standards:

- **USB 1.x:** USB 1.0 was the first release in 1996. It provided specified data rates of 1.5 Mbit/s (megabits per second, low bandwidth, low speed) and 12 Mbit/s at full bandwidth (also referred to as "full speed"). USB 1.1 followed in 1998 and corrected problems that had become apparent in 1.0, especially in hubs.

  In addition to fixing problems, USB 1.1 became widely accepted and implemented by computer manufacturers, leading to "legacy-free" PCs. A *legacy-free PC* is one in which the floppy drive controller, parallel printer port, RS-232 serial port, game ports and Industry Standard Architecture (ISA) expansion bus were all replaced by USB ports.

This enabled the building of simpler PCs and contributed to driving prices down, a major impact of USB.

- **USB 2.0:** This version arrived in 2001. It features a higher data transfer rate of 480 Mbit/s, which is 40 times faster than version 1.1.

- **USB 3.0:** In 2008 the USB standard got another huge speed increase, this time up to 5 Gbit/s (gigabits per second—that's fast). This version of the standard also had lower power consumption and increased power output, and it was backward compatible with USB 2.0. The first computers and other devices with actual 3.0 ports, called SuperSpeed ports, came out in 2010. If you see a USB port on your computer with a small SS over it and a blue plastic guide inside, it's a USB 3.0 port. Of course, if it is labelled "USB 3.0", that's a pretty good indicator as well. December 2014 saw the approval of USB 3.1 standards with increased speed, this time a blistering 10 Gbit/s.

USB Architecture

USB design includes a host controller that allows for numerous USB ports with multiple devices attached in a tiered star topology. Star networks (see Figure 12-3) are one of the most common arrangements, in which a central computer or hub controls communication with the devices around it. It is a client-server set up. This configuration's advantages emphasise reliability; if one client or connection drops out, the other connections are not affected.

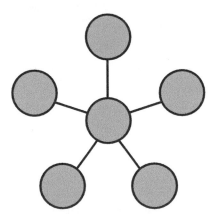

FIGURE 12-3: Star configuration

Adding to the flexibility of the network topology is the fact that any physical USB device may have subdevices, which makes it possible for one device to have several functions. For example, a webcam with a built-in microphone has a video device function and an audio function. We call these *composite* devices (that is, they're composed of more than one function).

The USB standard also includes *device classes*, which are software drivers for class codes and give the USB host the ability to connect easily to the various classes of devices supported. This gives the host the ability to recognise devices from different manufacturers so long as those devices provide the standard device codes.

Device classes include:

- **Audio:** Speaker, microphone, sound card, MIDI
- **Communications:** Modem, network adapter, Wi-Fi, RS232 serial adapter
- **Human interface:** Mouse, keyboard, joystick, trackball
- **Image:** Webcam, scanner
- **Printer:** Laser printer, inkjet, and CNC (Computer Numerical Control) using in automating machinery.
- **Mass storage:** USB flash drive, memory card reader, digital audio player digital camera, external hard drive
- **USB hub:** Controls connected USB devices that are connected to the hub
- **Video:** Webcam, surveillance cameras, consumer and professional video cameras and so on

In addition, there are other classes such as those for personal healthcare devices, compliance testing devices, smartcard readers, fingerprint readers and test measurements.

On the Raspberry Pi boards are two large surface mount chips. The largest is the Broadcom SoC 2835 on the first models and 2836 with four-core central processing unit (CPU) on the Raspberry Pi 2 and the new Raspberry Pi 3. The second, somewhat smaller chip is a SMSC LAN9512 USB hub and Ethernet controller. This latter chip handles the USB and networking services.

USB Powered Hubs

USB ports allow you to plug in and running a keyboard, a mouse and all sorts of other devices, including big hard drives. However, as we touched on in the introduction to this chapter, onboard USB also has current limits. In the case of the Model B, it should only be used for low-power devices.

When you exceed the power limits of the on-board USB, bad things happen, such as possible damage to components. Consider adding a powered USB hub for high current requirements. **WARNING**

If you've used the Model B, the lack of enough USB ports (the official name is "receptacle") is probably aggravating. After you plug in a keyboard and a mouse, you are stuck—there's no more room at the inn. In addition, if you use the wrong mouse or keyboard—that is, those with high current drain—it could cause the board's power supply to shut down.

USB Power

The USB 1.x and 2.0 specifications approved by the USB Implementers Forum allow for 5 volts direct current (VDC) from USB hubs on one wire for powering USB-connected devices. The variance in voltage is limited to a range of 4.75 VDC to 5.25 VDC. In USB 3.0, the variance increases to 4.25 VDC to 5.25 VDC.

As we have mentioned, the Raspberry Pi Model B current is limited compared to later models. The newer "+" models have proper USB power handling. A hub before 2.0 allocates a maximum of five unit loads (500 milliamperes [mA]) to a connected device or 750mA under USB 3.0. Slightly complicating these current limits, two types of devices exist: low power and high power. A low power device can draw at most only one unit load. A high power device usually operates as a low power one but can request more current and get it if available at the time from the hub.

> **NOTE** The current sourcing abilities of almost all USB ports differ from what the specs mention. The specs state, for instance, that without negotiation, a USB 2.0 device is allocated only 100mA (with negotiation up to 500mA). Negotiation for additional power comes through the Power Delivery protocols interfaced through a bidirectional data channel to control the power supply.
>
> The reality is most boards/power supplies ignore this spec and source whatever 5V VDC is available in the system. Devices such as high-speed external hard drives may require *more* power than is available via the Raspberry Pi's USB receptacles. In such cases, the device may have a Y-cable with two USB plugs. Connecting to two USB receptacles, in the USB specs at least, raises the maximum current load to 1 amp for USB 2.0 and earlier versions or 1.5 amp for USB 3.0.

Of course, the hub must be able to supply this amount of current. Using the USB controller on a Raspberry Pi, you *do not* have unlimited load. The solution involves adding an external hub with its own power supply and greater current-supplying capacity than the Raspberry Pi by itself.

Rapsberry Pi USB Power Solution

The Model B+ and the Raspberry Pi 2 come with four USB ports! Now, don't do a happy dance across the room just yet. Although having four USB ports instead of two does add flexibility and offers more current, there are still limitations. A good powered USB hub, like the one shown in Figure 12-4, is a way to work around those limitations.

FIGURE 12-4: A USB powered hub

Such hubs usually have seven or more ports and receive power through a wall plug. Thus, you get power to run hard drives and other juice-hungry devices without overtaxing your Raspberry Pi board's limited resources.

> Be sure to choose a powered USB hub that supports the Raspberry Pi. Do an Internet search for "powered USB hub" for lists of manufacturers and model numbers. **NOTE**

Ethernet

Ethernet in general consists of several computer-networking technologies. First introduced in 1980 and standardised in 1983 as IEEE 802.3, its development has been continuous since that time. Speeds have increased from 2.94 Mbit/s to 100 Gbit/s (gigabytes per second). By 2017, a speed of 400 Gbit/s is planned.

Networks enabled by Ethernet stream data in short pieces called "frames". A frame includes source addresses (where it comes from) and destination addresses (where it's going). Error-checking data causes the frame to be discarded if it arrives corrupted. In the case of a corrupted frame, a resend request can be triggered so that no data is lost.

Network Configurations

Similar to the way USB hubs control devices in a star configuration, networks (which were first to use the star topology) have clients connected to a hub. Hubs may be "bridged" (a connection made to another star configuration) to add more networks, both local and remote. The result is a vast collection of interconnected networks, which we call the Internet.

Raspberry Pi Networking

There are two ways to achieve network connectivity with the Raspberry Pi. The first is a wired connection that uses the Ethernet socket on the Raspberry Pi (excluding the Raspberry Pi Zero, which does not have an Ethernet socket). Figure 12-5 shows the socket, which accepts a standard network cable plug. The Ethernet port on the Raspberry Pi supports connections of 100 megabits per second (Mbit/s).

FIGURE 12-5: Ethernet port on the Raspberry Pi 2 Model B

The second way of connecting to the network involves the USB ports. You can use a wireless USB dongle (a dongle is a plug-in device) or a USB-to-Ethernet adapter. The USB wireless device allows easy connection to Wi-Fi networks in the area, and the USB-to-Ethernet effects a physical connection by providing a socket for a standard Ethernet cable.

A wireless dongle is handy if you want your Raspberry Pi to be portable. With an external battery power supply and wireless access, you can carry it anywhere! That is, you can carry it anywhere with wireless access, which is true for more and more places these days.

All sorts of tasks require a connection to both your local network and the Internet. Upgrading the operating system and the Raspberry Pi's firmware require Internet access, unless you decide to swap out the SD card as an alternative. Downloading and installing programs, web surfing, using the Raspberry Pi as a media centre to deliver movies to your flat-screen TV and many other tasks make networking a necessity.

Universal Asynchronous Receiver/Transmitters

Universal asynchronous receiver/transmitters (UARTs) use a set of registers to accept and output data. Older UARTs could translate data between parallel and serial formats, but modern UARTs do not have this capacity. The personal computers of yesteryear used to have serial ports as a standard feature. The now ancient (in computer years) RS-232 serial format (which ran these ports) is implemented via a UART. Serial ports such as these can still be found on various industrial instruments.

The UART works by breaking down bytes of data into their individual bits and sending those serially (one after the other). At the destination, the receiving UART reassembles the bytes. The advantage of serial transmission over parallel transmission lies in its cost; just a single wire is required. The Broadcom SoC on the Raspberry Pi has two UARTs.

A common use for UARTs is in microcontrollers, and the Raspberry Pi excels as a control device. The Raspberry Pi's onboard UART comes inside the Broadcom SoC containing the CPU (or CPUs), graphics processing units (GPUs) and all those other goodies. It's accessed and is programmable using the GPIO's pin 8 (transmit) and pin 10 (receive).

Read more on the GPIO in the last section of this chapter.

Small Computer Systems Interface

Small Computer Systems Interface (SCSI) provides standards for moving data to and from computers and peripherals, especially hard drives (although it's also good for scanners and other devices). SCSI has been around since the early 1980s and was once the gold standard of hard drive interfacing.

SCSI transfers data in parallel. To use it with a Raspberry Pi, such as by adding a SCSI drive, is possible via USB but a serial-to-parallel adapter cable is required. Such adapter cables cost about £15 and are readily available from major online computer parts retailers.

SCSI is very much on the way out, and it's unlikely that you'll find a use for it. **NOTE**

Parallel ATA

The Parallel Advanced Technology Attachment (PATA) standard is also known by several names:

- Integrated Drive Electronics (IDE)
- Extended Integrated Drive Electronics (EIDE)
- Ultra Advanced Technology Attachment (Ultra ATA)

No matter what you call it, PATA is an interface standard for connecting and passing data to and from hard disks, floppy disk drives and optical disc drives in computers. It has gone through many incremental developments and, like SCSI, it has been superseded by other standards. (See the next section on SATA.)

PATA cables have one significant limitation: they can be no longer than 18 inches. Because of this restriction, their primary use was as interfaces inside computer cases. Because PATA cables were the least-expensive solution for passing data to and from hard drives especially during the late 1980s to early 1990s, they were widely used.

If you have old PATA drives that you'd like to hang off your Raspberry Pi board, you can use a conversion cable to make the connection. The cables aren't expensive—less than £15 for a set of conversion cables that will handle IDE/PATA and/or SATA.

> **NOTE** Remember that any time you add something to the Raspberry Pi that draws the type of current a hard drive does, you should use a powered USB hub as discussed earlier.

Serial Advanced Technology Attachment

Serial Advanced Technology Attachment (SATA) devices communicate over a serial cable using two pairs of conductors. Its primary use connects computers and other devices to hard disk and optical drives. Two important advantages of SATA over SCSI and PATA are that it is speedier and uses less wiring, especially in the case of the older IDE interfaces.

In the late 1980s and 1990s, drives were installed in PCs with flat, grey, multi-conductor ribbon cables. The cables usually sported a red stripe on one side so people would know which way they plugged into the ribbon connector (to avoid possible damage to hardware). Because the data interchange was parallel, such cables required many conductors. SATA has replaced PATA in consumer and most business devices. However, some industrial and other uses of embedded flash memory still use the older PATA interfaces.

The current version of SATA, Revision 3.2, features communication speeds of 16 Gbit/s and actual data transfer of 1969 MB/s. As mentioned earlier, several inexpensive adapters exist for converting SATA drives to USB, which makes it possible to connect SATA devices to the Raspberry Pi via its USB receptacles. Here's another reminder that you should use a powered hub to make sure the drive gets adequate power and to reduce the chance of causing damage to the Raspberry Pi due to current overload.

RS-232 Serial

RS-232—a long-time standard for the serial transmission of data—was *the* standard and common on many personal computers in the 1980s and 1990s. Before PCs, RS-232 provided communications with terminals like the ones used to control mainframes and minicomputers.

All sorts of other peripherals once connected via RS-232 serial ports—printers, mice and other pointing devices, modems and more. However, RS-232 had some disadvantages:

- Variations in voltage due to long cables and mismatched transceivers

- Speed limitations

- Large, bulky connectors

USB came along in large part to cure these three disadvantages. RS-232 is still around, however, as connectors with industrial machines, as control ports in large networking devices and on various scientific instruments.

TTL (Transistor-Transistor Logic) level serial is what almost everyone uses these days. It's sometimes mistakenly referred to as RS2232.   **NOTE**

High Definition Media Interface

High Definition Multimedia Interface (HDMI) allows the transfer of video and audio from an HDMI-compliant display controller (think Raspberry Pi here) to compatible computer monitors, projectors, digital TVs or digital audio devices.

HDMI's high quality provides a marked advantage over composite video (such as what comes out of the composite video connector on the Raspberry Pi board). HDMI provides higher resolution instead of composite video's noisy and sometimes distorted picture.

Most TVs sold today include HDMI input ports, as do higher-end video monitors. If you don't have a TV that has an HDMI port, no problem. Here are two solutions for getting HDMI into non-HDMI devices:

- **Digital Video Interface (DVI):** You'll find computer monitors with DVI inputs more common than ones accepting HDMI. Just search online retailers for "hdmi to dvi" and you'll find several solutions (cables and adapter plugs) in the £4 to £7 range.

- **Video Graphics Array (VGA):** Most common of all are VGA monitors. A search for "hdmi female to vga male" will get you the right adapter in the £4 to £7 range. This is an active conversion; there is actually some circuitry inside the adapter cable that converts digital signals to analog. In the case of HDMI to DVI, it's just a remapping of digital signals; HDMI to VGA is more complicated and not as robust.

It is important to know that HDMI-to-HDMI connections include *both* video and audio. For connections converting HDMI to DVI or VGA, you will find only video goes through the connection. Your options for audio include a separate audio cable from the audio out port of the Raspberry Pi. Alternatively, some adapters have audio ports. You still need to run an audio cable from the converter's connector to the audio input on the monitor or to separate speakers. However, connecting the cable to the HDMI output of the Raspberry Pi gives better quality. This is the easy way to do it.

I²S

Inter-IC Sound (I²S), a communications protocol for carrying digital audio signals, is a type of serial bus interface standard that connects digital audio devices together. (You can read more about I²S in Chapter 11.) This protocol came from the Dutch technology giant Philips in 1986 as an internal feature of its CD players. The last revision happened in 1996 but this does not hamper its utility.

The following are some choices for good audio from the Raspberry Pi. Which is the correct answer?

A. Use audio output from the 3.5mm audio jack, which comes from Pulse Wave Modulation (PWM) in converting from digital to analog. It's limited to about 11 bits, a rate causing some to turn up their noses (or ears) at it.

B. HDMI, which is supposedly "high definition".

C. USB.

D. Hook a good digital audio converter (DAC) with I²S directly to the Raspberry Pi.

The answer, of course is "D".

However, where do you hook it? There's no discrete connector plug for I²S on the Raspberry Pi board. Instead, you use the GPIO pins, and you can do that the hard way or the easy way.

The hard way is by using jumper cables to directly access the needed GPIO pins. Four give you access to the I²S interface on the Broadcom SoC chip that has the CPU, GPU and so on.

The easy way is by purchasing one of the DAC units mentioned at the end of Chapter 11. They simply plug onto the GPIO pins and piggyback the Raspberry Pi board, providing a short, noise-free connection with that golden quality sound.

Some configuration is required to turn on and set up the I²S interface. One method is to use Python on Raspbian or a similar Linux-based operating system on the Raspberry Pi. You'll find a good deal of help on the web for achieving great sound from your Raspberry Pi on the Internet. You can search "raspberry pi sound" for tips and devices.

I²C

The I²C (Inter-Integrated Circuit) communications protocol also comes from Philips. I²C is a communications bus, providing communications between chips on a printed circuit board. One of its prime uses on the Raspberry Pi board and elsewhere lies in connecting sensors.

I²C is not initialised when the Raspberry Pi first comes out of the box. You have to tell the Raspberry Pi to use it. You accomplish this under the Raspbian OS (and other operating systems) with the `raspi-config` command in the terminal. On the command line, type

```
sudo raspi-config
```

Use the down arrow key to select 9 Advanced Options and press the Enter key. On the next screen, select A7 I2C to toggle the automatic loading of I2C on or off. (See Figure 12-6.) A reboot is required each time for the new state to take effect.

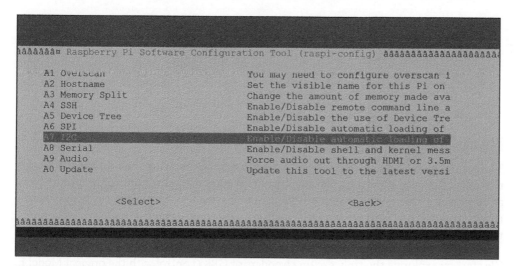

FIGURE 12-6: Enabling I²C on Raspberry Pi using `raspi-config`

As with most interfaces related to the GPIO pins, many of which enable connection to services on the Broadcom SoC, some programming is required. The steps in shell scripts or Python (one of the favoured methods of GPIO-programmed control) are beyond the scope of this book, but there are many examples on the web. You can search for "raspberry pi gpio python scripts".

Raspberry Pi Display, Camera Interface and JTAG

Before we get to GPIO, we have two more interfaces to mention. These two interfaces connect with ribbon cable connectors:

- **Camera Serial Interface (CSI)** (the MIPI CSI-2 standard): This interface allows the connection of a camera. Cameras for the Raspberry Pi are available. It is sometimes a bit irksome to connect the ribbon cable just right, but once things are hooked up properly you can program the Raspberry Pi to do all sorts of neat stuff with digital photography and video. Camera boards/modules cost about £25, so experimenting is possible at a reasonable cost.

- **Display Serial Interface (DSI):** This interface enables you to connect small displays to the Raspberry Pi board. This makes the Raspberry Pi, along with a battery power source, truly portable. A simple LED device costs about £9 whereas the official Raspberry Pi 7-inch touchscreen LCD monitor costs £65.

> **NOTE** The JTAG Header for debugging was on the older Raspberry Pi boards but isn't on the Raspberry Pi 2. JTAG provides facilities for debugging using techniques such as stepping through code and using break points (stopping at various places in the code). JTAG on newer boards is available via GPIO pins.

Raspberry Pi GPIO

The general purpose input output (GPIO) performs magic in tying the Raspberry Pi to the real world. Through these pins, the Raspberry Pi is programmed to control microcontrollers and real-world devices—such as doorbells, light bulbs, model aircraft controls, lawn mowers, robots, thermostats, electric coffeepots, motors of all sorts—that normally cannot connect to a computer or follow its orders.

We start by exploring the truly exciting wonders of GPIO control with the original Model B (as opposed to the current Raspberry Pi 3). The Model B (see Figure 12-7) has fewer GPIO pins than the two next releases—the Model B+ and Raspberry Pi 2. The extra pins on those versions work the same but give added capacity—but let's keep it simple for the moment. The pin assignments for the first 26 pins remain the same on all models of the Raspberry Pi.

FIGURE 12-7: GPIO pins on Raspberry Pi 2

GPIO Overview and the Broadcom SoC

The key to making the Raspberry Pi possible at such an incredibly low price is the Broadcom system-on-a-chip (SoC). As previously mentioned, in this one chip live CPU(s), GPUs and various interfaces, including UART, I²C, SPI (Serial Peripheral Interface) and so forth. The GPIO pins allow us to program these interfaces and also do much more.

The GPIO pins (P1 on the Raspberry Pi boards—either 26 on earlier models or 40 on the newer ones) allow configuration (that is, they are *programmable*) in several ways, such as:

- General-purpose input

- General-purpose output

- Up to six alternative settings, depending on the pin

The following items apply to most pins, but some are used as positive voltage sources or grounds:

- **Power-on states:** GPIOs (depending on the operating system and firmware in use) reset to general-purpose inputs when the board is rebooted.

- **Interrupts:** Each pin is programmable to generate an interrupt to the Broadcom's CPUs/GPUs. These interrupts can be configured as:

  - Level-sensitive

  - Rising/falling edge

  - Asynchronous rising/falling edge.

■ **Alternative functions:** As mentioned earlier, almost all of the GPIO pins have alternative functions in addition to simple switching operations. These involve direct connections (through the pins) to Broadcom IoC. The peripherals in the SoC, such as the UART and I²C buses, can be programmable to at least three sets of pins.

> **NOTE** For more information on connecting to these low-level peripherals, visit `http://elinux.org/RPi_Low-level_peripherals`.

GPIO Header 1

GPIO 1 refers to the P1 connector on Raspberry Pi boards—either the 26 pins on Model A and Model Bs or the 40 pins on the B+, Raspberry Pi 2 Model B and the new Raspberry Pi Zero.

GPIO Header 5

GPIO 5 provides additional GPIO connections on the Model A and Model B via the P5 header. This header does not have pins, so any connection to it has to be soldered to the board. From the Model B+ on, additional pins added to the P1 header replace the P5 header.

Meeting the GPIO

The GPIO performs magic in tying the Raspberry Pi to the real world. Through these pins, you can program the Raspberry Pi to control all sorts of real-world devices. First, we'll examine these pins and understand just how simple and powerful they are. Then we'll look at programming the Raspberry Pi to understand inputs, outputs and control devices.

Pin Layout

Figure 12-8 shows the GPIO pins on the Model B.

There are 26 pins—two rows of 13 each. The bottom row pins (left to right) consist of odd numbers: 1, 3, 5, 7, 9, 11, 13, 15, 17, 19, 21, 23 and 25. The top row pins (left to right) are even numbered: 2, 4, 6, 8, 10, 12, 14, 16, 18, 20, 22, 24 and 26.

The pins, when set as outputs, act like switches and provide power, enabling the Raspberry Pi to interact with other devices and—in some cases—supply the electricity those devices need to run. Later in this chapter is an example of using the Raspberry Pi to flash some lights.

The IO in GPIO stands for input/output. When you have a device connected to the Raspberry Pi and flip an external switch or, more likely, some electrical or mechanical gizmo opens or closes, that's *input*. It's a changed condition causing a program running on the Raspberry Pi to respond with some sort of action.

FIGURE 12-8: Close-up of the Raspberry Pi Model B's 26 GPIO pins

Here's an example of both input and output. You build a home security project using a Raspberry Pi. Someone opens an outside door. A wireless magnetic switch closes. The Raspberry Pi picks up the signal and closes a circuit, causing a chime to go off during the day or a siren at night. The door switch changes state from closed to open when it detects the door is ajar. A program on the Raspberry Pi outputs a switch closing, which causes the chime or siren to sound. Both tasks are accomplished through connections to GPIO pins—two different circuits were completed.

Thanks to the Raspberry Pi's ability to communicate in various ways—such as by wireless, Bluetooth or the Internet—inputs and outputs do not even have to be local. Devices and programs can be controlled from anywhere in the world!   **NOTE**

Circuits closing and opening describe electronic control. See the "Circuits" sidebar for additional explanation of circuits.

GPIO Operation

A GPIO pin, such as the 17 out of 26 pins on the Raspberry Pi B's board that are programmable switches, works in *binary* mode. Binary is just a fancy way of saying "on" or "off". That's how digital computers compute—they have bunches of circuits tied together, and those circuits are either on or off. In computer talk, 0 represents *off* and the number 1 represents *on*. Programmers call the *state* of the circuit—whether it's on or off—*high* (on) and *low* (off).

Circuits

Electricity works in circles. (A closed loop is called a *circuit*.) A very simple circuit, as shown in Figure 12-11, consists of a battery (voltage source) and a resistor (or load). The load performs work by resisting the voltage and consuming current as the battery overcomes the resistance to complete its circuit.

Putting a switch (a device that breaks the circuit when in the 'off' position and completes it when in the 'on' position) anywhere in the circuit gives us a way of controlling it.

If there is no load component (like a resistor), a wire from the positive to negative terminals of the battery creates a *short circuit* and quickly depletes all the energy stored in the battery.

To use the GPIO pins, we need to make complete circuits and avoid short circuits or otherwise overloading the Raspberry Pi's current-providing capacity. Don't worry, you'll be provided with safe guidelines for doing this later in this chapter.

Of the 26 GPIO pins on the Model B, 17 are programmable switches — specifically 3, 5, 7, 8, 10, 11, 12, 13, 15, 16, 18, 19, 21, 22, 23, 24 and 26.

Ground pins (places to complete a circuit) are 6, 9, 14, 20 and 25.

Pins 2 and 4 supply 5 volts (like the positive terminal on a battery). Pins 1 and 17 give 3.3 volts. Both require circuits that eventually come back to one of the ground pins noted earlier.

> **NOTE** The high/low terminology is not strictly true in hardware interfacing with terms "active low" and "active high". For instance, in SPI a chip select pin (CS) is "active low", meaning that the chip will only respond (i.e. be "on"), when CS is set low (0V).

So how would you expect the Raspberry Pi to communicate with real-world devices? The 17 GPIO pins work with the Raspberry Pi's internal voltage, 3.3VDC. When the logic state is high, the pin shows 3.3VDC. When the logic switches to low, the voltage is 0. By using this scheme, the Raspberry Pi can send commands out and/or receive incoming information.

Here's how simple it truly is. One of the most basic circuits we can build is a light and a battery or other power source. We can do this easily with the GPIO pins.

Figure 12-9 depicts a simple binary on/off circuit. To make it, we choose an output pin and hook one side of an LED light to it using a jumper cable. (LEDs are low current and fun to use as indicator lights, etc.) The other side of the light connects to a 220-ohm resistor (more about this in just a moment) and the other side of the resistor connects to a ground pin.

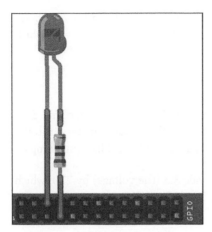

FIGURE 12-9: A GPIO simple LED circuit

When the output pin is high (has voltage), the LED lights; the LED goes out when the pin has 0 voltage. Later we look at writing programs in Python, which let the Raspberry Pi control the GPIO pins.

> The resistor we used in the circuit in Figure 12-12 is a *current limiting* component, which is a safeguard to prevent damaging both the Raspberry Pi and the LED.   **NOTE**
>
> Of course, you normally don't use all 17 pins. The accepted rule of thumb is to limit each pin to a maximum of about 16mA and not exceed a total of 50mA. No *exact* power specifications list exists for the Raspberry Pi. Such a list is impossible to create because there are too many variables, such as how the board gets its power and how it connects to a computer (using a USB port or by plugging into a converter connected to a wall socket). However, many smart Raspberry Pi experimenters have done measurements, and the figures we use in this chapter form a consensus of what's safe and what's not.

Managing Power

The issue with managing power on the Raspberry Pi stems from its main strength—its small size. On a board the size of a credit card, there is just no room for a massive power-handling circuit.

That makes it sound like there's not much power available, right? Don't worry; there's plenty of power available. If you are careful, you can run mighty machines with the Raspberry Pi. You just can't do it directly! Using GPIO requires using control circuits, which utilise relays, stepping switches and other types of external controllers, power transistors, microcontroller boards and other good stuff that lets the Raspberry Pi boss high-current devices.

There are two ways to make sure you are using damage-free current levels for the Raspberry Pi. You can *calculate* it or *measure* it. First, let's look at calculation. It's all about power, which we can measure using the following formula:

$I = V / R$

where I expresses current (in amps), V is voltage (in volts) and R is resistance in ohms. So if you know the voltage (3.3 VDC) and the resistance, you can plug those numbers into the formula to determine the current. Multiply the answer by 1,000 and you'll have milliamps.

Here's an example: say we have a 220-ohm resistor. Divide 3.3 (the voltage) by 220, which results in 0.015. Multiply .015 by 1,000 and you get 15, or 15mA. That's a safe current for one pin (so long as you do not exceed 50mA overall).

> **NOTE**   About the only device you can power safely directly from the GPIO pins is an LED light. However, be sure to put a 220-ohm resistor in series with the LED to limit the current to a safe level.

The formula we just used is called *Ohm's Law* (see Figure 12-10). It's a great tool for calculating safe limits for all your projects. Of course, with the Raspberry Pi, you'll be working in milliwatts and milliamps (thousandths of watts or amps) and mostly 3.3 VDC.

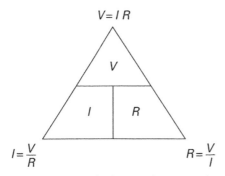

FIGURE 12-10: Ohm's Law, where V = voltage in volts, I = current in amps and R = resistance in ohms

The second way of testing for current level requires a test instrument—a *multimeter*—that measures voltage, current and resistance. You can find inexpensive digital readout multimeters online at Sparkfun (`www.sparkfun.com`), Adafruit (`www.adafruit.com`) and other online retailers for £4 to £15. Figure 12-11 shows a multimeter.

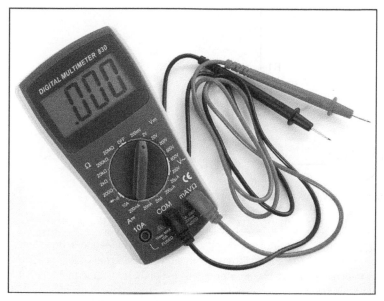

FIGURE 12-11: Multimeter

You use a multimeter *before* you connect the circuit. Two techniques work here:

- Measure the resistance of the circuit by connecting the multimeter (switched to ohms) across the positive and negative leads of the *unpowered* circuit. If it reads 220 ohms or more, the circuit is a safe one.

An infinite reading means your circuit is open and will not work. Check your connections. **TIP**

- Use a power supply set to 3.3 VDC. With the multimeter set to measure current (amps), put it *in series* (make it part of the circuit) and check the current. If your reading's greater than 16mA, add a resistor that limits the current to 16mA or less before connecting the circuit to the Raspberry Pi. Figure 12-12 shows an example of connecting a battery, resistor and amp meter (such as a multimeter switched to read current). When it's in series with the circuit, the multimeter reads the amount of current the resistor consumes. In Figure 12-12, R1 the resistor (right) is represented by the standard symbol for a resistor. The battery is on the left with a plus (+) showing its positive side, and the A in a circle denotes an amp meter for measuring current.

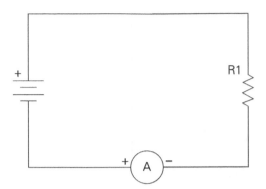

FIGURE 12-12: Measuring current with a multimeter

TIP   Another great reason for owning a multimeter is for measuring the value of resistors. Resistors have bands of colour indicating how many ohms they are. If you've lost the package a resistor came in and don't know the colour code, a multimeter comes in handy for finding that out. It's beneficial to learn the colour code, as you won't always have a multimeter with you.

All of the information provided in this section applies to the two 3.3V pins and the 17 switching pins. The two 5 VDC pins pull current through the Raspberry Pi's 5 VDC "rail"(where all the board's circuits get their power) and thus from the power source (USB port on a computer, external battery, a converter in a wall socket and so on). Because the current capacities vary widely, keep those current levels low. However, if you must have more power than the 3.3 VDC pins safely supply, the 5-volt pins might be useful.

CAUTION   Someone's likely to point out that you *could* disconnect the USB cable and run 5 VDC *into* one of the 5-volt GPIO pins. This setup powers the Raspberry Pi and gives you more current for GPIO operations. The problem is that this bypasses the built-in fuse protection of the Raspberry Pi, which *is not* a good thing and can result in current greater than a safe level, which can cause damage to the Raspberry Pi's components. We recommend against it.

On the other hand, the GPIO truly gives the Raspberry Pi (and you) fantastic capacity for controlling real-world devices. It's worth learning how to do this safely.

GPIO on the Model B+ and Raspberry Pi 2

If you have the new Model B+ or the Raspberry Pi 2 Model B, there are now 40 GPIO pins. For example, you will have 26 programmable pins overall instead of 17 (9 programmable pins have been added), two more grounds and a couple of pins (27 and 28) that are used as indexes by specialised plug-in boards. Figure 12-13 shows the GPIO pins on the Model B+.

FIGURE 12-13: Close-up of GPIO pins on the Raspberry Pi 2 Model B

Programming GPIO

The Python scripting language is the recommended and easiest method of programming GPIO. It's relatively easy to learn and comes standard in operating systems like Raspbian. To find out which version of Python you have, just go to the command line and type *python;* the version is returned, as shown here:

```
python
Python 2.7.9 (default, Mar 8 2015, 00:52:26)
[GCC 4.9.2] on linux2
```

When you update Raspbian (something you should do regularly), any newer version of Python downloads and installs along with the latest updates of everything else in Raspbian. To update and upgrade Raspbian, type the following from the command line (use the terminal if you run a GUI):

```
sudo apt-get update && sudo apt-get upgrade
```

> You should update Raspbian regularly for reasons of security and utility—that is, to keep your system secure while taking advantage of ongoing improvements in the hundreds of software packages on your Raspberry Pi. **TIP**

Also, if this is your first time using GPIO, you'll definitely want to install the Python GPIO library by using the following command:

```
sudo apt-get install rpi.gpio
```

> Python has many libraries of features and commands; you install only the ones needed for the tasks at hand. **NOTE**

Using Python, we write scripts to control the GPIO pins. The first step in writing one of these is to import the GPIO library, giving the script access functions concerning GPIO into your favourite editor, such as *nano*. Type the following command into the editor window:

```
import RPi.GPIO as GPIO
```

The next line specifies the layout of the GPIO pins (yes, you can change it). There are two choices: either match the layout on the board or use a numbering scheme matching the pins on the Broadcom SoC, as in:

```
GPIO.setmode(GPIO.BOARD)
```

Now we can start programming pins. Add the following lines to set pin 12 as an output:

```
GPIO.setmode(GPIO.BOARD)
GPIO.setup(12,GPIO.OUT)
```

or as an input:

```
GPIO.setup(12,GPIO.IN)
```

That's it. Three lines in a Python script and you've set up the GPIO to actually do something. For a good starting tutorial on programming GPIO pins, including alternative modes, see "Raspberry Pi GPIO Pins and Python" at http://makezine.com/projects/tutorial-raspberry-pi-gpio-pins-and-python/.

Using Raspbian Jessie (the latest release) on a Raspberry Pi 2 you can easily check GPIO pin settings. In the terminal, type:

```
gpio readall
```

and a table like the one shown in Figure 12-14 is generated.

Building a Simple Circuit

Are you ready to actually make something happen? How about turning on an LED and making it blink? We mentioned lighting an LED earlier but here we're providing more detail so you can do it yourself. You need the following components to follow along with this example:

```
+------+------+---------+------+---+---Pi 2---+---+------+---------+------+------+
| BCM  | wPi  |  Name   | Mode | V | Physical | V | Mode |  Name   | wPi  | BCM  |
+------+------+---------+------+---+----++----+---+------+---------+------+------+
|      |      |   3.3v  |      |   |  1 || 2  |   |      |  5v     |      |      |
|  2   |  8   |  SDA.1  | ALT0 | 1 |  3 || 4  |   |      |  5V     |      |      |
|  3   |  9   |  SCL.1  | ALT0 | 1 |  5 || 6  |   |      |  0v     |      |      |
|  4   |  7   | GPIO. 7 |  IN  | 1 |  7 || 8  | 1 | ALT0 |  TxD    | 15   | 14   |
|      |      |   0v    |      |   |  9 || 10 | 1 | ALT0 |  RxD    | 16   | 15   |
| 17   |  0   | GPIO. 0 |  IN  | 0 | 11 || 12 | 0 |  IN  | GPIO. 1 | 1    | 18   |
| 27   |  2   | GPIO. 2 |  IN  | 0 | 13 || 14 |   |      |  0v     |      |      |
| 22   |  3   | GPIO. 3 |  IN  | 0 | 15 || 16 | 0 |  IN  | GPIO. 4 | 4    | 23   |
|      |      |   3.3v  |      |   | 17 || 18 | 0 |  IN  | GPIO. 5 | 5    | 24   |
| 10   | 12   |  MOSI   |  IN  | 0 | 19 || 20 |   |      |  0v     |      |      |
|  9   | 13   |  MISO   |  IN  | 0 | 21 || 22 | 0 |  IN  | GPIO. 6 | 6    | 25   |
| 11   | 14   |  SCLK   |  IN  | 0 | 23 || 24 | 1 |  IN  | CE0     | 10   | 8    |
|      |      |   0v    |      |   | 25 || 26 | 1 |  IN  | CE1     | 11   | 7    |
|  0   | 30   |  SDA.0  |  IN  | 1 | 27 || 28 | 1 |  IN  | SCL.0   | 31   | 1    |
|  5   | 21   | GPIO.21 |  IN  | 1 | 29 || 30 |   |      |  0v     |      |      |
|  6   | 22   | GPIO.22 |  IN  | 1 | 31 || 32 | 0 |  IN  | GPIO.26 | 26   | 12   |
| 13   | 23   | GPIO.23 |  IN  | 0 | 33 || 34 |   |      |  0v     |      |      |
| 19   | 24   | GPIO.24 |  IN  | 0 | 35 || 36 | 0 |  IN  | GPIO.27 | 27   | 16   |
| 26   | 25   | GPIO.25 |  IN  | 0 | 37 || 38 | 0 |  IN  | GPIO.28 | 28   | 20   |
|      |      |   0v    |      |   | 39 || 40 | 0 |  IN  | GPIO.29 | 29   | 21   |
+------+------+---------+------+---+----++----+---+------+---------+------+------+
| BCM  | wPi  |  Name   | Mode | V | Physical | V | Mode |  Name   | wPi  | BCM  |
+------+------+---------+------+---+---Pi 2---+---+------+---------+------+------+
```

FIGURE 12-14: Table of GPIO pin assignments on Raspberry Pi 2

- A small LED (your choice of colour)

- A 200-ohm resistor

- A breadboard or alligator clips for making connections

- Some small-gauge wire or jumper wires

> You could use a lower value resistor, but 200 ohms allows the LED to light brightly and the circuit draws less current. Less is always better when using GPIO pins, so use the minimum that you can to make your project successful. **NOTE**

Use the following steps to build a simple circuit:

1. Use a jumper wire to connect GPIO pin 7 (the positive side of the circuit) to one end of the resistor.

2. Look at your LED. LEDs usually have one wire leg longer than the other, or one leg might have a bend in it. This is the positive side. Connect it to the other end of the resistor.

3. Hook the negative side of the LED to GPIO pin 6, which is ground in the GPIO layout we're using.

Your circuit is complete! It might look something like the one in Figure 12-15.

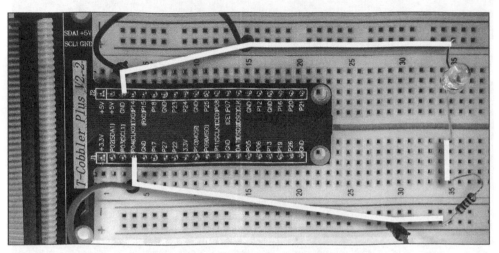

FIGURE 12-15: Simple breadboard circuit for flashing an LED; the white overlay shows the circuit

Example of Using Output

Now it's time to write the simple Python script that controls the LED's blinks. You use a text editor such as nano to write your Python script. Our script (with comments) is shown here.

```
## Blinking LED ##################################
import RPi.GPIO as GPIO    ## Import GPIO library
import time                ## Need this for blink delay
GPIO.setmode(GPIO.BOARD)   ## Use board pin numbering
GPIO.setwarnings(False)    ## Disable "Channel already
                           ## in use" warning

led = 7                    ## Variable for pin number
GPIO.setup(led, GPIO.OUT)  ## Set pin to output

## Blink the LED 60 times, once per second for 2 minutes

print "Blinking"           ## Blinking in progress
for x in range(0, 59):     ## repeats 60 times
    GPIO.output(led, 1)    ## Turn LED on
    time.sleep(1)          ## Keep it on for 1 second
    GPIO.output(led, 0)    ## Turn LED off
    time.sleep(1)          ## Wait 1 second

GPIO.cleanup()                 ## End program gracefully
```

A Closer Look at the Script

We want to give a little more detail about a few things in the script. Look first at the GPIO.setwarnings() line. If a GPIO script has been interrupted, the next script you run may cause this warning because the system thinks the crashed program still is using the GPIO service. It's only a warning and does not stop the script, but this line stops this minor annoyance.

Also, the GPIO.cleanup() command (the last line in the script) cleans up by releasing the GPIO to prevent the warning we just discussed. It's good programming practice to include in your scripts.

If this script doesn't work for you, check your circuit and also check for typos in the script. Typos are the most likely culprit. As with any code, things have to be exactly right for proper operation to occur.

TIP

Example of Using Input

Using a pin for output is perhaps not as simple as it might appear. When a pin is set to input, pressing a switch connected from the pin to ground closes a circuit and you get an input, right? The problem is that in actual use, the Raspberry Pi can become confused about whether a switch is open or closed. This phenomenon is called *floating*.

Input pins actually have three states—on, off and floating (where the logic is not clear). For practical results in using input logic, we need the Raspberry Pi detecting on or off states (true or false) only.

A solution to this problem of three states involves providing "pull up" and "pull down" reference voltages so the Raspberry Pi knows definitely when it gets an input. GPIO pins have an internal pull-up/pull-down resistor that can be enabled via programming, such as in a Python script.

Pull up means the switch or other input device connects to the negative end of the pull-up resistor. *Pull down* hooks the device to the positive end. A diagram of pull up and pull down is shown in Figure 12-16.

NOTE

In Figure 12-16, Vcc refers to a positive voltage supply. This would be 3.3 VDC on the Raspberry Pi. Because this connection and the pull-up resistor are internal, all that's required of you is a line in Python when you want to use a pin as an input.

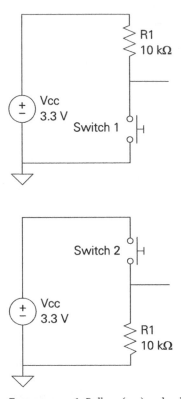

FIGURE 12-16: Pull up (top) and pull down (bottom)

For example, we can write a script detecting the press of a button like this:

```
## Input Using Pullup #########################################
import RPi.GPIO as GPIO                      ## Import GPIO library
import time                                  ## Need this for delay
GPIO.setmode(GPIO.BOARD)                     ## Use board pin
  numbering

GPIO.setup(15, GPIO.IN)
                                             ## Set pin 15 to input
  with pullup

## Let us know whenever button is pressed, please ################

print "Push this button"
```

```
while True:
    button_pressed = GPIO.input(15)
    if button_pressed == False:
        print("DING DONG, button pressed!")
        time.sleep(0.3)

GPIO.cleanup                        ## End program gracefully
```

The physical circuit using alligator clips or on a breadboard is minimal to construct. Run a jumper wire from pin 15 to one side of the switch and run another jumper wire from the other side of the switch to ground. Run the script, press the button three times and you get the following output:

```
Push this button
DING DONG, button pressed!
DING DONG, button pressed!
DING DONG, button pressed!
```

Alternative Modes

In the previous section we mentioned the alternative modes of the GPIO pins. Theoretically, there can be up to six alternative uses of a particular pin. The ALT functions are pin dependent. You can set individual pins to be in different ALT modes at any given time. In other words, not all pins need to be in ALT 1 mode at the same time; some pins can be in ALT 0 mode and a couple of others can be in ALT 4 mode.

> The "Raspberry Pi GPIO Pin Alternative Functions" article (www.dummies.com/how-to/ content/raspberry-pi-gpio-pin-alternative-functions.html) is good reading for a fast start in using alternative modes. Also check out the Broadcom documentation for the 2835 and 2836 (the latter is for the Raspberry Pi 2 Model B) for more detailed information. **TIP**

For the aforementioned detailed information concerning the 2835 chip, download the Broadcom 205-page PDF at www.alldatasheet.com/datasheet-pdf/pdf/502533/ BOARDCOM/BCM2835.html. Evidently, this level of detail is not available yet for the 2836.

GPIO Experimentation the Easy Way

We should mention that when using jumper cables on something as crowded with pins as P1, the GPIO header is a pin. Also you need to take great care to avoid shorts. Using such aids as breakout boards, breadboards and prototyping boards—many of which are available at low cost from major online retailers—offers a better solution.

These boards have connectors that plug into P1, and the additional board gives you much more room for adding jumpers, resistors and other components.

Index

Printed and bound by CPI Group (UK) Ltd, Croydon, CR0 4YY

27/10/2024

14580322-0004